ISAIAH 56–66

VOLUME 19B

THE ANCHOR BIBLE is a fresh approach to the world's greatest classic. Its object is to make the Bible accessible to the modern reader; its method is to arrive at the meaning of biblical literature through exact translation and extended exposition, and to reconstruct the ancient setting of the biblical story, as well as the circumstances of its transcription and the characteristics of its transcribers.

THE ANCHOR BIBLE is a project of international and interfaith scope: Protestant, Catholic, and Jewish scholars from many countries contribute individual volumes. The project is not sponsored by any ecclesiastical organization and is not intended to reflect any particular theological doctrine. Prepared under our joint supervision, THE ANCHOR BIBLE is an effort to make available all the significant historical and linguistic knowledge which bears on the interpretation of the biblical record.

THE ANCHOR BIBLE is aimed at the general reader with no special formal training in biblical studies; yet it is written with the most exacting standards of scholarship, reflecting the highest technical accomplishment.

This project marks the beginning of a new era of cooperation among scholars in biblical research, thus forming a common body of knowledge to be shared by all.

William Foxwell Albright
David Noel Freedman
GENERAL EDITORS

THE ANCHOR BIBLE

ISAIAH 56–66

◆

A New Translation
with Introduction and Commentary

JOSEPH BLENKINSOPP

THE ANCHOR BIBLE
Doubleday
New York   London   Toronto   Sydney   Auckland

THE ANCHOR BIBLE
PUBLISHED BY DOUBLEDAY
a division of Random House, Inc.
1540 Broadway, New York, New York 10036

THE ANCHOR BIBLE DOUBLEDAY, and the portrayal of an
anchor with the letters A and B are trademarks of
Doubleday, a division of Random House, Inc.

Library of Congress Cataloging-in-Publication Data

Bible. O.T. Isaiah LVI–LXVI. English. Blenkinsopp. 2003.
    Isaiah 56–66: a new translation with introduction and commentary /
By Joseph Blenkinsopp. — 1st ed.
    p. cm. — (The Anchor Bible; vol. 19)
    Includes bibliographical references and indexes.
    ISBN 0-385-50174-9 (v. 1 : alk. paper)
    1. Bible. O.T. Isaiah LVI–LXVI — Commentaries. I. Title: Isaiah
fifty-six–sixty-six. II. Blenkinsopp, Joseph III. Title. IV. Bible. English.
Anchor Bible. 1964; v. 19.

    BS192.2.A1 1964 .G3
    [BS1515.3]
    224′. 1077 — dc21

                                                    00–021326
                                                    CIP

for my sons
David and Martin

CONTENTS

◆

PREFACE

◆

On looking back over my notes, I was reminded that I began the draft of the commentary on Isa 56–66 on the Feast of the Epiphany 2001 and finished it on the same day a year later. The auspicious beginning notwithstanding, I cannot claim any special revelation; no star has guided my progress, but I was fortunate to be accompanied in the journey by wise men from many countries. I refer to the individual scholars, several of them personal friends, who have given their time and talents to the task of understanding and explaining this last section of Isaiah. It would be invidious to mention names; and, besides, they know who they are.

I can appreciate that some readers will think a year far too short a time to write a substantial commentary on a biblical text that bristles with problems including authorship, dating, formation, relation to the rest of the book, genres, and who knows what else. My only defense is that these chapters have engaged my attention many times over at least the past decade. I have had the opportunity to offer seminars on them to groups of outstanding doctoral students at the University of Notre Dame. During a leave of absence during the academic year 1997–1998, I had the privilege of lecturing on Isa 56–66 at the Biblical Institute, Rome, to some seventy students from about thirty countries. I have also over the last several years read papers on one or other aspect of the material to the Society of Old Testament Studies (United Kingdom), the Society of Biblical Literature, several institutions in the United Kingdom, the University of Oslo, the Free University of Amsterdam, and Hebrew University, Jerusalem. There were no doubt others, but these are the ones I can recall. There have also been several publications, some of them listed in the Bibliography. All this notwithstanding, I remain keenly aware how provisional the result is. Each generation has to engage the struggle anew, which certainly involves searching for solutions to problems, but even more so actualizing in new ways the enormous potential of a text like Isa 56–66.

As I said in the Preface to Volume 1, the bibliographies are extensive but by no means comprehensive. I wish to thank Ora Lipschitz of Ein Kerem, Jerusalem, for making his own bibliography of chs. 56–66 (arranged by chapter and verse) available to me. No one can, or should, read everything, and in trying to read everything (up to the end of 2001) that seemed to me to have something significant to say I am sure I have been guilty of sinning by omission and can only hope for forgiveness.

In this volume, unlike the two preceding it, I decided to use the transliteration of the Tetragrammaton (YHVH) rather than spelling it out. The reader can then supply the reading that seems to him or her most appropriate.

As on the previous two occasions, it is a pleasure to thank Professor David Noel Freedman for much valuable help. While his sight is unfortunately no longer unimpaired, his natural vigor is, at this writing, unabated. Thanks are also due to Mr. Andrew Corbin of Doubleday whose editorial skills and friendly encouragement were most helpful. I also thank, for the third time, doctoral student Angela Kim, whose research- and computer-related skills were much appreciated. Finally, a thank you to my wife, Jean, for love and support. She now knows more about the "Servants" and "Tremblers" than she ever thought she would need to know.

LIST OF ABBREVIATIONS

◆

AASOR	Annual of the American Schools of Oriental Research
AB	Anchor Bible
ABD	*Anchor Bible Dictionary.* Edited. D. N. Freedman. 6 vols. New York, 1992
ABR	*Australian Biblical Review*
AbrN	*Abr-Nahrain*
AcOr	*Acta Orientalia*
Adv. Marc.	*Adversas Marcionem,* Tertullian
Aeg	*Aegyptus*
Ag. Ap.	*Against Apion,* Josephus
AJSL	*Americal Journal of Semitic Languages and Literature*
AJT	*Australian Journal of Theology*
Akk.	Akkadian language
ANEP	*The Ancient Near East in Pictures Relating to the Old Testament.* Edited. J. B. Pritchard. Princeton,1954
ANET	*Ancient Near Eastern Texts Relating to the Old Testament.* 2d ed. Edited by J. B. Pritchard. Princeton, 1955
Ant.	*Jewish Antiquities,* Josephus
AP	*Aramaic Papyri of the Fifth Century* B.C. Edited. A. Cowley. Oxford, 1923
Aqu.	Aquila
AR	*Archiv für Religionswissenschaft*
ARAB	*Ancient Records of Assyria and Babylonia.* Edited by D. Luckenbill. 2 vols. Chicago, 1926–1927
Arab.	Arabic version
Aram.	Aramaic language
ASOR	American Schools of Oriental Research
ASTI	*Annual of the Swedish Theological Institute*
ATD	Das Alte Testament Deutsch
AThR	*Anglican Theological Review*
Aug	*Augustinianum*
AUSS	*Andrews University Seminary Studies*
AV	Authorized (King James) version
b.	Babylonian Talmud
BA	*Biblical Archaeologist*
BAR	*Biblical Archaeology Review*
Barn.	*Barnabas*
BASOR	*Bulletin of the American Schools of Oriental Research*
BAT	Die Botschaft des Alten Testaments
B.Bat.	*Baba Batra*
BeO	*Bibbia e Oriente*
BETL	Bibliotheca ephemeridum theologicarum lovaniensium

BFCT	Beiträge zur Förderung Christlicher Theologie
BHS	*Biblia Hebraica Stuttgartensia.* Edited by K. Elliger and W. Rudolph. Stuttgart, 1983
BI	*Biblical Illustrator*
Bib	*Biblica*
BibInt	*Biblical Interpretation*
BibLeb	*Bibel und Leben*
Bijdr	*Bijdragen: Tijdschrift voor filosofie en theologie*
BIOSCS	*Bulletin of the International Organization for Septuagint and Cognate Studies*
BJRL	*Bulletin of the John Rylands University Library of Manchester*
BK	*Bibel und Kirche*
BKAT	Biblischer Kommentar: Altes Testament. Edited by M. Noth and H. W. Wolff
BL	*Bibel und Liturgie*
BM	*Beth Mikra*
BN	*Biblische Notizen*
BR	*Biblical Research*
BRev	*Bible Review*
BSac	*Bibliotheca Sacra*
BT	*The Bible Translator*
BTB	*Biblical Theology Bulletin*
BWANT	Beiträge zur Wissenschaft vom Alten und Neuen Testament
BZ	*Biblische Zeitschrift*
BZAW	Beihefte zur Zeitschrift für die alttestamentliche Wissenschaft
CAD	*The Assyrian Dictionary of the Oriental Institute of the University of Chicago.* Edited by I. J. Gelb et al. Chicago, 1956–
CAH	Cambridge Ancient History. Edited by I. E. S. Edwards et al.
CANE	*Civilizations of the Ancient Near East.* Edited by J. Sasson. 4 vols. New York, 1995
CB	The Century Bible
CBC	The Cambridge Bible Commentary
CBQ	*Catholic Biblical Quarterly*
CD	Cairo (Genizah text of the) *Damascus Document*
CHJ	*The Cambridge History of Judaism,* vol. 1. Edited by W. D. Davies and L. Finkelstein. Cambridge, 1984
1–2 Clem.	*1–2 Clement*
Conc	*Concilium*
CTA	*Corpus des tablettes en cunéiformes alphabétiques découvertes à Ras Shamra–Ugarit de 1929 à 1939.* Edited by A. Herdner. Mission de Ras Shamra 10. Paris, 1963
CTR	*Criswell Theological Review*
DBAT	*Dielheimer Blätter zum Alten Testament und seiner Rezeption in der alten Kirche*
DBSup	*Dictionnaire de la Bible: Supplément.* Edited by L. Pirot and A. Robert. Paris, 1928–
DDD	*Dictionary of Deities and Demons in the Bible.* Edited by K. van der Toorn, B. Becking, and P. W. van der Horst. 2d ed. Leiden, 1999
Dial.	Justin, *Dialogue with Trypho*

Did.	*Didaskalia*
DJD	Discoveries in the Judaean Desert
DSD	*Dead Sea Discoveries*
EBib	Études bibliques
'*Ed.*	'*Eduyyot* (Testimonies)
En.	*Enoch*
EncJud	*Encyclopedia Judaica.* 16 vols. Jerusalem, 1972
'*Erub.*	'*Erubin* (tractate of the Mishnah)
EstBib	*Estudios bíblicos*
Eth.	Ethiopic version
ETL	*Ephemerides Theologicae Lovanienses*
EvT	*Evangelische Theologie*
EvQ	*Evangelical Quarterly*
ExpTim	*Expository Times*
fem.	Feminine
frg.	Fragment
FRLANT	Forschungen zur Religion und Literatur des Alten und Neuen Testaments
GKC	*Gesenius' Hebrew Grammar.* Edited by E. Kautzsch. Translated A. E. Cowley. 2d ed. Oxford,1910
HALOT	Koehler, L., W. Baumgartner, and J. J. Stamm. *The Hebrew and Aramaic Lexicon of the Old Testament.* Translated and edited under the supervision of M. E. J. Richardson. 5 vols. Leiden, 1994–2000
HAR	*Hebrew Annual Review*
HAT	Handbuch zum Alten Testament
Hen	*Henoch*
HeyJ	*Heythrop Journal*
HKAT	Handkommentar zum Alten Testament
HS	*Hebrew Studies*
HSAT	*Die Heilige Schrift des Alten Testaments.* Edited by E. Kautzsch and A. Bertholet. 4th ed. Tübingen, 1922–1923
HTR	*Harvard Theological Review*
HUCA	*Hebrew Union College Annual*
IB	*Interpreter's Bible.* Edited by G. A. Buttrick et al. 12 vols. New York, 1951–1957
IBS	*Irish Biblical Studies*
ICC	International Critical Commentary
IDB	*Interpreter's Dictionary of the Bible* Edited by G. A. Buttrick. 4 vols. Nashville, 1962
IDBSup	*Interpreter's Dictionary of the Bible: Supplementary Volume.* Edited by K. Crim. Nashville, 1976
IEJ	*Israel Exploration Journal*
IJT	*Indian Journal of Theology*
Int	*Interpretation*
ITC	International Theological Commentary
JAC	Jahrbuch für Antike und Christentum
JAOS	*Journal of the American Oriental Society*
JBL	*Journal of Biblical Literature*
JBQ	*Jewish Bible Quarterly*
JCS	*Journal of Cuneiform Studies*

JETS	*Journal of the Evangelical Theological Society*
JJS	*Journal of Jewish Studies*
JNES	*Journal of Near Eastern Studies*
JNSL	*Journal of Northwest Semitic Languages*
JPOS	*Journal of the Palestine Oriental Society*
JQR	*Jewish Quarterly Review*
JSem	*Journal of Semitics*
JSJ	*Journal for the Study of Judaism in the Persian, Hellenistic, and Roman Periods*
JSNTSup	Supplements to Journal for the Study of the New Testament
JSOT	*Journal for the Study of the Old Testament*
JSOTSup	Supplements to Journal for the Study of the Old Testament
JSP	*Journal for the Study of the Pseudepigrapha*
JSPSup	Journal for the Study of the Pseudepigrapha: *Supplement Series*
JSS	*Journal of Semitic Studies*
JTS	*Journal of Theological Studies*
K	Ketib (what is written)
KAT	Kommentar zum Alten Testament
KHC	Kurzer Hand-Commentar zum Alten Testament
KJV	King James Version
KTU	*Die keilalphabetischen Texte aus Ugarit.* Edited by M. Dietrich, O. Loretz, and J. Sanmartín. AAOT 24/1. Neukirchen-Vlyun, 1976
Leš	*Lešonénu*
Lev.Rab.	*Leviticus Rabbah*
Luc.	Lucianic family of LXX MSS
LXX	The Septuagint
m.	Mishnah
Magn.	Ignatius, *To the Magnesians*
masc.	Masculine
Meg.	*Megillah* (the Esther Scroll)
MH	Mishnaic Hebrew
MS(S)	Manuscript(s)
MT	Masoretic Text
MTZ	*Münchener theologische Zeitschrift*
Mus	*Muséon: Revue d'études orientales*
NAB	New American Bible
NCB	New Century Bible
NEAEHL	*The New Encyclopedia of Archaeological Excavations in the Holy Land.* Edited by E. Stern. 4 vols. Jerusalem, 1993
NEB	New English Bible
NIB	*The New Interpreter's Bible*
NICOT	New International Commentary on the Old Testament
NJPSV	New Jewish Publication Society version of the Holy Scriptures
NKZ	*Neue kirchliche Zeitschrift*
NRSV	New Revised Standard Version
NRTh	*Nouvelle revue théologique*
NT	New Testament
NTS	*New Testament Studies*
NTT	*Norsk Teologisk Tidsskrift*

OBO	Orbis Biblicus et Orientalis
OEANE	*Oxford Encyclopedia of Archaeology in the Near East.* Edited by E. M. Meyers. New York, 1997
OG	Old Greek Version
Or	*Orientalia*
OrChr	*Oriens Christianus*
OTE	*Old Testament Essays*
OTG	Old Testament Guides
OTL	Old Testament Library series
OtSt	*Oudtestamentische Studiën*
OTWSA	*Oudtestamentiese Werkgemeenskap van Suid-Afrika*
PEQ	*Palestine Exploration Quarterly*
PIBA	Proceedings of the Irish Biblical Association
Pirqe R. El.	*Pirqe Rabba;* Eliezer
PL	Patrologia Latina. Edited by J.-P. Migne. 217 vols. Paris, 1844–1864
pl.	Plural
POut	De Prediking van het Oude Testament
Q	Qere (what is read)
QC	*Qumran Chronicle*
Qere Or	Qere Orientale
RB	*Revue biblique*
RevistB	*Revista biblica*
RevExp	*Revue and Expositor*
RevQ	*Revue de Qumran*
RHPR	*Revue d'histoire et de philosophie religieuses*
RHR	*Revue de l'histoire des religions*
RivB	*Rivista biblica italiana*
RSR	*Recherches de science religieuse*
RSV	Revised Standard Version
Sabb.	*Sabbat* (tractate of the Mishnah)
Sanh.	*Sanhedrin* (tractate of Babylonian Talmud)
SANT	*Studien zum Alten und Neuen Testaments*
SB	Sources bibliques
SBLDS	Society of Biblical Literature Dissertation Series
SBLMasS	Society of Biblical Literature Masoretic Studies
SBLSP	Society of Biblical Literature Seminar Papers
SBS	Stuttgarter Bibelstudien
SBT	Studies in Biblical Theology
Scr	*Scripture*
SEÅ	*Svensk exegetisk årsbok*
Sem	*Semitica*
Sib.Or.	*The Sibylline Oracles*
sing.	Singular
SJOT	*Scandinavian Journal of the Old Testament*
SJT	*Scottish Journal of Theology*
ST	*Studia Theologica*
STDJ	Studies in the Texts of the Desert of Judah
SThU	*Schweizerische theologische Umschau*
Symm.	Symmachus

Syr.	*Vetus Testamentum Syriace* (The Peshiṭta Version)
TB	Theologische Bücherei
TBei	*Theologische Beiträge*
TBT	*The Bible Today*
TDOT	*Theological Dictionary of the Old Testament.* Edited by G. J. Botterweck and H. Ringgren. Translated by J. T. Willis, G. W. Bromiley, and D. E. Green. Grand Rapids, 1974–
Tg.	Targum
TGl	*Theologie und Glaube*
THAT	*Theologisches Handwörterbuch zum Alten Testament.* Edited by E. Jenni and C. Westermann. 2 vols. Munich, 1971–76 [for Eng. trans., see *TLOT*]
Theod.	Theodotion
ThViat	*Theologia Viatorum*
TLOT	*Theological Lexicon of the Old Testament.* Edited by E. Jenni and C. Westermann. Translated by M. E. Biddle. 3 vols. Peabody, Mass., 1997
TLZ	*Theologische Literaturzeitung*
TOTC	Tyndale Old Testament Commentaries
Transeu	*Transeuphratène*
TRu	*Theologische Rundschau*
TS	*Theological Studies*
TSK	*Theologische Studien und Kritiken*
TTZ	*Trierer theologische Zeitschrift*
TW	*Am Tisch des Wortes*
TynBul	*Tyndale Bulletin*
TZ	*Theologische Zeitschrift*
UF	*Ugarit-Forschungen*
Ug.	Ugaritic language
USQR	*Union Seminary Quarterly Review*
VC	*Vigiliae Christianae*
VD	*Verbum Domini*
Vet. Lat.	Vetus Latina version
VH	*Vivens Homo*
VT	*Vetus Testamentum*
VTSup	Vetus Testamentum Supplements
Vulg.	*Editio Vulgata*
WBC	Word Biblical Commentary
WC	Westminster Commentaries
WMANT	Wissenschaftliche Monographien zum Alten und Neuen Testament
WTJ	*Westminster Theological Journal*
WZ	*Wissenschaftliche Zeitschrift*
Yebam.	*Yebamot* (tractate of Babylonian Talmud)
ZAH	*Zeitschrift für Althebräistik*
ZAW	*Zeitschrift für die alttestamentliche Wissenschaft*
ZDMG	*Zeitschrift der deutschen morgenländischen Gesellschaft*
ZDPV	*Zeitschrift des deutschen Palästina-Vereins*
ZKT	*Zeitschrift für katholische Theologie*
ZNW	*Zeitschrift für die neutestamentliche Wissenschaft und die Kunde der älteren Kirche*
ZTK	*Zeitschrift für Theologie und Kirche*

ISAIAH 56-66:
A TRANSLATION

◆

REASSURANCE FOR THE MARGINAL (56:1–8)

56 ¹This is what YHVH says:
"Maintain justice, do what is right,
for my salvation is near at hand,
my deliverance will soon be revealed."
²Blessed is the one who does this,
the one who holds fast to it:
who observes Sabbath, who does not profane it,
who stays his hand from evildoing.
³The foreigner who adheres to YHVH must not say,
"YHVH will surely cut me off from his people";
and the eunuch must not say,
"I am just a withered tree."
⁴For this is what YHVH says,
"The eunuchs who observe my Sabbaths,
who choose what is pleasing to me
and hold fast to my covenant:
⁵to them I shall give in my house and within my walls
a memorial and a name
better than sons and daughters;
I shall give them a long-lasting name
that will not be cut off.
⁶The foreigners who adhere to YHVH,
to minister to him, to love YHVH's name,
to be his servants;
all who observe the Sabbath and do not profane it,
who hold fast my covenant:
⁷them I will bring to my holy mountain;
I will give them joy in my house of prayer.
Their burnt offerings and sacrifices
will be welcome on my altar;
for my house will be called a house of prayer
for all peoples."

⁸An utterance of the Sovereign Lord YHVH,
who gathers the dispersed of Israel:
"I shall gather yet more to him
besides those already gathered."

CORRUPT LEADERS INVITE DISASTER (56:9–12)

56 ⁹All you wild animals, come and devour,
all you animals of the forest!

¹⁰Israel's watchmen are blind, one and all,
they have no understanding.
They are all dumb dogs,
dogs that cannot bark;
panting, stretched out on the ground,
they love to slumber.
¹¹The dogs have a mighty appetite,
they never have enough.
[They are shepherds.]
They all go their own way,
to their own gain, one and all.
¹²"Come," says one, "I'll get the wine.
Let's drink strong drink to satiety.
Tomorrow will be like today,
or even better still!"

LAMENT FOR THE DEAD PROPHET
AND HIS DISCIPLES (57:1–2)

57   ¹The Righteous One has perished,
and no one takes it to heart;
the devout are swept away,
and no one gives a thought.
It was on account of evil
that the Righteous One was swept away.
²[He enters into peace.
They repose in their last resting places.
He is upright in his conduct.]

DENUNCIATION OF THE SORCERESS
AND HER CHILDREN (57:3–13)

i

57   ³As for you, draw near, children of the sorceress,
offspring of an adulterer and a whore!
⁴Of whom are you making fun?
At whom are you making faces
and sticking out your tongue?
Sinful brood, treacherous offspring!
⁵You who seek consolation with the shades of the dead
under every tree in leaf;

sacrificing children in the valleys,
under the clefts of the rocks.
Faced with all this, should I relent?

ii

[6]As for you, woman,
with the dead of the valley is your destiny,
it is they who are your portion;
to them you have poured out a libation,
you have made a cereal offering.
[7]On a high and lofty mountain
you have set up your bed;
there too you have gone up
to offer sacrifice.
[8]Beside the door and the doorpost
you have put up your sign;
for when I was absent you disrobed,
you lay down, made room in your bed
for those with whom you made bargains
for the pleasure of sleeping with them.
You gazed on them naked.
[9]You journeyed to Molech with oil,
you put on a lot of perfume;
you dispatched your envoys far afield,
you sent them down even to Sheol.
[10]You were worn out with all your journeying,
but you never said "It is in vain";
you found your vigor renewed,
and so you did not weaken.

iii

[11]Whom did you dread and fear
that you proved so false?
It was not me you kept in mind,
you never gave me a thought.
Did I not stay silent and avert my gaze
while you did not fear me?
[12]I will proclaim your conquests, all your doings,
but they will profit you nothing.
[13]When you cry out for help,
may your "gathered ones" come to your rescue.
The wind will carry them all off,
a breath of air will bear them away.

But the one who takes refuge in me will inherit the land,
will possess my holy mountain.

A CALL FOR A NEW BEGINNING (57:14–21)

57 [14]He said:

"Build up, build up the road and clear the way,
remove every obstacle from my people's path."
[15]For thus says the Exalted One,
who dwells in an eternal place,
whose name is holy:
"I dwell in a high and holy place
and with the contrite and humble in spirit,
to revive the spirits of the humble,
to revive the hearts of the contrite.
[16]I will not be forever accusing,
nor will I always be angry;
apart from me the spirit weakens,
for it was I made all creatures that breathe.
[17]I was angry at their sinful avarice;
I struck them, and in my anger I stayed hidden;
yet they kept turning back to their devices.
[18]Though I note their conduct, I will heal them,
give them respite, repay them with comfort,
[19]putting words of praise on the lips
of those among them that mourn.

Peace, peace, for those far off and for those that are near,
YHVH affirms it; yes, I will heal them.
[20]But the wicked are like the driven sea
that never can be still.
[Its waters dredge up slime and mud.]
[21]There is no peace, says my God, for the wicked.

TRUE FASTING, TRUE PIETY (58:1–14)

i

58 [1]Shout it out loud, do not hold back,
raise your voice like a trumpet!
Proclaim to my people their transgression,
to the household of Jacob their sins.
[2]Yet they seek guidance from me day after day
and take pleasure in knowing my ways,
like a nation that does what is right,
that has not abandoned the justice of its god.

They ask of me just decisions,
they take pleasure in approaching God.

ii

[3]"Why should we fast," they say, "when you take no notice?
Why should we afflict ourselves when you do not acknowledge it?"
"Look, on your fast days you pursue your own interests,
you oppress all your workers.
[4]Look, your fasting leads only to disputes and quarrels
and striking with vicious fists.
The fast you are keeping today
will not give you a hearing on high.

iii

[5]Is the fast that I favor
a day for humble self-affliction of this kind,
for bowing down the head like a bulrush,
making one's bed of sackcloth and ashes?
Is this what you call a fast,
a day acceptable to YHVH?
[6]Is not this the fasting that I favor:
to free those unjustly detained,
to loosen the straps of the yoke,
to release the oppressed into freedom,
pulling off every yoke?
[7]Is it not sharing your bread with the hungry,
bringing into your home the homeless,
clothing the one you see naked,
not hiding yourself from your neighbor?
[8]Then your light will break out like the dawn,
your wound will quickly be healed;
your vindication will precede you,
the glory of YHVH will be your rearguard.
[9]Then when you call, YHVH will answer;
when you cry out he will say, 'Here I am.'"

iv

"If you banish perverse conduct from among you,
pointing the finger, and malicious talk,
[10]if you offer your substance to the hungry
and satisfy the appetite of the afflicted,
your light will shine in the darkness,
your darkness will become like the noonday light.
[11]YHVH will always be your guide,
he will see to your needs in an arid land,
he will strengthen your bones.

You will be like a well-watered garden,
like a spring whose water never fails.
¹²Some of you will rebuild the ancient ruins,
you will build on foundations laid long ago;
you will be called repairer of the breach,
restorer of ruined dwellings.

v

¹³If you refrain from travel on the Sabbath,
from engaging in business on my holy day;
if you call the Sabbath a delight,
this holy day of YHVH most esteemed;
if you honor it, not following your inclinations,
or pursuing your own affairs
or engaging in idle talk;
¹⁴then you will take delight in YHVH.
I shall set you astride on the heights of the earth,
I shall give you the heritage of your ancestor Jacob to enjoy."

This is what YHVH has spoken.

WHY GOD REMAINS INACTIVE
AND SILENT (59:1–8)

59 ¹YHVH's arm is not so short that he cannot save,
nor his hearing so dull that he cannot hear.
²Your iniquities have created the rift
between you and your God;
your sins have concealed the Face from you,
so that he does not hear.
³Your hands are stained with blood,
your fingers with iniquity;
your lips utter what is false,
your tongue mutters what is perverse.
⁴No one issues a summons justly,
no one goes to law honestly.
Relying on worthless and fraudulent arguments,
they conceive trouble and bring forth iniquity.
⁵They hatch vipers' eggs,
they spin spiders' webs;
[if you eat their eggs you die.
The cracked egg hatches out as a poisonous snake.]

⁶Their webs will not serve for clothing,
[they will not be able to clothe themselves with what they produce.]
Their works are evil,
they perpetrate deeds of violence.
⁷Their feet run to evil,
they hasten to shed innocent blood.
Their scheming is all perverse,
bringing ruin and destruction in its wake.
⁸They are ignorant of the way of peace;
justice does not guide their conduct.
They have made their paths crooked for themselves;
none who walks in them knows peace.

A COMMUNITY COMPLAINT (59:9–15a)

59 ⁹Therefore, vindication remains far from us,
deliverance is not in our grasp.
We wait for daylight, and there is only darkness,
for light to dawn, and we walk in dark places.
¹⁰We grope like the blind along a wall,
we feel our way like the sightless;
we stumble at midday as at twilight,
like the walking dead among the healthy.
¹¹We all growl like bears,
like doves we keep on moaning.
We wait for vindication, but there is none,
for salvation, but it is far from us.
¹²Our transgressions against you are many,
our sins bear witness against us.
Our transgressions are present to us,
we know only too well our iniquities.
¹³We have transgressed, we have disavowed YHVH,
we have turned away from our God.
We utter threatening and rebellious words,
 we mutter lies conceived in the heart.
¹⁴Justice is turned around,
righteousness stays at a distance;
honesty stumbles in the street,
probity finds no entry.
^{15a}Honesty is nowhere to be found,
and whoever renounces evil is despoiled.

FINALLY, A REPLY (59:15b–20)

59 [15b]When YHVH saw it, he was displeased
that no retribution was in sight.
[16]He saw that there was no one else,
he was appalled that there was none to intervene.
So his own arm won him victory,
his triumphant power sustained him.
[17]He donned triumph like a coat of mail,
with the helmet of salvation on his head.
He clothed himself with garments of vengeance,
wrapped himself in rage like a robe.
[18]As their deserts are, so will he requite them,
wrath to his adversaries, requital to his enemies.
[To the coastlands and islands he will make requital.]
[19]They will fear the name of YHVH from the west,
from the rising of the sun, his glory.
He will come like a pent-up torrent,
driven on by YHVH's breath.
[20]He will come to Zion as Redeemer
for those in Israel who turn from transgression.
A saying of YHVH.

THE GIFT OF PROPHECY (59:21)

59 [21]As for me, this is my covenant with them, declares YHVH: my spirit that
rests upon you and my words that I have put in your mouth will not be absent
from your mouth or from the mouths of your descendants, or from those of the
descendants of your descendants declares YHVH, from this time forward and
for ever more.

AN APOSTROPHE TO ZION (60:1–22)

i

60 [1]Rise up, shine forth, for your light has come,
the glory of YHVH has dawned over you!
[2]Though darkness covers the earth
and deep gloom the nations,
YHVH shines over you like the dawn,
his glory appears over you.
[3]Nations will come to your light,
kings to the radiance of your dawn.

ii

⁴Lift up your eyes, look about you:
they are all assembling, they are coming to you!
Your sons will come from afar,
your daughters will be held on the hip.
⁵When you see it, you will be radiant,
your heart will thrill and dilate;
the sea's abundance will be lavished on you,
they will bring you the wealth of nations.
⁶Countless camels will cover your land,
young camels from Midian and Ephah;
all those from Sheba will come,
bearing gifts of gold and incense,
proclaiming the praise of Yahveh.
⁷All Kedar's flocks will be herded for you,
all Nebaioth's rams will be at your disposal;
they will be acceptable for offering on my altar,
and I will enhance the splendor of my house.

iii

⁸Who are these that fly like the clouds,
like doves to their dovecotes?
⁹The vessels from the coastlands are waiting,
ships of Tarshish in the lead,
to bring your sons from afar,
together with their silver and gold
for the name of YHVH your God,
for the Holy One of Israel;
for it is he has made you glorious.

iv

¹⁰Foreigners will build your walls,
their kings will minister to you.
In my wrath I struck you down,
but in my good pleasure I had compassion on you.
¹¹Your gates will always stay open,
day and night they will never be shut,
so they can bring you the wealth of nations,
with their kings leading the way.
[¹²For the nation or kingdom that will not serve you shall perish, and the nations
shall be utterly destroyed.]
¹³The glory of Lebanon will come to you,
cypress, fir tree, and box,
to adorn the place of my sanctuary;

I will honor the place where my feet rest.
¹⁴The children of those who oppress you
will come to you bending low;
all who despise you
will do homage at the soles of your feet.
They will address you as YHVH's City,
The Holy One of Israel's Zion.
¹⁵Instead of being abandoned and hated,
unheeded by those passing by,
I will make you an object of pride forever,
a joy for all generations.
¹⁶You will suck the milk of nations,
you will be suckled at the breast of royalty.
Then you will acknowledge
that I am YHVH your Savior,
your Redeemer, the Strong One of Jacob.

v

¹⁷In place of bronze, I bring gold;
in place of iron, I bring silver;
bronze in place of wood, iron in place of stone.
I assign Peace as your overseer,
Righteousness as your taskmaster.
¹⁸Never again will the sound of violence
be heard in your land;
there will be neither devastation nor destruction
within your borders;
you will name your walls Salvation,
Praise you will name your gates.
¹⁹No longer will the sun be your light in the daytime,
nor the moon give you light in the nighttime,
for YHVH will be your light everlasting,
your God will be your splendor.
²⁰Your sun will no longer go down,
your moon will not set,
for YHVH will be your light everlasting,
and your days of mourning will be ended.

vi

²¹Your people, righteous one and all,
will possess the land forever,
the shoot that I myself planted,
the work of my hands so that I might be glorified.
²²The least will become a thousand,

the youngest a numerous nation.
I am YHVH!
At its appointed time,
swiftly will I bring it about.

THE PROPHETIC DISCIPLE'S MISSION (61:1–7)

i

61 ¹The spirit of the Sovereign Lord YHVH is upon me,
because YHVH has anointed me.
He has sent me to announce good news to the poor,
to bind up the wounds of those broken in spirit;
to proclaim freedom to captives,
release to those in prison;
²to proclaim the year of YHVH's good pleasure,
a day of vindication for our God;
³to comfort all those who mourn,
to give to those who mourn over Zion
a turban in place of ashes,
festive oil in place of a mournful appearance,
a splendid garment in place of a drooping spirit.

ii

They will be called strong and sturdy oaks
that YHVH has planted for his glory.
⁴They will rebuild the ancient ruins,
restore the places long desolate,
repair the ruined cities
desolate for ages past.
⁵Foreigners will serve as shepherds of your flocks,
aliens will farm your land and dress your vines;
⁶but you will be called priests of YHVH,
you will be addressed as ministers of our God.
You will live off the wealth of nations,
you will revel in their riches.
⁷Instead of shame, they will have a double portion,
instead of disgrace, they will exult in their lot;
they will possess a double portion in their land,
everlasting joy will be theirs.

COVENANT OF BLESSING AND A HYMN OF THANKSGIVING (61:8–11)

i

61 8I, YHVH, love justice,
I hate rapine and wrongdoing.
I will give them a sure reward
and make with them a perpetual covenant.
9Their descendants will be known among the nations,
their offspring in the midst of the peoples;
all who see them will acknowledge
that they are a people blessed by YHVH.

ii

10I will rejoice in YHVH with all my heart,
my whole being will delight in my God,
for he has clothed me in the garments of triumph,
wrapped me in the robe of victory,
as a bridegroom puts on a turban like a priest,
or a bride adorns herself with her finery.
11As the earth brings forth its growth,
as a garden causes its plants to flourish,
so will the Sovereign Lord God make victory and renown
to flourish before all the nations.

THE NEW JERUSALEM (62:1–5)

62 1For Zion's sake I will not be silent,
for Jerusalem's sake I will not be still
till her vindication breaks out like the morning light,
her salvation burns bright like a flaming torch.
2Then nations will see your vindication,
all kings will witness your glory;
you will be called by a new name
that YHVH himself will bestow;
3you will be a splendid crown in YHVH's hand,
a royal diadem in the palm of God's hand.
4Nevermore will you be called "the Forsaken One,"
nevermore will your land be called "the Desolate One";
but you will be called "I Delight in Her,"
and your land will be called "Espoused,"
for YHVH will take delight in you,

and your land will indeed be espoused.
[5]As a young man weds a young woman,
so will your children be united with you;
as the bridegroom rejoices over the bride,
so will your God rejoice over you.

PROPHETS, GUARDIANS OF THE CITY (62:6–9)

i

62   [6]Upon your walls, O Jerusalem, I have posted watchmen;
they will never be silent, by day or by night.
O you who invoke YHVH's name, take no rest,
[7]and give no rest to YHVH,
until he establish Jerusalem solid and firm
and spread her renown throughout the earth.

ii

[8]YHVH has sworn with his own right hand,
with his mighty arm:
"Nevermore will I give your grain to feed your foes,
nor shall foreigners drink the wine
that you have toiled to produce;
[9]but those who harvest the grain shall eat it
and give praise to YHVH;
and those who gather the grapes shall drink the wine
within my sacred courts."

THE PROCESSIONAL WAY (62:10–12)

62   [10]Pass through, pass through the gates!
Clear a way for the people;
build up the highway, build it up,
clear away the stones,
raise a signal over the peoples!
[11]See, YHVH has proclaimed
from one end of the earth to the other:
"Tell daughter Zion,
See, your salvation comes;
see, his reward is with him,
his recompense precedes him."
[12]They will call them "the Holy People,"
"the Redeemed of YHVH,"

and you will be called "Sought Out,"
"City No Longer Forsaken."

A BLOODBATH IN EDOM (63:1–6)

63 ¹"Who is this that comes from Edom,
with glistening garments from Bosrah,
this person splendidly attired,
striding in the fullness of his power?"

"It is I who speak what is right,
who contend in order to save."

²"Why is your clothing all red,
your garments like those of the one
who treads grapes in the winepress?"

³"I have trod the wine vat alone,
no one from all the peoples was with me;
I tread them down in my anger,
I trample them in my fury.
Their lifeblood spatters my garments,
I have stained all my clothing.
⁴A day for vengeance is on my mind,
my year of redemption has arrived;
⁵I look for a helper, but there is none,
I am aggrieved that there is no one to sustain me;
so my own arm won me the victory,
my fury it was that sustained me.
⁶I trample peoples in my anger,
I make them drunk with my fury,
I pour out their lifeblood on the ground."

A COMMUNITY LAMENTS (63:7–64:11[12])

i

63 ⁷I will recite the benevolent acts of YHVH,
his deeds worthy of praise,
for all the favors he has shown us,
his abundant goodness to the household of Israel;
the favors he bestowed on them in his compassion
and in the abundance of his benevolence.

[8]He thought, "Surely they are my people,
children who will not play me false,"
so he became for them a savior.
[9]In all their afflictions he too was afflicted,
and the angel of his presence saved them.
In his love and his pity,
he himself redeemed them;
he lifted them up and carried them
for all the days of old.

ii

[10]Yet they rebelled and grieved his holy spirit,
so he turned against them and became their enemy;
he himself made war against them.
[11]Then they recalled the days of old:
[Moses, his people]
Where is the one who brought them up from the sea
together with the shepherd of his flock?
Where is the one who placed within him
his holy spirit;
[12]the one who sent his splendid power
to go at the right hand of Moses;
who divided the waters before them
to win himself a name everlasting;
[13]who led them through the watery depths
like horses through the desert without stumbling?
[14]Like cattle going down into the valley,
the spirit of YHVH gave them respite.
Thus did you lead your people
to win yourself a glorious name.

iii

[15]Look down from heaven and see,
from your holy, glorious, and exalted dwelling!
Where is your zeal, your power,
your abundant, tender compassion?
Do not stand aloof, [16]for you are our Father!
Were Abraham not to know us,
Israel not to acknowledge us,
yet you, YHVH, are our Father,
our Redeemer from old is your name.
[17]YHVH, why do you let us stray from your paths,
why harden our hearts, so that we do not revere you?
Return for the sake of your servants,
the tribes you have inherited.
[18]Why have the reprobates made light of your holy place?

Our adversaries have trampled down your sanctuary.
^{19a}We have long been like those over whom you do not rule,
as though we no longer bore your name.

iv

^{19b}Would that you might rend the heavens and come down,
that the mountains might quake in your presence,
64 ¹[like fire that ignites the kindling,
like fire that makes the water boil]
to make your name known to your adversaries;
so that nations will tremble before you
²when you do awesome deeds we could not hope for.
[When you came down, the mountains quaked in your presence.]
³From ages past no ear has ever heard or heeded,
no eye has ever seen any god but you,
who acts on behalf of those who wait for him.
⁴You come to meet those who rejoice to do what is right,
those who keep you in mind by observing your ways.
But when you grew angry, we sinned;
when you hid yourself, we transgressed.
⁵We have become like a thing unclean,
all our righteous acts like a filthy rag;
we all shrivel up like a leaf,
our iniquities bear us off like the wind.
⁶There is none who invokes your name,
who bestirs himself to hold on to you;
for you have hidden your face from us,
you have handed us over to our iniquities.

v

⁷Yet you, O YHVH, are our Father;
we are the clay, you are the one that shaped us;
we are all the work of your hand.
⁸Do not then be angry beyond measure,
nor forever bear iniquity in mind.
Consider, we are all your people!
⁹Your holy cities are a wilderness,
Zion, too, has become a wilderness,
Jerusalem a place of desolation.
¹⁰Our holy house, our pride and joy,
where our ancestors sang your praise,
has been consumed by fire;
our most precious possession has been turned into a shambles.
¹¹In view of all this, will you stand aloof, O YHVH?
Will you keep silent and afflict us beyond measure?

JUDGMENT ON THE SYNCRETISTS (65:1–7)

65 ¹I was ready to be sought out, but they did not ask for me,
I was ready to be found, but they did not seek me;
I said, "Here I am, here I am"
to a nation that did not invoke my name.
²All day long I spread out my hands
to a stubborn, rebellious people,
who go their evil way,
following their own devices;
³a people that provokes me
continually to my face.
They offer sacrifices in gardens,
they burn incense upon bricks;
⁴they squat among the tombs,
pass the night among the rocks.
They eat the flesh of pigs,
with broth of unclean things in their pots.
⁵They say, "Keep your distance;
do not approach me, for I have been set apart from you."
These are smoke in my nostrils,
a fire that burns all the time.
⁶Observe: it is recorded in my presence!
I shall not be silent; rather, I shall requite,
I shall requite in full measure ⁷their iniquities
and those of their forebears together.
[A saying of YHVH]
Since they burn incense on the mountains,
and on the hills they insult me,
I shall first take stock of their deeds
and then requite them in full measure.

WHO ARE AND ARE NOT GOD'S PEOPLE (65:8–12)

i

65 ⁸These are YHVH's words:
When there is still some juice in a bunch of grapes,
people say, "Don't destroy it; there's a blessing in it."
So shall I do for the sake of my servants,
so as not to destroy all the people.
⁹I shall bring forth descendants from Jacob,

from Judah heirs to inherit my mountains.
My chosen ones will inherit the land,
my servants will have their abode there.
¹⁰Sharon will be grazing for flocks,
the Vale of Achor pasture for cattle;
they will be for my people who seek me.

ii

¹¹But you who forsake YHVH
and neglect my holy mountain,
who spread a table for the god of good luck
and fill bowls of mixed wine for the god of destiny,
¹²I shall destine you for the sword;
you will all crouch down to be slaughtered—
because, when I called, you would not answer;
when I spoke, you would not listen;
but you did what was evil in my sight,
you chose what did not please me.

ESCHATOLOGICAL REVERSAL (65:13–16)

65   ¹³These, therefore, are the words of the Sovereign Lord YHVH:
My servants will eat, while you go hungry;
my servants will drink, while you go thirsty;
my servants will rejoice, while you are put to shame;
¹⁴my servants will exult with heartfelt joy,
while you cry out with heartache
and wail with anguish of spirit.
¹⁵You will leave your name behind as a curse for my chosen ones,
[May the Sovereign Lord YHVH put you to death!]
but his servants will be called by a different name,
¹⁶so that the one who blesses himself in the land
will do so by the God whose name is Amen,
and the one who swears an oath in the land
will do so by the God whose name is Amen,
for the former troubles are forgotten
and are hidden from my sight.

NEW HEAVEN, NEW EARTH, NEW CITY (65:17–25)

65   ¹⁷See, I am about to create new heavens and a new earth;
the former things will no more be remembered,

nor will they come to mind.
¹⁸Rejoice, rather, and take delight unending
in what I am about to create!
I shall create Jerusalem as a delight,
her people as a source of joy;
¹⁹I shall take delight in Jerusalem
and rejoice in my people.
No more will the sound of weeping be heard in her,
no more the cry of distress.
²⁰No child there will ever again live but a few days,
no old man fail to live out his full span of life.
Whoever dies at a hundred will be just like a youth,
whoever falls short of a hundred will be reckoned accursed.
²¹When they build houses, they will dwell in them,
when they plant vineyards, they will eat their produce;
²²they will not build for others to live in,
they will not plant for others to eat.
Like the life-span of a tree will the life-span of my people be,
my chosen ones will long enjoy the work of their hands.
²³They will not toil in vain
or bear children destined for disaster;
they will be a race blessed by YHVH,
they and their offspring with them.
²⁴Before they call out, I shall answer;
while they are yet speaking, I shall hear their prayer.
²⁵The wolf and the lamb will graze together,
the lion will eat hay like the ox.
[As for the snake, dust will be its food.]
No longer will they hurt or destroy
on all my holy mountain.
This is what YHVH says.

VINDICATION OF THE TRUE WORSHIPERS
OF GOD (66:1–6)

i

66 ¹This is what YHVH says:
Heaven is my throne, the earth is my footstool.
What kind of house could you build for me?
What kind of place for my abode?
²Did not my hand make all of these,
and all these things came to be?
[A pronouncement of YHVH]

But on these I look with favor:
the poor, the afflicted in spirit, and those who tremble at my word.

ii

³He who slaughters an ox kills a man;
he who sacrifices a sheep wrings a dog's neck;
he who makes a cereal offering (offers) the blood of a pig;
he who makes a memorial offering with frankincense
pronounces a blessing over an idol.
They too have chosen to go their own way,
they take delight in their idols;
⁴so I will choose to punish them
and bring on them the things that they dread;
for when I called, there was no one to answer,
when I spoke, they would not listen;
but they did what was evil in my sight,
choosing what was displeasing to me.

iii

⁵Hear the word of YHVH, you who tremble at his word!
Your brethren who hate you,
who cast you out for my name's sake, have said,
"May YHVH reveal his glory, that we may witness your joy!"
But it is they who will be put to shame.

iv

⁶That sound of tumult from the city,
that thundering from the temple,
it is the sound of YHVH dealing out
retribution to his enemies!

MOTHER ZION AND HER CHILDREN (66:7–16)

i

66 ⁷Before she went into labor, she gave birth,
before the birth pangs came on her, she bore a son.
⁸Who ever heard the like?
Who ever witnessed such events?
Can a land come to birth in a single day?
Can a nation be born all at once?
Yet, as soon as Zion was in labor,
she gave birth to her children!
⁹Shall I open the womb and not bring to birth?

[YHVH says]
Shall I, who bring to birth, close up the womb?
[Says your God]

ii

¹⁰Rejoice with Jerusalem, take delight in her,
all you who love her!
Be exceedingly joyful with her,
all you who now mourn over her;
¹¹that you may nurse and be satisfied
at her consoling breast;
that you may drink deeply with delight
at her splendid bosom.

iii

¹²For this is what YHVH says:
I will extend prosperity to her like a river,
the wealth of nations like a torrent in full spate.
Your infants will be carried on the hip,
dandled on the knees.
¹³As a mother comforts her son,
so will I comfort you;
you will find comfort in Jerusalem.
¹⁴You will witness it, your hearts will rejoice,
your bones will flourish like grass.
YHVH's power will be known among his servants
and his indignation among his enemies.

iv

¹⁵See, YHVH comes in fire,
his chariots like the whirlwind,
to requite with his furious anger,
to rebuke with a flame of fire.
¹⁶For with fire YHVH enters into judgment,
and with his sword on all humanity;
those slain by YHVH will be many.

A SENSE OF AN ENDING (66:17–24)

i

66 ¹⁷As for those who consecrate and purify themselves to enter the gardens
following the one in the center, who partake of swine's flesh, unclean things
and rodents, their deeds and their devices will together come to an end: a declaration of YHVH.

ii

¹⁸I am coming to gather together nations of every tongue, so that they can come and witness my glory. ¹⁹I shall place a sign among them, and I shall send some of them, the survivors, to the nations, to Tarshish, Put and Lud, Meshech and Tubal, Yavan and the distant coastlands and islands, those who have neither heard about me nor witnessed my glory. They will proclaim my glory among the nations. ²⁰They will bring all your brethren from all the nations as an offering for YHVH. They will bring them on horseback, in chariots and covered wagons, on mules and dromedaries, to Jerusalem my holy mountain, says YHVH, just as the Israelites themselves bring the cereal offering in ritually clean vessels to the house of YHVH. ²¹Some of them I shall take as priests, as Levites, says YHVH.

iii

²²For, as the new heavens and the new earth that I am about to make will endure in my presence—YHVH declares—so will your posterity and your name endure. ²³And each month at the new moon, and each week on the Sabbath, all flesh will come to worship in my presence: YHVH declares.

iv

²⁴They will go out and gaze on the corpses of the men who rebelled against me; for neither will the worm that consumes them die nor the fire that burns them be quenched; they will be an object of horror to all flesh.

[²³And each month at the new moon, and each week on the Sabbath, all flesh will come to worship in my presence: YHVH declares.]

INTRODUCTION

◆

INTRODUCTION TO
ISAIAH 56–66

◆

1. ISAIAH 56–66 AS PART OF THE BOOK OF ISAIAH

DUHM'S HYPOTHESIS AND ITS VICISSITUDES

The anonymous prophecies in chs. 56–66 have long been known by the title Trito-Isaiah. Understood as the production of a single author, these chapters first emerged as a distinctive work in the commentary of Bernhard Duhm, the first edition of which was published in 1892. Duhm's Trito-Isaianic hypothesis had a surprisingly large measure of success, considering how brief and laconic his arguments in its favor were. According to Duhm, the difference between chs. 40–55 and chs. 56–66 is largely a difference of subject matter, since the interest of the theocratic author of 56–66 in such legal matters as sacrifice and Sabbath is not shared by the prophetic author of 40–55. Concern with such matters requires a later date, with a community well established and having to deal with opposition from their Northern neighbors in Samaria, who were intent on building a schismatic temple. This suggested to Duhm a date shortly before Nehemiah's arrival in Jerusalem in the mid–fifth century. Deutero-Isaiah and Trito-Isaiah were first brought together around the beginning of the second century B.C.E., and the book of Isaiah achieved its final form under the Hasmonean Queen Salome (78–69 B.C.E.), the golden age of Pharisaism and scribalism.

The basic premise of Duhm's hypothesis imposed itself in spite of, or perhaps in part because of, its implicit contrast between a genuinely prophetic Deutero-Isaiah and his theocratic and legalistic successor, a bias characteristic of much biblical scholarship in the nineteenth and early twentieth century. But the hypothesis did not pass without criticism.

One of the most prominent dissenters was Charles Cutler Torrey, for whom chs. 34–35 and 40–66 represented a single literary work. Torrey lamented the fact that "the once great 'Prophet of the Exile' has dwindled to a very small figure, and is all but buried in a mass of jumbled fragments" (Torrey 1928, 4). Torrey saw the beginning of this fragmentation in an unjustified distinction between a Second Isaiah of Babylonian origin and the author of much or all of 49–66 or 56–66 of Palestinian origin—a distinction taken for granted rather than argued by many commentators since Torrey (e.g., Glahn 1934; Muilenburg

1956, 396–98; Haran 1963, 127–55). Torrey complained that the process of paring away bits from this great work, which he titled "The Second Isaiah," began with a penknife and ended with a hatchet, resulting in what he described as "an incomprehensible scrap-heap" (Torrey 1928, 13).

A more recent dissenter from the Duhmian consensus was James D. Smart. Smart was also concerned with distinguishing genuinely prophetic faith from ceremonial and legalistic religion. He succeeded in saving the unity of 40–66 by the simple expedient of reducing the legalistic element to 56:1–7 and 58:13–14, which insist on Sabbath observance, and then eliminating both passages. For Smart, the differences between 40–55 and 56–66 at the literary level can be explained in terms of different situations and genres without sacrificing unity of authorship. Isaiah 40–55 was conceived as one great work addressed to Israelites everywhere, while chs. 56–66 comprise a collection of shorter sayings from the same author addressed to his own congregation. All of this literary activity took place in Judah (Smart 1965, 228–36).

After summarizing the views of previous dissidents (Torrey, Smart, Morgenstern, Banwell, Haran), Fritz Maass (1967, 153–63) noted that Duhm's identification of 56–66 as the work of one individual was no longer in favor and argued that the prophetic career of the author of 40–55 could have continued for some time under changed circumstances. While chs. 56–66 contain many accretions, a Deutero-Isaianic core can be detected in the following passages: 57:14–19; 58:1–12; 59:1–3, 9–21, chs. 60–62; and 66:1–16.

At the time of writing, Christopher R. Seitz (1992, 501–7; 2001, 309–23) expressed misgivings about the propriety of giving independent treatment to chs. 40–66. In his ABD article, Seitz argues that the great theme of the restoration of Zion is not confined to 56–66 but has an important function throughout 40–66. Different subject matter rather than a quite different time period (for Duhm, the fifth rather than the sixth century) could account for the acknowledged differences, both literary and thematic, between 40–55 and 56–66 without necessarily surrendering unity of authorship. He suggests, finally, that once one abandons a Babylonian setting for 40–55, there may be no other compelling reason for dividing 40–66 into two segments of unequal length (sixteen and eleven chapters). In the introduction to his NIB commentary, however, he seems to be proposing a break between 40–53 and 54–66 based on the passage from discourse about the Servant to discourse of the Servants, understood to be disciples of the persecuted prophet of ch. 53 (Seitz 2001, 317). This gives him the following outline: 40:1–31; 41–48; 49–53; 54–66. It remains unclear whether this is taken to entail originally distinct collections or simply important points of passage in the development of a theme.

In the same NIB commentary (2001, 310–12), Seitz raises the question of the suitability of writing an introduction to one section of a biblical book which in the premodern period was read as a single work. As he sees it, the problem with this procedure is that the commentator easily overlooks the place and theological function of the section within the book as a canonical unit. On this point he is in agreement with Brevard S. Childs (1979, 325–30), who maintains that chs. 40–66 were deliberately dehistoricized to enable them to be read as the eschatological fulfillment of the prophecies in chs. 1–39. Childs's conclusion is that 40–66 makes sense theologically only if read in tandem with 1–39 and that the material in Second Isaiah probably never circulated independently of an earlier form of First Isaiah. It seems that Seitz, for whom the last 27 chapters of the book constitute "Isaiah's powerful conclusion" (2001, 312), presumably referring to the book rather than the prophet, is in agreement with this position.

Since this "canonical" approach to the Book of Isaiah was criticized in my previous two volumes (1, pp. 87–89; 2, pp. 48–50, 54–55), little need be added here. The view that Isa 40–55 (Deutero-Isaiah) was deliberately dehistoricized is not only unsupported by evidence but neglects the historical references actually present in it, conspicuously the career of Cyrus and the fall of Babylon. For both Childs and Seitz, it seems to be *theologically* necessary for biblical books to be coherent, well thought-out units so that, if it could be shown that a biblical book such as Isaiah is a compilation of disparate materials, a *mixtum compositum* (Lau 1994, 5), it would be impossible to extract theological meaning, or at least the proper canonical meaning, from its components.

But the canonicity of the book of Isaiah was, from the beginning, affirmed only because it was believed to have been composed by one divinely inspired author called Isaiah. Those who still hold this belief will continue to affirm unity on the basis of authorship, though to demonstrate it persuasively will not be easy. Those for whom it is critically impossible to do so will, in the first place, look for internal consistency and interconnections on literary grounds, as in any other ancient text, but without assuming that theological and canonical meanings necessarily presuppose literary unity. This brings us back to Isa 56–66 and the relation of these chapters to the other major components of the book of Isaiah.

ISAIAH 56:1: CONTINUITY AND A NEW BEGINNING

The fact that neither section 40–55 nor section 56–66 bears a title or superscription comparable to 1:1; 2:1; and 13:1 does not exclude the possibility that they constitute distinct sections of the book. These sections may well have had titles originally, at least of a kind comparable to those introducing Deutero- and Trito-Zechariah (Zech 9:1; 12:1), but once the entire book was put under the name of Isaiah (1:1), they may well have been removed. Most attentive readers will recognize that 56:1–8 sounds a new note, having little in common with what precedes—most but not all, for in this as in other respects Torrey (1928, 426–29) went his own way. He excised 56:2–6 as an insertion from a later hand, and read the rest of 55:1–56:8 as a unit, "a noble utterance, conceived in a truly catholic spirit."

Among more recent commentators, Steck (1987a, 228–46) attempted to connect 55 with 56–59 by the occasional verbal link (e.g., *qārôb*, "near," in

55:6) and 56:1, and by the suggestion, surely an improbable one, that the invitation to eat and drink in 55:1–3 is addressed sarcastically to the "wild animals," (i.e., Israel's enemies) in 56:9—thus establishing another verbal and thematic link between chs. 55 and 56.

The limitations of this rather desultory use of verbal parallels are also apparent in Beuken's presentation of 56–57 as a commentary on 55 (Beuken 1986a, 48–64). But it seems that the only clear and explicit connection between 56:1–8 and 55:1–13 is the phrase "A perpetual sign that shall not be cut off" in 55:13, a modified version of which appears in 56:5. What we can hold onto is that 55:1–13, one of the most theologically positive and satisfying chapters in the entire book, recapitulates chs. 40–54. (See Volume 2, pp. 367–73). Its final verses (55:10–13) form an inclusion with 40:3–5, 8 on the theme of return from foreign lands and the permanent validity of the (prophetic) word of God.

In a brief study of Isa 56:1, Rolf Rendtorff (1993a, 181–89) made the useful point that in biblical texts conclusions are generally easier to detect than beginnings, and that 55:1–13 is such a conclusion, recapitulating the preceding chapters. But from the twofold appearance of the word ṣĕdāqâ with different meanings in 56:1 ("what is right" and "deliverance," respectively, in my translation), the former of frequent occurrence in 1–39, the latter in 40–55, he went on to draw the conclusion that 56:1 was meant to create a deliberate continuity with the two preceding segments of the book while at the same time representing a new beginning. This is an important point. In subject matter, tone, and emphasis, chs. 56–66 are distinct enough to warrant separate treatment, yet they belong on the same textual and exegetical continuum as chs. 40–55. Their relationship with the heterogeneous material in 1–39, some of it certainly as late as if not later than 56–66, is not nearly so perspicuous, as we shall see.

ISAIAH 56–66 IN RELATION TO ISAIAH 40–55

Some of the ways in which chs. 56–66 mark a further stage of development and differentiation vis-à-vis chs. 40–55 will be apparent at first reading. While both sections are directed at Jewish communities, chs. 40–55 are concerned primarily with Judah's place on the international scene. YHVH's purposes are here seen to be implemented by human agents, Cyrus in the first place, and polemic is directed against cults practiced by foreign peoples. Literary forms and metaphoric language appropriate to these themes predominate, the most characteristic (especially in 40–48) being the trial scene together with much forensic terminology.

In 56–66, on the other hand, interest is focused on internal affairs. The prospect held out is that of direct divine action, whether in judgment or salvation, and no more is heard of the Persian conquests or other kinds of political agency. Alien (i.e., syncretic) cults practiced within the community are targeted rather than cults of foreign peoples.

But continuity is also in evidence. The theme of return and national reintegration is pursued in the last 11 chapters, especially in the central panel 60–

62, as it is in the 16 chapters preceding, and the destiny of Jerusalem becomes more insistently a concern as we move from one section to the next. To give a very rough idea in terms of usage: the names "Jerusalem" and "Zion" appear 5 times in 40–48, 11 times in 49–55, and 14 times in 56–66.

To expand this general statement into a fairly comprehensive, inner-Isaianic exegetical history would require a study of monograph length. As a *faute de mieux*, I will try to convey an idea of the continuities, occasional discontinuities, and developments within these chapters by looking briefly at some of the more prominent thematic terms occurring in both 40–55 and 56–66. For a more complete list of central themes, see Sekine 1989, 183–216.

COMFORT (verb *nḥm*). The promise at the outset of divine comfort for Jerusalem, ruined by the Babylonian invasion (40:1), comes prominently into view as we read through chs. 49–55 (49:13; 51:3, 12, 19; 52:9). It is promised to those who mourn for Zion (61:2–3) and rounds off the final section—and therefore the book, with the tender image of the mother comforting her child (66:13). The recurrence of this motif helps to draw together similar assurances that, for those who heed the prophetic message, all manner of things will be well.

THE WAY (substantive *derek, měsillâ*). In the early chapters, this seminal and multivalent term has a strongly physical connotation—a way through the wilderness, a way from the land of exile to the homeland (40:3; 43:19; 49:11), perhaps with the underlying sense of a processional route, a *via sacra* (cf. 35:8, *derek haqqōdeš*). In chs. 56–66 the same language is used, including repetition characteristic of 40–55, but this term, which is so easily spiritualized or eschatologized, is now a metaphor for a way out of the mess in which the community finds itself, a way in the direction of redemption. The physical obstacle that must be removed is now reinterpreted as a sinful way of life, which can then serve as an explanation for the delay in the fulfillment of the promises (Zimmerli 1963[1950], 217–33). The language consciously imitates 40:3: "Build up, build up, and clear the way / remove every obstacle from my people's path" (57:14 see also 62:10).

THE COMING OF GOD (WITH POWER). Toward the beginning of 40–55, the coming, and therefore the presence, of God is to be discerned in the political arena: "YHVH is coming with power / his strong arm affirms his rule" (40:10); hence the metaphor of God's arm, symbol of the power to rule, to bring about real changes as only rulers can (51:5). His arm will therefore be raised against the Babylonians (48:14) as it was in old times against Rahab (i.e., Egypt, 51:9). This metaphor, then, brings into play the canonical "mighty hand and outstretched arm" of the Exodus traditions (Deut 4:34; 5:15, etc). We notice here and throughout chs. 40–66 this tendency to "grid" the understanding of events and aspirations for the future on the narrative traditions. The metaphor continues to be used in 56–66 (59:16 = 63:5; 62:8), but it is becoming clearer that *the power of God is essentially and radically the power to overcome evil.* God will come in judgment—like a pent-up torrent (59:19), like fire (66:15)—but also in salvation (56:1; 59:20; 62:11–12), as a source of light (60:1).

The struggle for faith in the reality behind the language of God's advent and presence (*parousia* in early Christian texts) generates much of the energy we experience in reading these texts. It remains as much at the center of the religious life of the believer today as in the Persian province of Judah.

THE GLORY OF GOD (*kĕbôd YHVH*).   That the glory of God—the representation of the presence of the invisible God in some visible and apprehensible form—will be manifest to all peoples is proclaimed at the beginning of 40–55 (40:5) and further elaborated in 56–66, specifically at the beginning of the central panel, chs. 60–62. To see the glory is to pass from darkness to light, a prominent metaphor in 56–66 (58:8,10; 59:9; 60:1–2, 19–20). It is also clearer in this later formulation that the place where the glory will be manifested to nations and their rulers is Jerusalem (60:1–2; 66:18–19). In 40–55 God's agent will be "a light to the nations" (*'ôr gôyîm*, 42:6; 49:6, cf. *'ôr 'ammîm*, "a light to the peoples," 51:4). In keeping with the somewhat different view of divine action and human agency in 56–66, God's glory will appear over Jerusalem, and nations will come to the light (60:1–3).

Like the *melammu*, that is, the effulgence of divine origin surrounding Assyrian kings (cf. Isa 8:7), the divine *kābôd* is an attribute of YHVH as king. Allusions to YHVH as *melek hakkābôd* ("The King of Glory") in the processional Ps 24 and the frequent association of *kābôd* with divine kingship in other psalms (Pss 29; 102; 145) render a liturgical origin for this cluster of themes very probable. In Isa 1–39 the divine glory is associated with the royal title "YHVH Lord of the Hosts" (*YHVH ṣĕbā'ôt*, 6:3; 10:16; 24:23). In Isa 40–66 the focal point of much of the discourse is the complex metaphor of the coming of the God of Israel in glory to Jerusalem, where his kingship will be established, acknowledged, and proclaimed (Isa 40:5; 52:7; 60:1–2).

THE CREATOR GOD.   The emphasis in 40–55 on the God of Israel as universal creator (40:26, 28; 42:5; 45:7–8, 12, 18) was dictated by the polemic against the ostensibly more powerful gods of imperial Babylon and the religious ideology embodied in the canonical *Enuma Elish*. With the fall of Babylon, the rise of the Persian Empire, and the official acceptance by the court at Susa of the Zoroastrian state religion, less incompatible with "YHVH the God of heaven" than the Marduk cult, emphasis on this attribute of YHVH became less insistent. In place of the creation of the existing world, we hear that God will create new heavens and a new earth, replacing the old order ("the former things") that can now be forgotten (65:17–18). We note in passing that a term characteristic of 40–55, that is, *hāri'šōnôt* ("the former things") is given a new meaning and reference in 56–66.

JUSTICE, RIGHTEOUSNESS, SALVATION (*mišpaṭ, ṣĕdāqâ, yĕšû'â*).   It is well known that the terms "justice" and "righteousness" encapsulate the social ethic of the great eighth-century B.C.E. prophets: "Let justice roll down like water, and righteousness like an ever-flowing stream" (Amos 5:24). Both terms appear frequently with these meanings in all strata of Isa 1–39 (1:17, 21; 3:14; 4:14; 5:16, 23; 10:2; 16:5; 28:6; 30:18; 32:1), sometimes in combination, as a hendiadys (5:7; 9:6[7]; 28:17; 32:16–17; 33:5). They also appear with about the same frequency in 40–66 (40:14, 27; 42:1, 3, 4; 49:4; 51:4; 53:8; 54:14; 56:1; 58:2; 59:8, 14; 61:8). In later texts both terms, but especially ṣĕdāqâ, acquire an extended scope: broadening out from justice to justification or vindication to be brought about by divine intervention in a final act of judicial intervention; and from righteousness to the establishment of a righteous social order in the coming event of salvation. These changes can be observed only infrequently in 40–55. Thus, ṣĕdāqâ appears linked with yešaʿ or yĕšûʿâ ("salvation") in 45:8 and 56:1, 6, 8, with šālôm ("well-being") in 48:18, and with tĕšûʿâ(also "salvation") in 46:12–13, though it seems likely that this last passage is part of Hermisson's qārôb-Schicht assigned to Trito-Isaiah (Hermisson 1998:155; see Comments on the passage).

The same usage continues in 56–66 (56:1; 59:9,11,17; 61:10; 63:1) but is absent from 1–39, with the one significant exception of 1:27: "Zion will be saved in the judgment (mišpāṭ) / her penitents in the retribution (ṣĕdāqâ)," the opening line of the final stanza in the "Great Arraignment," which stands in conscious and deliberate parallelism with the last chapter of the book (see Volume 1, pp. 187–88).

THE SERVANT AND THE SERVANTS (ʿebed, ʿăbādîm).   The significance of this designation for understanding chs.56–66 has been increasingly recognized in recent publications (e.g., Beuken 1990, 67–87; Blenkinsopp 1997, 155–75). It seems that the language of servanthood was adopted by the Deuteronomists to express their ideas of instrumentality, primarily exercised by prophets and rulers. This will help to explain why in chs. 1–39 the term ʿebed appears in a religiously significant sense only twice, both in passages of Deuteronomic provenance (20:3; 37:35 = 2 Kgs 19:34; see Volume 1, pp. 321–32). In chs. 40–48, ʿebed occurs invariably in the singular and, setting aside the first of Duhm's four *Ebedlieder* (42:1–4), with reference to Jacob/Israel wherever an explicit identification is made (41:8–9; 44:1–2, 22; 45:4; 48:20). In the following section, chs. 49–55, the ʿebed is the individual referred to in the three remaining Duhmian passages (49:3, 5, 6; 52:13; 53:11) or in comments appended to them (49:7; 50:10).

The only exception to the individual reference in this section is 54:17 which speaks of the heritage of "the Servants of YHVH." Chapter 55 functions as a summation of 40–54 and the hinge between 40–54 and 56–66 (Volume 2, pp. 368–69). The reference to the Servants at the end of ch. 54 therefore functions, in rounding off the entire section, not only to signal a principal theme of 40–54 but to prepare the reader for the evolution of this theme, in the following chapters, which moves in the direction of a prophetic plurality. In 56–66, in fact, the term is used exclusively in the plural, either in a more general sense of devotees of YHVH (56:6; 63:17) or, in the last two chapters, with reference to a specific prophetic school or sect (65:8–9, 13–15; 66:14).

What we are observing in reading 56–66 in the light of 40–55 are developments along a textual and exegetical trajectory. The continuity is most clearly in evidence where a text in 56–66 reproduces, sometimes verbatim, entire verses or phrases from 40–55. Thus 62:11c quotes 40:10b verbatim, and the comparison of well-being with a river in the following verse (*kĕnāhār šālôm*) is taken from 48:18. Isaiah 60:9 combines phrases from 51:5b and 55:5b, suggesting the role of memory in transmission, not entirely unlike the way some early Christian texts combine different scriptural passages in a single quotation (e.g., Mark 1:2–3). The image of the glory of God as Israel's rearguard (verb *'sp*) in 58:8 replicates 52:12 together with its allusion to the Exodus tradition (Exod 14:19–20). In much the same way the repudiation of the idea of YHVH's hand (i.e., reach) being too short in 59:1 (verb *qṣr*) is taken from 50:2, here too with an echo of the narrative tradition of origins (Num 11:23). Among other motifs reproduced are: the lifting up of a signal (62:10 cf. 49:22), nursing at the breast (60:16 cf. 49:26), and the play on *bānîm/bônîm*, "children/builders" (62:5 cf. 49:17). Other examples will be noted in the commentary.

Interpretation of this kind is hardly ever simply reproduction, however. In almost all instances it involves a reactualization and therefore very often a problemization of the text, now considered to some degree authoritative, when introduced into a different situation. In 40–55 proselytes are acknowledged and accepted (44:5), but by the later stage represented by 56:1–8 the presence within the community of those who "join themselves to YHVH" has become a matter of dispute.

There are passages in 40–55 that reveal awareness that salvation is far off, 46:12–13 for example, but only in 56–66 (e.g., 59:9–15a) is the idea clearly expressed that the offer of salvation is contingent on removing the obstacle of individual and collective immorality. An important corollary of this shift is that the identity of God's people has become problematic. In *oratio recta* of the Deity, the phrase "my people" occurs unproblematically in chs. 40–55 beginning with the first verse, in the sense that the community addressed is essentially identical with the community of the historical traditions (e.g., 52:4–6). In 56–66 this can no longer be taken for granted. In the communal lament, YHVH expostulates that "surely they are my people" (63:8), but the response in 65–66 calls this statement into question: God recognizes as his people only those who seek him (65:10), those whom he acknowledges as his servants, his elect, those who tremble at his word (65:13–16; 66:5). We could read this as a step in the direction of the sectarian exegesis of the Qumran *pĕšārîm*.

ISAIAH 56–66 IN RELATION TO ISAIAH 1–39

While Isa 56–66, taken globally, can therefore be read productively as an exegetical extension or *Fortschreibung* of 40–55, no comparable relationship exists between 40–66 taken as a whole and the heterogeneous compilation of sayings in 1–39, some of which would be dated by many commentators later than 40–66. Chapters 1–39 are rhetorically quite different from 40–66, and, with respect to major themes, for example, polemic against false cults, divine titulary, and forms of human agency, the differences in treatment are more in evidence than the similarities (see further Volume 2, pp. 42–55).

The position adopted here, then, is as follows: (1) In terms of the great, general themes—the destiny of Jerusalem, the reality of judgment and salvation, the character of the God of Israel—all sections of the book have much in common. Concern with the destiny of Jerusalem, in evidence in Isaianic prophecies from the reigns of Ahaz and Hezekiah, not least in the final section, chs. 36–39, may have been an important reason for attaching chs. 40–55 to chs. 1–39. (2) The discourses in 56–66 reveal knowledge of early Isaianic sayings, but no more than of other earlier prophetic and nonprophetic material, and perhaps less than some non-Isaianic texts, especially Jeremiah. To cite one example: there are numerous points of contact, sometimes verbally identical, between Isa 40–66 and Jer 1–12. (3) A more complex and interesting relationship exists between the way certain exclusively Second Temple themes are treated in 1–39 and the way they are treated in 56–66; for example, Edom as reality and symbol (34:1–17; 63:1–6) and the admission of proselytes (11:11–12; 56:8).

There are relatively few sayings in 56–66 that betray familiarity with sayings in 1–39 that are deemed by most commentators to be proto-Isaianic. It has been proposed that the metaphor of the bunch of grapes, some good but most of them bad, in 65:8 has drawn on the vineyard song in 5:1–7, which is possible though hardly self-evident. Another example: It is striking that in 57:15 the YHVH discourse is introduced as emanating from *rām věnissā’*, "the One raised up on high," since the phrase occurs in the throne room vision (6:1). One might conclude from this to a strong thematic bond with proto-Isaiah, in the sense that the words of consolation in the second part of the book issue from the same God who was seen in vision by Isaiah centuries earlier. This is possible, but the allusion could be more casual.

We are on more solid ground with the unmistakable linguistic and thematic parallels between the first and last chapters of the book, or at least between 1:27–31 and 66:17–24. These have been the subject of much commentary in recent decades, which need not be documented once again, (see Volume 1, pp. 85–86, 187–88 and Comments on 66:17–24 below). It seems that this bracketing or enveloping editorial procedure, common in ancient texts, dates from the time when the prophetic corpus was being put together in its final form, the time in the Hellenistic period when books in something like the modern meaning of the term were beginning to be produced, and ancient texts were being assigned to authors. It implies that these 66 chapters were seen to comprise, *in some sense*, a literary and theological unity.

Of particular interest are the accounts of judgment on Edom in 34:1–17 and 63:1–6. At one point in these thematically similar passages, we come close to verbal parallelism:

kî yôm nāqām laYHVH / šěnat šillûmîm lěrîb ṣiyyôn

YHVH has a day of vengeance,
a year of reckoning for Zion's complaint. (34:8)

kî yôm nāqām bĕlibbî / ûšĕnat gĕ'ûlay bā'â

"A day of vengeance is on my mind,
my year of redemption has arrived." (63:4)

In other respects, however, the description of the horrors to be visited on Edom
is quite different in the two accounts. The language of ch. 34 is more overtly
apocalyptic, even more extreme than 63:1–6 and closer in detail to the predicted state of Babylon in ch. 13, featuring the "return to nature" theme. If,
moreover, chs. 34 and 35 belong together as two panels of a diptych, together
functioning as a recapitulation of the message of judgment and salvation in 1–
33, and, as such, derive from a late stage of redaction (as argued in Volume 1,
pp. 83, 450–51), 34:1–17 may as well have been borrowed from 63:1–6 as the
reverse.

An interesting example of intra-Isaianic exegesis occurs in the opening passage of 56–66: "An utterance of the Sovereign Lord YHVH, who gathers the
dispersed of Israel: 'I shall gather yet more to him besides those already gathered'" (56:8). The first half of the verse, in which the Sovereign Lord God is introduced as speaker (56:8a), is strikingly similar to the opening sentence of Isa
11:12–16, dealing with the same theme:

He will raise a *signal* for the nations,
and gather the dispersed men of Israel;
he will assemble the scattered women of Judah
from the four corners of the earth." (11:12)

But 11:12 is part of a larger exegetical unit. By means of the catchword *nēs*,
"signal," it is attached to 11:10, which is itself an addendum, that is, a comment on the "messianic" poem immediately preceding it (11:1–9): "On that
day the root of Jesse will stand as a *signal* for the peoples of the world; him will
the nations seek out; glory will rest on him." The signal is thereby reinterpreted
in 11:12 with a view to introducing the repatriation theme that is not present in
11:10. The same theme is introduced in the remaining gloss at 11:11, which interprets the signal as a hand signal given by YHVH: "On that day the Sovereign
Lord will raise his hand to recover the residue of his people. . . ." The shift from
a standard or ensign raised as a rallying point to a hand signal may have been
suggested by Isa 49:22:

Observe: I raise my hand to the nations,
I lift up a signal for the peoples;
they will carry your sons in their laps,
your daughters will be borne on their shoulders.

The author of 56:8 makes a significant contribution to this exegetical cluster in
two respects. The repatriation theme is eschatologized, in the sense of the final
ingathering of Israel, in keeping with the announcement at the beginning of

the passage (56:1); the ingathered people now include proselytes, "the others," whom the author has just assured of their good standing in the community.

2. THE LITERARY CHARACTER OF ISAIAH 56–66

STRUCTURE AS A CLUE TO MEANING

Isaiah 56–66 does not constitute what most people today would recognize as a literary work. To the extent that it exhibits coherence and unity, the effect is the result of redactional rather than authorial activity. At no point is it informed by purely aesthetic considerations, and thus, where a pleasing effect is obtained, it is more by accident than by design. It is what we might call *extreme writing*, a product of critical situations of which it was a part and to which it contributed. A complicating factor is that, at several points, it reproduces familiar types of oral performance, especially in those passages that are more clearly homiletic in character. But it hardly need be said that nothing in chs. 56–66 is a direct transcript of oral delivery.

The arrangement of the material can be construed in different ways. In this commentary it is divided into 25 passages, but the division is to some degree pragmatic and could be done otherwise. The familiar prophetic markers or speech formulas—*'āmar YHVH, koh 'āmar YHVH, nĕ'um YHVH* and others—are not frequent and not always indicative of distinct sayings since usage is often desultory, and some of these formulas occur within sayings. They are also confined to the first four and the last two chapters, where the shorter units occur. It is apparent that the classical prophetic genres (judgment-sayings, woe-sayings, sayings against foreign nations etc.) are breaking up and giving place to longer, less structured discourses.

The decisive influence in this process, both here and in 40–55, can be traced to the Deuteronomists (see Volume 2, pp. 51–54). The influence of the Deuteronomic theology on later prophecy is apparent in many ways: the redefinition of the prophet as "servant of YHVH" is the most obvious example, but it can also be seen in a more consistent appeal to the historical and legal traditions, fierce opposition to any kind of syncretism, and an uncompromising "YHVH alone" theology. A significant pointer in the same direction is the deliberate use of Deuteronomic language in the first-person divine address to a prophetic individual in 59:21, in which the choice of language ("covenant," "words placed in the prophet's mouth," "words that will not depart from the prophet's mouth") suggests an intent to align the Deutero-Isaianic prophetic succession with the "prophet like Moses" of Deut 18:15–18 (see Commentary ad loc.).

At several other points in the commentary we will note this strong Deuteronomic influence. Examples can easily be identified and verified: the description of the temple as a house of prayer (56:1–7 cf. 2 Kgs 8:41–43), reverence for the name of God (56:6 etc.), and the way in which covenant oaths are formulated (65:13–15, 21–22 cf. Deut 28:30, 47). The point to be made in this section is that these shifts in emphasis with respect to the prophetic function and agenda brought with them corresponding changes in the kind of discourse used. Volz puts it this way, if with some exaggeration: "The speaker [in chs. 56–66] is no longer elevated over the people and the community as a messenger of God; he is more a preacher, a pastor, a synagogue leader, a devout psalmist" (1932, 197). Thus: Isa 58:1–12 and Zech 7:1–19 can be read as sermons, or abstracts of sermons, on fasting; Isa 58:13–14 and Jer 17:19–27 as sermons on Sabbath observance; and Isa 59:1–15a, Zech 1:1–6, and Jer 7:1–26 as sermons on sin and its consequences—all in the Deuteronomic style. This is not to say that these passages are abstracts of sermons that were actually preached, since they could be literary imitations in the homiletic style. But the strongly oral character of this kind of discourse is difficult to explain if we exclude a plausible social situation for its original delivery.

Commentators have claimed to find many different macrostructural features in chs. 40–66—chiasmus, inclusio, ring arrangement, and so forth—some mutually incompatible and others lacking inevitability. Practically all scholars accept that the first chapter of Isaiah, or at least 1:27–31, forms an inclusio with the last chapter of the book, or at least 66:17–24. But it is less clear that 66:17–24, when read together with 56:1–8, forms an inclusio around 56–66. The two passages are quite dissimilar, and the only points of resemblance are the Sabbath (56:2, 4, 6; 66:23) and liturgical ministry (56:6–7; 66:21). But, since 55:1–13 recapitulates 40–54 and has its own inclusio (55:10–13 cf. 40:3–5, 8), 56:1–8 still clearly marks a new beginning.

In ancient texts, structure serves not just aesthetic ends but also as a vector of meaning. With respect to chs.40–66, it has been noticed, perhaps for the first time by Duhm (1922, 14), that the repetition of the phrase "there can be no well-being for the wicked" divides 40–66 into three equal segments of nine chapters each, ending with a lurid description of the ultimate fate of the wicked (48:22; 57:21; 66:24). Since the statement fits the context in 57:21 and not so well in 48:22, it may be that, at some point in the editorial history of the book, it was added at the end of ch. 48 precisely with a view to producing this triadic division. (1QIsaᵃ provides some support for this reading by leaving one-third of a line empty at 48:22 and most of a line after 57:21). But since 57:21, the original location of the phrase, does not seem to mark a major break in the text apart from serving as a fitting conclusion to 56–57, the division may have been purely practical and of no great significance otherwise.

There seems to be a consensus that chs. 60–62 form the central core of Trito-Isaiah and are quite distinctive compared with the four chapters that precede and the four that follow. The consensus is supported by the distribution of Masoretic *pisqôt* (paragraphs), since there are eight in 56–59 and eight in 63–66, all *sĕtûmôt* except the one *pĕtûḥâ* in 65:12c. This results in an a-b-a structure (56–59, 60–62, 63–66) by virtue of which the central panel presents the ideal situation in programmatic form, a kind of best-case scenario for the future. This structuring of the material provokes thought by juxtaposing and contrasting this ideal scenario with the real situation of a community going about its business, buying and selling, engaging in legal disputes, observing or not observing Sabbath, and beset by some severe problems. These problems are more severe in the third than in the first of the three sections (63–66), the tone more acrimonious, and the key term "Servants" (*'ăbādîm*) has a more restrictive scope, as we shall see,

I find a similar structure within chs. 60–62. The apostrophe to Zion in 60:1–22 is taken up again in 61:5–62:12, while the first-person declaration of a prophetic individual anointed with the spirit in 61:1–3 (extended form 61:1–7) is at the center, the *exact* center of chs. 60–62, since there are 44 stichometric lines preceding 61:1–3 and 44 following it. This arrangement is surely deliberate and reproduces the a-b-a pattern of 56–66 as a whole. I suggest that the point of this arrangement is that 61:1–3 is, in effect, the signature of the prophetic author of chs. 60–62. As such, it authenticates the "message" of 60–62, which the author is commissioned by God to announce in the spirit of the prophetic school to which he belongs (*lĕbaśśēr*, "announce," 61:1b; the same verb appears in 40:9; 41:27; 52:7). It also identifies those for whom the message is destined—the oppressed, the broken in spirit, the captives—and, in general, provides guidance regarding the way that 60–62 is to be read.

I add in parenthesis that this reading of the structure in the center of 56–66 has something in common with that of Pauritsch (1971), who proposed a cone-shaped model with two equal sections, 56–60 and 62–66, converging on ch. 61. He argues that it is in this chapter that the central message of God's concern for the outcast and poor (the *Ausgestossene und Arme* in Pauritsch's title) is heard. Pauritsch based his reading of Trito-Isaiah on the interesting but unverifiable hypothesis that the prophetic message, as encapsulated in the opening logion (56:1–8), was an authoritative response given in Jerusalem to a Judeo-Babylonian delegation of proselytes and eunuchs unsure of their good standing in the cult community.

Signs of deliberate structuring are not confined to chs. 60–62. YHVH is presented as warrior and vindicator of his people immediately before and after this central panel (59:15b–20; 63:1–6). There are laments, or at least complaints, before and after it (59:1–15a; 63:7–64:11); the former lament receives a positive response (59:15b–20), while the latter is given only an explanation why a positive response is not forthcoming (65:1–7). The denunciation of heterodox cult practices in 57:3–13 and 65:1–7 could also be seen as roughly symmetrical. Several scholars, finally, are convinced that 56:1–8 and 66:18–24 form an inclusio for the text as a whole (e.g., Sekine 1989, 228–33; Steck 1991a, 34–44). The injunction that closes 60–62—that is, 62:10–12 ("pass through, pass through the gates")—matches similar conclusions at 48:20–21 and 52:11–12 and provides confirmation that these three central chapters are in their original order. But the further away we get from the central panel, the less clear are such correspondences.

When we turn our attention to chs. 56–59, the first of the three major sections, we find that the author's signature is at the end rather than in the middle.

The strategic position of 59:21, a highly distinctive address to a prophetic individual in divine first-person speech, is indicated by the repetition of the key word *běrît* ("covenant") at the beginning and end of this first segment (56:4, 6; 59:21). The prophetic speech markers in 56:1–8, relatively rare elsewhere in 56–66, give us cause for believing that we are hearing an individual prophetic voice at the beginning and end of 56–59.

Further implications of these arrangements within chs. 56–66, including the last segment, 65–66, will be discussed in the section of the Introduction dealing with the formation of this segment of the book.

PROSODY AND GENRE IN CHAPTERS 56–66

With the exception of 59:21 and 66:18–20, chs. 56–66 are set off stichometrically in BHS. Without entering into the long and sometimes acrimonious debate about biblical poetry, it must suffice to note that, in 56–66 as elsewhere in the prophetic corpus, it is often impossible to distinguish between rhythmic prose and prosodically irregular verse. Moreover, the literary phenomenon of parallelism, which since Bishop Lowth's lectures of 1753 has been considered *the* characteristic of biblical poetry, occurs in cadenced prose as well as verse. There seems to have emerged a type of rhetorical and oratorical utterance, which can be appropriately called "recitative" (Volume 1, pp. 78–80), located on the spectrum between what is unmistakably prose and what is unmistakably verse, depending on the subject matter and the emotional charge that it generates.

An example of the range of possibilities must suffice. At one end of the band we have the short psalm in 61:10–11 ("I will rejoice in YHVH with all my heart"), in perfectly regular tricola (3–3), and the long psalm of communal lament and complaint in 63:7–64:11[12] in which we can see, through the various editorial additions and modifications, the intent to compose in the *qînâ* or limping measure (3–2) proper to the lament genre. While not belonging to a recognized verse genre, the emotionally charged apostrophe to Jerusalem in 60:1–22 maintains a high level of regularity in the 3–3 measure, omitting object marker, relative pronoun and, for the most part, definite article. At the other extreme, the 20 stichometric verses of 56:1–8 are very irregular, some of them do not scan at all, and no effort has been made to elide the object marker (*'et-*), definite article, or relative pronoun.

In recent decades the form-critical method seems to have lost its allure for many, perhaps most, biblical scholars. We are more attentive to the complexity of language and are aware that simply pinning a form-critical label on a text does not tell us much about it. It can also be misleading if it results in a positivistic and simplistic matching of text with social situation. There is the further point, made earlier, that in a text as late as Isa 56–66 the classical prophetic *Gattungen* have for some time been in a process of dissolution.

Some of the literary genres represented in chs. 56–66 are, nevertheless, recognizable, and their recognition can provide the first stage towards an eventual literary history of this section of the book. Some examples will be briefly mentioned here, leaving more detailed discussion to the commentary. Following the standard treatment of the hymns (Mowinckel 1962, 1:195–219), 63:7–64:11 [12] is seen to belong to the category of the psalms of communal lamentation. But then we note that the context has dictated the omission of the essential element of the "assurance of a hearing," an omission that is explained by the passage immediately following, which explains its absence from the psalm (65:1–7).

To take another example, the standard judgment-saying is represented by 56:9–12, 57:3–13, and 65:1–7, but we realize that this label does not measure up to the extremely vituperative language used in these passages, characteristic of much sectarian polemic. The opening passage, 56:1–8, is often categorized as a priestly or prophetic torah (instruction), but this leaves much unexplained, including the note of encouragement and exhortation that is not normally characteristic of this genre.

Chapters 58–59 have given rise to considerable form-critical conjecture. Muilenburg (1956, 686–87) described ch. 59 as a liturgy consisting in a sermon (vv 1–8), a public confession of sin (vv 9–15b), and absolution (vv 15c–20). But since, according to this hypothesis taken literally, the service in question would have lasted no more than five minutes (not impossible, but not probable either), we must assume that an abstract or summary of a service is intended.

This emended hypothesis would still not be free of the charge of form-critical positivism, since it neglects the possibility that 59:1–20 is a literary work modeled on such a service, always assuming that we knew what such a service was like or even whether it existed. More plausible is the identification of the chapter with a sermon (Kessler 1956, 337–38; Whybray 1975, 221: "a hell-fire sermon"), though here too we would have to assume either that it represents the very brief abstract of a sermon actually preached or a literary imitation of a homiletic style in vogue at that time.

It was common for earlier critical commentators to contrast the high literary and theological quality of Deutero-Isaiah (the presumed author of 40–55) with his less-gifted and less-inspired epigone, who produced all or most of 56–66. Not many of the scholars cited frequently in this commentary have paid much attention to the literary quality of these chapters. Among those who have done so we should mention Charles Cutler Torrey, who admittedly attributes all of 40–66, together with 34–35, to one author but loses no occasion to express appreciation for the aesthetic quality of much of this material. He praises, for example, ch. 59 as "this great poem *de profundis*" and is equally enthusiastic about ch. 60: "from the first verse to the last . . . one blaze of light" (Torrey 1928, 439, 443). Also deserving of special mention is the commentary of James Muilenburg, for whom the same ch. 60 is "a superb example of Hebrew literary style" (Muilenburg 1956:697).

Whatever opinion we form on their literary quality, it remains true that these chapters are not *belles lettres*. They fall into the category of polemical writing, produced to advance particular causes and to make an impact on the course of events, and should be judged accordingly.

3. ISAIAH 56–66 IN ITS HISTORICAL CONTEXT

THE POVERTY OF OUR KNOWLEDGE

Dating the last 11 chapters of Isaiah has not been easy, since they refer to no historical events and name no historical individuals. The lament for the destruction of Jerusalem and its temple (63:18; 64:9–10[10–11]) and the prediction of the rebuilding of "ancient ruins" (61:4) could suggest that a considerable amount of time had passed since the disastrous Babylonian campaign of 586 B.C.E., but it would still not provide an even approximate date for the composition of 56–66 as a whole or at least of the texts in which these statements appear. In another passage we hear that the city wall had not been rebuilt (60:10), but this could have been said anytime after 586 and prior to Nehemiah's administration in the mid-fifth century.

It would also be prudent to bear in mind that Jerusalem was subjected to attack and occupation more than once, under Persian, Ptolemaic, and Seleucid rule. A delegation to Nehemiah in Susa from Judah reported, sometime in 445 B.C.E., that the walls and gates of the city had been destroyed (Neh 1:1–3). This could hardly refer to the destruction of 586, which would not have been news in 445. The information was about a recent event, one that perhaps took place during the brief rebellion of the satrap Megabyzus, about which we are informed only by the unreliable Ctesias, or following on a Kedarite Arab raid on the city.

Jerusalem was also occupied briefly by Ptolemy I in 302/301 (Josephus, *Ant.* 12.4–10; *Ag. Ap.* 1.210), a circumstance that provided Steck (1991a, 237–38) with a fairly precise (but almost certainly mistaken) date for the composition or redaction of chs. 59–64. There were no doubt similar occasions during that long and troubled period of which we are ignorant. We simply do not have the information to locate the composition of these chapters within an absolute chronology with any degree of precision.

The same conclusion follows from the little that the texts tell us about the political and social condition of those addressed. Since the only references to political or religious leaders are metaphorical—they are good-for-nothing shepherds or dogs too lazy to bark (57:9–12)—we learn nothing *directly* about the political situation, including the impact of the imperial system on the province. The prevalence of syncretic religious practices (57:3–13; 63:1–7; 66:17) has, again, led some scholars (e.g., Volz, Steck) to opt for the Hellenistic period. But we shall see that these transgressive cults carried out in gardens, in tombs, and among the rocks can be viewed as well or better in continuity with well-documented religious practice during the last century of the Kingdom of Judah. For the most part, therefore, commentators are reduced to proposing dates based on the way they reconstruct the process of formation of these chapters in relation to chs. 40–55 (Deutero-Isaiah), on which there are practically as many hypotheses as there are commentators.

Most scholars today would, nevertheless, agree that the bulk of 56–66 reflects the situation in the province of Judah (Yehud) during the first century of Persian rule, corresponding more or less to the reigns of Darius I (522–486), Xerxes I (486–465), and Artaxerxes I (465–424). If we may take this as a reasonable working hypothesis, it will be useful to provide a brief summary of events during this epoch. We may then be in a better position to determine against this background at least the contours of currents and movements within contemporaneous Jewish communities as reflected in these chapters.

The source material for historical reconstruction is not abundant, and the information it provides is generally ideologically slanted and often unreliable. Much, too, has been lost or has survived only in fragments, including several histories or accounts of Persia written by Ctesias, Dionysios of Miletus, Hellanikos of Lesbos, and other Greek writers. The Greek historians, especially Herodotus, Xenophon, Thucydides, and what remains of Ctesias, are informative about Persian matters, and often entertaining, but betray no knowledge of the Palestinian hinterland, somewhat surprisingly in view of the archaeological evidence for Greek settlements along the Mediterranean coast and the import of Attic ware.

Royal inscriptions in Old Persian are important for royal ideology and for political, military, and social history but throw practically no light on the Trans-Euphrates region. The principal texts are as follows: the Behistun Inscription in Old Persian, Akkadian, and Elamite; the Naqš-I-Rustam mortuary texts; the Persepolis Fortification and Treasury tablets, written in Elamite with some dockets and glosses in Aramaic; and Xerxes' Daiva inscriptions.

Bearing on Cambyses and the early reign of Darius, we have, from Egypt, the inscription written on the statue of Udjahorresnet in the Vatican Museum and the Demotic Chronicle from the Ptolemaic period dealing with the codification of Egyptian laws under Darius I. The Aramaic texts from the Jewish military colony on the island of Elephantine at the first cataract of the Nile cover a good part of the fifth century and are of prime historical significance. The so-called Passover Papyrus written in 419, during the reign of Darius II, merits special mention.

Even more important for our purposes is the letter written in 408 to Bigvai (Bagoas), Persian governor of Judah, requesting permission to rebuild the Jewish temple on the island of Elephantine (Jeb) destroyed in a pogrom a few years earlier. Permission was received in a memorandum dispatched jointly by Bigvai and Delaiah of Samaria, couched in language that closely resembles the edict cited in Ezra 6:2–5.

With respect to the biblical texts: Ezra–Nehemiah covers only the first and last quarter of the century, leaving a gap between the completion of the rebuilding of the temple in 515 and the arrival of Ezra in 458. Scholars differ in assessing the historical reliability of its narratives (first and third person) and the official documents it cites. The Books of Chronicles, written in the late Persian or (less likely) the early Ptolemaic period, do not cover the period at all but could be expected to reflect some aspects of religious life in Judah under

Persian rule. While clearly fictional, Esther shows considerable knowledge of life and manners at the Persian court.

Among prophetic texts assigned to this period, Haggai and Zechariah 1–8 provide important information on one reaction within Jewish communities to the critical events of 520–518 (see below), while Malachi testifies to neglect of the normative cult and a general condition of disorientation and *anomie*, probably during the half-century preceding the activity of Ezra and Nehemiah. Joel, cult prophet or priest, writes about a public fast occasioned by a plague of locusts. Since it provides no clues at all to the date of composition, it could as well come from the second Persian century or even later.

A HISTORICAL SURVEY

From the beginning, prophecy in Israel, Judah, and the other relatively small west-Asian states was concerned with the rise and fall of the great Near Eastern empires, first the Assyrians (911–612 B.C.E.), then the Babylonians (626–539), and then the Persians (539–333). Since the earlier period, forming the background to Isa 40–55, was dealt with in the previous volume (2, pp. 92– 104; see also, even more recently, Baltzer 2001, 26–30), our survey can begin with the struggle for succession to the Persian throne following the death of Cambyses, successor to Cyrus, in 522.

Darius I (Dārayavauš), belonging to the cadet branch of the Achaemenid dynasty, seized control after disposing of a rival claimant, a certain Gaumata who claimed to be Bardiya, brother of Cambyses. Since Darius's legitimacy was contested, not without justification, he spent the first two years of his reign putting down revolts in many parts of the empire. His version of these events is presented in the propagandistic inscription carved out of the rock at Behistun, on the main caravan route from Baghdad to Tehran. Though his account is supported by the Greek historians, who are uniformly hostile to his predecessor, Cambyses, there is good reason for skepticism. As the historian J. M. Cook succinctly put it, "the story smells" (Cook 1983, 52).

During the critical years 522–520, and for long afterwards, the city of Babylon was one of the most resolute centers of opposition to Persian rule. The first revolt under Nidintu-Bel, who claimed descent from the great Nebuchadrezzar, took place in the autumn of 522 and was followed by another "messianic" uprising by a claimant to the Babylonian throne, an Armenian called Arkha, a year later (August to November 521). Both of these revolts were crushed and their leaders put to death. During most of this time, Darius himself resided in Babylon.

Close contact between the Judean homeland and expatriate Judeans settled in southern Mesopotamia was facilitated by the fact that Judah belonged to the same satrapy as Babylon. It is therefore not surprising that, within a year, prophets in Judah were predicting the collapse of the Persian Empire and the restoration of the native Judean dynasty in the person of Zerubbabel, grandson of Jehoiachin. second-last king of Judah (Hag 2:6–7, 20–23; Zech 6:9–15).

With the consolidation of Darius's power, these "messianic" aspirations petered out, and Zerubbabel disappeared from the scene under circumstances unknown to us. It is interesting to note that there seems to be no place for the national dynasty in the future projected in Isa 56–66.

The disturbances in Babylon in the early years of Darius's reign could have provided motivation for Judean settlers to emigrate to Judah, especially if the Jewish ethnic minority in and around Babylon and Nippur had come out in support of the native rebellions. That this actually happened is suggested by the exhortation to flee from the land of the north (i.e., Babylon) and escape to Zion, in Zech 2:10[6]. The result would have been a significant increase in the Judeo-Babylonian element in the province of Judah at that time. How many had already immigrated into Judah before the accession of Darius we do not know. The list of about 50,000 who are said to have returned following immediately on a decree of Cyrus (Ezra 2:1–67 = Neh 7:6–68) is probably a census of the province from a considerably later date.

No doubt some did trickle back following on the fall of Babylon in 539, and others in connection with the invasion of Egypt in 525 (the Udjahorresnet inscription tells us that many foreigners came to Egypt with the Persian army), but the main movement into the province took place during the period subsequent to 520. Such a displacement of population may even have been mandated by the Persian authorities with a view to creating a buffer zone against endemic disturbances in the Persian satrapy of Mudriya (Egypt). Though the decree of Cyrus cited in Ezra 1:2–4, and dated to 539/538, specifically mandated the rebuilding of the temple, two decades later no progress had been made in completing the task (Hag 1:1–6).

There was also a revolt against Darius in Egypt (*Behistun* col. II 7; Kent 1953, 123) that was suppressed by the satrap Aryandes. But Egypt continued to be the most restive of Persian provinces, often in alliance with the Athenians, eventually achieving temporary independence (405–343). Darius may have visited Egypt in 517, and this was about the same time that he gave orders for the codification of Egyptian laws in force up to the time of the Persian conquest in 525. The Demotic Chronicle from the Ptolemaic period (papyrus 215 of the Bibliothèque Nationale in Paris; Briant 1996, 488–500), which provides this information, states that the task was assigned to a commission of priests, sages (scribes), and warriors, that it took 16 years to complete, and that the final text was written up in demotic Egyptian and Aramaic. Since this project was part of Darius's overall organization of the empire after the critical first 2 years of his reign, it is possible that similar measures were taken elsewhere, including Judah. Some scholars think that a decree to codify local laws could have contributed to the redaction of the Pentateuch, or at least the Pentateuchal laws. This is not impossible, but hard evidence is lacking (Blenkinsopp 2001, 41–62).

At all events, the proximity of Judah to this rich but problematic province of the empire gave it an importance that it otherwise would not have had, and made it the object of special attention on the part of the imperial authorities in Susa. One example may be cited. If the basic historicity of Ezra's mission is accepted, and if it took place in the seventh year of Artaxerxes I (465–424), therefore in 458, it could well have been occasioned by the critical situation created at that time by the revolt of Inaros in Egypt (460–454), the defeat and death of the local satrap, and a formidable Athenian fleet of 200 vessels prowling the Aegean and looking to take advantage of the Persian defeat.

Contact between Persians and mainland Greeks came about as a result of the Persian conquest of Ionia (the western coastal area of Turkey) in 520–519 and of Thrace in 513–512. Conflict between Persia and Athens was inevitable after the Athenians supported the Ionian revolt (498–493) and refused to submit by offering earth and water to Darius. As every schoolboy used to know, the Persian invasion of the mainland was famously defeated at Marathon in September 490, and the expedition of Xerxes a decade later fared no better. Both Greeks and Judeans defined themselves politically, culturally and ethnically in relation to Persian imperial power, but in profoundly different ways.

Once the revolts had been crushed, Darius set about organizing the empire, dividing it, according to Herodotus (3.89–97), into twenty satrapies. The small province of Judah was part of the fifth, *Babirush-Ebernari*, comprising the entire former Neo-Babylonian Empire. This situation continued until after the Babylonian revolts against Xerxes, when Babylon and the Trans-Euphrates region became distinct satrapies. An Akkadian contract tablet from the early years of Darius gives us the name Ushtani, satrap of Babylon-Abar-Nahara (*piḫat babili u ebirnari*), who would have been the immediate superior of Tattenai, governor of the Trans-Euphrates region (Ezra 5:3).

Within this overall imperial system the political status of Judah has been long disputed, and is still not entirely clear. The biblical texts refer to it as a province (*yĕhûd mĕdîntā'*, Ezra 2:1; 5:8 etc.), and there are allusions to governors preceding Nehemiah (Neh 5:15; Mal 1:8), including Sheshbazzar and Zerubbabel (Ezra 5:14; Hag 1:1 etc.), and one following him, the Bigvai or Bagoas of AP 30 and 31, mentioned above. Other names of governors of the province have turned up on seals and seal impressions (Yehoʿezer, Aḥzai, Elnathan) and one (Yehezqiyah) on coins from the late Persian period. While the chronological sequence is not clear enough to allow us confidently to fill in all the gaps in the sequence of governors, these data make it difficult to accept the older view that Judah remained administratively subject to Samaria until it achieved autonomy under Nehemiah.

Something must now be said about the religious implications of Judah's political status under Iranian rule. After the Babylonian conquest, the administrative center was moved to Mizpah, a few miles north of Jerusalem. There may have been some religious activity on the site of the ruined temple, somewhat similar to praying at the *kōtel* today, but it is probable that an alternative sanctuary was set up in connection with the provincial administration, perhaps at Bethel, in close proximity to Mizpah, which had survived the Assyrian conquest as a cult center (2 Kgs 17:27–28).

As long as Babylonian control lasted, there was no likelihood of restoring either Jerusalem itself, that "rebellious city harmful to kings and provinces"

(Ezra 4:15), or its temple which had provided religious sponsorship for the revolts. But the knowledge that Persian rulers, beginning with Cyrus in his famous Cylinder Inscription, claimed to favor the cults of their subject peoples, inspired some elements, most of them in the diaspora, to foresee the possibility of restoring the Jerusalem temple and its cult. Since it is so overwhelmingly represented in the biblical texts, this "Zionist" movement now seems to have been predestined and inevitable. But the careful reader of Isa 56–66 and the other sources listed earlier will find evidence for different views. It is always prudent to bear in mind that it is generally the winners, in this instance the "Zionists," who write the history.

It is difficult to realize in retrospect how deeply problematic this step, the restoration of the Jerusalem cult, must have been. During the Judean monarchy, the temple was the property of the royal dynasty, its functionaries were royal appointees, and its cult, the cult of the national deity, YHVH, was the religious expression and legitimation of state policies. One implication of this function was that the temple priesthood provided the religious underpinning for successive revolts against Assyrian and Babylonian overlords. This was the rule rather than the exception throughout the Near East. It explains, for example, why Xerxes destroyed the great Esagila sanctuary in Babylon after the revolts in that city toward the beginning of his reign (484–482). It also explains why, after the fall of Jerusalem, Nebuzaradan the Babylonian generalissimo returned to burn the temple as a deliberate, ideological act, and why the leading priests were among the first to be executed (2 Kgs 25:8–9, 18–21).

According to our principal biblical source, the temple was eventually completed in the sixth year of Darius (516/515), after the original rescript of Cyrus was rediscovered in the archives at Ecbatana (Hamadan) and reissued with additions (Ezra 6:1–18). This source is insistent that the project of rebuilding was the result of a direct initiative of the Persian central authority and was financed out of the imperial and satrapal exchequers.

In view of available sources illustrative of Persian policy toward the cult centers of other deities (Marduk, Apollo, Leto, Neith, et al.), this information does not appear basically incredible, even if the documents cited are free compositions of one or more Jewish authors worded so as to further their own political agenda (Blenkinsopp 1991, 22–53). The new status of the Jerusalem temple, according to which the Iranian king in distant Susa took the place of the local dynast, was given symbolic expression by means of prayers and sacrifices for the royal family that were now incorporated into the temple liturgy (Ezra 6:10). The implication was that from now on the temple and its personnel had to serve the interests of the empire, represented by its local officials.

The course of the struggle among different factions and families of priests to control the operations of the newly constituted temple is obscure and, in the absence of new information, is likely to remain so. In any case, none of these families is mentioned by name in Isa 56–66. The relevant genealogies and other indications here and there suggest that, at some point, a compromise was reached between Aaronites, originally associated with the Bethel sanctuary, and Zadokites represented, during the early years of Darius's reign, by Jeshua ben Jehozadak (Blenkinsopp 1998, 25–43).

Competition with respect to both building the temple (Ezra 4:1–4) and serving in it was understandable, since control of the temple and its operations translated into a considerable amount of social and economic control. In the first place, temple personnel, according to the census list in Ezra-Nehemiah constituting about 12 percent of the population (Ezra 2:1–67 = Neh 7:6–69), were tax exempt (Ezra 7:24) and were supported by the temple tax and other perquisites (Neh 10:32–39; 13:12–13). The sacrificial system was another type of subvention for the temple staff. Though there is no explicit reference to lands owned by the Jerusalem temple, temples in Mesopotamia, Asia Minor, and the Greek mainland owned estates, and the Levitical regulations governing land vowed to the temple (Lev 27:16–25) suggest that the Jerusalem temple also owned land from which, presumably, it drew revenue.

The proclamation summoning the běnê haggôlâ to convene in front of the temple to resolve the intermarriage issue contained a stipulation threatening absentees with confiscation of their property and exclusion from the group (Ezra 10:8). The term rěkûš ("property") has a wide range of meanings, including "real estate" (1 Chr 27:25–31), and the verb ḥrm has the sense of dedicating property by transferring its ownership to the deity, that is, to the temple and priesthood, a point made more explicitly in parallel passages in 1 Esd 9:4 and Josephus, Ant. 11.148. The Jerusalem temple was therefore, in all probability, similar except in scale to Mesopotamian temples well documented for the Achaemenid and Hellenistic periods.

Like other temples known to us from that time, the Jerusalem temple would also have served as a center of economic redistribution, as it did in the Hellenistic and Roman periods. We recall that during Nehemiah's absence in Susa, the ubiquitous Tobiah obtained space in the temple precincts through the connivance of a clerical relative, no doubt with a view to promoting his commercial interests (Neh 13:4–5).

Though the province, including the temple and its operations, was under the control of a governor and not that of the priests—priestly hegemony came about only in the Hellenistic period—the exercise of political rights as Judeans within the province was inseparable from membership in good standing in the temple cult community. The point is made obliquely in the promise addressed to sexually mutilated proselytes in Isa 56:5 of secure status "in my house and within my walls"—that is, as a member in good standing of the Judean cult and the civic community. Other outsiders threatened with expulsion were assured of free access to the Jerusalem cult (56:7).

By the same token, the absentees from the plenary assembly called to resolve a crucial religious matter were threatened with loss of civic status and forfeiture of immovable property (Ezra 10:8). This type of kārēt procedure, a form of exclusion that was both political and religious, was not a uniquely Jewish affair. At the end of the Pisistratid tyranny in Athens (510–509), a revision of the citizen roster led to the exclusion of "those of impure descent," that is, those unable to prove their membership in one of the phratries (Aristotle, *The Constitution of Athens* 13.5). The threat of exclusion in Ezra 10:8 inevitably calls to mind the excommunication of the *ḥărēdîm* in Isa 66:5, on which more will be said in due course.

A major problem in our attempt to get some idea of the nature of Judean society in the early Achaemenid period is the distinction in Ezra–Nehemiah, but not in the other relevant biblical sources, between the Judean-Babylonian immigrants and the rest of the population that had lived continually in Judah and adjacent provinces and had survived the Babylonian campaign. According to this source, the Judeo-Babylonian element—described as *běnê haggôlâ* ("those of the dispersion"), *qěhal haggôlâ* ("the dispersion community"), or simply *haggôlâ* ("the dispersion")—formed a distinctive collectivity that took sole responsibility for building the temple (Ezra 3:8–9; 4:1–4), thereafter controlled its operations, insisted on ritual segregation from the local population (Ezra 6:19–21; 9:1–2; 10:6–8), and yet welcomed recruits on condition of their accepting the same restrictions (Ezra 6:21). We have the distinct impression that these people came to be recognized as the political, social and religious elite in the province. Their distinctive social status probably explains the complaint of the common people and their wives against "their fellow-Jews" in Neh 5:1. But their distinctive, quasi-sectarian character vis-à-vis the indigenous population is exaggerated for well-known ideological reasons in Ezra–Nehemiah, a point to be borne in mind in reading the polemical passages in Isa 56–66.

By the end of 521, Darius had crushed most of the revolts, and in the course of the next three years he put an end to Elamite resistance and settled affairs in Egypt—for the time being, at any rate. The empire continued to expand. The Indian satrapy (Hindush) was added in 517, after campaigns in what is now Pakistan, and a Persian army pushed back the Scythians and crossed into Europe, winning territory in Thrace. During the latter part of his reign, Darius's energies were concentrated on suppressing the Ionian revolt centered on Miletus. Athenian support for the rebels led to a punitive expedition into the Greek mainland, which was repulsed at Marathon. During this entire period, from Darius's sixth year when the temple was completed (516/515) to his death (486), we have no information relevant to Yehud (the province of Judah).

Another Egyptian revolt broke out before the accession of Xerxes (Khšayarša; Ahasuerus in Ezra 4:6 and Esther). The history of the Persian Empire is the history of the fomenting and stifling of one rebellion after another, due principally to the crushing burden of tribute needed to pay for military campaigns, the Persian addiction to magnificent palaces, and the luxurious lifestyle at the court reflected, with some exaggeration, in the book of Esther. After the Egyptian revolt was put down in 484, Xerxes reversed the policy of his predecessors by confiscating temple lands and, in general, showing scant regard for Egyptian religious susceptibilities.

The same policy was pursued after the suppression of revolts in Babylon instigated by Bel-shimanni in 484 and Shamash-eriba in 482. The great Esagila sanctuary was destroyed, the solid gold statue of the god Marduk was, according to Herodotus (1.183) and other Greek historians, taken away and melted down, and Babylon lost its special status, becoming a mere satrapy cut off from the Trans-Euphrates territory. Meanwhile, the campaign against the mainland Greeks, left to Xerxes as a heritage from Darius, went ahead. The defeat of the Persians by land and sea, at Salamis, Plataea, and Mykale (480–479), led to the withdrawal of the Persian armies and inaugurated a long period of hostilities between the Persians and the Delian League, ending with the Peace of Callias in 449.

The biblical texts provide only one piece of information for the reign of Xerxes, an obscure notice that the adversaries of the gôlâ-group lodged a complaint or accusation against them at the beginning of the reign (Ezra 4:6). The failure of this text to say what the complaint was about led Morgenstern (1956, 101–79; 1957, 15–47; 1960, 1–29) to create a lion out of a claw, reading this uncommunicative notice (with the help of equally obscure archaeological data) as indicating a revolt in Judah resulting in extensive devastation in the province and Jerusalem. It is possible that there was some support in the province for the Babylonian rebels, as there may have been in the early years of the reign of Darius, and the fierce suppression of the revolts may have motivated some among the Jewish ethnic minority in Babylon to emigrate to Judah. The high cost of putting down revolts and mounting campaigns, including the less successful ones on the Greek mainland, would have put an additional burden on the agrarian subsistence economy on which the province rested.

The same pattern continued following another episode of palace intrigue, for which the Persian court was notorious, which led to the assassination of Xerxes and the accession of his son Artaxerxes (Artakhšassa, meaning in Old Persian "Possessing a kingdom of justice," Hebrew 'artaḥšaśtā'; 465–424). The frequency of revolts by satraps, noticeable from about this time, indicates a weakening of the traditional bonds of loyalty that had so far held the empire together. The most serious threat came from Egypt with the revolt led by the Lybian Inarus in 460. The Egyptian satrap, Achaemenes, was defeated and killed, the Athenians took Cyprus, their fleet destroyed the Persian fleet, and their ground forces penetrated the heart of Lower Egypt. Persian control was reestablished only after Megabyzus, son-in-law of Xerxes and satrap of the Trans-Euphrates region, was brought in by Artaxerxes to deal with the crisis. He defeated the rebels, annihilated the Athenian fleet, and by 454 the revolt was at an end. A new satrap, Arsames, whose personal correspondence has survived (G. R. Driver 1957), was appointed and remained in office until near the end of the century.

The history of yĕhûd mĕdîntā' during the four decades of the reign of Artaxerxes is almost impenetrably obscure. Ezra 4:7–24 reports two letters from Samaria to the imperial authorities in Susa accusing the Jerusalem Jews of seditious intent in rebuilding the city and its defenses. The first was from a certain Tabeel, with the concurrence of Mithredath, a Persian satrapal official (4:7). The second was dispatched by provincial officials in Samaria. This second missive was sent by a certain Rehum, who held the office of bĕʿēl-ṭĕʿēm (i.e., the one authorized to issue decrees; framānakara in Old Persian), together with the secretary (*sāpar*) Shimshai, with other satrapal officials named as co-signatories. In reply, Artaxerxes agreed with their assessment of the situation and authorized them to terminate the activity going on in Jerusalem, which they lost no time in doing.

This flurry of diplomatic activity is unfortunately not dated but would best fit the early years of the reign. The letters may have been written with the idea of exploiting the unrest and uncertainty immediately following the accession of Artaxerxes in 465. On the assumption that Ezra's caravan arrived in Jerusalem in the seventh year of the same monarch (Artaxerxes I, nicknamed "Long Arm") the year would be 458. Nehemiah's mission began in the twentieth year of the same reign, therefore thirteen years later, in 445.

It is hardly necessary to add that neither of these conclusions would pass uncontested, and the historical value of the narratives in which these chronological indications occur has also been questioned. But if we are going to use these texts at all as potential source material, we should at least ask how they fit with data from nonbiblical sources and with information from other biblical texts. The reference in the correspondence to "the Jews who came up from you to us" (Ezra 4:12) could conceivably refer to a group arriving from Babylon or Iran even earlier in the reign of Artaxerxes but more likely alludes to earlier immigrants from Babylonia.

Hanani's report to his brother Nehemiah in Susa about the sad state of affairs in Yehud, with the wall of Jerusalem broken down and its gates gutted by fire (Neh 1:1–3), is what could be expected as a result of the forcible termination of the rebuilding project by the Samarians (Ezra 4:23). Another possibility is that, since this situation appears to have developed not long before 445, it may have been connected with the revolt of the Trans-Euphrates satrap Megabyzus referred to above. (Ctesiô does not give an exact date, but the revolt, which did not last long, probably took place between 450 and 448.) It may also have resulted from hostile action on the part of Judah's immediate neighbors, which is to say enemies—for example, an Arab raid on Jerusalem as suggested by Morton Smith (1971, 127–28).

HISTORICAL CLUES IN CHAPTERS 56–66

In both Isa 66 and Ezra 9–10 we hear of a group of people who are said to tremble at God's word (Isa 66:2, 5; Ezra 9:4; 10:3). They are named four times, and in each case a qualification is attached to the designation *ḥărēdîm* ("Tremblers"), as follows:

- *ḥārēd ʿal-dĕbārî*, "those who tremble at my word" (Isa 66:2)
- *haḥărēdîm ʾel-dĕbārô*, "you who tremble at his [God's] word" (Isa 66:5)
- *kol ḥārēd bĕdibrê ʾĕlohê-yiśrāʾēl*, "all those who tremble at the words of Israel's God" (Ezra 9:4)
- *haḥărēdîm bĕmiṣvat ʾĕlohēnû*, "those who tremble at the commandment of our God" (Ezra 10:3)

These qualifications exclude the possibility of aligning the term with descriptive titles such as "Pharisee" or "Essene," but we see from the contexts that they were a group that could act in concert on a matter of policy (in Ezra 9:4 and 10:3) and was well enough defined for its adherents to be excommunicated (in Isa 66:5). The claim advanced by the group of an imminent and catastrophic divine intervention in human history that would bring joy to them and shame to their adversaries is also clearly sectarian in nature (66:5 cf. 65:13–16).

Since the term ḥārēd, ḥărēdîm occurs only in these four texts as a religious category, comparable to "Quakers," "Shakers," and the ʿēdâ ḥărēdît in contemporary Jerusalem, we are justified in asking whether there may be a connection of a historical nature between the Isaianic and Ezra contexts in which the term occurs. In Isa 66 the ḥărēdîm are linked with the poor (ʿăniyyîm) and the broken in spirit as those on whom the God of Israel looks with favor. They are hated (i.e., shunned, by their fellow-Jews) and excommunicated on account of their devotion to the divine name, which is to say, the true worship of the God of Israel as they understood it. For this reason they, and not their adversaries, will rejoice on judgment day. They were motivated by the belief that this day would come in the near future.

The eschatological beliefs of the ḥărēdîm come more sharply into focus when we note that the claim of the ʿăbādîm ("Servants") in 65:13–16 could have either provoked the taunt of their adversaries in 66:5 or served as the reply to it. The theme of reversal ("My servants will eat, but you will go hungry," etc.), characteristic of sectarian thinking, marks them out as an eschatological-prophetic group, and the designation "Servants" suggests adherence to the person and teaching of the Servant whose death is lamented in Isa 53. The ḥărēdîm and the ʿăbādîm are clearly one and the same entity.

Who, then, are the opponents of these "Tremblers" and "Servants"? In Isa 66:5 they are simply alluded to as "your brethren" (i.e., fellow-Jews), but if the ḥărēdîm were officially banned from the community (verb niddâ; see Comments ad loc.), those banning them must have included the temple priesthood. This is confirmed by the larger context. First, a contrast is set up between the temple and its operations on the one hand and "those who tremble at my word" on the other, in the first of the four texts (66:1–2). In the two verses immediately following, temple functionaries are either compared to or identified with idolaters who take delight in their "abominations," a code word for non-Yahvistic cults. Since excommunication entailed exclusion from participation in temple worship, the official priesthood must have been involved.

There is nothing in Ezra 9–10 that would lead us to question this profile of the opponents. In Ezra 9–10 the crisis, precipitated by Ezra himself, is about exogamous marriage. The temple priests were found to be among the leading transgressors (9:1–2; 10:5), forming about 20 percent of the total of those who had married women outside the group (10:18–22). Among them were members of the family of Jeshua the high priest, whose involvement in deviant cults is elsewhere hinted at (Zech 3:1–5). Priestly intermarriage and associated "abominations" are also prominent issues in Malachi, generally thought to be roughly contemporaneous. The pledge that the transgressive priests were coerced by Ezra and his supporters into signing by no means put an end to the practice of exogamous marriage (e.g., Neh 13:28; Josephus, *Ant.* 11.302–12).

Isaiah 66:1–6 puts the *ḥărēdîm* in opposition to the temple priesthood, as we have seen, and there are indications elsewhere in chs. 56–66 that priests are prominent among the practitioners of deviant cults. In this respect, there is continuity between religious practice under the late Judean monarchy and what was happening in the province in the early Persian period (2 Kgs 23:4–7, 10–12; Jer 7:9; Ezek 8:1–18).

So far, then, there is no contradiction between the profile of the *ḥărēdîm* and their opponents in Isa 66 and Ezra 9–10. However, the actual situation of this group is not identical in the two texts. In Ezra 9–10 those who "tremble at the words [i.e., commandments] of the God of Israel" (9:4 cf. 10:3) form the nucleus of Ezra's support group. The qualifications added to the designation *ḥărēdîm* and the insistence that the issue should be resolved "according to the law" (10:3) indicate a strong attachment to law or, since there is no law governing coercive separation from wife and children, to a rigorist interpretation of law. The real concern, however, focuses not so much on marital separation as on the adoption of alien cults as a consequence of marriage outside of the community of the elect. The text on which, in all probability, the interpretation is based is explicit on this point: "Do not intermarry with them . . for that would turn your children away from following me to serve other gods" (Deut 7:3–4).

At this point, a common misconception must be set aside. The history of religious sectarianism shows that, far from being opposed to prophetic and eschatological consciousness, legal rigorism often goes in tandem with it. The Qumran sect would be a good illustration of this sectarian ethos. There is no reason to believe that the prophetic author who enjoined observance of the Sabbath in view of an imminent eschatological event (Isa 56:1–6) was any less of a legal rigorist than Ezra and his supporters are said to have been. "The word" that, in Isa 66:2 and 5, induced the trembling could therefore be the legal as well as the prophetic word, that is, the divine teaching that the prophet is commissioned to impart.

By the same token, we should not assume that Ezra's *ḥărēdîm* were indifferent or hostile to prophecy. The term *ḥārēd* itself intimates the kind of intense state of consciousness generally associated with prophecy. As described in Ezra 9–10, Ezra's conduct may even suggest that he himself belonged to the ranks of the *ḥărēdîm*. His emotional reaction to the bad news (9:3–5), his prolonged stupor (*mĕšômēm* cf. Ezek 3:15 emended text), fasting and mourning (9:4; 10:6 cf. the "mourners" in Isa 57:18; 61:2–3; 66:10), and penitential prayer (9:6–15) reproduced aspects of the "hasidic" milieu common to Isa 56–66, Daniel, and the Qumran sectarians.

A reading of these two texts together suggests that they are addressing the same historical and social situation but from different perspectives and at different points in a developing situation. In Ezra 9–10 the *ḥărēdîm*, in alliance with Ezra, are in a position to dictate policy, whereas in Isa 65–66 they are a persecuted and shunned minority. Whether the marginalization of the ḥărēdîm took place before or after the religious "reforms" of Ezra we can only speculate. All the indications point to the conclusion that Ezra's drastic solution to inter-marriage succeeded only in alienating the priestly and lay aristocracy and probably led to his recall after a fairly short stay in the province. If this is so, his supporters would have been exposed to the kind of hostility reflected in the last two chapters of Isaiah. Their excommunication would be repayment for the ostracism and confiscation of property threatened against those who stood aloof from Ezra's reforming measures (Ezra 10:8).

What can be concluded, if provisionally and tentatively, from consideration of the changing fortunes of these "Tremblers" is that the last section of Isaiah, that is, chs. 65–66, or the greater part of it, reflects the situation in the province of Judah from shortly before the activity of Ezra (458) to the arrival of Nehe-miah in the province (445). The first passage in this section, 56:1–8, could like-wise be read as reflecting opposition to Nehemiah's controversial aim of creating an ethnically and religiously homogeneous community, especially by aggres-sive enforcement of Sabbath observance (see especially Neh 13:1–3).

With the possible exception of one or two brief scribal addenda, to be noted in the Commentary, the rest of the material in chs. 56–66 would be earlier. The absence of polemic in the central block (chs. 60–62) may be the result of a deliberate authorial or editorial decision, but its close thematic and linguistic association with 40–55 nevertheless suggests chronological priority. For the rest, we can only very uncertainly attempt to locate it on a trajectory covering the obscure period from the completion of the temple to Ezra's arrival in the province (516/515–458). Much depends on how one reconstructs the literary history of these 11 chapters, and to this we now turn.

4. THE FORMATION OF ISAIAH 56–66

A BRIEF SURVEY OF RESEARCH

The formation of a biblical book, a fortiori of any part of it, becomes an issue only when traditional authorial attributions are questioned and eventually aban-doned. With respect to Isaiah, we can detect the beginnings of this process in the commentary on Isa 40 of the twelfth-century Jewish scholar Abraham Ibn Ezra. Doubts about the separate dating and authorship of 40–66 were expressed from time to time during the early-modern period, but credit for the first clear affirmation of the distinction between 1–39 and 40–66 goes to Johann Chris-toph Döderlein, professor at the University of Altdorf, writing in 1781. While conservative scholars both Jewish and Christian continued, and still continue, to argue for the authorial unity of the book, the issue of the distinction between these two major sections of the book has ceased to be a subject of debate among critical commentators and readers (see further Volume 2, pp. 69–71).

The so-called Trito-Isaiah as the author of chs. 56–66 emerged for the first time in the commentary of Bernhard Duhm published in 1892. (In the present commentary references and quotations are from the 4th edition of 1922.) Duhm's thesis was not entirely original; he simply went a few steps farther than earlier scholars (Stade, Kuenen, Cornill) who argued that the last three or four chapters of the book could not have been written by the author of 40–55. Duhm's theses about the formation of the book are stated clearly and succinctly (1922, 14–15, 19, 418–19). Isaiah 40–66 is a redactional composite with three major sections: Deutero-Isaiah (40–55) from ca. 540, written in one of the Phoenician cities; the "Servant Songs" (41:1–4; 49:1–6; 50:4–9; 52:13–53:12), all from one author writing a few years later; and Trito-Isaiah (56–66) composed in Jerusalem shortly before the activity of Ezra and Nehemiah.

Apart from some few editorial additions (especially 58:13–14; 59:5–8; 66:23–24), 56–66, not excluding 60–62, is the work of one author writing in the tradition of Ezekiel, Haggai, and Zechariah, and described by Duhm as "a theocrat of the first water" (*Theokratiker vom reinsten Wasser*, p. 418). Since Trito-Isaiah had the same basic concerns as Deutero-Isaiah, while dealing with them in a very different spirit, it was natural that these chapters should be attached to 40–55. But the distinctive character of Trito-Isaiah remains fully in evidence, corresponding to a different and later situation with different problems and opponents, principally schismatic "brethren," whose aim was to build a temple that would rival the Jerusalem temple.

As succinct and relatively undeveloped as they were, these conclusions of Duhm set the agenda for the study of these 11 chapters, and the questions he posed and answered are still with us after more than a century. We shall deal with them briefly in turn.

The first, that *56–66 is a composition or compilation distinct from 40–55*, was accepted by most but not all scholars. It was vigorously rejected by Torrey, who read 40–66 together with 34–35 as one coherent work, exhibiting the same style and prosodic form throughout. Torrey removed what he took to be the only obstacles to identifying basically one and the same background throughout 40–66 by the simple expedient of eliminating the references to Cyrus, Babylon, and the Chaldeans (43:14; 48:14, 20) as unwarranted glosses. Torrey took the view that the main reason for a distinct Third Isaiah was that scholars assigned different locations for 40–55 and 56–66: Babylon for the former, Judah for the latter. This problem disappears, he claimed, once one accepts that the entire work was produced in Palestine (Torrey 1928, 3–110).

Other commentators maintained authorial unity by taking these two locations as corresponding to successive phases of the one prophet's career: chs. 40–55 and 56:1–8 written in Babylon, 56:9–66:24 in Judah (Glahn 1934), or 40–48 in Babylon, 49–66 in Judah (Haran 1963, 127–55). Maass (1967, 153–63) also argued that the proponents of Trito-Isaiah had neglected to consider the possibility that differences of subject matter could be explained by different situations facing the prophet throughout his career, evidently a rather long career.

Smart (1965, 13–33, 115–20, 230) took a leaf out of Torrey's book by eliminating the references to Cyrus and allusions to Babylon and the Babylonians as clumsy insertions from the time of the Book of Chronicles. Since, in addition, insistence on Sabbath observance could only proceed from "a later writer, orthodox and legalistic in contrast to Second Isaiah" (p. 230), 56:1–7 and 58:13–14 must also be expunged as inappropriate insertions into the text.

A threat to the distinctive character of 56–66 of a different nature could also be envisaged from the work of the redactional maximalists for whom 40–55 and 56–66 are both made up of a congeries of literary fragments, the productions of many hands. There are also exponents of a less radical option that blurs rather than removes the distinction by dividing the second part of the book into multiple blocks, each with its own distinctive contribution: 40–48, 49–54(55), 60–62, 56–59, 63–66. A very recent variation on this option is offered by Christopher R. Seitz in the Introduction to his *NIB* commentary, in which he divides the second half of the book as follows: 40–48, 49–52:12, 52:13–53:12 (the Suffering Servant passage), and 54–66. As was noted above, Seitz entertains serious doubts whether a break between chs. 55 and 56 is at all warranted (1992; 2001, 309–23).

Variations on the arguments for the unity of 40–66 have appeared in a few other commentators during the past century (e.g., König 1926, Kissane 1960), but for most critical scholars the distinct contours of chs. 56–66, not excluding the core section 60–62, thematically close to 40–55 as it is, are sufficiently in evidence to justify adopting Trito-Isaiah as the most productive working hypothesis available.

If, then, this first and basic thesis of Duhm is accepted, we can go on to the related proposition that *chs. 56–66 are essentially ordered to and dependent on chs. 40–55.* That this conclusion could not simply be taken for granted is apparent from the opening remarks of the commentary on 56–66 by Paul Volz:

In these chapters we are standing on quite different ground with respect to both external historical events and the history of the community, as well as with regard to the entire ethos. Nothing is said about redemption, return from exile and restoration, and in most passages Jerusalem is rebuilt and the people are living in Palestine. Those addressed are not the people as a whole, viewed in their national identity, but rather certain groups are prominent, and the community has taken the place of the nation. Even though Deutero-Isaiah often endows the word "Israel" with spiritual meaning, he never loses sight of its national character. Here, on the other hand, it is often the community of the devout that is the recipient of the word of God and the eschatological promise. The kind of prophetic consciousness in evidence is no longer as it was with Deutero-Isaiah who enunciated oracles and religious principles in an elevated style, of fundamental and abiding character. Here, in these chapters, we are continually immersed in the details of community organization and conflicts within the people and community. The speaker no longer resembles Deutero-Isaiah in standing out from the people as a messenger of God; he is rather a preacher, a pastor of souls, a synagogue leader, a devout psalmist. (Volz 1932, 197)

Volz's characterization of chs. 56–66 could be questioned at certain points, but it at least accents the need to acknowledge the distinctiveness of these chapters before relating them to 40–55. According to Duhm (1922, 19), chs. 56–66 were appended to 40–55 because they shared the same concerns, especially the restoration of Jerusalem to its former eminence. The differences are accounted for by the later situation (mid–fifth century) of the community addressed in chs. 56–66.

Close affinity with 40–55 can easily be verified, especially but not exclusively with regard to chs. 60–62. For example: the repatriation theme in 60:4 follows from 49:18, 22, the subjection of foreigners in 60:14–16 takes up where 49:23 leaves off, and the image of goods pouring in through the open gates of Jerusalem in 60:11 echoes 45:1. There are several instances where Deutero-Isaianic texts are cited practically verbatim (60:9 = 51:5; 60:13 = 41:19; 60:16 = 49:26; 62:11 = 40:10). The exhortation with which 60–62 concludes (62:10–11) functions as a structural parallel to 40:1–3 and 48:20–21. Themes prominent in 40–55, discussed in a previous section of the Introduction, are taken up and developed in different directions in 56–66 in keeping with changing situations. (Zimmerli 1963 [1950], 217–33). It is clear, for example, that the admission of proselytes is still an issue but has become problematic (58:1–8 cf. 44:5), and it seems that, in 56–66, it is no longer anticipated that God will intervene in Israel's affairs through human intermediaries, whether native or foreign.

The question must then be asked: *How are we to understand the relationship of 56–66 to 40–55?* According to Duhm, and those who agree with him in reading 56–66 as a literary unity, preeminently Elliger, the relationship was one of prophet and disciple. For those, on the other hand, who concluded that "Trito-Isaiah" was a code name for a compilation of texts that could not possibly be ascribed to one author, it was represented as a simple matter of a prophetic school or circle reproducing and adapting the teaching of "Deutero-Isaiah" in accordance with the needs of their own time, a view well represented in the commentary tradition (e.g., Cheyne 1895; Muilenburg 1956; Hanson 1975).

In recent scholarship, however, we note a growing sense that starting out with the concept of author is not the most useful approach to this material. The point has been made most forcibly by Odil Hannes Steck, whose numerous essays on Isa 56–66 practically defy documentation. Steck argued that we must begin by setting aside the Duhmian dogma of a completely distinct Trito-Isaian collection, and therefore a distinct Trito-Isaian prophetic author, since 56–66 consists in an accumulation of expansive comment (*Fortschreibung*) the formation of which, covering a period from the sixth to the third century B.C.E., must be understood in the context of the book of Isaiah as a whole, not just the 16 chapters immediately preceding it.

In several of his publications Steck elaborated a detailed picture of the successive stages in this incremental build-up, leading to the final form of 56–66

as an integral part of the book. Without attempting a comprehensive reproduction of Steck's complex arguments and conclusions, I will briefly mention
the main points. (A useful diagram of the successive redactional stages can be
consulted in Steck 1991a, 278–79.) Most of 60–61 is a supplement or literary
expansion of 40–55 added in the first half of the fifth century; the exhortation
to go through the gates and build up the highway in 62:10–12 is the finale to
the redactional unit dealing with return from exile, that is, 1:1–62:12; later in
the Hellenistic period 63:1–6, judgment on Edom, and several passages in 1–39
were added in a penultimate redaction; later still, the situation was rendered
seriously problematic by the addition of the lament in 63:7–64:11[12], a reaction to the traumatic event of Ptolemy I's capture of Jerusalem in 302/301
B.C.E.; and finally, the addition of chs. 65–66, in which Hellenistic cults are
condemned and the servant motif is applied to the devout members of the Jewish community, brought the long and complicated process to its completion
(1:1–66:24).

Taken all in all, Steck's many essays of detailed analysis and synthesis represent one of the most sustained attempts at a critical understanding of these last
eleven chapters of the book of Isaiah. One can learn much from his work even
while disagreeing with most of his conclusions. Steck was a redactional maximalist, and his reconstruction is based on arguments many of which are arbitrary and unpersuasive. This is the case with dating, especially the correlation
with the political history of the Ptolemies, and the rather casual way in which
one text is said to be a deliberate *Fortschreibung* of another, sometimes on the
basis of the occurrence of a single word. Steck would, of course, have agreed
that these *Fortschreibungen* had to be written by somebody, but he rejects
rather too quickly the idea of oral tradition. Though he vigorously denied the
charge, he tended to speak of redaction as a gradual, anonymous build-up,
rather like barnacles on the keel of a ship.

Steck was criticized somewhat along these lines by Wolfgang Lau (1994,
15–16), who insisted on maintaining the distinction between tradition and redaction, between the author and the editor, though in fact the nature of the distinction never emerges very clearly in his own redactional analysis. He too
abandons the idea of authorship as a starting point for the investigation, since
(with the analysis of his teacher Hans-Jürgen Hermisson) neither 40–55 nor
56–66 forms a literary unity. Those to whom we owe the compilation of the
material in 56–66, formed as the result of an incremental exegetical process,
recognized themselves to be prophets, but were also tradents, forerunners of
the scribes of the Greco-Roman period, and their productions are learned,
scribal works presented as prophetic (*Schriftgelehrte Prophetie*). Lau's own solution is to identify 60–62 as the core Trito-Isaianic prophecy around which three
compilations produced by circles of tradents (*Tradentenkreise*) progressively
accumulated. The compilations were distinguished according to shared theological ideas, and were united in the final redaction with the individual traditions (*Einzelüberlieferungen*) that stand by themselves (56:1–8; 63:1–6; 63:7–
64:11).

Perhaps the most distinctive feature of 56–66, compared with 40–55, is religious polemic, often quite vitriolic, directed by one group within the community against another. A note of reproof is heard from time to time in 40–55 (42:19–20; 43:22–24; 45:9–11; 46:12; 48:1–5) but mild and low key by comparison with the diatribe in 56–66 and not yet indicative of serious division within the community addressed. This feature has suggested to several scholars a way to identify as the Trito-Isaianic core of 56–66 the passages from which the polemical element is absent and that are therefore, in this respect, closest to Deutero-Isaiah. While there are numerous variations in detail, wide agreement exists about the following passages: all or most of chs. 60–62; 57:14–20; 65:16b–24(25); 66:7–16; and perhaps 58:3–12 (see, for example, Westermann 1969, 296– 97; Sekine 1989, 182; Koenen 1990, 215–21). The rest is consigned to one or more redactional stages, though more often than not without clarifying the respective roles of prophet and redactor and what is implied in passing from one to the other.

It will be clear by now that *chs. 56–66 do not come from one hand or from one time period*. Duhm's statement of preference (rather than sustained argument) for the unity of 56–66 has had its appeal, though the difficulty of sustaining this thesis became apparent with the need to make exceptions. Marti (1900, 362, 377, 399, 414), for example, had to exempt 59:5–8, 64:9–11 and 66:23–24, and others since have felt obliged to make other concessions (e.g., Odeberg 1931; Kessler 1956; Bonnard 1972). The strategy of reading these chapters as a compilation of disparate materials that could have been put together by one person (Zillessen 1906, 231–76) comes up against the evidence for a degree of coherence both in subject matter and organization and is no longer in favor.

The most systematic and detailed attempt to support the Duhmian unity hypothesis was made by Karl Elliger in his monograph *Die Einheit des Tritojesaja* published in 1928. In the pursuit of his thesis, Elliger brought together a vast amount of lexical, stylistic, and prosodic data purporting to show that the bulk of 56–66 was composed by one prophetic author, a contemporary of Haggai and Zechariah. One admires Elliger's meticulous approach to the task, but in working through this material it is difficult to avoid the impression that he missed the wood for the abundance of trees. The reader must judge for himself or herself whether the author of the lament psalm in 63–64 could plausibly have written the virulent polemic of 57:3–13; or whether the comforting words of 57:14–19 could have come from the same source as 63:1–6; or, to make an end, whether the attitude to foreigners in 56:1–8 is consistent with 60:10 and 61:5–6. Elliger's arguments were subjected to detailed critique by Sekine (1989, 239–84), to whom the reader is referred.

Many recent commentators would agree to identifying chs. 60–62 as the production of an individual prophet, a disciple of Deutero-Isaiah who could, for convenience, be referred to as Trito-Isaiah (e.g., Vermeylen 1978, 503–4; Sekine 1989, 230–31). A recent variation is that of P. A. Smith (1995, 173–86, 204–7), who postulates two Trito-Isaiahs. The first was the author of 60:1–63:6, and this core was somewhat later expanded by a second Trito-Isaianic hand with the addition of 56:1–8; 56:9–57:21; 58:1–59:20; 65:1–66:17, to which the exilic lament in 63:7–64:11 was appended. Most of this literary activity took place between 538 and 515. We shall see that there are reasons for not including the bloodbath in Edom (63:1–6) in the core section, and the material assigned to the second Trito-Isaiah is too diverse to permit a persuasive case for unity of authorship.

HINTS OF MEANINGFUL ARRANGEMENT IN ISAIAH 56–66

In recent critical studies of 56–66 a great deal of energy has been expended on working out a detailed diachronic breakdown or, using an archaeological metaphor, a stratigraphy of these chapters. We may take as an example the work of Jacques Vermeylen (1978, 503–17), who sorts out the material into seven stages covering a period from the sixth century—or, if one includes 56:9–12 and 57:6–13a, from pre-exilic times—to the final *retouches* in the third century B.C.E. Unlike Westermann, he does not see the process originating in a Trito-Isaianic collection; there is therefore no core—only layers. The sorting out is done exclusively by identifying a dominant theme, or themes, and a corresponding *état d'ésprit* proper to each layer or strand. There is therefore a missionary strand (the fourth, from the late Persian period) and a strand emphasizing Sabbath observance and polemic against false cults (the fifth, from the early Hellenistic period). As the title of Vermeylen's book indicates—(*Du Prophète Isaïe à l'Apocalyptique*) these are stages on the way to a fully developed apocalyptic world view. Individual verses and fractions of verses are surgically removed from one context and assigned to another in keeping with what the author takes to be their place on the diachronic scale. Vermeylen's work is admittedly an extreme example of redactional criticism but not entirely uncharacteristic of much recent writing on Third Isaiah.

Redactional criticism has, so to speak, been sanctified by usage, though much of the aura has worn off in recent years. There is certainly a place for it when used judiciously as a way of getting some idea under what circumstances and for what readership a text came into existence. But any analysis of an ancient text that aspires to adequacy should combine synchrony with diachrony rather than be under constraint to choose between these two approaches. Practically speaking, one might begin by looking for significant structural elements, for clues to meaning, in the way that the text to be interpreted is organized.

In a previous section of the Introduction (pp. 38–39), we saw that 56–66 is set out in a tripartite arrangement with chs. 60–62 as the central panel and the prophetic signature (61:1–3) as its center, and therefore as the central point of the entire compilation. Indications of symmetrical arrangement are more difficult to detect the further the distance from 60–62—not surprisingly, since we must allow for the possibility that 56–66 has undergone several expansions, editings, and restructurings over the course of time. It is nevertheless possible to discern the outline of a pyramidal structure converging at its apex on the apostrophe to Jerusalem in 60–62 and the first-person declaration of the prophetic author's identity and mission in 61:1–3:

61:1–3

60—61—62

59:15b-20   63:1–6

59:1–15a   63:7–64:11

56:9–58:14   65:1–16

56:1–8   66:18–24

Key: YHVH as warrior and vindicator (59:15b–20; 63:1–6); communal lament (59:1–15a; 63:7–64:11); condemnation of heterodox cult practices and the religious life of the community in general (56:9–58:14; 65:1–16); positive attitude to proselytes and mission to the Gentile world (56:1–8; 66:18–24).

With respect to the last set of parallels (56:1–8 and 66:18–24): We frequently come across the idea in the commentary tradition that these two passages form, as it were, bookends to the compilation (e.g., Sekine 1989, 228–33; Steck 1991a, 34–44). Few if any of these parallels are completely symmetrical or correspond very closely in genre, style, and lexicon, but the outlines are clear enough to permit us to conclude, first: that the diverse material in 56–66 has been deliberately arranged according to a certain aesthetic and thematic plan; second: that chs. 60–62 constitute the central statement in the compilation; and, finally, that the prophetic statement at its center indicates, in addition to a conviction of prophetic authorship, the nature of the "message" and those to whom it is addressed.

With respect to 56–59: that these chapters form a redactional unit of some kind is suggested by the reference to covenant (*bĕrît*) at the beginning and end (56:4, 6; 59:21). Isaiah 59:21 reads as follows:

> As for me, this is my covenant with them: my spirit that rests upon you, and my words that I have put in your mouth, will not be absent from your mouth, or from the mouths of your descendants, or from those of the descendants of your descendants, declares YHVH, from this time forward and for ever more.

The prophetic author of 59:21 in effect puts his signature to this first section, in the same way that 61:1–3 indicates the prophetic author of 60–62. This brief first-person statement is therefore neither the introduction to 60–62 (Pauritsch 1971, 94; Sekine 1989, 135; Stuhlmueller 1990, 345) nor, primarily at least, a link between 56–59 and 60–62 (Lau 1994, 225–26). Endowment with the spirit combined with the placement of words in the mouth clearly indicate an individual prophetic figure (cf. Jer 1:9; Deut 18:18; 34:9–10). We are therefore hearing an individual prophetic voice at the beginning and end of 56–59. One implication is that those for whose benefit the covenant is promised in 59:21 include the marginal classes who receive prophetic reassurance in 56:1–7— not essentially different, therefore, from the oppressed to whom the good news is addressed in 61:1–3.

In the first two chapters (56–57), we detect an alternation of promise and threat, salvation and judgment as we move, somewhat unevenly and fitfully, from one passage to the next (56:1–8; 56:9–12; 57:1–2; 57:3–13; 57:14–21), ending, however, on a high note. In the following two chapters, with the exception of 59:15b–20, which sounds the theme of vindication together with 63:1–6, the tone is strongly homiletic. The almost total absence of prophetic speech formulas (the exception is 58:14b "For the mouth of YHVH has spoken") reinforces the impression that 58:1–59:15a constitutes in effect a homily or, more precisely, a kind of distillate of several homilies—whether actually delivered or a literary composition in the homiletic style we cannot say for sure.

We come now to the third major division, chs. 63–66: What one might expect to find toward the end of the book is either a series of appendices comparable to the eschatological "on that day" sayings with which Zechariah concludes, some of them strongly reminiscent of Isa 66 (Zech 14:4–21), or a conflation of different conclusions comparable to the final chapters of the book of Job (Job 38:1–40:5; 40:6–42:6). One partitioning of this final section proposed by Beuken (1991, 204–21) is as follows: 66:7–14 concluded chs. 56–66; 66:15–20 (21) served as the finale to chs. 40–55 and chs. 56–66 when these were joined together; 16:22–23 (with v 24 as a later addition) were added to bring the entire book to a close.

We therefore have a cumulative process corresponding to stages in the formation of the book of Isaiah. If this reading is correct, it would seem to suggest that 40–55 and 56–66 were brought together without reference to 1–39 and prior to the coupling of 40–66 with 1–39. The close parallelism between 66:7–14 and 54:1–17, both of which begin with Jerusalem and end with the Servants, the two principal themes of Isa 40–66, indicates a close redactional linking of these two major sections, with ch. 55 serving as a transition between them. It therefore confirms Beuken's reading of 66:7–14 as the first of three conclusions.

That 66:15–21 was intended to serve as the conclusion to 40–66 is rather more problematic on account of the evident differences among vv 15–16, v 17, and vv 8–21 (see Commentary ad loc.). The conclusion to these 27 chapters would more likely have been limited to the prediction of fiery judgment in vv 15–16, to which were appended at some point in time the prose addenda in vv 17–21.

The last three verses (66:22–24) form the capstone to the entire complex structure of the book but repeat themes and language primarily from chs. 40–66. The creation of a new heaven and earth draws on the eschatological logion of 65:17a together with the language of newness that pervades chs. 40–48 (42:9;

43:19; 48:6). The promise of name (*šēm*) and offspring (*zeraʿ*, "seed") is thematic in the second section of the book (41:8; 44:3; 45:19, 25; 48:19; 54:3; 58:5; 61:9; 62:2; 65:15, 23). It is also noteworthy that the expression *kol-bāśār*, "all flesh," appears, with one exception (49:26), only at the beginning and end of 40–66 (40:5–6; 66:23). The intent to bring the entire book to a conclusion and definition is less prominent but can be detected in the consigning of the "rebels" (*pōšĕʿîm*) to inextinguishable fire (cf. 1:27–31), perhaps also in the reference to the new moon and Sabbath now, finally, to be celebrated in due manner (cf. 1:13–14).

The movement of thought in the rest of this third major section is determined by the psalm of communal lamentation and complaint in 63:7–64:11 (63:7–64:12; hereafter 63–64). To this extent I agree with Steck's parsing of this segment of Trito-Isaiah without accepting the consequences that he draws from it, including a date in the Ptolemaic period (Steck 1989a, 394–404; 1991a, 38–44). The psalmist asks why God continues to be silent and inactive faced with the distress of his people, and complains that this is so even though they are all God's holy people (63:8; 64:8), his servants (63:17), children of Abraham and Jacob (63:16). In place of the assurance of response, a normal component of this kind of psalm, there follows an explanation for why a response is not forthcoming (65:1–7). From this explanation ensues a radical rejection of the psalmist's assumption that all those in whose name he is speaking are God's people.

In terms reminiscent of the old prophetic idea of the remnant, 65:8–12 distinguishes, on the one hand, between the servants and the elect who are the true descendants of Jacob–Israel, and, on the other, the reprobates who forsake their God and practice false cults. This distinction will become apparent on judgment day when the roles will be reversed, a typical sectarian belief (65:13–66:6). This entire sequence of sayings (65:1–66:6) is held together to form a single discourse by the theme of calling and responding or not responding that recurs throughout (65:1, 12, 24; 66:4b).

THE BEARERS OF THE DEUTERO-ISAIANIC PROPHETIC TRADITION: FROM TEXT TO SOCIAL REALITY

The passage from text to social reality is always problematic, even with texts more cooperative than Isa 56–66. There are large gaps between biblical texts and social realia; some of these gaps may be bridgeable and others may not, but the best we can hope for is not a suspension bridge but a pontoon put together with whatever material lies at hand.

We would not expect to find much usable material in the central panel (chs. 60–62), in which the author imagines what the future might be like, a kind of best-case scenario. In the remaining chapters we have a picture of a settled community in which there are rich and poor, those close to the sources of power and those deprived of it—a community in which the poor are exploited

by the wealthy as always, a community going about its civic and religious business, and especially a community under severe stress. It is safe to assume that
not all of this material was composed at the same time. The political and social
background is noticeably different from that of chs. 40–55, though the effects
of the Babylonian punitive campaigns and occupation are still in evidence.
There hangs over the entire corpus a cloud of anxiety and disquietude.

Given this situation, is it possible to get behind the texts with a view to explaining more fully the numerous indications of dependence on Isa 40–55 discussed above? We have seen that in 56–66 individual texts from 40–55 have
been given a future, a new lease on life, by being taken over, expanded, adapted
to the needs of a later generation of listeners or readers. Since this did not happen sporadically, the view presupposes an exegetical tradition and therefore
the existence of bearers of the tradition, tradents for whom 40–55, or the core
of the Deutero-Isaianic corpus, possessed permanent authority and contemporaneous validity and relevance. The question then arises whether we can say
anything about this tradition and these tradents, understood as the social matrix within which "Trito-Isaiah" was generated.

One approach would be to follow up on proposals already in place and focus
on first-person discourse. In 61:1–3 we hear an individual speak of his prophetic endowment and the responsibilities that flow from it. The suggestion
was made earlier that the position of this statement at the precise center of 60–
62 invites the conclusion that it served, at least for the redactor of the material,
as the signature of the prophetic author of 60–62.

The statement has close thematic and linguistic affinity with first-person
prophetic discourse in 40–48. Endowment with the divine spirit recalls 42:1
(*nātattî rûḥî ʿālâv*, "I have put my spirit upon him"), no doubt understanding
the one endowed here to be no longer Cyrus but a prophetic figure. It is
aligned even more closely with the fragmentary 48:16 ("and now the Sovereign
Lord YHVH has sent me, and his spirit . . ."), where the designation *ʾădōnay
YHVH* ("the Sovereign Lord YHVH") also appears, as it does in Duhm's third
Servant passage (50:4–9) but rarely elsewhere in 40–66. Moreover, both 61:1–3
and 48:16 speak of the prophet's being sent on a mission (verbal stem *šlḥ*). The
proclamation of good news to the oppressed and imprisoned, in the manner of
a herald, is equally familiar from these earlier chapters (see Beuken 1989b for
a more detailed discussion).

Much the same language is used in the prophetic colophon with which the
first section ends (59:21), matching the strong prophetic asseveration at the beginning of 56–66, liberally provided as it is with prophetic speech formulas
(56:1–8). The anonymous speaker in 59:21 is certainly a prophet conscious of
spirit-endowment. But he is not a solitary prophetic figure, since the divine
spirit and the prophetic word are promised also to his "seed" (*zeraʿ*) which, in
the context, can only mean a succession of individuals, bearers of the same
prophetic tradition. The connection with the promised "seed" of the Servant,
the Righteous One (*ṣaddîq*, 53:11 cf. 57:1–2) who, being dead, will see posterity (*zeraʿ*) and prolong his days (53:10), is unmistakable.

The assurance given the prophet in 59:21 speaks of words placed in the speaker's mouth, an expression that refers back to the Deuteronomic "prophet like Moses" of Deut 18:18 (*nātattî děbāray běpîv* cf. Jer 1:9: *nātattî děbāray běpîkâ*). That the words must not "depart from your mouth" (*lo' yāmûšû mippîkâ*) likewise recalls the injunction addressed to Joshua, direct successor to the protoprophet: *lo' yāmûš sēper hattôrâ hazzeh mippîkâ* (Josh 1:8). The intent in this clearly deliberate choice of language is to align the Trito-Isaianic prophetic *diadochē* with the Deuteronomic prophetic succession to Moses, the protoprophet. The numerous indications in 40–66 of affinity with the Deuteronomic corpus might in fact suggest that the bearers of the tradition represented by the prophetic individual in 59:21 originated within, or were in some way originally associated with, the Deuteronomic school in the post-destruction phase of its existence.

We seem to be able to make out in the texts the faint imprint of prophetic and scribal activity carried on over several generations by a movement or school owing allegiance to the prophetic leader and teacher responsible for the core of 40–55, whose voice we are hearing in 48:16; 49:1–6; and 50:4–9, and whose death is recorded in the threnody of 52:13–53:12. This activity was scribal as well as prophetic, since it seems that the claim to authority of these prophetic tradents rested on the interpretation of existing prophecy, in the first place that of the prophetic Servant of 40–55.

Moreover, we can speak of a group phenomenon, a *school*, since the texts refer to a prophetic plurality. The so-called Deutero-Isaiah opens with a summons to prophets (five imperatives in the plural, one in the singular, 40:1–8; see Volume 2, pp. 179–80), and prophetic groups are referred to under the metaphor of sentinel or lookout (*ṣōpîm, šōměrîm*) in 40–66 and elsewhere (52:8; 56:10–11; 62:6–7; Jer 6:17; 29:8; Ezek 3:17). The voice we are hearing in the comment attached to the third of Duhm's Servant passages (50:10–11) would most naturally be that of a disciple, and we are surely hearing the voice of a disciple also in the lament and panegyric for the dead prophet in 53:1–11. The mysterious allusion to a teacher in Isa 30:20–21 whose admonishing voice is heard from behind, that is, from the past, may also belong to the same context (see Volume 2, pp. 349–57).

To summarize: The proposal is that, by careful attention to prophetic first-person speech throughout chs. 40–66, we can detect stages in the development of a prophetic succession leading to the emergence of an eschatologically oriented sect within the Iranian province of Judah some time in the mid–fifth century B.C.E. As is generally the case with religious sects, its origins can be traced back to a charismatic individual, the anonymous prophetic individual whose voice is heard and whose fate is described in Isa 49–55. (He may also be referred to in Isa 30:19–21 and in the reference to the dead *saddîq* in 57:1–2.)

Hostility between this prophetic group and the religious authorities, whose control of the Jerusalem temple translated into a large measure of social and economic control, was fueled by the sect's radical rejection of the syncretist option, its rigorist interpretation of the laws (which however did not exclude the admission of proselytes), and an eschatological doctrine inherited from the Servant and his first adherents. The result was the exclusion of the group from the cult community and its consequent social and economic marginalization.

Unfortunately, we cannot say whether this group continued in existence after the epoch of Ezra and Nehemiah and, if so, for how long. For those who date the last two chapters of the book to the time of the *diadochoi* (e.g., Volz, Steck), it would not be difficult to link these *ḥărēdîm*/*ʿăbādîm* with the *ḥăsîdîm* (*asidaioi*) of the Seleucid period and the world of sectarian piety reflected in the book of Daniel. But, while there are features shared by these two "worlds," a more cautious approach would be to view this process by which a prophetic school, and eventually a sect, forms around the person and teaching of a charismatic individual as a recurring feature of Second Temple history, including the "Teacher of Righteousness" and the Qumran community, and Jesus and the early Christian movement.

The frequent attempts that have been made (e.g., by Plöger, Hanson) to trace the development of apocalyptic and its sectarian matrix through Second Temple history—with Isa 24–27, 56–66; Zech 12–14; Ezek 38–39; and Joel as points marking the trajectory—and the book of Daniel as the finishing post—seem to me to be misguided. Sects can form and apocalyptic world views can be generated at any time, given the right set of circumstances. Here, as elsewhere, we have to acknowledge the poverty of our knowledge of the past.

5. TEXT AND ANCIENT VERSIONS

The Hebrew text now commonly in use, *Biblia Hebraica Stuttgartensia* (BHS), is based on the so-called Leningrad Codex (MS B19ᴬ) in the St. Petersburg Public Library, copied in 1009 C.E. from exemplars produced by the famous Ben Asher family. Since 1995, students of the book of Isaiah are fortunate to have available for their use the first volume of the Hebrew University Bible Project, prepared by the late Professor Moshe Goshen-Gottstein. It consists in a reproduction of the Aleppo Codex of Isaiah with full critical apparatus, including variant readings from the ancient versions, the abundant Qumran material, readings from Cairo geniza fragments, rabbinic quotations, and medieval manuscripts.

The Aleppo Codex, now in Jerusalem, is about half a century older than the Leningrad Codex. It was prepared meticulously by Aaron ben Asher in Tiberias and received the seal of approval from Maimonides. Also relevant for the textual history of the book are the Cairo Codex of the Former and Latter Prophets (895 C.E.) and the St. Petersburg MS of the Latter Prophets with the small and large Masora (*masora parva, masora magna*; (916 C.E.).

The Ben Asher family claimed to stand in a tradition of biblical learning—dealing with the consonantal text, its punctuation, and its preparation for liturgical use—originating in the time of the Second Temple. Though unverifiable, the claim of intellectual continuity between the Second Temple Levitical scholars and the medieval Masoretes is not implausible. A significant amount of earlier textual material has come to light, some from the geniza (storeroom) of the Karaite synagogue in Old Cairo in the late nineteenth century, and a great deal more from Qumran and other sites in the Judean Wilderness.

The study of this material has convinced most specialists that a text tradition not essentially different from that of the Masoretes flourished even before the fall of Jerusalem, and that in the years following the destruction, the Tannaitic period, the dominance of this text type became almost total. With respect to Isa 56–66, this conclusion is reinforced by the relative infrequency of variant readings in the *Great Isaiah Scroll* (1QIsa[a]) and their almost total absence in 1QIsa[b] and the fragments from the fourth Qumran cave. In general, variants based on the versions are considerably more numerous that those deriving from early Hebrew textual material.

Though the Hebrew text of Isa 56–66 has been well preserved, commentators will often find it difficult to resist the temptation to improve it, sometimes in brilliant and ingenious ways (see, e.g., the Notes on Lagarde's proposal for 63:1a and Torrey's for 65:7c). But the task of the text critic is not to improve the text but to establish as accurately as possible what it says, and to do so by removing the corruptions that may have been introduced consciously or unconsciously in the process of transmission. Following this guideline, I have found relatively few instances in chs. 56–66 where emendation of the Masoretic text seemed to be called for. In general, the Hebrew Text of Isa 40–66 has been well preserved.

Evidence for at least 21 copies of Isaiah discovered at Qumran and one in the Wadi Murabbaʿat testify to the importance of the book in the Judaism of late antiquity. To judge by the Qumran finds, only Psalms and Deuteronomy enjoyed a higher esteem. The complete *Isaiah Scroll* from the first cave (1QIsa[a]) is 7.34 meters in length with 54 columns, the last 9 of which contain chs. 56–66. One large fragment of a second, incomplete scroll from the same cave, designated 1QIsa[b], reproduces part of chs. 55:2–66:24 on 5 columns. Seven of the Isaiah fragments from cave 4, dated to the first century B.C.E., contain parts (sometimes only one word) of 54 of the 202 verses in chs. 56–66. The complete list is as follows:

4QIsa[b] = 4Q56	61:1–3; 64:5–65:1; 66:24
4QIsa[c] = 4Q57	66:20–24
4QIsa[d] = 4Q58	57:9–17; 57:18–58:3; 58:5–7
4QIsa[e] = 4Q59	59:15–16
4QIsa[i] = 4Q62a	56:7–8; 57:5–8
4QIsa[m] = 4Q66	60:20–61:1; 61:3–6
4QIsa[n] = 4Q67	58:13–14

Most of the variants in the fragments are orthographic and do not affect the sense at all. In the majority of instances in which 1QIsa[a] differs from MT, the reading in a fragment supports the latter against the former, although there are nine or ten cases of agreement between a fragment reading and 1QIsaᵃ against MT and eight in which the fragment reading differs from both MT and 1QIsaᵃ (see further 1997 DJD 15:19–134). What is most striking about the Qumran Isaiah fragments in general is that, with few and unimportant exceptions, they are identical with the medieval Masoretic text.

In the complete *Isaiah Scroll* from the first Qumran cave, the scribe indicated divisions in the text by gaps of different lengths. These do not always correspond with divisions in MT. There is no space preceding and following 56:1–8, though 56:3–5 is set off by small gaps in the scroll. Section 57:1–2 is attached to the preceding chapter, permitting a new beginning at 57:3, the polemic against the Sorceress and her children; and the final phrase, "But the one who takes refuge in me will inherit the land, will possess my holy mountain" (57:13c), is set off with spaces before and after (below). In the central section, the scribe read 60:1–61:9 as one passage, likewise isolating 62:10–12 ("Pass through, pass through the gates") and following it with 63:1–64:11, also presented without a break. The approach is quite different in the last two chapters, which are broken up into numerous small passages. It is not clear that these divisions correspond to any deliberate and meaningful arrangement of these chapters.

For the most part, the 1QIsaᵃ variants are either simply orthographic or are grammatical, with differences in number, gender, or person that in most instances have little effect on the meaning. The 1QIsaᵃ scribe made occasional minor alterations to produce a smoother reading and also seems to have been partial to the use of the conjunction. Changes introduced for theological reasons are rare but not without interest. In the opening passage (56:6), the scribe omitted *lĕšārĕtô* ("to minister to him"), perhaps because he found the idea of foreigners serving as cult personnel disturbing, and in the same verse a blessing on the Name of God replaces the love of the Name.

In 57:15b, a slight change (*bĕmārôm ûbĕqōdeš*, "on high and in the sanctuary") allowed him to introduce the sanctuary as God's dwelling rather than just the heavens, as in MT,. The stones to be cleared away from the route in 62:10 undergo a metaphorical transformation in 1QIsaᵃ into "the stone of stumbling" (*'eben hannegep*, as in 8:14, and cf. 57:14), and the simple omission of a *mem* (pl. ending in *ûmē 'ammîm*) in 63:3a removed the idea that God would look to Gentiles ("the peoples") for assistance (reading *ûmē 'ammî 'ên-'îš 'ittî*, "And among *my people* there was no one with me").

But the most surprising of the variants occurs in the indictments of 65:1–5, where those addressed are described as sacrificing in gardens, in addition to which *ynqv ydym 'l h'bnym* (65:3b), literally, "They suck hands on the stones." This is close enough to the consonantal text of the corresponding half-verse in MT, *mqtrym 'l hlbnym*, to justify the conclusion, reached in the Commentary, that MT has circumspectly replaced a reference to an obscene practice in the *Vorlage* of the Qumran version with a less objectionable ritual.

Use of the term *Septuagint* for the Greek translation of the Hebrew text of Isaiah is inexact, since it more properly applies to a collection of translations and recensions differing considerably among themselves in quality and time of composition. (For details, see M. K. H. Peters 1992). But since the application of the term to the preeminent Old Greek translation (OG) has been sanctioned by usage, "the Septuagint" (LXX) and "the Old Greek version" (OG) are used interchangeably in all three volumes of the AB Isaiah commentary.

A date around the middle of the second century B.C.E. is usually assigned to the OG of Isaiah. Several attempts to fix the date more precisely on the basis of supposed allusions to contemporaneous political events have been made by various scholars. A reference to the death of Antiochus IV in 164 B.C.E. has been detected in the mock-lament on the death of a Babylonian king in 14:4–24 LXX; an echo of the conquest of Babylon by Mithridates I in 141 B.C.E. has been picked up in the same poem ("I will make Babylon desolate," 14:23 LXX); and some have found an allusion to the destruction of Carthage by the Romans (146 B.C.E.) in 23:1 LXX ("Wail, you ships of Carthage, for she has perished"). This last, in which Carthage (*karchēdōn* translates Hebrew Tarshish, *taršîš*), is the most promising, but all are speculative.

The purpose and function of LXX continue to be disputed. While the provision of a reliable translation for the liturgical use of Greek-speaking Jews in Egypt, in the manner of the Targums, still seems the most likely hypothesis, other suggestions have been made.

The Septuagint Isaiah has not generally been held in high esteem *qua* translation (see Volume 2, p. 123). Based on a *Vorlage* close to MT, it stays close to the original for the most part but becomes paraphrastic or vague where the Hebrew text is difficult or obscure. This is so with the obscure allusion to the *ṣaddîq* in 57:1–2 ("His burial shall be in peace, he is removed out of the midst," LXX). In 57:76–79 the translator deliberately blurred the erotic innuendo of the language. A similar impulse may have led to the rewording of 66:3 to avoid the idea of human sacrifice.

Rare words (e.g., *'ašmannîm*, 59:10b) or unfamiliar usage of familiar words (e.g., *nepeš* in 58:10a) also caused problems. A particularly interesting example occurs in 66:7 where MT, referring to Jerusalem/Zion, reads: "Before the birth pangs came on her, she bore a son." The translator was clearly not familiar with the rare meaning of the verb *mlṭ* Hiphil, "to give birth," the only other occurrence of which is in Isa 34:15, and assigned the more usual sense of "escape" to it; hence, "she escaped (*exephugen*) and bore a son." This mistranslation then became part of the dramatic narrative of the Woman Clothed with the Sun in the Christian Apocalypse, who "gave birth to a son and fled (*ephugen*) into the wilderness" (Rev 12:5–6).

Scholars have detected a contemporizing tendency throughout the translation. Small-scale examples are the substitution of Syene, a familiar location in Upper Egypt, for Seba (43:3) and "Persians" for "Sinim" in 49:12. The identification of those who are to "comfort my people" as priests rather than prophets in 40:2 has been taken to indicate that the learned translator belonged to the circle of the high priest Onias (van der Kooij 1981, 60–65). In 59:5b the translator, perhaps unfamiliar with the word *'ep'eh* ("adder?"), introduced the mythical basilisk. Other examples will be given in the Notes.

The Aramaic Targum, attributed traditionally to Jonathan ben Uzziel, disciple of the great Hillel, and therefore known as *Targum Jonathan*, aimed to make the text intelligible not just on the linguistic level but also on the contemporaneous theological level. Metaphorical language is spelled out, for example, by identifying the wild animals of 56:9 with foreign kings, and those far off and near with, those who observe the law and those who have repented and returned to the law respectively (57:19). The Targum explicitly identifies certain sayings as having been spoken by a prophet (58:3; 61:1; 62:10; 63:7), and there are numerous instances of small-scale additions for the purpose of clarification. The *methurgeman* ("author of the Targum") had no hesitation in paraphrasing or simply rewriting expressions judged to be indelicate or theologically problematic. The diatribe against the Sorceress in 57:3–13 is therefore practically rewritten, and in 65:2 YHVH sends his prophets to an unresponsive people rather than pleading with outstretched hands.

In other respects, the Targum loses no opportunity to update the text in the light of the more-developed theological ideas current in the early rabbinic period. Wherever possible the concept of "repentance" (*tĕšûbâ*) is introduced (e.g., 57:18; 58:12), and in one instance the merits of the ancestors take the place of prophetic intercession (62:6). Isaiah 57:16b is rewritten to testify to the resurrection of the dead ("I am about to restore the spirits of the dead and the souls I have made"), as also is 58:11b ("Your body will live with everlasting life.") The ultimate fate of the reprobate is to undergo "the second death" (*môtā' tĕnînā'*, 65:5, 15), and in the final verse of the book the targumist has substituted the spirits of the rebellious for the worm that does not die (66:24).

The strongly interpretative and paraphrastic character of the Targum therefore limits its value as a text-critical resource. The relatively rare instances in which the Aramaic Targum supports OG against MT are noteworthy; they include the following: *rā'îm* for MT *rō'îm* (56:12), *ûlĕhāšîb* for MT *ûlĕšābê* (59:20), *tanēḥēnû* for MT *tĕnîḥānû* (63:14), *vattĕmaggĕnēnû* for MT *vattĕmûgēnû* (64:6), *qārā'* for MT *qorā'*. For the very few other cases in which a Targum reading may have some text-critical value, the reader is referred to the Notes.

Many of the variant readings in the Peshiṭta, the standard Syriac version used by the Syrian Orthodox and Maronite churches, agree with LXX (29 out of the 45 in BHS) and with Targum (21 in BHS), with which the Peshitta has much in common. In chs. 56–66 I have found only 3 or 4 instances in which a reading unique to the Peshitta merited consideration (58:7a, 65:5a, 66:17b; on 63:3c cf. Aqu. and Symm.).

Jerome's *editio vulgata* stays close to MT, a particularly valuable trait in the difficult places in which the other ancient versions tend to be paraphrastic (e.g., 57:8, 17; 59:5–6, 10; 63:7; 64:5b; 65:16). In his commentary on the opening verse of 56–66 (56:1), Jerome writes that Isaiah's hearers are being urged to prepare themselves for the advent of the Savior, *quia ipse est iustitia et misericordia Dei* ("for he is the justice and mercy of God"). On the basis of this equivalence, he took every opportunity in his translation to render the abstract terms *ṣedeq* and *yeša'* ("righteousness," "salvation") as *iustus* and *salvator*, respectively

(45:8; 51:5; 62:1–2, 11), with reference to Christ. The key Isaianic term *kābôd* ("glory"), parallel with *yeša'* in 62:2, is translated *inclitus* ("eminent"), and the genitival phrases *rûaḥ qodšô* ("his holy spirit" 63:10) and *'ārê qodšĕkâ* ("your holy cities" 64:9[10]) as , *spiritum sancti eius* ("the spirit of his Holy One") and *civitas sancti tui* ("the city of your Holy One") respectively—the latter in agreement with LXX.

6. CHAPTERS FROM THE EARLY HISTORY OF THE INTERPRETATION OF ISAIAH 56–66

ISAIAH 56–66 AND JEWISH-CHRISTIAN POLEMIC

Jewish and Christian readers of Isaiah in antiquity did not separate Isa 56–66 from the rest of the book or make any of the structural or chronological distinctions familiar to modern scholarship. As far as we know, the issue of authorship never arose; the readers of the book simply assumed that all 66 chapters were the work of Isaiah ben Amoz, whose name appears in the superscription. So, for example, Sirach (Sir 48:20–25) praises Isaiah for having foreseen hidden things before they happened and for comforting the mourners in Zion, which appears to refer to passages in both Second and Third Isaiah (Sir 48:6; 61:2–3). Josephus (*Ant.* 13.62–73) relates that Onias the high priest was inspired to build a temple in Egypt after reading Isa 19:19, written more than six centuries earlier, and Cyrus knew what he had to do on behalf of his Jewish subjects because he had read it all in Isaiah written 210 years before his time (*Ant.* 11.5–7).

These assumptions about the authorship of biblical books depended on ideas about soul-loss and -possession common in the Greek-speaking world, according to which divine inspiration was thought to inhere in individuals rather than texts. At the same time, there are indications that specific authorial attributions were not in themselves a matter of great theological concern. There seems to have been an element of fluidity or indeterminacy in assigning titles to the Twelve prophetic books, to judge by double or multiple attributions of individual sayings (e.g., Isa 2:2–5 = Mic 4:1–5) and the fictitious title Malachi, assigned to the last of the Twelve. The Qumran *pĕšārîm* ("interpretations") on Isaiah include commentary on Hos 6:9 and Zech 11:11 without distinct identification, and the Gospel according to Mark opens with a quotation attributed to Isaiah but comprised Isa 40:3 and Mal 3:1 (Mark 1:2).

The first stage in the history of the interpretation of a biblical text begins within the text itself. This stage therefore falls under the heading of the formation of the text, including editorial additions, expansions and rearrangements. At some point, it was no longer considered appropriate to insert additions or modifications into the text. At this juncture, any further interpretative elaboration or comment had to be external to the text.

The capacity to generate commentary therefore came to be recognized as one of the surest signs of canonical status. The earliest commentaries on Isaiah are the Qumran *pĕšārîm*. They comprise mostly brief and fragmentary interpretations of passages from twelve chapters of 1–39, two from 40–55 (40:11–12; 54:11–12), and none from 56–66. In the much-discussed 11QMelchizedek text, however, Isa 61:1–3 is one of several texts reinterpreted apocalyptically to refer to the final liberation of the Sons of Light from Belial.

Something was said about the interpretation of the book as a whole in early Judaism in the first volume of this commentary (1, pp. 92–95) and, with special reference to the Servant, in the second (2, pp. 81–87), to which the reader is referred. In the section of the Introduction on The Formation of Isa 56–66 (above, pp. 54–66), some of the salient features of the theology of the Targum were mentioned: messianism, the world to come, repentance, the law, and the destiny of Israel. For the Targumist, the book of Isaiah was a powerful resource for Jewish spiritual resistance against pagan Rome, though for obvious reasons the note of political protest is muted.

Edom is identified with Rome in the Targum's paraphrase of 34:9 and 54:1, while in Ibn Ezra's commentary on the second Edom passage in Isaiah (63:1–6) Edom stands for the Christian empire that arose on the foundations of Rome. The treading of the wine press could then be read as a prediction of the eventual defeat and disappearance of the Christian religion.

The last 11 chapters of Isaiah have provided more ammunition for polemicists in the long history of Jewish-Christian debate than any of the previous sections of the book. One obvious reason is that the book of Isaiah lent itself to Christian reinterpretation more readily than other prophetic books. In the prologue to his commentary *In Esaiam*, Jerome refers to all three sections of the book in noting that it "contains the totality of the mysteries of the Lord: Immanuel born of a virgin, worker of famous deeds and signs, his death, burial, and resurrection from the lower regions, together with the proclamation of the Savior to all the nations" (*PL* 24.18–21).

His contemporary Augustine makes the same point in his *Confessions* (11.5), recalling that "he (Ambrose) recommended Isaiah the prophet to me; for this reason I believe that he more clearly foreshadows the gospel and the calling of the Gentiles than the rest of the prophets." But it is also apparent that the acrimonious polemical language of some early Christian writings matches the kind of language that the "Servants" directed at their opponents in Isa 56–66. While regrettable, this is hardly surprising, since the social situation—the painful separation of a group of dissidents from the parent body—was the same in both cases. One can think of many other examples in the history of religious movements—for example, the Protestant Reformation of the sixteenth century.

In this context Isa 65:1–2 was to achieve a certain notoriety (OG rendered here):

I was found by those who did not seek me,
I was revealed to those who did not ask for me.

I said, "Here I am, here I am"
to a nation that did not call on my name.
I spread out my hands all the day
to a disobedient and stubborn people
to them that do not walk in a way that is true,
but follow their own devices.

In Rom 10:20–21, Paul relied on the OG translation (above) in applying the first couplet to the offer of salvation to the Gentiles, and the rest of the passage to those among the Jewish people who had rejected the Christian claims. The same text served the author of *The Epistle of Barnabas* (12:4), writing about half-century later, and Justin in his *Dialogue with Trypho* approximately 160 C.E. It became, sadly, a *locus classicus* in Christian anti-Jewish polemic. On the instructions of Pius IX, an inscription with this same text was set up in Latin and Hebrew on the facade of the church of San Gregorio a Ponte Quattro Capi in Rome, facing into the Jewish ghetto, where it can still be seen (see the illustration in Sawyer 1996: plate 30).

Isaiah 65:1–2 was not the only text from chs. 56–66 that could serve as ammunition in the ongoing Jewish-Christian polemic. The Christian strategy was to appropriate the language of the dissident minority in these chapters for themselves and identify the opponents of the *ʿăbādîm/ḥărēdîm* with the members of the Jewish community who rejected the Christian claims. In Jerome's commentary *In Esaiam*, for example, the Servants who announce their ultimate vindication in 65:13–15 ("My servants will eat, while you go hungry," etc.) are the Christians, and their opponents are the Jews. He then interprets 66:5 as reflecting the rejection of the Christian message by the great majority of their Jewish "brethren," while at the same time insisting that Christians must love Jews as their brothers (*In Esaiam* 18).

The homiletic passage about fasting in 58:1–12 provides another example of the practice of reading the Isaianic text in the light of the Christian Gospels. *The Epistle of Barnabas* (3:1–5) applied the reproach about false fasting to the Jews and the description of the authentic way of fasting to the Christian practice. The approach of Justin (*Dial.* 15) was similar, and both he and Jerome referred, inevitably, to the Gospel parable of the Pharisee who fasted twice a week and the publican who presumably did not (Luke 18:9–14). That the need to differentiate the Christian from the Jewish practice was a factor is apparent from the ruling in *Didache* 8:1: "Let not your fasts be with the hypocrites, for they fast on Mondays and Thursdays; you must fast on Wednesdays and Fridays."

In the Targum, the *ʿebed* of Isa 53 is explicitly identified with *měšîḥâ* ("Messiah"; 43:10; 52:13), though without the suffering and death. This view was strongly represented throughout the rabbinic period, though the collective interpretation came to prevail, perhaps in reaction to the Christian appropriation of ch. 53. Hence, the disciples of the Servant whose voice we hear in chs. 56–66 constituted, for Jewish interpreters, the holy remnant, the purified Israel whose ultimate vindication is guaranteed by the prophet.

The Christian appropriation of this "Suffering Servant" chapter (Volume 2, pp. 88–92), on the other hand, made it inevitable that the Servants of chs. 56–66 would be identified with the followers of Jesus. Once this was accepted, everything else fell into place. The promise of land and city could be spiritualized (e.g., Jerome, *In Esaiam* 16 on Isa 57:14), 66:1–4 could be read as a rejection of the temple and the sacrificial cult (e.g., *Barn.* 2:4–10; 16:1–4), those who are to be gathered from all nations and tongues (66:18) are the new people of God from the Gentile world (Ignatius, *Magn.* 10:3), and the scene portrayed in the final verse describes the fate of those who reject the Christian message (e.g., 2 *Clem.* 7:6; 17:4–6).

ISAIAH 56–66 IN EARLY CHRISTIANITY

A reading of the Servant passages in Isaiah, generally in the OG translation, provided for the first generations of Christians essential clues to the identity of Jesus. The need to explain in scriptural terms the suffering and death of Jesus and the redemptive value of the death gave these texts a unique function in the presentation of the Christian message (Matt 26:54; Mark 9:12; Luke 22:37; Rom 4:25; 1 Cor 15:3–4; 1 Pet 2:18–25). Philip catechized the Ethiopian eunuch "beginning with this scripture," that is, Isa 53:7–8 (Acts 8:35), and dependence on the Servant texts is apparent in the language that early Christian preachers and missionaries used about Jesus. Of particular significance is the term *pais theou*, which combines the idea of servanthood in the Isaianic sense with divine sonship (Matt 12:18; Acts 3:13, 26; 4:27, 30; *Did.* 9:2–3; 10:2–3; *Barn.* 6:1; 9:2). Though the Servant is not explicitly identified as Messiah in the New Testament, as in the Targum (on Isa 43:10 and 52:13), both qualifications were united in the person of Jesus. For further discussion, see Volume 2, pp. 87–92.

Since early Christians were not concerned to distinguish successive stages in the development of a Deutero-Isaianic prophetic tradition, the first-person prophetic statement in 61:1–3, with which the Lukan Jesus inaugurates his public activity (Luke 4:16–21), was read simply as an extension of the Servant sayings in Isa 40–55. Hence, following this text, Jesus could be referred to as the *anointed* prophet in early Christian teaching (Acts 4:27; 10:38). The title *ho dikaois*, "The Righteous One" (Acts 7:52; 1 John 2:1), may have had the same associations with the prophetic Servant, reflecting the *ṣaddîq* of Isa 53:11 and possibly also 57:1–2.

The emergence of the first Christian group as, historically considered, a Palestinian Jewish sect, can be viewed within a recurring pattern in the Second Temple period. Following this pattern, a body of disciples forms around a prophetic-charismatic individual and then develops to the point of severing relations more or less definitively with the parent body. The process is therefore from prophetic discipleship to sect. The formation of the Qumran sect around the person and teaching of the *mōreh haṣṣedeq* ("The Legitimate Teacher" or

"The Teacher of Righteousness") in opposition to the authorities in control of the temple is one conspicuous example, but no doubt there were others.

Seen from within, that is to say, in Gospel sayings attributed to Jesus, the profile of the disciple is so close to the description of the faithful adherent of the Servant's teaching in Isa 56–66 that it suggests a deliberate modeling of the former on the latter. The Beatitudes (Matt 5:3–12; Luke 6:20–26) embody the theme of eschatological reversal, the classical expression of which is Isa 65:13–15 ("My servants will eat, while you go hungry," etc.).

The affinity is particularly clear in the Lucan version, which adds *nun* ("now"): "Blessed are you who weep *now*, for you will laugh." The last of the Lucan blessings are on those—disciples—who are hated (verb *miseō*) and cast out (*aphorizō*); and to be hated (that is, shunned) and cast out is precisely what happened to the *ḥărēdîm* of Isa 66:5. Luke also balances the blessings with woes on the rich, those already consoled, those who have eaten their fill and who have present cause to laugh (20:24–26). This, again, corresponds to the antitheses of Isa 65:14b–15a. And, finally, we can without much difficulty find in Isa 56–66 the equivalent of most of the categories of people on whom blessing is bestowed in the Beatitudes.

Adherence to the person and teaching of Jesus as a way of life is no doubt encapsulated in the title "The Way," used by disciples for themselves in The Acts of the Apostles (9:2, 9, 23; 22:4; 24:14, 22). While more than one explanation is possible, this too may have been suggested by the term *derek* ("way"), one of the key metaphors in the second part of Isaiah (40:3; 57:14; 62:10 cf. 35:8). The same term can stand for the teaching of the master to be observed among the disciples, as in the admonition of the mysterious Teacher in Isa 30:21: "This is the way; keep to it" (see Volume 1, pp. 420–21).

Orientation to a decisive and imminent divine intervention in human affairs was an essential element in the self-understanding of most of the first Christian generation and came to expression in good part in terms taken from Deutero- and Trito-Isaiah. The announcement of the good news that now the Kingdom of God is at hand, the first words spoken by the Markan Jesus (Mark 1:14), can be parsed as simply an abstract reformulation of the proclamation of the herald (*měbaśśēr*) in Isa 52:7: *mālak 'ĕlohāyik*, "Your God has inaugurated his reign," addressed to Jerusalem. Therefore both the gospel as the vehicle by which the message is communicated (Isa 40:9; 41:27; 52:7; 60:6; 61:1) and the message itself (52:7) are based on these passages in the second and third major segments of Isaiah.

The Lucan account of the inauguration of Jesus' public activity draws on the same source. The occasion was his reading of the words of the anointed prophet in Isa 61:1–2, the *haftara* for that day, in the Nazareth synagogue, and announcing its present fulfillment. The message that there is good news for the poor, freedom for the imprisoned and oppressed, and sight for the blind provides the key to the Gospel miracles as signs that the new age is at hand (cf. Matt 11:2–6).

Anticipation of the proximate return of Jesus in glory, expressed in terms of a royal *parousia* (Matt 24:3; 1 Cor 15:23; 2 Thess 2:8), echoes the many announcements of the coming of God, of the glory of God, or of salvation in Isa 56–66 (59:19–20; 60:1; 62:11; 63:1, etc.). These texts also provide the background for the description of the triumphant entry into Jerusalem, in fulfillment of Scripture and, specifically, of Isa 62:11 and Zech 9:9 (Matt 21:5 cf. John 12:15). Like the disciples of the Servant, the Jesus group had to deal with the disconfirmation of their belief in an imminent divine intervention. Since in both cases the principal reason for delay was a sinful way of life (Isa 59:1–15a; 2 Pet 3:9), it was also possible to hasten the coming of the day by leading godly lives (2 Pet 3:11–12). There remains also the prospect of a final judgment described in terms of the undying worm and inextinguishable fire of Isa 66:24 (Mark 9:48).

The debt to the last 11 chapters of Isaiah in this imaging of the future in early Christianity is especially in evidence in the Christian Apocalypse. The transformation of nature (Rev 21:23; 22:5), new heaven and new earth (21:1 cf. Gal 6:15; 2 Cor 5:17; 2 Pet 3:13), a new name for the elect (Rev 2:17; 3:12), judgment as grape harvesting (14:19–20; 19:15), an end to weeping (21:4), and the new Jerusalem as a bride (21:2), are all Trito-Isaianic motifs that have been given a new context.

This last section of Isaiah also provided the terms of reference for articulating the mission of early Christianity. It seems that the Jesus group first emerged as a revitalization movement within Palestinian Judaism and then, at a certain point, embarked on a mission beyond the confines of Judaism. It was at this point that these last chapters of Isaiah made their most distinctive contribution to the understanding of the identity and mission of early Christians. A mandate for the Gentile mission was readily available in Isa 65:1–2 read in the Greek: "I was found by those who did not seek me / I revealed myself to those who did not ask for me" (Rom 10:20–21). According to Acts of the Apostles, this new departure was effected by Paul and Barnabas after they experienced local opposition from Jewish groups in Pisidian Antioch (Acts 13:44–49). Paul may have been convinced from early in his career as a disciple of Christ that he was destined to be, like Jeremiah, a "prophet to the nations" (Acts 9:15; 26:17–18).

According to the Gospels, the idea of a twofold mission, to Jews first and then to Gentiles, came from Jesus himself, in keeping with the dual mission placed on the Servant of the Lord (Isa 49:6). The mandate of the Jesus of Matthew's Gospel is that the good news is to be proclaimed throughout the world as a testimony to all the nations, and then the end will come (Matt 24:14). This idea, that the Gentile mission is a function of the eschatological perspective, a necessary prelude to the *parousia*, is one of the most distinctive contributions of Isa 56–66 (56:1–8; 66:18–19, 21) to early Christianity.

·

7. ASPECTS OF THE THEOLOGY OF ISAIAH 56–66

TRADITION AND SITUATION

The title assigned to this section of the Introduction could give the impression that Isa 56–66 contains a coherent theological "message." For those who defend the essential authorial unity of these chapters a certain degree of coherence could perhaps be argued, but for most contemporary scholars it makes better sense to read 56–66 as a deposit of reflection and elaboration on existing prophetic teaching regarded as authoritative—first of all on the preceding section of the book.

There is no term in English corresponding exactly to the German *Fortschreibung* often used to characterize this type of literary activity. What is implied in this idea of "ongoing writing" is the transmission of a complex of themes and beliefs, in the course of which they undergo development, modification, reinterpretation, and reconfiguration to meet the demands of new situations as they arise. Whether its practitioners are conscious of it or not, or whether they acknowledge it or not, theology is always done in the context of a particular tradition and is always a matter of mediating between situation and tradition— understanding "tradition" (with Shils 1981, 13) as "a sequence of variations on received and transmitted themes."

The possibility of describing the situation, or the successive situations, addressed in chs. 56–66 rests on one's prior decision about dating the material in these chapters, on which, as we have seen, there is more than one opinion. On the assumption that much of it reflects the vicissitudes of the Persian province of Judah from the late sixth to the mid–fifth century B.C.E., that is, during the reigns of Darius I, Xerxes I, and Artaxerxes I, the long-term effects of the Babylonian conquest and the crisis of faith in traditional religious resources that it induced would still have been felt. The reader of 56–66 soon becomes aware that the dominant frame of mind of the people being addressed is one of disorientation and disillusionment (see especially 59:9–15a and 63:7–64:11). Even if we make all due allowance for homiletic hyperbole, the message is that engagement in traditional religious practices—fasting, sacrifice, Sabbath—remains at the level of mere formality (see especially 58:1–14). There are few if any signs of moral regeneration. Religious leaders are self-indulgent and neglect their responsibilities (56:9–12). There is rampant injustice in the workplace and in the exercise of the judicial system. Murder is being committed, and there is no thought for the poor (58:3–4, 6–10; 59:1–15a). Worst of all, from the point of view of the prophetic author or preacher, the syncretised state religion of the last decades of the Judean Kingdom, including mortuary rites and cults with a strong sexual orientation, is still being practiced, and the practitioners still include the temple priesthood (57:3–13; 65:1–12; 66:17).

These chapters refer to no known historical events on the international scene, and allusions to situations within the province are seldom clear or unambiguous. In the long lament toward the middle of the section (63:7–64:11), Jerusalem, its temple, and the cities of Judah lie in ruins (63:18; 64:9–10), but elsewhere either the rebuilding of the temple is being contemplated (66:1–2) or it is actually in process (56:5, 7; 60:7, 13; 66:6). We can nevertheless conclude that the people addressed in these chapters had inherited and had themselves been prey to successive disappointments. Expectations aroused by the campaigns of Cyrus, culminating in the fall of Babylon in 539, had not been fulfilled. Darius had survived the crisis of 521–520 and, in consequence, the Judean dynasty had not been reestablished in the person of Zerubbabel. Attempts to achieve a degree of autonomy had been thwarted by external opposition and internal dissension during the reigns of Darius, Xerxes, and Artaxerxes I (Ezra 4:4–24; 9–10; Neh 1:1–3). It is therefore hardly surprising that the syncretist option—including the worship of the Queen of Heaven and the propitiation of chthonic deities—was alive and well at all levels of the population, including the religious leadership. We recall that the attempt to suppress the traditional cult of the goddess, probably a reference to the short-lived religious reforms of Josiah, was cited by Jeremiah's contemporaries in Egypt as an alternative explanation of the disaster (Jer 44:15–19).

The question now arises: how did the different speakers and authors in 56–66 address this situation, and what resources did the religious tradition within which they operated make available to them? The first and most obvious thing to be said about this tradition is that it was prophetic. Acquaintance with a wide range of prophetic texts, among which texts from Isa 1–39 are present but not particularly prominent, is demonstrated in the commentary. One striking example may be mentioned here, namely, the close and at times verbatim dependence on texts in Jer 1–12: Jerusalem as a bride (Jer 2:1, 32 cf. Isa 61:10; 62:4–5), as a faithless wife with her children (Jer 2:9; 3:20–22 cf. Isa 57:3–13), as a whore (Jer 4:30–31 cf. Isa 57:3) engaged in an exhausting pursuit of strangers (Jer 2:25, 33–37 cf. Isa 57:10), as shedding innocent blood (Jer 2:34 cf. Isa 57:5; 59:3). The figure of the land devastated by wild animals while its shepherds and guardians either sleep or carouse in Isa 56:9–12 is borrowed, sometimes with the same words, from Jer 12:7–13. There are also close parallels between Isa 56–66 and the numerous references to heterodox open-air rites in the early chapters of Jeremiah.

That this tradition was not only prophetic but, for want of a better term, Deutero-Isaianic, was demonstrated in our discussion of the formation of chs. 56–66 and is assumed in what follows. It has also been established that the Deutero-Isaianic prophetic legacy was mediated by disciples of the Servant, identified with the author of the prophetic deposit or the core of 40–55. We have also established that affinity with 40–55 is especially in evidence in chs. 60–62, the central panel of this last major segment of the book.

An essential component of the tradition within which the Deutero- and Trito-Isaianic authors did their thinking and speaking derived from the Deuteronomistic movement. Whatever the origins of this movement, it is generally agreed that it came into prominence in the last century of the Judean monarchy and survived the disasters of the early sixth century B.C.E. Apart from the book of Deuteronomy itself, its principal literary expressions are the History of the Kingdoms, usually referred to as the Deuteronomistic History, and editorial expansions to several prophetic books, most clearly and extensively Jeremiah. There are some significant differences of emphasis among these sections of the corpus that suggest an origin in different branches of the movement or school. To take one example: Deuteronomistic passages in Jeremiah emphasize the disastrous effects of social injustice, whereas the History attributes the collapse of the state exclusively to cultic irregularity.

In any case, what we can call the Deuteronomistic option survived the disaster, and it did so because it offered a cogent theological explanation for why the disaster took place, by digging deeper into the traditions. In formulating this explanation prophecy played a crucial role, because not only were "his servants the prophets" sent to warn of the consequences of neglecting the (Deuteronomistic) law, thus exonerating YHVH of responsibility for the disaster, but their predictions were spectacularly fulfilled. It is this "argument from prophecy" that is taken up and developed in a new direction in Isa 40–55—the first of many indications of a close thematic link between the Deuteronomistic and Deutero-Isaianic traditions. A more pragmatic reason for survival has been plausibly suggested, namely, the alliance of the Deuteronomists with the pro-Babylonian faction at the Judean court, one of whose representatives, Gedaliah, was appointed ruler of the province after the conquest (2 Kgs 25:22–26; Jer 40:5–6).

In Isa 40–66 in general, and in 56–66 in particular, Deuteronomistic influence is apparent in the first place in the prevalence of a homiletic and exhortatory style reminiscent of the sermons attributed to Moses in Deuteronomy and in marked contrast to Isa 1–39. Good examples of this style can be found in 48:17–19 and 58:1–14. To this distinctive kind of discourse corresponds a transformation in understanding the prophetic function, the main features of which can be deduced from what Deuteronomy has to say about prophecy (Deut 18:15–22).

A prophet was always in some respects a preacher (*maṭṭîp* → verb *nṭp* Hiphil: Amos 7:16; Mic 2:6, 11; Ezek 21:2, 7), but now preaching is more directly about law observance and moral regeneration based on the law. Prophecy is becoming a more learned, scribal and textual activity, with its predictive aspects less in evidence. All of this is encapsulated in the description of the prophet as "the Servant of YHVH" (*'ebed YHVH*), attached in the first place to Moses as both lawgiver and protoprophet, and then to the prophetic "Servants" who continued the mission of Moses throughout the history. This is without a doubt the clearest and most significant indication of Deutero- and Trito-Isaianic affinity with the post-disaster Deuteronomists.

DEALING WITH ISSUES THEOLOGICALLY
IN ISAIAH 56–66

We can now go on to ask how the authors of Isa 56–66, thinking and working in the context of the Deuteronomistic–Deutero-Isaianic theological tradition so described, express themselves in relation to the issues of their own day. We begin with the basic political but also religious question of the nature of the community and its civic leadership.

A striking feature of Isa 40–66 is that nowhere in the aspirations for and dreams of a future restoration is there place for *the monarchy*. A foreign ruler is now the Lord's anointed one (45:1), and the Davidic covenant is transferred to the people as a whole (55:3–5). This is in stark contrast to the aspirations focused on Zerubbabel, scion of the royal Judean dynasty, voiced by Haggai during the *annus mirabilis* of Darius (Hag 2:20–23). There were others in those years who envisaged a restored nation under an ideal Davidic ruler (Jer 23:5–6; 33:14–26; Ezek 37:24–28; Amos 9:11–15; probably Isa 11:1–9), sometimes referred to in cryptic fashion by the code name ṣemaḥ ("sprout," "branch": Zech 3:8, ʿabdî ṣemaḥ, "my servant ṣemah"; 6:12; Jer 23:5; 33:15).

Within the Deuteronomistic movement, the attitude toward the monarchy seems to have been somewhat more ambivalent. In the History (1 Sam 8–12), the establishment of kingship represents an affront to YHVH as divine ruler but is accepted with some reluctance, while the Lawbook prescribes, in effect, a constitutional monarchy, a monarchy under the law (Deut 17:14–20). At the same time, the monarchy is primarily responsible for the liquidation of both kingdoms and therefore stands under divine judgment.

In Isa 40–55 God as king has taken the place of the dynastic ruler. YHVH is king of Israel (41:21; 43:15; 44:6), and the proclamation of his rule ("Your God has inaugurated his reign" 52:7) is one of the climactic points in these chapters. The language draws richly on the mythical theme of victory over the monsters of chaos (e.g., Pss 74:12–14; 89:6–19) and is reinforced by interposed hymns of praise (Isa 42:10–13; 44:23; 45:8; 49:13). In this respect, Isa 40–55 represents a kind of mirror-image of the ideology of royal power expressed in the Babylonian *akitu* festival and the creation myth *Enuma Elish* ("Marduk is king!" IV 28; see Volume 2, pp. 105–10).

Though explicit political language associated with kingship is infrequent in 40–55 and completely absent from 56–66, perhaps the most fundamental symbol uniting both sections is the procession to Jerusalem culminating in the proclamation of divine rule. A close analogy would be the use of the term *parousia* in the New Testament for the anticipated coming of Christ in glory (Matt 24:3; 1 Cor 1:8; 2 Pet 3:4 etc.). Elsewhere, *parousia* can refer both to a theophany (a solicited or unsolicited visit from a deity) and to the solemn visit of a ruler to a city (an event calling for repair of the approach route, a welcoming delegation to escort the distinguished guest into the city, and other appropriate rituals). In Deutero-Isaiah, the theme is announced in the opening paragraph which speaks of preparing the highway and announces the coming of God with power in salvation and judgment (40:1–11). Associated with the theophany is the revelation of the *kābôd* ("glory") associated with divine kingship and comparable to the effulgence (*melammu, melam šarruti*) surrounding Assyrian kings (40:5; 60:1–3).

Throughout chs. 40–66, the same theme of the inauguration of divine kingship underlies the frequent references to the coming of God, the dawn of salvation, the movement from darkness to light, but also the prospect of judgment (45:8; 51:5–6; 59:20; 62:11; 66:15–16). It is emphasized that in some capacity all nations are to participate in this event (40:5; 52:7; 60:3, 11; 62:2). That the theme of divine kingship takes the place of political aspirations for the restoration of the native dynasty is one of several indications that the bearers of the prophetic tradition in 40–55, and their successors in 56–66, were looking for transformation beyond the more or less calculable or imaginable course of political movements and events.

With the liquidation of the Judean state and its institutions, primarily the monarchy and the state priesthood, Judah was reduced to a small province at the western edge of the Babylonian Empire. Since the Babylonians, unlike the Assyrians, did not practice cross-deportation, the way was left open for the eventual return of some of the deportees or their descendants to Judah. It was also fortunate that the imperial authorities found it more cost-effective to settle the deportees as tenant farmers and fief-holders in areas due for redevelopment rather than reducing them to slavery. The situation following the liquidation of the state in 586 B.C.E. therefore evidenced some features relevant to our understanding of the nature of the *community* addressed in chs. 56–66.

The first and most obvious of these features is decentralization, or in other words, a passage from monocentrism to pluricentrism (Talmon 1986, 165–201). There were now significant Jewish communities in foreign territory, of which the largest were situated in Babylonia and Egypt. Some diaspora communities were no doubt in existence before the Babylonian conquest, but the situation changed quantitatively and qualitatively after the deportations of the early sixth century.

This important shift is reflected in the evolution of the term *yĕhûdîm* in Biblical Hebrew. As Josephus observed (*Ant.* 11.173), this gentilic originally applied to members of the tribe of Judah and inhabitants of the Kingdom of Judah (therefore "Judeans") and, as such, it appears as early as the eighth century in Assyrian records and in the biblical account of the reign of Ahaz (2 Kgs 16:6). It continued in use with the same meaning down to and after the fall of Jerusalem (2 Kgs 25:25; Jer 32:12; 34:9; 38:19 etc.). The beginnings of a shift from the purely territorial to the ethnic-religious sense is apparent in references to *yĕhûdîm* in Babylon (Ezra 4:12, 23; Dan 3:8, 12), in Egypt (Jer 43:9; 44:1), and elsewhere. Members of the Jewish colony on the island of Elephantine, at the first cataract of the Nile, not descended from Judeans, also called themselves *yĕhûdāyē'* (Aram.) By the time Esther came to be written, the term was being used in much the same way as it is today, and it was possible to speak of "becoming Jewish" (or perhaps, in the context, "pretending to be Jewish": verb *hityāhēd* Hithpael, Esth 8:17).

The passage from ascriptive status as members of a nation state would lead eventually to a kind of social organization in which criteria for membership remained to be determined. It would also leave open the possibility of admitting, or even soliciting, adherents from outside the group. In chs. 40–55, those addressed are frequently taken to task for various failings (40:27–31; 42:18–20; 43:22–24; 45:9–11; 46:12–13; 48:1–2; 50:1–3, 11), but there is no doubt that one people is being addressed, which bears the names Jacob and Israel. Even though spiritually deaf and blind (43:8), they are God's chosen people, one and undivided (40:1; 43:20; 52:4–6). But it is also anticipated that new adherents, elsewhere referred to as *gērîm*, and as "God-fearers" in the Targum, will affiliate with the community and take a new name. The text in question is as follows:

> I will pour out water on the thirsty ground,
> streams of water on the parched land;
> I will pour out my spirit on your descendants,
> my blessing on your offspring.
> They will flourish like well-watered grass,
> like willows by the runnels of water.
> This one will say, "I belong to YHVH,"
> another will take the name Jacob,
> yet another will write YHVH's name on the hand,
> and add the name Israel to his own. (44:3–5)

Behind this and several other references to the new people of God in 40–66 there lies the Abrahamic blessing (Gen 12:1–3 and passim in Gen 12–50), here reinterpreted by prophetic authority in the light of a new situation—that of a confessional community, adherence to which can come about by personal decision.

The change in status is reflected in the use of the designation *gēr/gērîm*. During the time of the kingdoms, the *gērim* constituted a purely social category—that of resident aliens; but, by the time Isa 40–55 came to be written, the meaning "proselyte" was already beginning to be attached to the term (e.g., Isa 14:1; see Volume I pp. 281–82), reflecting the change in status of the community in question.

With Isa 56–66 we move into a different situation. As we read on through these chapters it becomes clear that membership in the group, and indeed its very identity, have become problematic. In the central panel (chs. 60–62) there is as yet no sign of any change. All of the people addressed are still God's holy people (62:12) and inheritors of the Abrahamic blessing (60:21–22). In the opening passage, however, foreigners and eunuchs have to be assured of their good standing in the community (56:1–7), and this is followed by a strong assertion that God will gather into his people others besides diaspora Jews (56:8). Toward the end (66:18–19), we hear that missionaries will go out and proclaim the fame and glory of YHVH in foreign lands—and will do so in preparation for the final theophany, the *parousia.*

The open admissions policy expressed at the beginning and toward the end of section 56–66 called for a definition or clarification of criteria for affiliation with and good standing in the community. These chapters contain no formal halakic statement about such matters. In 56:1–7 the ethnic and physical dis-qualifications of the Deuteronomistic law (Deut 23:2–9) are set aside in favor of a general statement about adherence to the covenant ratified by Sabbath observance. Interestingly, there is no allusion to circumcision, and we are not told under what circumstances these foreigners and eunuchs became mem-bers of the community in the first place.

When we turn to the last two chapters, it is clear that a critical point has been reached. In the long lament immediately preceding, the psalmist keeps on reassuring the community addressed that, in spite of their sins, they are still God's people (63:8, 14, 18; 64:8[9]), but the reassurances are brushed aside in the following statement that explains why the lament remained unanswered (65:1). Appeal to the prophetic idea of the holy remnant under the figure of the grape cluster (65:8) leads to the assertion that God will create a new people beginning with his servants, his elect, the people who seek him (65:9–10). The irony of the situation is that a prophetic-eschatological group, now excommu-nicated (66:5), is stating that those who have excluded them are no longer part of the household of Israel. The true situation will be clearly discerned only at the final judgment, when the roles are reversed (65:13–16), but the matter has already been decided in principle.

The situation underlying chs. 56–66, in which the location and identity of Israel and the conditions for membership and good standing in it have become problematic, points to a recurring feature in the history of Second Temple Juda-ism. It was customary at one time to present this issue in terms of a dichotomy or contrast between a universalist and an integrationist perspective. Typically, the policies of Ezra and Nehemiah would be cited as illustrative of the former and the book of Ruth or Jonah of the latter, which would often, for Christian scholars, lead to a contrast between early Christian universalism and the par-ticularism, integrationism, and legalism (all pejorative terms) of the Judaism of that time.

It is clear by now that this way of presenting the issue was greatly oversimpli-fied and misleading. Use of the notoriously slippery term *universalism* was rarely clarified, and dubious conclusions were drawn from a reading of the relevant texts. The situation appears to have been that openness to proselytes was the norm, well documented in the relevant biblical texts not excluding Ezra–Nehemiah. Furthermore, the notable demographic increase of Judaism between the Persian and Roman periods suggests that the adherence of prose-lytes was of frequent occurrence. The degree of receptivity would of course vary according to circumstances. The beginning and end of Isa 56–66 testify to a remarkably open and generous attitude to outsiders: the temple of Jerusalem is to be a house of prayer for all peoples (56:7), proselytes will qualify as temple personnel (66:21; perhaps 56:7), and missionaries will be sent out to proclaim YHVH to the nations (66:18–19).

As was noted above, Isa 56:1–7 disregards the disqualifications of the *tôrat qĕhal YHVH* ("the law of the community of YHVH") of Deut 23:2–9, but the absolute exclusion of Moabites and Ammonites is also disregarded in the story of Ruth, the Moabite, and the incident involving Achior, the Ammonite (Jdt 14:10), both of whom embraced the Jewish religion.

In the absence of an effective central authority during the time of the composition of chs. 56–66, criteria for membership in the community were still undefined. The basic issue was group maintenance. In the opening passage of 56–66, the condition for maintaining one's status is to hold fast to the covenant and observe the Sabbath as the external and visible sign of the observant life, and this in view of the proximate advent of salvation (56:1–7). In Exod 12:43–49 (P) circumcision is the essential precondition for participation in Passover, and therefore for civil and religious status in the group, whereas according to Ezra 6:21, probably from the school to which the author of Chronicles belongs, outsiders may participate on condition of repudiating idolatry ("the uncleanness of the peoples of the land").

Elsewhere there are hints that a confession of faith may in some circumstances have been made. Certain affirmations of the unity and incomparability of the God of Israel in Isa 40–55 come to mind in this respect (e.g., 45:14, 22–25). In the historical narratives, similar confessional statements are put into the mouths of certain individuals, some of them introduced with the formulaic *ʿattâ yādaʿtî* ("Now I know . . ."). Thus Jethro is catechized by Moses, pronounces a blessing, and says, "Now I know that YHVH is greater than all the gods" (Exod 18:8–12). Healed of his disease, Naaman makes the extraordinary confession, "Now I know that there is no god in all the earth except in Israel" (2 Kgs 5:15). Rahab of Jericho recites what sounds like a piece of catechetical instruction, and then makes this confession: "YHVH your God is the one who is God in heaven above and on earth beneath" (Josh 2:9–11). Perhaps these formulations go back to practice attending the reception of proselytes into the Jewish faith.

The question where and how to worship was the central issue in Judean communities during the seven decades between the destruction of city and temple (586) and the rebuilding and rededication of a temple in Jerusalem (516). Under the monarchy, the Jerusalem temple was a state institution associated with the dynasty, and its personnel were state functionaries. The building of the temple, its upkeep, and its operations were financed out of state funds (1 Kgs 5:15–32; 7:51; 9:10–14; 2 Kgs 12:1–17). As is clear from the liturgical hymns performed in the temple, the possibility of national salvation, cohesion, and even survival was tied in with the temple and dynasty. The destruction of the temple by the Babylonians and the execution of the leading priests (2 Kgs 25:9, 13–18) were dictated by the fact that the primary function of the temple cult was to legitimate state policies, in this instance, the decision to rebel.

What, then, do these eleven chapters of Isaiah have to say about *temple, priesthood,* and *worship?* As long as the Babylonian Empire lasted, there was little or no possibility of rebuilding the temple. Though direct evidence is lacking, there are some indications that an alternative, imperially approved cult place was set up in connection with the administrative center at Mizpah a few miles north of Jerusalem, in something of the same way that the Assyrians set up a cult center at Bethel after the conquest of Samaria 136 years earlier (2 Kgs 17:24–28; Blenkinsopp 1998, 25–43). But it must in any case have been unclear what the function of a rebuilt temple would be in the absence of a nation state under a monarch. For the deportees there was, in addition, the old problem of whether YHVH could be worshiped outside of his own territory (cf. 1 Sam 26:19; 2 Kgs 5:17; Ps 137:4 "How can we sing hymns to YHVH on foreign soil?"), though places of worship were eventually established in various diasporic locations, of which the best known is the temple of YHV (YHVH) in Elephantine (Jeb).

While the restoration of the Jerusalem cult is not a major concern in Isa 40–48, the task of at least laying the foundations of the temple is assigned to Cyrus (44:28). In chs. 49–55 the focus shifts more directly to the city that is to be rebuilt, repopulated, and cleansed of anything impure (52:1, 11). All of this is in preparation for the inauguration of the reign of God in Jerusalem (52:7). Though the temple is not mentioned in this connection, affinity with the so-called enthronement psalms (Pss 93, 95–97, 99) leaves no doubt that this eschatological event is envisaged as taking place in a rebuilt temple.

There is no consensus about whether Cyrus permitted, and even encouraged and materially supported the project of temple building, as stated in Ezra 1:1–4 and 3:7. The debate over the historical value of Ezra 1–6 has been going on for a long time, with no resolution in sight. According to the Aramaic source incorporated into the Ezra narrative, it was Darius who granted definitive approval for the task and subsidized it from the imperial and satrapal treasuries (Ezra 6:6–12). The outcome was that the work was completed by the sixth year of his reign, either 516 or 515 B.C.E. (Ezra 6:13–18).

This notice is consistent with what we know of Achaemenid imperial policy in other parts of the empire and provides the essential clue to the function of the rebuilt Jerusalem temple. The provision of financial and other assets for the task, and especially the incorporation of prayers and sacrifices for the royal family in the temple liturgy (Ezra 6:10), indicate that the Jerusalem temple was under imperial sponsorship and was, in effect, an instrument of imperial control. It also meant that the emperor in distant Susa had taken the place of the local dynast, from which fact his subjects in Yehud were invited to draw the appropriate conclusions. YHVH's title, "the God of Heaven," used in official documents (Ezra 1:2; 7:12, 21, 23; cf. AP 30:2, 15, 27–28), which corresponds to a designation of the Zoroastrian deity Ahura Mazda, is another indication of imperial sponsorship of the restored Jerusalem cult.

The central panel of section 56–66, that is, chs. 60–62, speaks of the adornment of "my glorious house" (60:7) and the provision of choice timber for its construction (60:13). These are aspects of a scenario, a projection into the future, envisaged at a time when both city and temple still lay in ruins (cf. 61:4). The same situation forms the background to the lament in 63:7–64:11[12]): Jerusalem is a wilderness and the temple has been burned to the ground (63:18; 64:10[11]). The setting for passages at the beginning and end of 56–66 appears, however, to be quite different. Eunuchs are promised permanent status "in my house and within my walls" which I take to refer to religious and civic status, respectively. The preacher also mentions "dubiously belonging" members of the community engaging in prayer and sacrifice in "my holy mountain" (*har qodšî*, cf. 57:13; 65:7, 11, 26; 66:20) and does so in a way to suggest that this is a present possibility. More controversial is the saying with which the last chapter of the book opens:

Heaven is my throne; the earth is my footstool.
What kind of house could you build for me?
What kind of place for my abode?
Did not my hand make all of these,
and all these things came to be? (66:1–2a)

To summarize the position taken in the Commentary: This is not an outright, ideological rejection of temple worship, since the same sentiments are expressed in Solomon's prayer at the dedication of the First Temple (1 Kgs 8:27). It is not a rejection of a project to build a temple elsewhere — in Samaria, according to Duhm — nor is it directed against the proposal to rebuild the Jerusalem temple. It could, however, be directed against expectations of miraculous political and social transformation to follow automatically on the rebuilding, expectations of the kind expressed in Hag 2:6–9, 19, 20–23 and no doubt shared by many at that time.

I believe that here, as so often elsewhere in chs. 40–66, the essential clues are to be found in the work of the Deuteronomists. We note in the Lawbook a concern to avoid the idea of the temple as the dwelling of the Deity in a literal and magical sense. The authors therefore introduce the theological topos of the divine Name (*šēm*) placed in, or dwelling in, the temple (Deut 12:5, 11, 21; 14:23–24; 16:2, 6, 11; 26:2). The adoption of this language made it possible to combine presence and immanence with transcendence, but without subscribing to magical ideas about temples common in the ancient Near East.

We note in passing the Deuteronomistic campaign against a multiplicity of cult centers, especially open-air shrines (Deut 7:5–6; 12:2–4 etc.), of which we hear echoes in Isa 56–66. The other side of the coin is the much-discussed centralization of worship in the Lawbook, a requirement that makes a better fit with the period following 586 (when Judah was greatly reduced in size) than with the monarchy. The Deuteronomistic divine name theology also dictates what the History has to say about the construction and ongoing history of the

Jerusalem temple (1 Kgs 5:5; 8:27, 29; 9:3). Finally, both the History and the Deuteronomistic edition of Jeremiah warn against taking the temple as an unconditional pledge of divine presence and benign activity—in other words, against dissociating temple worship from the striving for personal righteousness and the creation of a just society (1 Kgs 9:6–9; Jer 7:1–15, 21–26; 26:1–6). This, too, is entirely compatible with the fragments of social preaching we hear in Isa 56–66.

Another way of assigning a function to the temple in keeping with prophetic-Deuteronomistic ways of thinking is by reviving the old commonplace of the sky as the place where gods live. This reaffirmation of transcendence is for obvious reasons most commonly encountered in liturgical hymns (Pss 2:4; 11:4; 33:13–14; 102:20; 150:1) but is found elsewhere (1 Kgs 8:38–39, 42–43; Isa 58:4; 63:15). In keeping with this topos, the entire earth (Isa 66:1), or the land of Israel (Lam 2:1), or the ark of the covenant (Ps 132:7; 1 Chr 28:2) serves as the footstool for the enthroned Deity. This is the image of the royal audience chamber (e.g., the *apadama* of the Persian emperors), most familiar from the great vision of Isaiah (6:1–13).

In Solomon's prayer at the dedication of the First Temple, the devotee prays in or facing toward the temple, and God hears from heaven (1 Kgs 8:38–39, 42–43, 49). The temple therefore serves as a kind of sounding board, the place where this form of intercommunication can best be effected. It is also significant that, while this representation appears to remove God from human contact more than magical ideas of presence and activity do, God in this way of thinking is also present to the poor, the broken-spirited, and the oppressed, including people marginalized by the religious authorities (Isa 57:15; 66:2).

Isaiah 56–66 also provides a window into some characteristic aspects of exilic and early postexilic *piety*. Hymns, prayers, and invocations had always accompanied sacrifice, but the professional pray-er, the one who interceded in national crises and in response to individual need, was the prophet not the priest. This is the role assigned to the prophets in 62:6–7 who engage in round-the-clock intercessory prayer for Jerusalem. Communal prayer apart from sacrificial ritual is also characteristic of this age, and the consciousness of a failed history help to move it in the direction of the confession of sin. In 56–66 the communal confession of 59:9–15a receives an answer (59:15b–19), while the lament of 63:7–64:11 does not. Communal confession of sin will continue to be prominent throughout the entire Second Temple period (Ezra 9:6–15; Neh 9:6–37; Dan 9:4–19; 1QS 1:4–2:1; 4QDibHam[a]).

The description of the temple as "a house of prayer for all peoples" (56:7) is an early indication that in the general religious consciousness of this time prayer is gaining at the expense of sacrifice. This process is accelerated then, and more so in the early Hellenistic period, by the decline in prestige of the Jerusalem priesthood and therefore of sacrifice as the one religious act for which priests are indispensable. Solomon's prayer at the dedication of the First Temple, acknowledged to be from the post-destruction period, provides examples of temple-based prayer for various eventualities, including natural and military disasters, and for the forgiveness of sin (1 Kgs 8:31–53). This long prayer also attests the practice, common in the diaspora, of praying toward the temple. At a later time, we will find Daniel in distant Susa praying three times a day facing Jerusalem (Dan 6:10). The practice will eventually be given a more permanent institutional expression in the orientation of synagogues toward Jerusalem.

Confession of sin as a first step toward conversion, turning one's life around (verbal stem *šûb*), is also expressed in the practice of fasting (58:3–12) and mourning (57:18; 61:2–3; 66:10). In reading 56–66, we have the sense that the emphasis is falling more than previously on the moral regeneration of the individual. But what is most clearly in view in 56–66 is that individual and social salvation, or redemption, or transformation, is conditional on the struggle for moral regeneration, both social and individual. This is announced from the start:

> Maintain justice, do what is right,
> for my salvation is near at hand,
> my deliverance will soon be revealed. (56:1)

The preacher takes up the old prophetic theme, one still relevant, that the practice of religion (fasting, sacrificing, Sabbath observance, etc.) is of no avail whatsoever unless accompanied by striving for a just and compassionate social order (see especially chs. 58–59).

WHAT KIND OF THEOLOGY?

It is hardly necessary to labor the point that, in this context, we are not talking about theology as a set of theoretical considerations but as a way of reacting to critical situations from a specific religious point of view. The point of view in question has sometimes been characterized as eschatological and sometimes as apocalyptic. Both words support more than one explanation, but the term *apocalyptic* tends to defy precise definition and, in any case, the phenomenon is thought by most scholars to arise only in the Hellenistic period, beginning with sections of Enoch and Daniel. This limitation seems arbitrary, however, because one would think that the right set of circumstances could generate an apocalyptic world view at any time. In any case, apocalyptic writing is not limited to Judaism. It may help, nevertheless, to ask to what extent, if at all, Isa 56–66 qualifies as apocalyptic writing, measured against the standard texts and descriptions.

In the first place Isa 56–66 lacks a well-articulated dualism, or theory of two ages. This characteristic theme could perhaps be seen to be adumbrated in the prediction of a new heaven and new earth (65:17; 66:22), picked up in early Christian writings (2 Pet 3:5–13; Rev 21:1). But in the Isaianic texts, the context in which the prediction is made puts the emphasis on social rather than cosmic transformation.

Moreover, we see how, typically, this motif can be read as an exegetical development from Deutero-Isaianic sayings about "new things" (42:9; 48:6) together with the prediction about the sky's vanishing like smoke and the earth's wearing out like a garment (51:6). Isaiah 60:19–20, envisaging a world in which the sun and moon will no longer be necessary (cf. 24:23), has likewise inspired Rev 21:23 and 22:5. It thereby affords another indication that Isa 56–66, rather than being part of a complex apocalyptic structure, is one of several texts that have provided material for the apocalyptic "rebirth of images" at a later time.

Also absent from 56–66 is the periodization of history so prominent in Daniel. There is no semblance of a narrative framework common to most texts deemed to belong to the apocalyptic genre. The revelation (*apokalupsis*) is not mediated through a supernatural being (an angel in Rev 1:1–2, Uriel in *4 Ezra*), there are no angels and demons, and no dominion of Satan. Mythical motifs are also lacking, and, with the exception of the bloodbath in Edom (63:1–6) and the undying worm and inextinguishable fire of the last verse (66:24), the imagery is fairly subdued compared with the surreal visualizations in parts of *Enoch* and Daniel. Isaiah 56–66 does indeed speak of a final judgment (59:20; 63:1–6) but, with the possible exception of 66:24, not a postmortem judgment—again, in contrast to these later texts (e.g., Dan 12:2).

A final point: apocalypses are generally pseudepigraphs; and though 56–66 is attributed to the Isaiah of the first superscription (1:1), who was not its author, it is not in itself a pseudepigraphal work, as are Daniel, *Enoch*, and other works attributed to ancient worthies, all the way back to Adam.

On the other hand, everything in 56–66 is decisively oriented to the future. The future, in the sense of the expectation of a discontinuity in the historical process, a "singularity," determines life in the present. This refers in the first place to the moral life of the individual and community, which is clearly affirmed right from the outset (56:1). God will appear with power, and the power of God is essentially the power to overcome evil. Projecting the future can be delusive and self-deceptive, but it can also give meaning and direction to present action. The self-indulgent conduct of both community leaders (56:9–12) and those who have settled for the syncretistic option (57:3–13; 65:1–12; 66:17) illustrates the antieschatological attitude in much the same way as the attitude of the apostate Jews in Egypt during a later age, as described in Wis 2:1–20.

While the future intervention presented in Isa 56–66 is, literally, an act of God, its effects lie for the most part within the bounds of historical plausibility, including physical reconstruction, freedom from oppression, and the repopulation of province and city with immigrants from the diaspora. On the whole, then, the world view of chs. 56–66 is best described as that of prophetic eschatology but with elements that serve as material for the divinely scripted apocalyptic dramas of the Greco-Roman period. These include judgment by fire (66:15–16), the lurid description of the fate of the reprobate (66:24), new heavens and new earth (65:17; 66:22), the imminence of divine intervention (56:1 cf. 51:4–5), and an ultimate reversal of fortune and of roles (65:13–15).

THE NAMES OF GOD

None of the divine names or titles in Isaiah serves as a reverential substitute for the proper name YHVH (Yahveh) or "The Sovereign Lord YHVH" (*'ădonāy YHVH*, 56:8; 61:1, 11; 65:13, 15), a practice introduced only much later. The titles borrowed from chs. 40–55, especially "Redeemer" (*gô'ēl*, 59:20; 60:16; 63:16), "Savior" (*môšî'â*, 60:16; 63:8), and "Creator" (*bôrē'*, 65:17–18), represent attributes and aspects of divine activity of particular relevance for the critical situation addressed in those chapters. Other titles are taken over less deliberately either from 40–55 — "The Strong One of Jacob" (*'ăbîr ya'ăqob*, 60:16 cf. 49:26) — or from the proto-Isaianic collection — "The Holy One (of Israel)" (*qādôš, qĕdôš yiśrā'ēl*, 57:15; 60:9, 14), "The Exalted One" (*rām vĕniśśā'*, 57:15 cf. 6:1).

Of particular interest in this context is 65:15b–16:

> his servants will be called by a different name,
> so that the one who blesses himself in the land
> will do so by the God whose name is Amen,
> and the one who swears an oath in the land
> will do so by the God whose name is Amen.

Most modern translations have found "Amen" as a divine title implausible and have therefore emended the Masoretic Text (see Notes ad loc.). However, the author of the Christian apocalypse did not find it incredible as a title (Rev 3:14, applied to Jesus), and in 2 Cor 1:17–20 it encapsulates for Paul the essence of God as faithful, one of the root meanings of the verbal stem *'mn*. Nor have commentators found unacceptable the verbal form *'ehyeh* ("I am") used in divine titles (Exod 3:14; Hos 1:9). As the context of Isa 65:15–16 suggests, *'āmēn* is pronounced in oath-taking as a solemn asseveration and expression of commitment (Num 5:22; Deut 27:15–26; Jer 11:5; Neh 5:13). It is also used in liturgical hymns to express congregational assent to the praises of God (Pss 41:14; 72:19; 89:53; 106:48; Neh 8:6; 1 Chr 16:36.) In this context, it occurs as a designation or title in order to provide the different name promised to the faithful Servants — the Amen people, a people that says Yes to God.

Equally interesting, and in terms of its impact more significant, is that in the communal lament God is addressed as "father" (*'ābînû*, "our father," 63:16; 64:7[8]). This title, which seems so prominent to Jews, Christians, and no doubt others today, does not occur frequently in the Hebrew Bible. This may be due to the desire to avoid ideas about the physical paternity of the deity (e.g., the Ugaritic El is "father of the gods," and in Jer 2:27 Israelites address a tree-deity as "father"), but more likely because it did not fit widespread perceptions of YHVH at that time. Israel as YHVH's firstborn son (Exod 4:22; Hos 11:1; Jer 31:9) implies divine paternity but only in a purely formal way. The idea of the Davidic king as adoptive son of God (2 Sam 7:14; Ps 2:7; 89:27) is also a special case and almost certainly an import from Egyptian court protocol.

It would be consoling, and may even be correct, to suggest that, in a time of physical and spiritual collapse and godforsakenness, people began to address God as "father" because of the pervasively emotional connotations of the word. It is understandable that in the aphoristic literature the father is the one who disciples and reproves (e.g., Prov 3:12), and there is much emphasis on the honor due to the father in the laws, didactic writings, and elsewhere (e.g., Mal 1:6), all of which can be transferred to God as father. But YHVH is also the father who carries his small son through the desert (Deut 1:31), who extends his protection as *paterfamilias* of the household to orphans and widows (Ps 68:6 [5]), who is compassionate toward his children (Ps 103:13), who can be addressed as "the friend of my youth" (Jer 3:4), and who is saddened when his children repudiate or ignore him (Jer 3:19). In chs. 56–66 the connection is not made explicitly, but the appeal to God as father in the lament recalls the theme of the readiness of God as father to respond when the children call out, and even when they refuse to do so.

BIBLIOGRAPHY

◆

ISAIAH 56–66

◆

COMMENTARIES

Achtemeier, E.
1982   *The Community and Message of Isaiah 56–66: A Theological Commentary.*
        Minneapolis: Augsburg.
Begrich, J.
1963   *Studien zu Deuterojesaja.* 2d ed. Munich: Chr. Kaiser.
Beuken, W. A. M.
1989a   *Jesaja: Deel III A/B.* Nijkerk: Callenbach.
Bonnard, P.-E.
1972   *Le Second Isaïe: Son disciple et leurs éditeurs Isaïe 40–66.* EBib. Paris:
        Gabalda.
Bredenkamp, C. J.
1887   *Der Prophet Jesaia.* Erlangen: Andreas Deichert.
Budde, K.
1922   *Das Buch Jesaja.* 4th ed. Tübingen: Mohr.
Calvin, J.
1979   *Commentary on the Book of the Prophet Isaiah.* Volume 2. Grand Rapids,
        Mich.: Baker.
Cheyne, T. K.
1882   *The Prophecies of Isaiah.* Volume 2, 2d ed. London: Kegan, Paul,
        Trench.
1895   *Introduction to the Book of Isaiah.* London: Adam & Charles Black.
Childs, B. S.
2000   *Isaiah.* OTL. Louisville: Westminster.
Delitzsch, F.
1889   *Commentar über das Buch Jesaia.* 4th ed. Leipzig: Dörfling & Franke.
        [English trans., *Biblical Commentary on the Prophecies of Isaiah.* Edin-
        burgh: T. & T. Clark, 1890]
Dillmann, A.
1890   *Der Prophet Jesaja.* 5th ed. Leipzig: Hirzel.
Duhm, B.
1922   *Das Buch Jesaja übersetzt und erklärt.* 4th ed. Göttingen: Vandenhoeck
        & Ruprecht.
Emmerson, G. I.
1992   *Isaiah 56–66.* OTG. Sheffield: JSOT Press.
Feldmann, F.
1925–26 *Das Buch Isaias.* Münster.
Finkelstein, L.
1926   *The Commentary of David Kimhi on Isaiah.* New York: Columbia Uni-
        versity Press.

Fischer, J.
    1939   Das Buch Isaias. Part 2. Bonn: Peter Hanstein.

Fohrer, G.
    1964   Das Buch Jesaja, 3 Band: Kapitel 40–66. Zurich: Zwingli.

Guinot, J.-N.
    1980   Commentaire sur Isaïe de Theodoret du Cyr: Introduction, texte critique,
                traduction et notes. Paris: du Cerf.

Hanson, P. D.
    1995   Isaiah 40–66. Interpretation Commentaries. Louisville: John Knox.

Herbert, A. S.
    1975   The Book of the Prophet Isaiah: Chapters 40–66. Cambridge: Cambridge
                University Press.

Ibn Ezra, A.
    1964   The Commentary of Ibn Ezra on Isaiah. Translated by M. Friedlander.
                Volume 1. New York: Feldheim.

Jones, D. R.
    1974   Isaiah 56–66 and Joel: Introduction and Commentary. Philadelphia:
                Westminster.

Kessler, W.
    1960   Gott geht as um das Ganze: Jesaja 56–66 und Jesaja 24–27 übersetzt und
                ausgelegt. Stuttgart: Calwer.

Kissane, E. J.
    1960   The Book of Isaiah. Volume 2. 2d ed. Dublin: Browne & Nolan.

Knight, G. A. F.
    1985   The New Israel: A Commentary on the Book of Isaiah 56–66. ITC 5.
                Grand Rapids, Mich.: Eerdmans / Edinburgh: Handsel.

König, E.
    1926   Das Buch Jesaja. Gütersloh: Bertelsmann.

Koole, J. L.
    1995   Jesaja III vertaald en verklaard. Kampen: Kok.

Leslie, E. A.
    1963   Isaiah. New York: Abingdon.

Lowth, R.
    1833   Isaiah: A New Translation. 10th ed. Dublin: T. T. & J. Tegg.

Marti, K.
    1900   Das Buch Jesaja. Tübingen: Mohr Siebeck.

McKenzie, J. L.
    1968   Second Isaiah: Introduction, Translation and Notes. Garden City, N.Y.:
                Doubleday.

Miscall, P.
    1993   Isaiah. Readings: A New Biblical Commentary. Sheffield: Sheffield Aca-
                demic Press.

Motyer, J. A.
    1993   The Prophecy of Isaiah: An Introduction and Commentary. TOTC.
                Downers Grove, Ill.: InterVarsity.

Muilenburg, J.
    1956   Isaiah 40–66. Pages 381–773 in vol. 5 of IB.

Odeberg, H.
1931   *Trito-Isaiah (Isaiah 56–66): A Literary and Linguistic Analysis*. Uppsala: Lundequistska.
Orelli, C. von
1889   *The Prophecies of Isaiah*. Edinburgh: T. & T. Clark.
Oswalt, J. N.
1998   *The Book of Isaiah Chapters 40–66*. NICOT. Grand Rapids, Mich.: Eerdmans.
Penna, A.
1958   *Isaia*. Turin: Marietti.
Ridderbos, J.
1985   *Isaiah*. Grand Rapids, Mich.: Zondervan.
Rosenburg, A. J.
1982–83   *Isaiah: A New English Translation, Rashi and Commentary*. New York: Judaica.
Sawyer, J. F. A.
1986   *Isaiah: Volume 2. The Daily Study Bible*. Philadelphia: Westminster.
Schoors, A.
1972   *Jesaja*. Roermond: Romen & Zonen.
Scullion, J. J.
1982   *Isaiah 40–66*. Old Testament Message 12. Wilmington, Del.: Glazier.
Seitz, C. R.
2001   *The Book of Isaiah 40–66*. Pages 309–552 in vol. 6 NIB. Edited by L. E. Keck. Nashville: Abingdon.
Skinner, J.
1915   *The Book of the Prophet Isaiah. Chapters XL–LXVI*. Volume 2. Cambridge: Cambridge University Press.
Smart, J.
1965   *History and Theology in Second Isaiah: A Commentary on Isaiah 35,40–66*. Philadelphia: Westminster.
Smith, G. A.
1889   *The Book of Isaiah*: London: Hodder & Stoughton.
Stuhlmueller, C.
1990   Deutero-Isaiah and Trito-Isaiah. Pages 329–48 in *The New Jerome Biblical Commentary*. Edited by R. E. Brown et al. Englewood Cliffs, NJ: Prentice Hall.
Torrey, C. C.
1928   *The Second Isaiah: A New Interpretation*. New York: Scribner's.
Volz, P.
1932   *Jesaja II, Zweite Hälfte: Kapitel 40–66*. Leipzig: Deichert.
Watts, J. D. W.
1987   *Isaiah 34–66*. WBC. Waco, Tex.: Word.
Westermann, C.
1969   *Isaiah 40–66: A Commentary*. OTL. Philadelphia: Westminster.
Whitehouse, O. C.
1908   Isaiah XL–LXVI. C. B. Edinburgh: T. C. & E. C. Jack.
Whybray, R. N.
1975   *Isaiah 40–66*. NCB. Grand Rapids, Mich.: Eerdmans.
1983   *The Second Isaiah*. OTG. Sheffield: JSOT Press.

Young, E. J.
1972   *The Book of Isaiah. Volume 3: Chapters 40 through 66.* NICOT. Grand
        Rapids, Mich.: Eerdmans.
Youngblood, R. F.
1993   *The Book of Isaiah: An Introductory Commentary.* Grand Rapids, Mich.:
        Baker.
Ziegler, J.
1948   *Isaias.* Die Heilige Scrift. Würzburg: Echter.

MONOGRAPHS, ARTICLES, SPECIAL STUDIES

Abramowski, R.
1925   Zum literarischen Problem des Tritojesaja. *TSK* 96–97:90–143.
Ackerman, S.
1990   Sacred Sex, Sacrifice and Death: Understanding a Prophetic Poem. *BR*
        6/1:38–44.
Ackroyd, P. R.
1977   Isaiah I–XII: Presentation of a Prophet. Pages 16–48 in *Congress Volume:
        Göttingen, 1977.* VTSup 29. Leiden: Brill.
1986   "יד *yād.*" Pages 397–426 in vol. 5 of *TDOT.*
Aejmelaeus, A.
1995   Der Prophet als Klageliedsänger: Zur Function des Psalms Jes 63,7–64,11
        in Tritojesaja. *ZAW* 107:31–50.
Albertz, R.
1990   Das Deuterojesaja-Buch als Fortschreibung der Jesaja-Prophetie. Pages
        248–56 (esp. 241–56) in *Die Hebräische Bibel und ihre zweifache Nach-
        geschichte.* Festschrift R. Rendtorff. Edited by E. Blum et al. Neukirchen-
        Vluyn: Neukirchener Verlag.
Anderson, B. W.
1988   The Apocalyptic Rendering of the Isaiah Tradition. Pages 17–38 in *The
        Social World of Formative Christianity and Judaism. Fst. H. C. Kee.* Edited
        by J. Neusner et al. Philadelphia: Westminster.
Anderson, T. D.
1986   Renaming and Wedding Imagery in Isaiah 62. *Bib* 67:75–80.
Auld, A. G.
1980   Poetry, Prophecy, Hermeneutic: Recent Studies in Isaiah. *SJT* 33:567–81.
Aus, R. D.
1976   The Relevance of Isaiah 66:7 to Revelation 12 and 2 Thessalonians 1.
        ZNW 67:252–68.
1977   God's Plan and God's Power: Isaiah 66 and the Restraining Factors of
        2 Thess 2:6–7. *JBL* 96:537–53.
Ausin, S.
1999   El Espíritu Santo en la comunidad escatológica (Is 61:1–11). *EstBib*
        57:97–124.
Baechli, O.
1966   Die Erwählung des Geringen im Alten Testament. *TZ* 22:385–95.

Baillet, M.
1982   *Qumrân grotte 4.III (4Q482–4Q520)*. DJD 7. Oxford: Clarendon.
Baldacci, M.
1978   Due antecedenti storici in Is. 65,11. *BeO* 20:189–91.
1980   Due misconosciuti parallelismi ad Isaia 59,10. *BeO* 22:237–42.
Baltzer, K. H.
1992   Stadt Tyche oder Zion Jerusalem? Die Auseinandersetzung mit den Göttern der Zeit bei Deuterojesaja. Pages 114–19 in *Fst. für Horst Dietrich Preuss zum 65. Geburtstag*. Edited by J. Hausmann and H.-J. Zobel. Stuttgart: Kohlhammer.
1994   The Polemic against the Gods and Its Relevance for Second Isaiah's Conception of the New Jerusalem. Pages 52–59 in *Second Temple Studies Vol. 2: Temple and Community in the Persian Period*. Edited by T. C. Eskenazi and K. H. Richards. Sheffield: JSOT Press.
2001   *Deutero-Isaiah*. Minneapolis: Fortress.
Banwell, B. D.
1964–65 A Suggested Analysis of Isaiah xl–lxvi. *EvT* 76:166.
Barker, M.
1978   The Evil in Zechariah. *HeyJ* 19:12–27.
Barré, M. L.
1985   Fasting in Isaiah 58:1–12: A Reexamination. *BTB* 15:94–97.
Barrick, W. B.
1982   The Meaning and Usage of RKB in Biblical Hebrew. *JBL* 101:481–503.
Bartlett, J. R.
1989   *Edom and the Edomites*. Sheffield: JSOT Press.
Bastiaens, J., W. A. M. Beuken, and F. Postma
1984   *Trito-Isaiah—An Exhaustive Concordance of Isa. 56–66, Especially with Reference to Deutero-Isaiah: An Example of Computer-Assisted Research*. Amsterdam: Free University Press.
Becker, J.
1968   *Isaias: Der Prophet und sein Buch*. Stuttgart: Katholisches Bibelwerk.
Beek, M. A.
1973   Das Mitleiden Gottes: Eine masoretische Interpretation von Jes 63:9. Pages 23–30 in *Symbolae Biblicae et Mesopotamicae: Fst. F. M. T. de Liagre Böhl*. Edited by M. A. Beck et al. Leiden: Brill.
1978   De vreemdeling krijgt toegang (Jesaja 56:1–8). In *De knecht: Studies rondom Deutero-Jesaja door collega's en oud-leerlingen aangeboden aan Prof. Dr. J. L. Koole*. Kampen: Kok.
Begg, C. T.
1985   Foreigners in Third Isaiah. *TBT* 23:90–108.
1988   The Absence of YHWH ṣĕbā'ôt in Isaiah 56–66. *BN* 44:7–14.
Begrich, J.
1934   Der priestliche Heilsorakel. *ZAW* 52:81–92.
1938   *Studien zu Deuterojesaja*. Stuttgart: Kohlhammer.
Berges, U.
1998   *Das Buch Jesaja: Komposition und Endgestalt*. Freiburg: Herder.
Bergmeier, R.
1969   Das Streben nach Gewinn—des Volkes עוֹן. *ZAW* 81:93–97.

Beuken, W. A. M.
1985   Trito-Jesaja: Profetie en schriftgeleerdheid. Pages 71–85 in *Profeten en profetische gestalten: Fst. A. van der Woude*. Edited by F. García Martínez et al. Kampen: Nijkerk.

1986a   Isa. 56.9–57.13: An Example of the Isaianic Legacy of Trito-Isaiah. Pages 48–64 in *Tradition and Reinterpretation in Jewish and Early Christian Literature: Fst. J. C. H. Lebram*. Edited by J. W. van Henten et al. Leiden: Brill.

1989b   Servants and Heralds of Good Tidings: Isaiah 61 as an Interpretation of Isaiah 40–55. Pages 411–42 in *The Book of Isaiah / Le Livre d'Isaïe*. Edited by J. Vermeylen. Leuven: Leuven University Press.

1989c   Does Trito-Isaiah Reject the Temple? An Intertextual Inquiry into Isaiah 66:1–6. Pages 53–66 in *Intertextuality in Biblical Writings: Essays in Honour of Bas van Iersel*. Edited by S. Draisma. Kampen: Kok Pharos.

1990   The Main Theme of Trito-Isaiah: The "Servants of YHWH." *JSOT* 47:67–87.

1991   Isaiah Chapters LXV–LXVI: Trito-Isaiah and the Closure of the Book of Isaiah. Pages 204–21 in *Congress Volume: Leuven, 1989*. Edited by J. A. Emerton. VTSup 43. Leiden: Brill.

Biddle, M. E.
1995   Lady Zion's Alter Ego: Isaiah 47,1–15 and 57,6–13 as Structural Counterparts. Pages 124–39 in *New Visions of Isaiah*. Edited by R. F. Melugin and M. A. Sweeney. JSOTSup 214. Sheffield: Sheffield Academic Press.

Blank, S. H.
1952   "And All Our Virtues": An Interpretation of Isa 64:4b–5a. *JBL* 71:149–54.

Blenkinsopp, J.
1981   Interpretation and the Tendency to Sectarianism: An Aspect of Second Temple History. Pages 1–26 in *Jewish and Christian Self-Definition*. Vol. 2. Edited by E. P. Sanders. Philadelphia: Fortress.

1983   The "Servants of the Lord" in Third Isaiah. Pages 1–23 in PIBA 7. [Reprinted, pp. 392–412 in R. P. Gordon (ed.), *"The Place Is Too Small for Us": The Israelite Prophets in Recent Scholarship*. Sources for Biblical and Theological Study 5. Winona Lake, Ind.: Eisenbrauns, 1995].

1987   The Mission of Udjahorresnet and Those of Ezra and Nehemiah. *JBL* 106:409–21.

1988a   *Ezra–Nehemiah: A Commentary*. Philadelphia: Westminster.

1988b   Second Isaiah: Prophet of Universalism? *JSOT* 41:83–103.

1990   A Jewish Sect of the Persian Period. *CBQ* 52:5–20.

1991   Temple and Society in Achaemenid Judah. Pages 22–53 in *Second Temple Studies 1: Persian Period*. Edited by P. R. Davies. Sheffield: Sheffield Academic Press.

1996   *A History of Prophecy in Israel*. Louisville: Westminster/John Knox.

1997   The Servant and the Servants in Isaiah and the Formation of the Book. Pages 155–75 in vol. 1 of *Writing and Reading the Scroll of Isaiah*. Edited by C. C. Broyles and C. A. Evans. 2 vols. VTSup 70. Leiden: Brill.

1998   The Judaean Priesthood during the Neo-Babylonian and Achaemenid Periods: A Hypothetical Reconstruction. *CBQ* 60:25–43.

2000a   *Isaiah 1–39: A New Translation with Introduction and Commentary*. AB 19. New York: Doubleday.

2000b   Judah's Covenant with Death (Isaiah XXVIII 14–22). *VT* 50:472–83.
2001   Was the Pentateuch the Constitution of the Jewish Ethnos? Pages 41–62 in *Persia and Torah: The Theory of Imperial Authorization of the Pentateuch.* Edited by J. W. Watts. Symposium Series. Atlanta: Society of Biblical Literature.

Bloch-Smith, E. M.
1992   *Judahite Burial Practices and Beliefs about the Dead.* Sheffield: Sheffield Academic Press.

Botterweck, G. J.
1965   Sehnsucht nach dem Heil: Is 64:1–7. *BibLeb* 6:280–85.

Bratcher, R. G.
1983   Biblical Words Describing Man: Breath, Life, Spirit. *BT* 34:201–13.

Brayley, I. F. M.
1960   Yahweh Is the Guardian of His Plantation: A Note on Is. 60:21. *Bib* 41:275–86.

Brettler, M. Z.
1998   Incompatible Metaphors for YHWH in Isaiah 40–66. *JSOT* 78:97–120.

Briant, P.
1996   *Histoire de l'Empire Perse de Cyrus a Alexandre.* Paris: Fayard. Eng.: *From Cyrus to Alexander: A History of the Persian Empire.* Translated by P. T. Daniels. Winona Lake, Ind.: Eisenbrauns, 2002.

Brongers, H. A.
1975a   Jes 56:10a. *VT* 25:791–92.
1975b   Einige Bemerkungen zu Jes 58:13–14. *ZAW* 87:212–16.

Brown, S. G.
1993   The Intertextuality of Isaiah 66:17 and 2 Thessalonians 2:7: A Solution for the "Restrainer Problem." Pages 254–78 in *Paul and the Scripture of Israel.* Edited by C. A. Evans and J. A. Sanders. JSNTSup 83. Sheffield: Sheffield Academic Press.

Brownlee, W. H.
1964   *The Meaning of the Qumrân Scrolls for the Bible: With Special Attention to the Book of Isaiah.* New York: Oxford University Press.

Buchheit, V.
1990   Tierfriede bei Hieronymus und seinen Vorgängern. *JAC* 33:21–35.

Budde, K.
1891   Zum hebräischen Klagelied. *ZAW* 11:234–47.
1892   Zum hebräischen Klagelied. *ZAW* 12:31–37.

Bultmann, C.
1992   *Der Fremde in antiken Juda: Eine Untersuchung zum sozialen Typenbegriff "ger" und seinem Bedeutungswandel in der alttestamentlichen Gesetzgebung.* FRLANT 153. Göttingen: Vandenhoeck & Ruprecht.

Burghardt, W. J.
1990   Isaiah 60:1–7, Expository. *Int* 44:306–400.

Buse, I.
1956   The Markan Account of the Baptism of Jesus and Isaiah 63. *JTS* 7:74–75.

Butterworth, M.
1975   The Revelation of the Divine Name. *IJT* 24:45–52.

Cannon, W. W.
1929   Isaiah 61:1–3: An Ebed-Jahweh Poem. *ZAW* 47:284–88.

1934   Isaiah c. 57:14–21, cc. 60–62. ZAW 52:75–77.

Carr, D. M.
1996   Reading Isaiah from Beginning (Isaiah 1) to End (Isaiah 65–66): Multiple Modern Possibilities. Pages 188–218 in *New Visions of Isaiah*. Edited by R. F. Melugin and M. A. Sweeney. JSOTSup 214. Sheffield: Sheffield Academic Press.

Carroll, R. P.
1978   Second Isaiah and the Failure of Prophecy. *ST* 32:119–31.
1979   *When Prophecy Failed: Cognitive Dissonance in the Prophetic Traditions of the Old Testament*. New York: Seabury.
1982   Eschatological Delay in the Prophetic Tradition? *ZAW* 94:47–58.

Caspari, W.
1929   Der Geist des Herrn ist über mir. *NKZ* 40:729–47.

Castagno, A. M.
1982   "Un nuovo cielo ed una nuova terra": L'esegesi di Is 65:17 e 66:22 nei Padri. *Aug* 22:337–48.

Causse, A.
1939   La vision de la nouvelle Jérusalem (Esaïe 60) et la signification sociologique des assemblées de fête et des pèlerinages dans l'orient sémitique. Pages 739–50 in vol. 2 of *Mélanges syriens offerts à monsieur René Dussaud par ses Amis et ses élèves*. 2 vols. Paris: Geuthner.

Cheyne, T. K.
1905   A Dark Passage in Isaiah. *ZAW* 25:172.

Childs, B. S.
1979   *Introduction to the Old Testament as Scripture*. Philadelphia: Fortress.

Clements, R. E.
1982   The Unity of the Book of Isaiah. *Int* 36:117–29.
1997   "Arise, Shine, for Your Light Has Come": A Basic Theme of the Isaian Tradition. Pages 441–54 in *Writing and Reading the Scroll of Isaiah*. Edited by C. C. "Broyles and C. A. Evans. VTSup 70. Leiden: Brill.

Clifford, R. J.
1989   Narrative and Lament in Isaiah 63:7–64:11. Pages 93–102 in *To Touch the Text: Biblical and Related Studies in Honor of Joseph A. Fitzmyer, S.J.* Edited by M. P. Horgan and P. J. Kobelski. New York: Crossroad.

Collins, J. J.
1994   The Works of the Messiah. *DSD* 1:98–112.
1997   A Herald of Good Tidings: Isaiah 61:1–3 and Its Actualization in the Dead Sea Scrolls. Pages 225–40 in *The Quest for Context and Meaning: Studies in Biblical Intertextuality in Honor of James A. Sanders*. Edited by C. A. Evans and S. Talmon. Leiden: Brill.

Conrad, D.
1968   Zu Jes 64,3b. *ZAW* 80:232–34.

Conrad, E. W.
1988   Isaiah and the Abraham Connection. *AJT* 2/1: 382–93.
1991   *Reading Isaiah*. Minneapolis: Fortress.

Cook, J. M.
1983   *The Persian Empire*. London: Dent.

Coppens, J.
1977a   Miscellanées bibliques 84: L'oint d'Is. LXI,2 et les prêtres d'Is. LXI,6. *ETL* 53:186–87.
1977b   Miscellanées bibliques 87: Le Psaume cx. *ETL* 53:191–92.
Crenshaw, J. L.
1972   WEDOREK ʿAL-BAMOTE ʾARES. *CBQ* 34:39–53.
Cresson, B. C.
1972   The Condemnation of Edom in Postexilic Judaism. Pages 125–48 in *The Use of the Old Testament in the New and Other Essays*. Edited by J. M. Efird. Durham, N.C.: Duke University Press.
Croatto, J. S.
1997a   El Origen isaiano de las bienventuranzas de Lucas: Estudio exegetico de Isaias 65:11–16. *RevistB* 65:1–16.
1997b   Wie ist die Befreiung anzukündigen? Hermeneutischer Kommentar zu Jes 61:1–3. Pages 148–65 in *Ihr Völker alle, klatscht in die Hände! Fst. E. S. Gerstenberger*. Edited by R. Kessler et al. Münster: LIT.
Crüsemann, F.
1969   *Studien zur Formgeschichte von Hymnus und Danklied in Israel*. WMANT 32. Neukirchen-Vluyn: Neukirchener Verlag.
Dahood, M.
1965   Hebrew-Ugaritic Lexicography III. *Bib* 46:311–32.
1967   Hebrew-Ugaritic Lexicography V. *Bib* 48: 421–38.
1968   Hebrew-Ugaritic Lexicography VI. *Bib* 49:355–69.
1969   Hebrew-Ugaritic Lexicography VII. *Bib* 50:337–56.
1971   Hebrew-Ugaritic Lexicography IX. *Bib* 52:337–56.
1974   Hebrew-Ugaritic Lexicography XII. *Bib* 55:381–93.
1976   The Chiastic Breakup in Isaiah 58:7. *Bib* 57:105–8.
1977   The Ugaritic Parallel Pair QRA//QBA in Isaiah 62:2. *Bib* 58:527–28.
1982   'Sangue', 'DM, Fenico-Punico, Isaja 63:2. Page 155 in vol. 2 of *Sangue e antropologia biblica nella patristica: Atti della settimana, Roma 23 novembre 1981*. Edited by F. Vattioni. 2 vols. Rome: Pia unione Preziosissimo Sangue.
Daris, S.
1978   Isaia 58:6–9 in uno scritto anonimo. *Aeg* 58:106–9.
Darr, K. P.
1994   *Isaiah's Vision and the Family of God*. Literary Currents in Biblical Interpretation. Louisville: Westminster.
Davies, P. R.
1975?   Who Can Join the "Damascus Covenant"? *JJS* 46:134–42.
Day, J.
1989   *Molech: A God of Human Sacrifice in the Old Testament*. Cambridge: Cambridge University Press.
2000   *Yahweh and the Gods and Goddesses of Canaan*. Sheffield: JSOT Press.
Delcor, M.
1967   Two Special Meanings of the Word יד in Biblical Hebrew. *JSS* 12:230–40.
Diebner, B. J.
1998   Mehrere Hände—ein Text: Jes 58 und die Grenzen der Literarkritik. *DBAT* 29:139–56.
Dietrich, W.
1976   Rache: Erwägungen zu einem alttestamentlichen Thema. *EvT* 36:450–72.

Donner, H.
  1985   Jesaja 56,1–7: Ein Abrogationsfall innerhalb des Kanons—Implikationen
              und Konsequenzen. Pages 81–95 in *Congress Volume. Salamanca, 1983*.
              VTSup 36. Leiden: Brill.

Driver, G. R.
  1922   Some Hebrew Roots and Their Meaning. *JTS* 23:69–73.
  1934a   Studies in the Vocabulary of the Old Testament VII. *JTS* 35:380–93.
  1934b   Hebrew Notes. *ZAW* 52:51–56.
  1935   Studies in the Vocabulary of the Old Testament IV. *JTS* 36:293–301.
  1939   Hebrew *'al* ('high one') as a Divine Title. *ExpTim* 50:92–93.
  1940   Hebrew Notes on Prophets and Proverbs. *JTS* 41:162–75.
  1957   *Aramaic Documents of the Fifth Century* B.C. Oxford: Clarendon.
  1958   Notes on Isaiah. Pages 42–48 in *Von Ugarit nach Qumran; Beiträge zur
              alttestamentlichen und altorientalischen Forschung. Fst. Otto Eissfeldt*.
              Edited by J. Hempel and L. Rost. BZAW 77. Berlin: Alfred Töpelmann.
  1967   Isaianic Problems. Pages 43–57 in *Fst. für Wilhelm Eilers*. Edited by
              G. Wiessner. Wiesbaden: Harrassowitz.

Easley, K. H.
  1989   Ancient Winepresses. *BI* 16/1:65–69.

Ebach, J.
  1992   "Hoch und heilig wohne ich—und bei dem Zermalmtem und Geis-
              terniederten": Versuch über die Schwere Gottes. Pages 85–113 in *Auf
              Israel hören: sozialgeschichtliche Bibelauslegung*. Edited by R. Jost et al.
              Luzern: Edition Exodus.

Eerdmans, B. D.
  1937   Reflections on a Synagogue Inscription (Isaiah 66). Pages 35–40 in *Quan-
              tulacumque. Fst. Kirsopp Lake*. Edited by R. P. Casey et al. London:
              Christophers.

Ego, B.
  1998   "Der Herr blickt herab von der Höhe seines Heiligtums": Zur Vorstel-
              lung von Gottes himmlischem Thronen in exilisch-nachexilischer Zeit.
              ZAW 110:556–69.

Ehrlich, E. L.
  1953   *Der Traum im Alten Testament*. BZAW 73. Berlin: de Gruyter.

Elliger, K.
  1928   *Die Einheit des Tritojesaja*. Stuttgart: Kohlhammer.
  1931   Der Prophet Tritojesaja. *ZAW* 49:112–40.
  1933   *Deuterojesaja in seinem Verhältnis zu Tritojesaja*. Stuttgart: Kohlhammer.

Emerton, J. A.
  1980a Notes on Two Verses in Isaiah (26:16 and 66:17). Pages 12–25 in *Prophecy:
              Fst. G. Fohrer*. Edited by J. A. Emerton. BZAW 150. Berlin: de Gruyter.
  1980b Notes on the Text and Translation of Isaiah 22:8–11 and 65:5. *VT* 30:437–51.

Epstein, J. N.
  1913   Zu dem Ausdruck ארץ בעולה *Jes* 62:4. *ZAW* 33:82–83.

Evans, C. A.
  1982   The Citation of Isaiah 60:17 in 1 Clement. *VC* 36:105–7.
  1988   On the Unity and Parallel Structure of Isaiah. *VT* 38:129–47.

Everson, A. J.
  1978   Is 61:1–6. To Give Them a Garland Instead of Ashes. *Int* 32:69–73.

Ferris, P. W., Jr.
1992   *The Genre of Communal Lament in the Bible and the Ancient Near East.* Atlanta: Scholars Press.

Festinger, L. et al
1964   *When Prophecy Fails.* New York: Harper & Row.

Firmage, E.
1992   Zoology (Animal Profiles). Pages 1143–44 in vol. 6 of *ABD.*

Fischer, I.
1989   *Wo ist Jahwe? Das Volksklagelied Jes 63,7–64,11 also Ausdruck des Ringens um eine gebrockene Beziehung.* Stuttgart: Katholisches Bibelwerk.

Fishbane, M.
1985   *Biblical Interpretation in Ancient Israel.* Oxford: Clarendon.

Fitzgerald, A.
1967   Hebrew YD- 'Love' and 'Beloved'. *CBQ* 29:368–374.

Fitzmyer, J.
1967   *The Aramaic Inscriptions of Sefire.* Rome: Pontifical Biblical Institute.

Fohrer, G.
1970   Kritik an Tempel, Kultus und Kultusausübung in nachexilischer Zeit (Jes 56,9–57,13; 65,1–7; Hag; Mal). Pages 101–16 in *Archäologie und Altes Testament: Fst. Kurt Galling.* Tübingen: Mohr (Siebeck). [Reprinted, pp. 81–95 in *Studien zu alttestamentlichen Texten und Themen.* Berlin: de Gruyter, 1981]

Frankemölle, H.
1989   Jesus als deuterojesajanischer Freudenbote? Zur Rezeption von Jes 52:7 und 61:1 im Neuen Testament durch Jesus und in den Targumim. Pages 34–67 in *Vom Urchristentum zu Jesus: Fst. J. Gnilka.* Edited by H. Frankemölle and K. Kertelge. Freiburg im Breisgau: Herder.

Frankena, R.
1966   Einige Bemerkungen zum Gebrauch des Adverbs כן על im hebräischen. Pages 94–99 in *Studia Biblica et Semitica. Fst. Th. C. Vriezen.* Edited by W. C. van Unnik and A. S. van der Woude. Wageningen: H. Veenman.

Gelston, A.
1965   The Missionary Message of Second Isaiah. *SJT* 18:308–18.
1992   Universalism in Second Isaiah. *JTS* 43:377–98.

Gerstenberger, E.
2001   "ענה" Pages 230–52 in vol. 11 of *TDOT.*

Gevaryahu, H.
1989–90   Isaiah: How the Book Entered Holy Writ. *JBQ* 18:202–12.

Ginsberg, H. L.
1971   The Book of Hosea. *EncJud* 8:1010–25.

Glahn, L.
1934   Die Einheit von Kap. 40–66 des Buches Jesaja. Pages 25–65 in *Der Prophet der Heimkehr.* Edited by L. Glahn and L. Köhler. Giessen: Alfred Töpelmann.

Glueck, N.
1936   The Boundaries of Edom. *HUCA* 11:141–57.

Goergen, A.
1990   Das grosse Sammeln, das es noch nie gab: Der Ausgang einer prophetischen Vision (Jesaja Kapitel 66). *TGl* 33:98–106.

Gordis, R.
1937   Studies in Hebrew Roots of Contrasted Meanings. *JQR* 27:33–58.
Gordon, C. H., and E. J. Young
1951   ʾgʾlty: Isaiah 63:3. *WTJ* 14:54.
Gosse, B.
1989   L'alliance d'Isaïe 59,21. *ZAW* 101:116–18.
1990a   Detournement de la vengeance du Seigneur contre Edom et les nations
            en Isa 63,1–6. *ZAW* 102:105–10.
1990b   Isaïe 21:11–12 et Isaïe 60–62. *BN* 53:21–22.
1990c   L'emploi de Ṣ'Ṣ'YM dans le livre d'Isaïe. *BN* 56:22–24.
1992   Sur l'identité du personnage d'Isaïe 61:1. *Transeu* 5:45–48.
1993a   Isa 59,21 et 2 Sam 23,1–7: l'opposition entre les lignées sacerdotales et
            royales à l'époque post-exilique. *BN* 68:10–12.
1993b   Le Psaume 83, Isaïe 62:6–7 et la tradition des Oracles contre les Nations
            des livres d'Isaïe et d'Ezechiel. *BN* 70:9–12.
1994   Les introductions des Psaumes 93–94 et Isaïe 59,15b–20. *ZAW* 106:303–6.
1997a   L'universalisme de la Sagesse face au Sacerdoce de Jérusalem au retour
            de l'exil (Le don de "mon Esprit" et de "mes Paroles" en Is 59,21 et Prov
            1,23). *Transeu* 13:39–45.
1997b   Isaïe 56–59. *Hen* 19:267–81.
Gowan, D. E.
1981   Isaiah 61:1–3, 10–11. *Int* 35:404–9.
Greenfield, J. C.
1961   The Prepositions B . . . TAḤAT . . . in Jes 57:5. *ZAW* 73:226–28.
Grelot, P.
1957   Un parallèle babylonien d'Isaïe 60 et du Psaume 72. *VT* 7:319–21.
1963   L'exégèse Messianique d'Isaïe 63:1–6. *RB* 70:371–80.
1972   Deux tosephtas targonmiques médites sur Isaïe 66. *RB* 79:511–43.
1990   Sur Isaïe LXI: La première consécration d'un grand-prêtre. *RB* 97:414–31.
Gressmann, H.
1898   *Über die in Jes LVI–LXVI vorausgesetzen Verhältnisse.* Göttingen: Van-
            denhoeck & Ruprecht.
Gross, H.
1967   A Ṣion Egli viene in qualità di redentore: Is 59:20. *Conc* 3:97–109; 619–
            31.
Gross, W.
1993   Israel und die Völker: Die Krise des YHWH-Volk-Konzepts im Jesa-
            jabuch. Pages 149–67 in *Der Neue Bund im Alten. Studien zur Bundesthe-
            ologie der beiden Testamente.* Edited by E. Zenger. Freiburg im Breisgau:
            Herder.
Grunwaldt, K.
1992   *Exil und Identität: Beschneidung, Passa und Sabbat in der Priesterschrift.*
            Frankfurt-am-Main: Anton Hain.
Gunkel, H.
1933   *Einleitung in die Psalmen.* Edited by J. Begrich. Göttingen: Vandenhoeck
            & Ruprecht.
Halpern, B.
1998   The New Names of Isaiah 62:4. Jeremiah's Reception in the Restoration
            and the Politics of "Third Isaiah." *JBL* 117:623–43.

Hanson, P. D.
1975   *The Dawn of Apocalyptic*. Philadelphia: Fortress.
1988   Third Isaiah: The Theological Legacy of a Struggling Community. Pages 91–103 in *Reading and Preaching the Book of Isaiah*. Edited by C. Seitz. Philadelphia: Fortress.
Haran, M.
1963   The Literary Structure and Chronological Framework of the Prophecies in Isa XL–XLVIII. Pages 127–55 in *Congress Volume: Bonn, 1962*. VTSup 9. Leiden: Brill.
1983   Priesthood, Temple, Divine Service: Some Observations on Institutions and Practices of Worship. *HAR* 7:121–35.
Harding, F. C.
1914   The Oracle against Edom (Isa 63:1–6 and 59:16–17). *JBL* 33:213–17.
Hauret, C.
1962   Lo stendere il dito. *BeO* 4:164–68.
Heider, G. C.
1985   *The Cult of Molek: A Reassessment*. Sheffield: JSOT Press.
1992   Molech. Pages 895–98 in vol. 4 of *ABD*.
1999   Molech. Pages 581–85 in *DDD*.
Hermisson, H.-J.
1998   *Studien zu Prophetie und Weisheit*. Tübingen: Mohr Siebeck.
Hessler, B.
1961   Şion im Glanze der Herrlichkeit Jahwes nach Is 60,1–3. *BK* 16:101–4.
Hoaas, G.
1997   Passion and Compassion of God in the Old Testament: A Theological Survey of Hos 11:8–9; Jer 31:20 and Isa 63:9–15. *SJOT* 11:138–59.
Hoeffken, P.
1991   Tritojesaja in redaktionsgeschichtlicher Sicht. *BeO* 48:735–42.
Hoffer, H. A.
1974   אוב Pages 130–34 in vol. 1 of TDOT.
Holladay, W. L.
1997   Was Trito-Isaiah Deutero-Isaiah After All? Pages 193–217 in *Writing and Reading the Scroll of Isaiah*. Edited by C. C. Broyles and C. A. Evans. VTSup 70. Leiden: Brill.
Holmgren, F.
1974   Yahweh the Avenger: Isaiah 63:1–6. Pages 133–48 in *Rhetorical Criticism: Fst. J. Muilenburg*. Edited by J. J. Jackson and M. Kessler. Pittsburgh: Pickwick.
Hoppe, L. J.
1983   Isaiah 58:1–12: Fasting and Idolatry. *BTB* 13:44–47.
1985   The School of Isaiah. *BT* 23:85–89.
Huesman, J. E.
1956   Finite Uses of the Infinitive Absolute. *Bib* 37:271–95.
Huonder, V.
1975   *Israel Sohn Gottes: Zur Deutung eines alttestamentlichen Themas in der jüdischen Exegese des Mittelalters*. Freiburg Universitätsverlag/Göttingen: Vandenhoeck & Ruprecht.
Hurowitz, V.
1997   A Forgotten Meaning of *nepeš* in Isaiah LVIII 10. *VT* 47:43–52.

Irwin, W. H.
1967   "The Smooth Stones of the Wadi"? Isaiah 57:6. *CBQ* 29:31–40.

Jacob, E.
1983   Le Dieu souffrant: Un thème théologique véterotestamentaire. *ZAW* 95:1–8.

Japhet, S.
1991   The Temple in the Restoration Period: Reality and Ideology. *USQR* 44:195–251.
1992   YD VŠM (Isa 56:5): A Different Proposal. *Maarav* 8 (*Let Your Colleagues Praise You: Fst. S. Gevirtz.* Edited by R. J. Ratner et al.): 69–90.

Jefferson, H. G.
1949   Notes on the Authorship of Isaiah 65 and 66. *JBL* 68:225–30.

Jepsen, A.
1974   "אמן 'aman." Pages 322–23 in vol. 1 of *TDOT.*

Jeremias, J.
1971   Lade und Zion: Zur Entstehung der Ziontradition. Pages 183–93 in *Probleme biblischer Theologie: Gerhard von Rad zum 70. Geburtstag.* Edited by H. W. Wolf. Munich: Kaiser.

Johns, C. H. W.
1899   Isaiah 65:12. *EvT* 10:423; 526–27.

Jones, I. H.
2000   Once More, Isaiah 66: The Case of 2 Thessalonians. Pages 235–55 in *The Old Testament in the New Testament: Fst. J. L. North.* Edited by S. Moyise. JSNTSup 189. Sheffield: Sheffield Academic Press.

Jüngling, H.-W.
1993   "Die Eichen der Gerechtigkeit": Protojesajanisches in Jes. 61. Pages 199–219 in *Biblische Theologie und gesellschaftliche Wandel: Für Norbert Lohfink, S.J.* Edited by G. Braulik. Freiburg im Breisgau: Herder.

Junker, H.
1962   Sancta Civitas, Jerusalem Nova: Eine formkritische und überlieferungs-geschichtes, Pages 29–35 in *Ekklesia: Fst. für M. Wehr.* Edited by H. Gross. Trier: Paulinus.

Kedar-Kopfstein, B.
1988   Synästhesien im biblischen Althebräisch in Übersetzung und Auslegung. *ZAH* 1:47–60; 147–58.

Kellas, J.
1907   Note on Isaiah 63:9. *EvT* 18:384.

Kellermann, U.
1991   Tritojesaja und das Geheimnis des Gottesknechts: Erwägungen zu Jes 59,21; 61,1–3; 66:18–24. *BN* 58:46–82.

Kendall, D.
1984   The Use of *Mišpat* in Isaiah 59. *ZAW* 96:391–405.

Kennedy, C. A.
1989   Isaiah 57:5–6: Tombs in the Rocks. *BASOR* 275:47–52.

Kent, R. G.
1953   *Old Persian Grammar, Texts, Lexicon.* New Haven: American Oriental Society.

Kessler, W.
1956–57   Studien zur religiösen Situation im ersten nachexilischen Jahrhundert und zur Auslegung von Jes 56–66. *WZ* 6:41–74.
1956   Zur Auslegung von Jes. 56–66. *TLZ* 81:335–58.
Kiesow, K.
1979   *Exodustexte im Jesajabuch: Literarkritische und Motivgeschichtliche Analysen.* Freiburg Universitätsverlag/Göttingen: Vandenhoeck & Ruprecht.
Kingsbury, E. C.
1964   The Prophets and the Council of Yahweh. *JBL* 83:279–86.
Klein, H.
1981   Die Aufnahme Fremder in die Gemeinde des Alten und des Neuen Bundes. *TBei* 12:21–34.
Knight, G. A. F.
1988   Is "Righteous" Right? *SJT* 41:1–10.
Koch, R.
1946   Der Gottesgeist und der Messias. *Bib* 27:241–68; 376–403.
Köbert, R.
1986   Heisst syr. HAŠQBOL duplex? *Bib* 67:555–56.
Koehler, L.
1921   Jes 63:4. *ZAW* 39:316.
1925   Emendation. Pages 173–80 in *Vom Alten Testament: Fst. Karl Marti.* Edited by K. Budde. BZAW 41. Giessen: Alfred Töpelmann.
Koenen, K.
1988a   Sexuelle Zweideutigkeiten und Euphemismen in Jes 57,8. *BN* 44:46–53.
1989a   Zur Aktualisierung eines Deuterojesajawortes in Jes 58,8. *BZ* 33:255–58.
1990   *Ethik und Eschatologie in Tritojesajabuch.* Neukirchen-Vluyn: Neukirchener Verlag.
1994   *Heil den Gerechten—Unheil den Sündern! Ein Beitrag zur Theologie der Prophetenbücher.* BZAW 229. Berlin: de Gruyter.
1998   "Wem ist Weh? Wem ist Ach? . . . Wer hat trübe Augen?" Zur Funktion von Rätselfragen im Alten Testament. *BN* 94:79–86.
Korpel, M. C. A.
1996   Metaphors in Isaiah lv. *VT* 46:43–55.
Kosmala, H.
1967   Form and Structure in Isaiah 58. *ASTI* 5:69–81.
Kraus, H.-J.
1966   Die ausgebliebene Endtheophanie: Eine Studie zu Jes 56–66. *ZAW* 78:317–32.
1990   *Das Evangelium der unbekannten Propheten: Jesaja 40–66.* Neukirchen-Vluyn: Neukirchener Verlag.
Kruger, H. A. J.
1997   Who Comes—Yahweh or Nahar? A Few Remarks on the Tradition of Isaiah 59:19c–d and the Theological Meaning of the Passage. *OTE* 10:84–91; 268–78.
Kselman, J. S.
1981   A Note on *w'nḥhw* in Isa 57:18. *CBQ* 43:539–42.
Kuntzmann, R.
1977   Une relecture du "salut" en Is 63:7–14: Étude du vocabulaire. *RSR* 51:22–39.

Lack, R.
1973 *La Symbolique du livre d'Isaïe: Essai sur l'image littéraire comme élément de structuralisme*. Rome: Pontifical Biblical Institute.

Landersdorfer, S. K.
1919 Is 62:4. *ZKT* 43:355–57.

Langer, B.
1989 *Gott als "licht" in Israel und Mesopotamien: eine Studie zu Jes 60:1–3, 19–20*. Kosterneuburg: Österreichisches Katholisches Bibelwerk.

Lau, W.
1994 *Schriftgelehrte Prophetie in Jes 56–66: Eine Untersuchung zu den literarischen Bezügen in den letzten elf Kapiteln des Jesajabuches*. BZAW 225. Berlin: de Gruyter.

Lescow, T.
1992 *Das Stufenschema: Untersuchungen zur Struktur alttestamentlicher Texte*. BZAW 211. Berlin: de Gruyter.

Lewis, T. J.
1987 Death Cult Imagery in Isaiah 57. *HAR* 11:267–84.
1989 *Cults of the Dead in Ancient Israel and Ugarit*. Atlanta: Scholars Press.

Liebreich, L. J.
1955–56 The Compilation of the Book of Isaiah. *JQR* 46:259–77.
1956–57 The Compilation of the Book of Isaiah. *JQR* 47:114–38.

Lindblom, J.
1962 *Prophecy in Ancient Israel*. Philadelphia: Muhlenberg.

Lipiński, E.
1969 *La Liturgie Pénitentielle dans la Bible*. Paris: du Cerf.
1973 Garden of Abundance, Image of Lebanon. *ZAW* 85:358–59.
1999 "Nāqam; nāqām; něqāmâ." Pages 1–9 in *TDOT*.

Lofthouse, W.
1937–38 Isaiah 65,11. *ExpTim* 49:102–5.

Loretz, O.
1989 Stelen und Sohnespflicht im Totenkult Kanaans und Israels: *škn* (KTU 1.17. I 26) und *jd* (Jes 56,5). *UF* 21:241–46.

Lupieri, E.
1978 Agostino e Ireneo. *VC* 15:113–15.

Maass, F.
1967 Tritojesaja? Pages 151–63 in *Das ferne und nahe Wort: Fst. Leonhard Rost*. Edited by F. Maass. BZAW 105. Berlin: Alfred Töpelmann.

Maier, J.
1979 Ergänzend zu Jes 62:9. *ZAW* 91:126.

Maier, W. A.
1992 Gad (Deity). *ABD* 2:863–64.

Martin-Achard, R.
1979 L'espérance des croyants d'Israël face à la mort selon Esaïe 65,16c–25 et selon Daniel 12,1–4. *RHPR* 59:439–51.

Mauser, U.
1982 Isaiah 65:17–25. *Int* 36:181–86.

McCarter, P. K.
1999 Zion. Pages 940–91 in *DDD*. Edited by K. van der Toorn et al.

McCullough, W. S.
1948   A Re-examination of Isaiah 56–66. *JBL* 67:27–36.
McKane, W.
1980   Poison, Trial by Ordeal and the Cup of Wrath. *VT* 30:474–92.
Meinhold, J.
1901   Miscellen. *ZAW* 21:203–8.
1922   Jes 59:10. *ZAW* 40:156–57.
Melugin, R. F., and M. A. Sweeney, (eds.)
1996   *New Visions of Isaiah.* Sheffield: Sheffield Academic Press.
Michel, D.
1965–66 Zur Eigenart Tritojesajas. *ThViat* 10:213–30.
Monaci, C.
1982   "Un nuovo cielo ed una nuova terra": L'esegesi di Is 65.17 e 66.22 nei
        Padri. *Aug* 22:337–48.
Moor, J. C. de
1997   Structure and Redaction: Isaiah 60,1–63,6. Pages 325–46 in *Studies in
        the Book of Isaiah: Fst. W. A. M. Beuken.* Edited by J. van Ruiten and
        M. Vervenne. Louvain: Leuven University Press / Peeters.
Morgenstern, J.
1950   Isaiah 63:7–14. *HUCA* 00:187–203.
1956   Jerusalem—485 B.C. *HUCA* 27:101–79.
1957   Jerusalem—485 B.C. *HUCA* 28:15–47.
1960   Jerusalem—485 B.C. *HUCA* 31:1–29.
1969–70 Isaiah 61. *HUCA* 40–41:109–21.
Mowinckel, S.
1931   Die Komposition des deuterojesajanischen Buches. *ZAW* 49:87–112;
        242–60.
1938   Neuere Forschung zu Deuterojesaja, Tritojesaja und dem Aebäd-Jahwe
        Problem. *AcOr* 16:1–40.
1946   *Prophecy and Tradition.* Oslo: Dybwad
1953   Der metrische Aufbau von Jes 62:1–12 und die neuen sogennante "Kurz-
        verse." *ZAW* 65:167–87.
1962   *The Psalms in Israel's Worship.* 2 vols. New York: Abingdon.
Munos, L. D.
1962   Un Reine de Sacerdotes y una nacion santa (ex 19,6). *EstBib* 37:149–212.
Murtonen, A.
1980–81 Third Isaiah: Yes or No? *AbrN* 19:20–42.
Myers, J. M.
1971   Edom and Judah in the Sixth–Fifth Centuries B.C. Pages 377–92 in *Near
        Eastern Studies: Fst. W. F. Albright.* Edited by H. Goedicke. Baltimore:
        Johns Hopkins Press, 377–92.
Nebe, G.
1978   Noch einmal zu Jes 62:9. *ZAW* 90:106–11.
Neirynck, F.
1997   Q 6:20–21; 7:22 and Isaiah 61. Pages 27–64 in *The Scripture in the Gos-
        pels.* Edited by C. M. Tuckett. Leuven: Leuven University Press.
Nestle, E.
1899   Isaiah 65:11. *EvT* 10:475.

Neufeld, T. R. Y.
  1989   *God and the Saints at War: The Transformation and Democratization of the Divine Warrior in Isaiah 59, Wisdom of Solomon 5, 1 Thessalonians 5, and Ephesians 6.* Ph.D. dissertation. Harvard University.

Newman, J. H.
  1999   *Praying by the Book: The Scripturalization of Prayer in Second Temple Judaism.* Atlanta: Scholars Press.

Niebuhr, U.
  1984   Glory. *BTB* 14:49–53.

Nielsen, A.
  1924   Studies in Hebrew Lexicography. *AJSL* 40:153–85.

Nielsen, K.
  1989   *There Is Hope for a Tree.* Sheffield: JSOT Press.

Oesterley, W. O. E.
  1916   *Studies in Isa. XL–LXVI.* London: Scott.

Ollenburger, B. C.
  1987   *Zion, the City of the Great King.* Sheffield: JSOT Press.

Olley, J. W.
  1983   Notes on Isaiah 32:1, 45:19, 23 and 63:1. *VT* 33:446–53.
  1999   "No Peace" in a Book of Consolation: A Framework for the Book of Isaiah? *VT* 49:351–70.

Orlinsky, H. M., and N. H. Snaith
  1977   *Studies in the Second Part of the Book of Isaiah.* Leiden: Brill.

Oswalt, J. N.
  1997   Righteousness in Isaiah: A Study of the Function of Chapters 55–66 in the Present Structure of the Book. Pages 177–91 in *Writing and Reading the Scroll of Isaiah.* Edited by C. C. Broyles and C. A. Evans. VTSup 70. Leiden: Brill.

Page, S. H. T.
  1985   The Suffering Servant between the Testaments. *NTS* 31:481–97.

Pardee, D.
  1988   *Ugaritic and Hebrew Poetic Parallelism: A Trial Cut ('nt I and Proverbs 2).* VTSup 39. Leiden: Brill.

Pascal, E.
  1984   *Is 63:7–64:11: Étude littéraire et théologique.* Ph.D. dissertation. Strasbourg.

Paschen, W.
  1970   Rein und unrein: Untersuchung zur biblischen Wortgeschichte. SANT 24:219.

Paul, S. M.
  1992   Polysensuous Polyvalency in Poetic Parallelism. Pages 147–63 in *"Sha'arei Talmon": Studies in the Bible, Qumran, and the Ancient Near East Presented to Shemaryahu Talmon.* Edited by M. Fishbane, E. Tov, and W. W. Fields. Winona Lake, Ind.: Eisenbrauns.

Pauritsch, K.
  1971   *Die neue Gemeinde. Gott sammelt Ausgestossene und Arme (Jesaja 56–66). Die Botschaft des Tritojesaja.* Rome: Pontifical Biblical Institute.

Peels, H. G. L.
1995 *The Vengeance of God: The Meaning of the Root NQM and the Function of the NQM-Texts in the Context of Divine Revelation in the OT.* Leiden: Brill.

Perles, F.
1912 A Miscellany of Lexical and Textual Notes on the Bible. *JQR* 2:97–132.
1913 A Miscellany of Lexical and Textual Notes on the Bible. *JQR* 3:313–14.
1917–18 Neue Analekten zur Textkritik des Alten Testaments. *Orientalische Studien* 2:125–35.

Petersen, D.
1977 *Late Israelite Prophecy: Studies in Deutero-Prophetic Literature and in Chronicles.* Missoula, Mont.: Scholars Press.

Ploeg, J. P. M. van der
1948 Notes Lexicographiques. *OtSt* 5:142–50.

Plöger, O.
1957 Reden und Gebet im deuteronomistischen und chronistischen Geschichtswerk. Pages 35–49 in *Fst. G. Dehn.* Edited by W. Schneemelcher. Neukirchen-Vluyn: Kreis Mohrs.
1968 *Theocracy and Eschatology.* Richmond: John Knox.

Podella, T.
1989 *SOM—Fasten: Kollektive Trauer um den verborgenen Gott im Alten Testament.* Neukirchen-Vluyn: Neukirchener Verlag.

Polan, G. T.
1986 *In the Ways of Justice towards Salvation: A Rhetorical Analysis of Isaiah 56–59.* Frankfort am Main: Peter Lang.

Ponset, H.
1983 D'Isaie, LXIV,3 à I Corinthiens, II,9. *RB* 90:229–42.

Porteous, N. W.
1967 Jerusalem–Zion: The Growth of a Symbol. Pages 93–111 in *Living the Mystery.* Oxford: Blackwell.

Poznanski, S.
1913 Zu dem Ausdruck ארץ בעולה Jes 62:4. *ZAW* 33:81–82.

Rad, G. von
1966 The City on the Hill. Pages 232–42 in *The Problem of the Hexateuch and Other Essays.* Edinburgh: Oliver & Boyd.

Ravasi, G.
1997 Le vesti, le nozze, i germogli: Lettura simbolice-teologica di Isaia 61,10–11. *Vivens Homo* 8:47–60.

Reider, J.
1935 Contributions to the Hebrew Lexicon. *ZAW* 53:270–77.
1940 Substantival ʿAL in Biblical Hebrew. *JQR* 30:263–70.

Reiterer, F. V.
1976 *Gerechtigkeit als Heil: ṢDQ bei Deuterojesaja.* Graz: Akademischer Druck.

Renaud, B.
1977 La morte du juste, entrée dans la paix (Is 57,1–2). *RSR* 51:3–21.

Rendtorff, R.
1993a Isaiah 56:1 as a Key to the Formation of the Book of Isaiah. Pages 181–89 in *Canon and Theology.* Minneapolis: Fortress.

1993b   The Composition of the Book of Isaiah. Pages 146–69 in *Canon and Theology*. Minneapolis: Fortress.

Ribichini, S.
1999   "Gad, גד." Pages 339–41 in *DDD*.

Rinaldi, G. M.
1961   'Gli Scampati' di Is 66:18–22. Pages 109–18 in *À la rencontre de Dieu: Fst. A. Gelin*. Edited by A. Barucq et al. Paris: Mappus.

Ringgren, H.
1963   Einige Schilderungen des göttlichen Zorns. Pages 107–13 in *Tradition und Situation: Studien zur alttestamentlichen Prophetie. Fst. A. Weiser*. Edited by E. Würthwein. Göttingen: Vandenhoeck & Ruprecht.

Roberts, J. J. M.
1982   Zion in the Theology of the Davidic-Solomonic Empire. Pages 93–108 in *Studies in the Period of David and Solomon and Other Essays*. Edited by T. Ishida. Winona Lake, Ind.: Eisenbrauns.

Robinson, G.
1976   The Meaning of *yd* in Isaiah 56,5. *ZAW* 88:282–84.

Rofé, A.
1985   Isaiah 66:1–4: Judean Sects in the Persian Period as Viewed by Trito-Isaiah. Pages 205–17 in *Biblical and Related Studies presented to Samuel Iwry*. Edited by A. Kort and S. Morschauser. Winona Lake, Ind.: Eisenbrauns.

1989   Isaiah 59:19 and Trito-Isaiah's Vision of Redemption. Pages 407–10 in *The Book of Isaiah. Les oracles et leur relectures unité et complexité de l'ouvrage*. Edited by J. Vermeylen. Leuven: Leuven University Press.

1993   The Piety of the Torah-Disciples at the Winding-up [*sic*] of the Hebrew Bible: Josh 1:8; Ps 1:2; Isa 59:21. Pages 78–85 in *Bibel in jüdischer und christlicher Tradition: Fst. Johann Maier*. Edited by H. Merklein et al. Frankfurt am Main: Anton Hain. [Reprinted in Hebrew, Rofé 1994]

1994   The Devotion to Torah-Study at the End of the Biblical Period: Joshua 1:8; Psalm 1:2; Isaiah 59:21. Pages 622–28 in *The Bible in the Light of its Interpreters*. Edited by S. Japhet. Jerusalem: Magnes.

1995   Promise and Covenant: The Promise to the Patriarchs in Late Biblical Literature. Pages 52–59 in *Divine Promises to the Fathers in the Three Monotheistic Religions: Proceedings of a Symposium held in Jerusalem, March 24–25th 1993*. Edited by A. Niccacci. Jerusalem: Franciscan Printing Press.

Rooker, M. F.
1996   Dating Isaiah 40–66: What Does the Linguistic Evidence Say? *WTJ* 58:303–12.

Room, H. J.
1993   Een Woord gesproken in welke tijd? Enkele opmerkingen over het auteurschap van Jesaja 56–66. Pages 124–36 in *Een sprekend begin: opstellen aangeboden aan Prof. Dr. H. M. Ohmann*. Kampen: van den Berg.

Rosendal, B.
1994   "Gerechtigkeit" und "Werke" in Jesaja 57,12. *SJOT* 8:152–54.

Rubinstein, A.
1963   Word Substitution in Is LXIII.5 and LIX.16. *JSS* 8:52–55.

Rudolph, W.
1976   Zu Jes 62:9. ZAW 88:282.
Ruiten, J. van
1992   The Intertextual Relationship between Isaiah 65,25 and Isaiah 11,6–9. Pages 31–42 in *The Scriptures and the Scrolls: Studies in Honour of A. S. van der Woude*. Edited by F. García Martínez et al. Leiden: Brill.
Ruppert, L.
1994   Das Heil der Völker (Heilsuniversalismus) in Deutero und "Trito" Jesaja. MTZ 45:137–59.
Ruszkowski, L.
2000   *Volk und Gemeinde im Wandel: Eine Untersuchung zu Jesaja 56–66.* FRLANT 191. Göttingen: Vandenhoeck & Ruprecht.
Sanders, J. A.
1975   From Isaiah 61 to Luke 4. Pages 75–106 in *Christianity, Judaism and Other Greco-Roman Cults*. Edited by J. Neusner. Leiden: Brill.
1982   Isaiah in Luke. *Int* 36:144–55.
Sasson, J. M.
1976   Isaiah LXVI 3–4a. *VT* 26:199–207.
Saviv, A.
1985–86   Clarification of the Word *šem* in the Bible. *BM* 31:31–38. [Hebrew]
Sawyer, J. F. A.
1989   Daughter of Zion and Servant of the Lord in Isaiah: A Comparison. *JSOT* 44:89–107.
1996   *The Fifth Gospel: Isaiah in the History of Christianity.* Cambridge: Cambridge University Press.
Saydon, P. P.
1955   Assonance in Hebrew as a Means of Expressing Emphasis. *Bib* 36:36–50; 287–304.
Scharbert, J.
1983   "Erwählung" im AT im Licht von Gen 12,1–3. Pages 13–33 in *Dynamik im Wort: Fst. aus Anlass des 50 jahrigen Bestehens des Katholischen Bibelwerks in Deutschland*. Stuttgart: Katholisches Bibelwerk.
Schildenberger, J.
1965   Die Gottestadt Jerusalem (Is 60,1–6). *TW* 7:21–26.
Schmid, H.
1968   *Mose, Überlieferung und Geschichte.* BZAW 110. Berlin: de Gruyter.
Schmidt, B. B.
1994   *Israel's Beneficent Dead: Ancestor Cult and Necromancy in Ancient Israelite Religion and Tradition.* Tübingen: Mohr Siebeck. [Reprinted, Winona Lake, Ind.: Eisenbrauns, 1996]
Schmidt, M.
1948   *Prophet und Tempel.* Zurich: Zollikon.
Schmitt, J. J.
1980   L'oracle d'Isaïe 61:1ff.: Et sa relecture par Jésus. *RSR* 54:97–108.
1985   The Motherhood of God and Zion as Mother. *RB* 92:557–69.
Schneck, R.
1994   *Isaiah in the Gospel of Mark I–VIII.* Vallejo, Calif.: Bibal.
Schneider, S., and J. H. Berke.
1995   שד: Breast, Robbery, or the Devil? *JBQ* 23:86–90.

Schottroff, W.
1997   "Unrechtmässige Fesseln auftun, Jochstricke lösen," Jesaja 58:1–2: Ein
          Textbeispiel zum Thema Bibel und Ökonomie. *BI* 5:263–78.

Schramm, B.
1995   *The Opponents of Third Isaiah.* Sheffield: Sheffield Academic Press.

Schult, H.
1974   Jes 63:1—MI ZH BA. *DBAT* 7:31–32.

Schwarz, G.
1975   ". . . trinken "in meinen heiligen Vorhöfen?" Eine Emendation. *ZAW*
          87: 216–17.

Schwartz, J.
1993   Treading the Grapes of Wrath. The Winepress in Ancient Jewish and
          Christian Traditions. *TZ* 49:215–28.

Scullion, J. J.
1971   *Ṣedeq-Ṣedaqah* in Isaiah cc. 40–66. *UF* 3:335–48.
1972   Some Difficult Texts in Isaiah 56–66 in the Light of Modern Scholar-
          ship. *UF* 4:105–28.

Secombe, D.
1981   Luke and Isaiah. *NTS* 37:252–59.

Sehmsdorf, E.
1972   Studien zur Redaktionsgeschichte von Jesaja 56–66 (Jes 65:16b–25 66:1–
          456:1–8). *ZAW* 84:517–76.

Seitz, C. R.
1988   Isaiah 1–66: Making Sense of the Whole. Pages 105–26 in *Reading
          and Preaching the Book of Isaiah.* Edited by C. R. Seitz. Philadelphia:
          Fortress.
1992   Isaiah, Book of (Third Isaiah). Pages 501–7 in vol. 3 of *ABD.*
1996   How Is the Prophet Isaiah Present in the Latter Part of the Book? The
          Logic of Chapters 40–66 within the Book of Isaiah. *JBL* 115:219–40.

Sekine, S.
1989   *Die Tritojesajanische Sammlung (Jes 56–66) redaktionsgeschichtlich unter-
          sucht.* BZAW 175. Berlin: de Gruyter.

Sheppard, G. T.
1992   The "Scope" of Isaiah as a Book of Jewish and Christian Scriptures.
          Pages 257–81 in *New Visions of Isaiah.* Edited by R. F. Melugin and
          M. A. Sweeney. Sheffield: Sheffield Academic Press.

Shils, E.
1981   *Tradition.* Chicago: University of Chicago Press.

Smart, J.
1935   A New Interpretation of Isaiah 66:1–6. *ExpTim* 46:420–32.

Smith, M.
1971   *Parties and Politics That Shaped the Old Testament.* New York: Colum-
          bia University Press.

Smith, P. A.
1995   *Rhetoric and Redaction in Trito-Isaiah: The Structure, Growth and Author-
          ship of Isaiah 56–66.* VTSup 62. Leiden: Brill.

Smith-Christopher, D. L.
1996   Between Ezra and Isaiah: Exclusion, Transformation, and Inclusion of
              the "Foreigner" in Postexilic Biblical Theology. Pages 117–42 in *Ethnic-
              ity and the Bible*. Edited by M. Brett. Leiden: Brill.
Snaith, N. H.
1977   Isaiah 40–66: A Study of the Teaching of the Second Isaiah and Its Con-
              sequences. Pages 139–46 in *Studies on the Second Part of the Book of
              Isaiah*. Edited by H. Orlinsky and N. H. Snaith. Leiden: Brill.
Sommer, B. D.
1998   *A Prophet Reads Scripture: Allusion in Isaiah 40–66*. Stanford: Stanford
              University Press.
Sperling, S. D.
1999   Meni; מני; 'Fortune'. Pages 566–68 in *DDD*.
Stade, B.
1902   Emendationen. ZAW 22:328.
Steck, O. H.
1985a   Jesaja 60,13: Bauholz oder Tempelgarten? *BN* 30:29–34.
1985b   *Bereitete Heimkehr: Jesaja 35 also redaktionelle Brücke zwischen dem
              Ersten und dem Zweiten Jesaja*. Stuttgart: Katholisches Bibelwerk.
1986a   Der Grundtext in Jesaja 60 und sein Aufbau. *ZTK* 83:261–96.
1986b   Der Rachetag in Jesaja lxi 2: Ein Kapitel redaktionsgeschichtlicher
              Kleinarbeit. *VT* 36:323–38.
1986c   Heimkehr auf der Schulter oder/und auf der Hüfte: Jes 49,22b/60,4b.
              ZAW 98:275–77.
1987a   Beobachtungen zu Jesaja 56–59. *BZ* 31:228–46.
1987b   Jahwes Feinde in Jesaja 59. *BN* 36:51–56.
1987c   Beobachtungen zur Anlage von Jes 65–66. *BN* 38/39:103–16. [Reprinted,
              pp. 217–33 in *Studien zu Tritojesaja*, 1991]
1987d   Lumen gentium. Exegetische Bemerkungen zum Grundsinn von Jesaja
              60:1–3. Pages 1279–94 in *Weisheit Gottes—Weisheit der Welt: Fst. J. K.
              Ratzinger*. Edited by W. Baier et al. 2 vols. St. Ottilien: EOS.
1988   Zur literarisches Schichtung in Jes. 51. *BN* 44:74–86.
1989a   Tritojesaja im Jesajabuch. Pages 361–406 in *The Book of Isaiah: Les ora-
              cles et leur relectures unité et complexité de l'ouvrage—Le Livre d'Isaïe*.
              Edited by J. Vermeylen. BETL 81. Leuven: Leuven University Press.
1989b   Zion also Gelände und Gestalt: Überlegungen zur Wahrnehmung Je-
              rusalems also Stadt und Fraus im Alten Testament. *ZTK* 86:261–81.
              [Reprinted, pp. 126–45 in *Gottesknecht und Zion*. Tübingen: Mohr Sie-
              beck, 1992]
1991a   *Studien zu Tritojesaja*. BZAW 203. Berlin: de Gruyter.
1991b   Anschlussprobleme einer redaktionellen Entstehung von Tritojesaja.
              Pages 269–79 in *Studien zu Tritojesaja*. Edited by O. H. Steck. Berlin:
              de Gruyter.
1991c   Zu jüngsten Untersuchungen von Jes 56,1–8; 63,7–66,24. Pages 229–65
              in *Studien zu Tritojesaja*.
1991d   Zu jüngsten Untersuchungen von Jes 56,9–59,21; 63,1–6. Pages 192–214
              in *Studien zu Tritojesaja*.
1991e   Jesaja 62,10–12 als Abschluss eines Grossjesajabuches. Pages 143–66 in
              Studien zu Tritojesaja.

1991f   Jüngste Untersuchungen zu Jes 66 und zur Endredaktion des Jesa-
             jabuches. Pages 262–65 in *Studien zu Tritojesaja*.
1991g   Zu jüngsten Untersuchungen von Jes 60–62. Pages 119–40 in *Studien zu
             Tritojesaja*.
1992a   *Gottesknecht und Zion*. Tübingen: Mohr Siebeck.
1992b   ". . . ein kleiner Knabe kann sie leiten": Beobachtungen zum Tierfrieden
             in Jesaja 11,6–8 und 65,25. Pages 104–13 in *Alttestamentliche Glaube
             und biblische Theologie: Fst. für Horst Dietrich Preuss zum 65. Geburtstag*.
             Edited by J. Hausmann and H.-J. Zobel. Stuttgart: Kohlhammer.
1993   Der sich selbst aktualisierende "Jesaja" in Jes 56,9–59,21. Pages 215–30 in
             Biblische Welten: Fst. für Martin Metzger zu seinem 65. Geburtstag. Edited
             by W. Zwickel. OBO 123. Göttingen/Fribourg: Editions universitaires.
1997a   Autor und/oder Redaktor in Jesaja 56–66. Pages 219–59 in *Writing and
             Reading the Scroll of Isaiah*. Edited by C. C. Broyles and C. A. Evans.
             VTSup 70. Leiden: Brill.
1997b   Der Neue Himmel und die neue Erde: Beobachtungen zur Rezeption
             von Gen 1–3 in Jes 65:16b–25. Pages 349–65 in *Studies in the Book of
             Isaiah: Fst. W. A. M. Beuken*. Edited by J. T. A. van Ruiten and M. Ver-
             venne. Leuven: Leuven University Press.

Stegemann, U.
1969   Der Restgedank bei Isaias. *BZ* 13:161–86.
Stummer, F.
1926   Einige Keilschriftliche Parallelen zu Jes. 40–66. *JBL* 45:171–89.
Sweeney, M. A.
1988   *Isaiah 1–4 and the Postexilic Understanding of the Isaianic Tradition*.
             BZAW 171. Berlin: de Gruyter.
1993   The Book of Isaiah in Recent Research. Pages 141–62 in *Currents in Re-
             search: Biblical Studies I*. Edited by A. J. Hauser and P. Sellow. Sheffield:
             JSOT Press.
1996   The Book of Isaiah as Prophetic Torah. Pages 50–67 in *New Visions of
             Isaiah*. Edited by R. F. Melugin and M. A. Sweeney. Sheffield: Sheffield
             Academic Press.
1997   Prophetic Exegesis in Isaiah 65–66. Pages 455–74 in *Writing and Read-
             ing the Scroll of Isaiah*. Edited by C. C. Broyles and C. A. Evans. VTSup
             70. Leiden: Brill.

Talmon, S.
1984   *Yad wašem*: An Idiomatic Phrase in Biblical Literature and Its Variations.
             HS 25:8–17. [Reprinted in *Literary Studies in the Hebrew Bible — Form
             and Content: Collected Studies*. Jerusalem: Magnes, 1993]
1986   The Emergence of Jewish Sectarianism in the Early Second Temple
             Period. Jerusalem: Magnes. Pages 165–201 in *King, Cult and Calendar
             in Ancient Israel: Collected Studies*.

Tangberg, K. A.
1987   *Die Prophetische Mahnrede: Form und traditionsgeschichtliche Studien
             zum prophetischen Umkehrruf*. Göttingen: Vandenhoeck & Ruprecht.

Tate, M. E.
1996   The Book of Isaiah in Recent Study. Pages 22–56 in *Forming Prophetic
             Literature: Essays on Isaiah and the Twelve in Honor of John D. W. Watts*.
             Edited by J. W. Watts and P. R. House. Sheffield: JSOT Press.

Thackeray, H. St. J.
1911   "A New Name" (Not "Another Name"): Isaiah 65:15. *JTS* 12:112–14.
Thornton, T.
1974   Stephen's Use of Is. 66:1. *JTS* 25:432–34.
Tomasino, A. J.
1993   Isaiah 1.1–2.4 and 63–66 and the Composition of the Isaianic Corpus. *JSOT* 57:81–98.
Toorn, K. van der (ed.)
1996   *Family Religion in Babylonia, Syria and Israel.* Leiden: Brill.
1999   *Dictionary of Deities and Demons in the Bible (DDD).* 2d ed. Leiden: Brill / Grand Rapids, Mich.: Eerdmans.
Torrey, C. C.
1929   The Influence of Second Isaiah in the Gospels and Acts. *JBL* 48:24–36.
Tournay, R. J.
1997   Polemique Antisamaritaine et le Feu du TOFET. *RB* 104:354–67.
Tropper, J.
1989   *Nekromantie: Totenbefragung im Alten Orient und im Alten Testament.* Kevelaer: Butzon & Bercker / Neukirchen-Vluyn: Neukirchener Verlag.
Vanoni, G.
1995   *"Du bist doch unser Vater" (Jes 63:16): Zur Gottesvorstellung des Ersten Testaments.* Stuttgart: Katholisches Bibelwerk.
Vaux, R. de
1958   Le sacrifices des porcs en Palestine et dans l'Ancien Orient. Pages 250–65 in *Von Ugarit nach Qumran: Fst Otto Eissfeldt.* Edited by J. Hempel and L. Rost. BZAW 77. Berlin: Alfred Töpelmann. [Reprinted, pp. 252–69 in *The Bible and the Ancient Near East.* Garden City, N.Y.: Doubleday, 1971]
Veijola, T.
1985   Das Klagegebet in Literatur und Leben der Exilsgeneration am Beispiel einiger Prosatexte. Pages 286–307 in *Congress Volume: Salamanca, 1983.* VTSuppl 36. Leiden: Brill.
Vermeylen, J.
1978   *The Book of Isaiah—Le Livre d'Isaïe: Les Oracles et leur Relecture.* Volume 2. Leuven: Peeters and Leuven University Press.
Wallis, G.
1957   *Die Gemeinde des Tritojesaja-Buches: Eine traditionsgeschichtliche Untersuchung.* Berlin: de Gruyter.
1971   Gott und seine Gemeinde: Eine Betrachtung zum Trito-jesaja-Buch. *TZ* 27:182–200.
Watts, J. W., and P. House (eds.)
1996   *Forming Prophetic Literature: Essays on Isaiah and the Twelve in Honor of John D. W. Watts.* Sheffield: Sheffield Academic Press.
Webster, E. C.
1986   A Rhetorical Study of Isaiah 66. *JSOT* 34:93–108.
1990   The Rhetoric of Isaiah 63–65. *JSOT* 47:89–102.
Weinfeld, M.
1995   KABÔD. Pages 22–38 in vol. 7 of *TDOT*.
Weise, M.
1960   Jesaja 57,5–6. *ZAW* 72:25–32.

Weissert, D.
　1967　　Der Basilisk und das Windei in LXX—Jes 59:5: Ein textuales und ein folkloristisches Problem. ZAW 79:315–22.

Wells, R. D.
　1996　　"Isaiah" as an Exponent of Torah: Isaiah 56.1–8. Pages 883–96; SBL Seminar Papers, 1996. SBLSP 33. Atlanta: Scholars Press. [= Pages 140–55 in New Visions of Isaiah. Edited by R. F. Melugin and M. A. Sweeney. Sheffield: Sheffield Academic Press, 1996]

Werline, R. A.
　1998　　Penitential Prayer in Second Temple Judaism: The Development of a Religious Institution. Atlanta: Scholars Press.

Werlitz, J.
　1997　　Vom Knecht der Lieder zum Knecht des Buches: Ein Versuch über die Ergänzungen zu den Gottesknechtstexten des Deuterojesajabuches. ZAW 109:30–43.

Wernberg-Møller, P.
　1954　　A Note on ZVR 'To Stink'. VT 4:322–25.

Westermann, C.
　1964　　Sprache und Struktur der Prophetie Deuterojesajas. Pages 92–170 in Forschung am Alten Testament: Gesammelte Studien. Edited by C. Westermann. Munich: Kaiser.
　1981　　Praise and Lament in the Psalms. Atlanta: John Knox.
　1991　　Basic Forms of Prophetic Speech. Louisville: Westminster.
　1997　　KBD "To Be Heavy". TLOT 2:590–602.

Whitley, C. F.
　1972　　Deutero-Isaiah's Interpretation of ṣedeq. VT 22:469–75.

Whitt, W. D.
　1992　　The Divorce of Yahweh and Asherah in Hos 2:4–7, 12ff. SJOT 6:31–67.

Widengren, G.
　1976　　The Gathering of the Dispersed. SEÅ 41:224–34.

Wieringen, A. L. H. M. van
　1993　　Analogies in Isaiah: Computerized Analysis of Parallel Texts—Concordance of Analogies between Isaiah 56–66 and 40–66. 2 Vols. Ph.D. Dissertation. Cath. Nijmegen, Amsterdam.
　1996　　Parallel Clauses between Third and Second Isaiah: A New Kind of Computer Concordance. BN 82:21–26.

Williamson, H. G. M.
　1987　　Did the Author of Chronicles Also Write the Books of Ezra and Nehemiah? BR 3:56–59.
　1990a　　Isaiah 63,7–64,11: Exilic Lament or Postexilic Protest? ZAW 102:48–58.
　1990b　　Laments at the Destroyed Temple. BRev 6/4:12–17, 44.
　1994　　The Book Called Isaiah. Oxford: Clarendon.
　1995　　Synchronic and Diachronic in Isaian Perspective. Pages 211–26 in Synchronic or Diachronic? A Debate on Method in Old Testament Exegesis. Edited by J. C. de Moor. Leiden: Brill.

Winkle, D. W. van
　1997a　　Isaiah 56:1–8. Pages 234–52 in SBL 1997: Seminar Papers. SBLSP 36. Atlanta: Scholars Press.
　1997b　　The meaning of yad wašem in Isaiah lvi 5. VT 47:378–85.

1997c   An Inclusive Authoritative Text in Exclusive Communities. Pages 423–40 in vol. 1 of *Writing and Reading the Scroll of Isaiah*. Edited by C. C. Broyles and C. A. Evans. VTSup 70. Leiden: Brill.

Winter, P.
1954   Ou dia cheir presbeos oude cheir seraph oude cheir angelou: Isa. 63:9 (Gk) and the Passover Haggadah. *VT* 4:439–41.

Wodecki, B.
1982   Der Heilsuniversalismus bei Trito-Jesaja. *VT* 32:248–52.

Wu, S. J. T.
1995   *A Literary Study of Isaiah 63–65 and Its Echo in Revelation 17–22*. Ph.D. Dissertation. Trinity Evangelical Divinity School.

Yahuda, A. S. E.
1947   Hebrew Words of Egyptian Origin. *JBL* 66:83–90.

Zaleman, L.
1997   The Eternal City: Rome or Jerusalem? *JJS* 48:312–13.

Zillessen, A.
1906   "Tritojesaja" und Deuterojesaja: Eine literarkritische Untersuchung zu Jes 56–66. *ZAW* 26:231–76.

Zimmerli, W.
1950   Zur Sprache Tritojesajas. *SThU* 20:110–22. [Reprinted, pp. 217–33 in *Gottes Offenbarung: Gesammelte Aufsätze zum Alten Testament. Fst. Ludwig Köhler*. Munich: Kaiser, 1963]

1970   Das "Gnadenjahr des Herrn." Pages 321–22 in *Archäologie und Altes Testament. Fst. K. Galling*. Edited by A. Kuschke et al. Tübingen: Mohr (Siebeck).

Zimmermann, R.
2000   "Bräutigam" als frühjüdisches Messias-Prädikat? Zur Traditionsgeschichte einer urchristlichen Metapher. *BN* 103:85–100.

Zorell, F.
1922   Isaiae prophetae de recto modo ieiunandi instruction (Is 58:1–14). *VD* 2: 68–70.

1925   Annus benevolentiae Domini (Is 61). *VD* 5:11–15.

Zwickel, W.
1991   MOTAH = 'Jochhaken'. *BN* 57:37–40.

TEXT AND VERSIONS

Abegg, M. G., Jr.
1994   Messianic Hope and 4Q285: A Reassessment. *JBL* 113:81–91.

Aus, R. D.
1977   God's Plan and God's Power: Isaiah 66 and the Restraining Factors of 2 Thess 2:6–7. *JBL* 96:537–53.

Barthélemy, D.
1986   *Critique textuelle de l'Ancien Testament, 2: Isaïe, Jérémie, Lamentations*. Göttingen: Vandenhoeck & Ruprecht.

Betz, O.
1995   The Servant Tradition of Isaiah in the Dead Sea Scrolls. *JSem* 7:40–56.

Bewer, J. A.
1908 Textual Suggestions on Isa 2:6; 66:3; Zeph 2:2,5. *JBL* 27:163–66.
Birnbaum, S. A.
1949 The Date of the Isaiah Scroll. *BASOR* 113:33–35.
Brock, S. P.
1985 Text History and Text Division in Peshitta Isaiah. Pages 49–80 in *The Peshitta: Its Early Text and History*. Edited by P. B. Dirksen and M. J. Mulder. Monographs of the Peshitta Institute, Leiden 4. Leiden: Brill.
Bronno, E.
1956 The Isaiah Scroll DSIa and the Greek Transliterations of Hebrew. *ZDMG* 106:252–58.
Brooke, G. J.
1994 Isaiah 40:3 and the Wilderness Community. Pages 117–32 in *New Qumran Texts and Studies*. Leiden: Brill.
1995 4Q500 1 and the Use of Scripture in the Parable of the Vineyard. *DSD* 2:268–94.
Burrows, M.
1948–49 Variant Readings in the Isaiah Manuscript. *BASOR* 111:16–24; 113:24–32.
1950 *The Dead Sea Scrolls of St. Mark's Monastery, Vol. 1: The Isaiah Manuscript and the Habakkuk Commentary*. With J. C. Trever and W. H. Brownlee (eds.). New Haven: American Schools of Oriental Research.
Byington, S. T.
1957 יהוה and אדני. *JBL* 76:58–59.
Carmignac, J.
1968 Six passages d'Isaïe éclairés par Qumran. Pages 37–46 in *Bibel und Qumran: Fst. H. Bardtke*. Edited by S. Wagner. Berlin: Evangelische Hauptbibelgesellschaft.
Chilton, B.
1982 *The Glory of Israel: The Theology and Provenance of the Isaiah Targum*. Sheffield: JSOT Press.
Collins, J. J.
1997 A Herald of Good Tidings: Isaiah 61:1–3 and Its Actualization in the Dead Sea Scrolls. Pages 225–40 in *The Quest for Meaning: Studies in Biblical Intertextuality—Fst. J. A. Sanders*. Leiden: Brill.
Dahood, M. J.
1957 Some Aphel Causatives in Ugaritic. *Bib* 38:62–73.
1958 Some Ambiguous Texts in Isaias. *CBQ* 20:41–49.
1960 Textual Problems in Isaiah. *CBQ* 22: 400–409.
Delekat, L.
1957 Die Peschitta zu Jesaja zwischen Targum und Septuaginta. *Bib* 185–99; 321–35.
Derenbourg, J. and H. Derenbourg
1896 *Version arabe d'Isaïe de R. Saadia ben Josef al-Fayyoûmi*. Paris: Societé Asiatique.
Díez Macho, A.
1960 A New Fragment of Isaiah with Babylonian Pointing. *Textus* 1:132–43.
Driver, G. R.
1935 Linguistic and Textual Problems: Isaiah xl–lxvi. *JTS* 36:396–406.

1937 Linguistic and Textual Problems: Isaiah 1–39. *JTS* 38:36–50.

Eissfeldt, O.
1949 Varianten der Jesaia-Rolle. *TLZ* 74:221–26.

Elliger, K.
1971 Textkritisches zu Deuterojesaja. Pages 113–19 in *Near Eastern Studies in Honor of William Foxwell Albright*. Edited by H. Goedicke. Baltimore: Johns Hopkins University Press.

Giese, R. L.
1988 Further Evidence for the Bisection of 1QIsᵃ. *Textus* 14:61–70.

Ginsberg, H. L.
1950 Some Emendations in Isaiah. *JBL* 69:51–60.
1958 The Arm of YHWH in Isaiah 51–63 and the Text of Isa 53:10–11. *JBL* 77:152–56.

Gordis, R.
1950 "NA'LAM" and other Observations on the Ain Feshka Scrolls. *JNES* 9:44–47.

Goshen-Gottstein, M. H.
1954a Die Jesaiah-Rolle im Lichte von Peschitta und Targum. *Bib* 35:51–71.
1954b Die Jesaja-Rolle und das Problem der hebräischen Bibelhandschriften. *Bib* 35:429–42.
1995 *The Book of Isaiah*. Jerusalem: Magnes.

González, A.
1960 La lengua y la base lingüística del Rollo de Isaías. *EstBib* 19:237–44.

Grelot, P.
1972 Deux Tosephtas Targoumiques Inédites sur Isaïe 66. *RB* 79:511–43.
1973 Deux Tosephtas Targoumiques Inédites sur Isaïe 66. *RB* 80:363.

Guillaume, A.
1957 Some Readings in the Dead Sea Scroll of Isaiah. *JBL* 76:40–43.

Hegermann, H.
1954 *Jesaja 53 in Hexapla, Targum, und Peschitta*. BFCT 56. Gütersloh: Bertelsmann.

Hempel, J.
1951 Beobachtungen an der "syrischen" Jesajarolle vom Toten Meer (DSIa). *ZDMG* 101:138–73.

James, F. D.
1959 *A Critical Examination of the Text of Isaiah, Based on the Dead Sea Scroll of Isaiah (DSIa), the Masoretic Text, the Septuagint*. Ph.D. Dissertation. Boston: Boston University.

Katz, E.
1963 Qumran Text und eine schwierige Maimonides Stelle. *RevQ* 4:107–10.

Kedar-Kopfstein, B.
1964 Divergent Hebrew Readings in Jerome's Isaiah. *Textus* 4:176–210.

Kister, M.
1992 Biblical Phrases and Hidden Biblical Interpretations and Pesharim. Pages 27–39 in *The Dead Sea Scrolls. Forty Years of Research*. Edited by D. Dimant and U. Rappaport. Jerusalem: Magnes.

Köbert, R.
1986 Heisst syr. Hašqbōl duplex? *Bib* 67:555–56.

Koenen, K.
1988b   Textkritische Anmerkungen zu schwierigen Stellen im Tritojesajabuch.
           Bib 69:564–73.
1988c   Zum Text von Jes. 63,18. ZAW 100:406–9.
1989b   Zum Text von Jesaja lvii 12–13a. VT 39:236–39.
Koenig, J.
1982   L'Herméneutique analogique du Judaïsme antique d'après les témoins tex-
           tuels d'Isaïe. VTSup 33. Leiden: Brill.
1983   Réouverture du débat sur la première main rédactionnelle du rouleau
           ancien d'Isaïe de Qumrân (1QIsaᵃ) en 40,7–8. RevQ 11:219–37.
Kooij, A. van der
1981   Die alten Textzeugen des Jesajabuches: Ein Beitrag zur Textgeschichte des
           Alten Testaments. Göttingen: Vandenhoeck & Ruprecht.
1989   The Septuagint of Isaiah: Translation and Interpretation. Pages 127–33
           in The Book of Isaiah—Le Livre d'Isaïe: Les Oracles et leur relecture. Ed-
           ited by J. Vermeylen. Leuven: Peeters and Leuven University Press.
Kraft, R. A.
1961   Barnabas' Isaiah Text and the "Testimony Book" Hypothesis. JBL
           79:336–50.
Kuhl, C.
1952   Schreibereigentümlichkeiten: Bemerkungen zur Jesajarolle (DSIa). VT
           2:307–33.
Kutscher, E. Y.
1974   The Language and Linguistic Background of the Isaiah Scroll (1QIsᵃ).
           Leiden: Brill.
Loretz, O.
1993   Ugaritisch-hebräisch hmr/hmr und msk (/mzg). Neu- und Mischwein in
           der Ägäis und in Syrien–Palästina. UF 25:247–58.
Maori, Y.
1982   The Tradition of Pesqaʾot in Ancient Hebrew MSS: The Isaiah Texts and
           Commentaries from Qumran. Textus 10: 1–50. [Hebrew]
1992   The Text of the Hebrew Bible in Rabbinic Writings in Light of the
           Qumran Evidence. Pages 283–89 in The Dead Sea Scrolls: Forty Years
           of Research. Edited by D. Dimant and U. Rappaport. STDJ 10. Leiden:
           Brill / Jerusalem: Magnes Press.
Miller, M. P.
1969   The Function of Isa 61:1–2 in 11Q Melchizedek. JBL 88:467–69.
Morrow, F. J.
1973   The Text of Isaiah at Qumran. Ph.D. dissertation. Catholic University of
           America.
Noetscher, F.
1951   Entbehrliche Hapaxlegomena in Jesaia. VT 1:299–302.
Olley, J. W.
1979   "Righteousness" in the Septuagint of Isaiah: A Contextual Study. Missoula,
           Mont.: Scholars Press.
1983   Notes on Isaiah XXXII 1, XLV 19,23 and LXIII 1. VT 33:446–53.
Ottley, R. R.
1909   The Book of Isaiah according to the Septuagint. 2 vols. Cambridge: Cam-
           bridge University Press.

Peters, M. K. H.
  1992   Septuagint. Pages 1093–1104 in vol. 5 of *ABD*.
Praetorius, F.
  1913   Zum Texte des Tritojesajas. ZAW 33:89–91.
Qimron, E.
  1979   *The Language and Linguistic Background of the Isaiah Scroll (1QIsᵃ).*
           Indices and Corrections. Leiden: Brill.
Rossi, J. B. de
  1786   *Variae Lectiones Veteris Testamenti III.* Parma.
Rowlands, E. R.
  1959   The Targum and the Peshitta Version of the Book of Isaiah. *VT* 9:178–
           91.
Rubinstein, A.
  1953   Notes on the Use of the Tenses in the Variant Readings of the Isaiah
           Scroll. *VT* 3:92–95.
  1954   Isaiah 17:75: הסתד ואקצף and the DSIa Variant. *VT* 4:200–201.
Ruiten, J. T. A. G. M. van
  1992   The Intertextual Relationship between Isa 11,6–9 and Isa 65,25. Pages
           31–42 in *The Scriptures and the Scrolls: Studies in Honour of A. S. van*
           der Woude on the Occasion of His 65ᵗʰ Birthday. Edited by F. García Mar-
           tínez, A. Hilhorst, and C. J. Labuschagne. Leiden: Brill.
Schaller, B.
  1984   EXEI EK SION HO RUOMENOS: Zur Textgestalt von Jes 59:20–21 in
           Röm 11:26–27. Pages 201–6 in *De Septuaginta. Fst. J. W. Wevers.* Edited
           by A. Pietersma and C. E. Cox. Mississauga, Ont.
Seeligmann, I. L.
  1948   *The Septuagint Version of Isaiah: A Discussion of Its Problems.* Leiden:
           Brill.
Siegel, J. P.
  1975   *The Severus Scroll and 1QIsᵃ.* SBLMasS 2. Missoula, Mont.: Scholars Press.
Skehan, P. W.
  1960   Some Textual Problems in Isaiah. *CBQ* 22:47–55.
Smolar, L. and M. Aberbach
  1983   *Studies in Targum Jonathan to the Prophets.* New York: Ktav.
Starkova, K. B.
  1992   The Ideas of Second and Third Isaiah as Reflected in the Qumran Lit-
           erature. *QC* 2:51–62.
Stummer, F.
  1937   Beiträge zur Lexicographie der Lateinischen Bibel. *Bib* 18:23–50.
Syren, R.
  1989   Targum Isaiah 52:13–53:12 and Christian Interpretation. *JJS* 40:201–12.
Talmon, S.
  1964   Aspects of the Textual Transmission of the Bible in the Light of Qumran
           Manuscripts. *Textus* 4:95–132. [Reprinted, pp. 71–116 in *The World of*
           Qumran from Within: Collected Studies. Jerusalem: Magnes/Leiden: Brill,
           1989]
Tov, E.
  1992   The Textual Base of the Corrections in the Biblical Texts Found at
           Qumran. Pages 299–314 in *The Dead Sea Scrolls: Forty Years of Research.*

　　　　　　　Edited by D. Dimant and U. Rappaport. Leiden: Brill / Jerusalem:
　　　　　　　Magnes.

Troxel, R. L.
　1992　　　Eschatos and Eschatology in LXX–Isaiah. *BIOSCS* 25:18–27.

Ulrich, E. C., and P. W. Skehan
　1996　　　An Edition of 4QIsa^e, Including the Former 4QIsa^l. *RevQ* 17:23–36.

Ulrich, E. C., et al.
　1997　　　*Qumran Cave 4.X: The Prophets.* DJD 15. Oxford: Clarendon.

Weissert, D.
　1967　　　Der Basilisk und das Windei in LXX—Jes 59,5: Ein textuelles und ein
　　　　　　　folkloristisches Problem. *ZAW* 79:315–22.

Wernberg-Møller, P. C. H.
　1958　　　Two Notes. *VT* 8:305–8.

Woude, A. S. van der
　1965　　　Melchisedek als himmlische Erlösergestalt in den neugefundenen es-
　　　　　　　chatologischen Midraschim aus Qumran Höhle XI. *OtSt* 14:354–73.

　1999　　　Fifty Years of Qumran Research. Pages 1–45 in *The Dead Sea Scrolls
　　　　　　　after Fifty Years: A Comprehensive Assessment.* 2 vols. Edited by P. W.
　　　　　　　Flint and J. C. VanderKam. Leiden: Brill.

Yadin, Y.
　1980　　　A Note on the Title of the Verso of the Genizah MS 1134. *HUCA* 51:61.

Ziegler, J.
　1934　　　*Untersuchungen zur Septuaginta des Buches Isaias.* Münster: Aschendorff.

Zijl, J. B.
　1979　　　*A Concordance to the Targum of Isaiah.* Missoula, Mont.: Scholars Press.

TRANSLATION,
NOTES AND
COMMENTS

◆

ISAIAH 56–66

◆

REASSURANCE FOR THE MARGINAL (56:1–8)

(Begg 1985, 90–108; Beuken 1989a, 19–39; Delcor 1967, 230–40; Donner 1985, 81–95; Japhet 1992, 69–90; Koenen 1990, 11–32; Odeberg 1931, 32–62; Pauritsch 1971, 31–51; Polan 1986, 43–90; Rendtorff 1993a, 181–89; Robinson 1976, 282–84; Schramm 1995, 115–25; Scullion 1971, 335–48; Sehmsdorf 1972, 544–56; Sekine 1989, 31–42; Steck 1991a, 34–44, 169–86, 229–65 (242–48); Talmon 1984, 8–17; Wells 1996, 140–55; van Winkle 1997b, 378–85; 1998, 423–40)

TRANSLATION

56   [1a]This is what YHVH says:
"Maintain justice, do what is right,
for my salvation is near at hand;
my deliverance will soon be revealed."[b]
[2]Blessed is the one who does this,
the one who holds fast to it:
who observes Sabbath, who does not profane it,[c]
who stays his hand[d] from evildoing.
[3e]The foreigner who adheres to YHVH[f] must not say,
"YHVH will surely cut me off from his people";
and the eunuch must not say,
"I am just a withered tree."
[4]For this is what YHVH says,
"The eunuchs who observe my Sabbaths,
who choose[g] what is pleasing to me
and hold fast to my covenant:
[5]to them I shall give in my house and within my walls
a memorial and a name
better than sons and daughters;
I shall give them[h] a long-lasting name
that will not be cut off.
[6]The foreigners who adhere to YHVH,
to minister to him, to love YHVH's name,
to be his servants;
all who observe the Sabbath and do not profane it,[i]
who hold fast to my covenant:
[7]them will I bring to my holy mountain;
I will give them joy in my house of prayer.

Their burnt offerings and sacrifices
will be welcome[j] on my altar;
for my house will be called a house of prayer
for all peoples."

[8]An utterance of the Sovereign Lord YHVH,
who gathers the dispersed of Israel:
"I shall gather yet more to him
besides those already gathered."

NOTES

a   1QIsaiah[a] adds *ky*ʾ, "for," presumably to connect with the preceding saying,
     but 1QIsa[b], LXX, and other versions support MT.
b   LXX acknowledges the different meanings of *ṣĕdāqâ* (here translated "what
     is right" in v 1a and "deliverance" in v 1b) by the use of different terms:
     dikaiosunē ("righteousness") in v 1a and *eleos* ("mercy") in v 1b.
c   Literally, "so as not to profane it"; 1QIsa[a] has fem. suffix for MT masc. since
     šabbāt is fem.; Ibn Ezra takes it to refer to *yôm haššabāt*, "the day of Sab-
     bath" (*yôm* masc.), and the Masoretes probably did too.
d   1QIsaiah[a] has *ydyv*, "his hands."
e   Omitting the conjunction with 1QIsa[a], LXX, and Syr.; MT has the support of
     1QIsa[b], Vulg., Tg.
f   Literally, "the one who has joined himself [to YHVH]"; MT *hannilvāh*
     should be Niphal active participle *hannilveh* cf. LXX *proskeimenos* and
     Theod., Syr., Tg.
g   1QIsaiah[a] has imperfect *vybḥvrv*, for MT perfect, either read as a vav con-
     secutive or as a result of yod/vav confusion.
h   For MT *lô*, "to him," read pl. with LXX (*autois*), 1QIsa[a] (*lhmh*), and other
     ancient versions.
i   1QIsa[a] read *ûbĕnê hannēkār hannilvîm ʾel YHVH / lihyôt lô lĕʿăbādîm/
     ûlĕbārēk ʾet šēm YHVH / vĕšōmĕrîm ʾet haššabāt*: the scribe wrote *ʾel YHVH*
     for MTMT *ʿal YHVH*; omitted "to minister to him," perhaps troubled by
     the prospect of foreigners functioning as liturgical ministers; substituted
     "bless" for "love" for the same reason; transposed two of the phrases; and
     substituted *šōmĕrîm* for MT *kol-šōmēr*; LXX has pl. too.
j   Some versions supply a verb: LXX *esontai* → *yihyû*, "will be [acceptable]";
     as also 1QIsa[a] *yʿlv*, "will go up," but MT is supported by 1QIsa[b], 4QIsa[i],
     Syr., and Vulg.

COMMENTS

This opening passage of the third major segment of the book of Isaiah consists
in three distinct but connected oracular statements identified by traditional
prophetic speech formulas. The first (v 1) is followed by an interpretative comment of the seer explaining what the injunction to maintain justice and do

what is right implies and how broad its scope is (vv 2–3). The seer's inclusive vision of the community addressed is then confirmed by a second declaration in which the concerns of the two categories, those of foreign descent and the sexually mutilated, are addressed in inverse order (vv 4–7). As the prophetic incipit indicates, the final oracle (v 8) is a distinct saying but thematically an expansion of the word addressed to the foreigners; hence, the inversion of the two declarations: foreigners, eunuchs (3); eunuchs, foreigners (4–7).

The passage is coherent and well organized and makes its point elegantly and economically. None of the attempts to split it up into "primary" and "secondary" layers, for example, by designating anything that looks somewhat *de trop* as the work of a redactor (e.g., "better than sons and daughters" and "that will not be cut off" in v 5 by Sekine 1989, 39–40) can be said to be successful. Nor does it seem necessary to separate vv 1–2 from vv 3–8 as an editorial prologue to chs. 56–66 (Volz 1932, 203–4). As we shall see, the entire passage nevertheless forms an inclusio of sorts when read together with 66:15–24.

Isaiah 56:1–8 signals for most scholars a new departure and therefore justifies marking off chs. 56–66 as a separate text. This conclusion would now be widely accepted, but it does not exclude lines of continuity between 40–55 and 56–66 that are not difficult to identify. Both sections may have had their own superscriptions, which were removed at the final stage of the making of the book of Isaiah. Some exegetes have argued for a close linkage between 55:1–13 and 56:1–8, in the sense that the latter gives a more concrete and explicit expression to and interpretation of the former (Beuken 1986a, 50–52; 1989a, 19; Steck 1991a, 41–42, 170–71). Along the same lines, Torrey (1928, 255–57, 426–29) proposed that 55:1–56:8 minus 56:2–6 forms one unit. There is at least one linguistic link between 55:13b and 56:5b:

věhāyāh lāYHVH lěšēm / lě'ôt 'ôlām lo' yikkārēt

All this will be a memorial/name for YHVH,
a perpetual sign that shall not be cut off. (55:13b)

věnātattî lāhem . . . yād vāšēm . . . šēm 'ôlām 'ăšer lo' yikkārēt

To them I shall give . . . a memorial and a name . . . a long-lasting name that will not be cut off. (56:5)

Since 56:5 is more securely embedded in its context than 55:13b, it appears that the latter was added to 55:1–13a precisely to create a nexus with what follows—a not uncommon way of threading texts together.

Apart from this obvious instance, the parallels between these successive passages are not particularly impressive. The most distinctive vocabulary of 56:1–8, beginning with *mišpāṭ*, *ṣědāqâ*, and *yěšû'a*, is absent from 55:1–13 (for a more complete listing, see Polan 1986, 44–52). Both passages speak of a covenant (*běrît*), but they do so in quite different ways. The theme of the permanent efficacy of the (prophetic) word of God in 55:10–11 and that of return from exile and the regeneration of nature in 55:12–13 are likewise absent from 56:1–18. Salvation is offered in both passages (55:1–5; 56:1), but it is immediately available in the former and conditionally imminent in the latter. The genre and the exhortative tone of ch. 55 are also quite different from the more pointed and prescriptive language of 56:1–8.

While exegetes can always be counted on to find points of contact and continuity between almost any two juxtaposed passages in Isaiah, there is insufficient evidence that 56:1–8 was composed with 55:1–13 in mind. A more plausible view is that 54:17b, which speaks of the heritage of the Servants of YHVH, deliberately anticipates a major theme of 56–66, and that ch. 55 serves as a theological summary of chs. 40–54.

On the other hand, the many points of linguistic and thematic similarity between 56:1–8 and 66:15–24 suggest a deliberate intent at creating a framework for these last 11 chapters, a point on which most commentators would agree. This well-attested technique of "bracketing" makes the point that the material enclosed within the brackets is in some respects one text with a distinctive point of view. This matter will call for discussion again when we reach the last section of the Commentary, but for the moment the main points of overlap may be listed: Servants of YHVH appear in both passages (66:14; 56:6); an imminent intervention in salvation and judgment is foreseen (66:15–16; 56:1), which will be preceded by the gathering in (verbal stem *qbṣ*) of all nations (66:18; 56:8); symbolically central is "my holy mountain" (*har qodšî*, 66:20; 56:7), also known as YHVH's house (*bêt YHVH*, *bêtî*, 66:20; 56:5, 7); foreigners are qualified to serve (verbal stem *šrt*) as cult ministers (66:21; 56:6); and, not least, the observance of Sabbath is the principal criterion for adherence to the Jewish faith and Jewish observance (66:23 cf. 56:2, 4, 6).

The point of view is therefore similar at both extremities of chs. 56–66, and it is not only different from but at variance with voices heard elsewhere in the section. We the readers have the task of distinguishing between the different speaking voices in these last 11 chapters of the book. It seems that one of these voices can be heard at the beginning and the end.

The initial oracle (v 1) urges the practice of justice and righteousness in view of an imminent salvific intervention in human affairs by the God of Israel. At this broad thematic level, continuity with 40–55 is apparent from the beginning. The prospect for a dramatic change in the fortunes of the Jewish community addressed, as it struggled to survive the destruction of the state and the subsequent deportations, is the central theme of the previous 16 chapters, as it is of all the writings that have survived from that time and place. In 40–55 salvation was announced in traditional religious terms—God's glory will be revealed (40:5), God will be present with them (40:9), God will come with power (40:10), God will reign as king (52:7)—but these were terms that had to be converted into the currency of political realities. Specifically, Cyrus had to fulfill his commission to rebuild Jerusalem and the cities of Judah, bring back the descendants of the deportees (44:26, 28; 49:16–21), and enable Judah to become a major player on the stage of history (41:14–16).

This was the dream, but none of it seemed to be happening, or appeared likely to happen, and the crisis of confidence and faith arising out of the prophetic author's failure to persuade is apparent in increasing complaints on the one side (40:27; 49:14) and increasing reproaches on the other (42:18–19; 43:8, 22–28; 46:8, 12–13; 48:1–8). This corresponded to a widening division in the community between the prophet's adherents, the "Servants of YHVH," and the skeptics—those who, in anachronistic Hasidic terms, might be called the *mitnaggědîm*, "the opponents" (50:10–11; 51:7–8). Isaiah 56–66 reflects the process by which this division widened into open schism, perhaps most clearly visible in 66:5 where "those who tremble at God's word," who are also YHVH's Servants, are shunned and cast out by their "brethren," that is, their fellow-Jews.

We are therefore hearing the author of this passage, whom we take to be a disciple of the prophetic author of the core of chs. 40–55, attempting to deal with the problem of the delay in the fulfillment of prophecy. The tone is more positive than some earlier exhortations; for example:

> Listen to me, you stubborn people,
> far removed from deliverance as you are:
> "I bring my deliverance near, it is not far off,
> my salvation will not be delayed." (46:12–13a)

The delay is not to be attributed to the lack of God's power or will to intervene (50:2) but to a sinful inattention to the law:

> If only you had heeded my commandments!
> Your prosperity would have flowed like a river,
> your vindication like the waves of the sea. (48:18)

It seems likely that at least some of the passages in 40–55 assigned by Hermisson to his *qārôb-Schicht*, passages in other words that speak of divine intervention on behalf of Israel as imminent, or attempt to explain why intervention is delayed (especially 46:12–13 and 51:5–6; see Hermisson 1998, 139–41, 153–55), are from the same hand as 56:1–8.

Isaiah 56:1–8 opens with an exhortation to practice justice and righteousness *in view of* an imminent divine intervention of salvation and judgment (v 1). We can read this as an anticipation of early Christian *Interimethik*, that is, ethics in the light of eschatology, a way of living in a world or world order that is about to come to an end. The term *mišpāṭ*, usually translated "justice," can refer to legal process, judicial procedure, a verdict handed down by a judge (Isa 3:14; 34:5; 41:1; 53:8; 54:17; 58:26), or the bringing of a grievance to law, in particular a just cause calling for redress (Isa 40:27; 50:8). The maintenance of order based on justice is the primary responsibility of rulers and governments (Isa 16:5; 28:6; 32:1; 42:1), who must see to it that the rights of all classes, especially the most marginal and vulnerable, are respected (Isa 42:1–4). From this point, it is a short step to attributing *mišpāṭ* to God, with regard to God's way of acting on humanity and safeguarding the human practice of justice (Isa 26:8–9; 51:4); God is a God of justice (*'ĕlōhê mišpāṭ*, 30:18).

In early prophecy, *mišpāṭ* is preeminently a social concept and has particular reference to the protection of the classes in society that are least able to look after themselves—widows, fatherless, destitute (Isa 1:17; 10:2). Of particular importance is the task of safeguarding the access of the powerless in society to judicial process (Amos 5:10–13; Mic 3:9–12; Isa 5:23; 33:15). With this meaning, the term occurs either by itself or, as here, in combination with *ṣĕdāqâ*, "righteousness"—that is, doing what is right in the sphere of social relations (Isa 5:7; 9:6; 28:17; 32:16; 33:5; 58:2). The demand for justice is so peremptory that, in the view of these early prophets (Amos, Micah, and Isaiah in particular), a society that does not practice it does not deserve to survive.

By the same token, the sad experience that the demand so often goes unanswered can give rise to severe problems of faith in God as the guarantor of justice. For many, the line of thought would have been: If justice is not done and seen to be done, then if God exists he might as well not exist. This more explicitly theological aspect contributed to a semantic shift, as a result of which the term *mišpāṭ*, or the hendiadys *mišpāṭ ûṣĕdāqâ* ("justice and righteousness"), which encapsulates the entire prophetic ethic, came to connote a final settling of accounts, an eschatological judgment in which the righteous victims of injustice would at last find vindication (Isa 1:27; 5:16; 59:9–15) and the unjust, the oppressor of the poor and weak, would be called to account.

The point of this opening statement in 56:1, which sets the tone for the section as a whole, is made by exploiting the semantic ambivalence of the term *ṣĕdāqâ*, which can carry either an ethical ("righteousness," "doing what is right") or eschatological meaning ("deliverance," "final vindication"). With this eschatological meaning, it occurs in late contexts throughout Isaiah, in parallelism with *mišpāṭ* (1:27; 5:16; 59:9, 14) or, as here, with *yĕšûʿâ*, "salvation" (45:8; 46:12–13; 51:6, 8; 59:17).

Rendtorff (1993a, 181–89) sees the combination of the two meanings of the term *ṣĕdāqâ* and its incidence throughout the book as structurally significant, but perhaps goes too far in concluding that chs. 56–66 could never have existed independently of 1–39 and 40–55. The theological implication, at any rate, is that in prophetic discourse ethical conduct is never enjoined on general and abstract grounds but always as a function of particular religious convictions. In this respect it differs from the traditional didactic and aphoristic type of moralism attested throughout the ancient Near East, inclusive of Israel.

The point is made more specifically as the prophet goes on to state in what maintaining justice and doing what is right consist (v 2). He begins by pronouncing a blessing on the one who accepts the invitation. Translating *'ašrê 'ĕnôš* "Happy is the man . . ." (as in NRSV), is perhaps not entirely adequate since here, as in Ps 1 (*'ašrê hā 'îš 'ăšer lōʾ hālak baʿăṣat rĕšāʿîm*, literally: "Blessed is the man who does not walk in the counsel of the reprobate"), there is something more than a sense of satisfaction at the performance of good deeds. As in the Gospel Beatitudes (Matt 5:3–12), in which we detect a strong echo of the reversal of fortune promised the "Servants" in Isa 65:13–14, there is a sense of ultimate fulfillment. This reading will be tested and verified as we continue working through this section.

It will seem somewhat surprising that the quite general injunction to avoid evildoing is linked with the very specific point of Sabbath observance. An explanation is at hand in the reassurance addressed to the eunuchs, a reassurance conditional on observing Sabbath and holding fast to the covenant (v 4). Moreover, the fact that Sabbath observance can stand, by metonymy, for covenant observance has roots in a particular tradition of holy history. At the conclusion of the work of constructing the wilderness sanctuary, observance of Sabbath was enjoined in imitation of the Sabbath of God following the creation of the world, and its observance was described as a perpetual covenant (*běrît ʿôlām*, Exod 31:12–17). To this extent, the passage betrays affinity with the perspective of the priest-scribes who authored the Priestly History (P) in the Hexateuch.

It will not be necessary to trace the history of this institution of the Sabbath, beyond noting that it only attained a position of central importance as a "sacramental symbol" (Marti 1900, 363), the position that it has held ever since among observant Jews, in post-destruction piety (Ezek 45:17; 44:24; Isa 58:13–14; 66:23; 1:13; Num 15:32–36). It must be sanctified (verbal stem *qdš*), and not profaned (*ḥll*) by carrying burdens, lighting fires, buying and selling, or any kind of unnecessary work (e.g., Isa 58:13–14; Ezek 20:12–13; 22:8; Jer 17:19–27, probably postexilic; Neh 10:32–34[31–33]; 13:15–22).

Sabbath observance was an important aspect of Nehemiah's campaign to create a strong ethnic consciousness in the province of Yehud in the mid–fifth century B.C.E. It is the second among the stipulations of his covenant (*ʾămānâ*) sealed with an oath (*šěbûʿâ*), consistent with the view of Sabbath as significative of covenant (Neh 10:1–40[9:38–10:39]). That Sabbath became one of the focal points of early Jewish religious consciousness is also apparent in the occurrence of the name Shabbetai attested in late biblical texts (Ezra 10:15; Neh 8:7; 11:16), as well as among Babylonian Jews and in the Jewish settlement on the island of Elephantine at the first cataract of the Nile (e.g., AP 58:3).

It is of interest to note that, in contrast to the Priestly prescriptions in the Pentateuch (Gen 17:9–14; Exod 12:43–49), Sabbath observance and not circumcision is here the criterion of membership in the community. We have no reason to believe that the author of this passage would challenge the exclusion of the uncircumcised and ritually unclean from the Jerusalem of the future (Isa 52:1), but it is interesting nevertheless that Isa 56–66 and Ezra–Nehemiah pass over it in silence.

This last section of the book of Isaiah (chs. 56–66) provides a prime example of the theory of cognitive dissonance, introduced into the social sciences and, inevitably in due course, into biblical studies about half a century ago (Festinger 1964; Carroll 1979). (With equal inevitability the term is now being used loosely and inaccurately for any kind of dissent or disaccord.) As originally formulated, the theory claims to account for the stratagems by means of which a group (faction, sect, cult) attempts to reduce or eliminate the inconsistency caused by the disconfirmation of its beliefs and convictions. So understood, it applies preeminently to group reaction to unfulfilled predictions—those, for example, that even the casual reader can detect in the book of Daniel and in certain New Testament texts.

In Isa 56–66, we shall find that frustrated expectations led to division in the community, redefinitions of the "redemptive media"—that is, the conditions necessary for access to redemption—by groups deprived of political and religious power within the community, and conflict about ethnic and religious identity. This situation inevitably brought to the fore the crucial issue of qualification for membership in the community, one aspect of which is raised in this first passage in chs. 56–66.

After the blessing pronounced in v 2, the seer goes on to speak to the fears of two "dubiously belonging" classes in the Jewish community (3). He addresses to them a solemn prophetic word, assuring them of their good standing in the community (4–7). This address does not seem to fit the pattern of an authoritative priestly *tôrâ*, as some commentators suggest, because the tone is more exhortative than prescriptive. The repetition of the injunction to observe Sabbath and hold fast to the covenant in v 6 also makes it unnecessary to consider vv 3–7 or 3–8 an independent saying (as does Westermann 1969, 312). The term usually translated "foreigner" (*ben-hannēkār*, elsewhere *nokrî*) can refer to one who is not a member of the household (Gen 17:12, 27; 31:15) but more commonly designates a non-Israelite (e.g., 2 Sam 15:19; 22:45–46) and therefore a worshiper of "foreign" gods (Gen 35:4; Deut 31:16; Josh 24:20 etc.).

The related term *zār* ("foreigner, outsider") has a somewhat broader connotation, since it is used not only of foreigners in the usual sense (e.g., Isa 1:7; 25:2, 5; 61:5) but also of outsiders vis-à-vis a particular household or family (Deut 25:5) or even the priesthood—a layman, therefore (e.g., Exod 29:33; Lev 22:10–16; Num 1:51; the closest equivalent to "lay person" in early Christian texts is *idiōtēs*).

The foreigners addressed here are those who have, literally, "joined themselves to YHVH" (*hannilvîm ʿal-YHVH*). They are therefore non-Israelites who have embraced the cult of YHVH. In texts from the time of the kingdoms, the term *gēr* connotes a resident alien who has left his own country for whatever reason—famine, military disaster, bloodguilt—and lives in Israel or Judah as the client of an individual or family. The *gēr* is therefore are intermediate between the *ben-nēkār* and the *'ezraḥ* (native-born Israelite), and, though recommended to the general care in the legislation (Exod 20:10; 22:20; 23:9), still belongs on the margins of society together with widows, the fatherless, and the destitute (e.g., Jer 7:6; 22:3).

The term will eventually acquire a predominantly religious connotation, in the sense of a proselyte's adherence to the worship of the God of Israel (in LXX *prosēlutos, paroikos*). To this change corresponds the shift from ascriptive membership in a national, ethnic group to an elective, voluntarist community or, in other words, from a group based on ties of blood (*Blutgemeinschaft*) to a confessional community (*Bekenntnisgemeinschaft*). In Isa 56–66 and other texts from the same period we can detect the beginnings of this process, but it was still basically a question of determining the *civil* status of different categories of people living in the province of Judah and in Jewish communities in other lands.

The foreigners of 56:1–8 are quite different from those who will be put to work at menial tasks in the imagined Jewish commonwealth of the future (60:10; 61:5), a fortiori, from the foreigners who occupy the country and live off it (62:8).

Since the celebration of Passover is a highly visible sign of membership in the community of Israel, it is understandable that it should provide the context for stating conditions for membership in the household of Israel. The Priestly legislation emphasizes circumcision as a criterion for membership (Exod 12:48–49), and the account of the first Passover after the "return to Zion" lists as participants Israelites together with "all those who had joined them, separating themselves from the impurity [i.e., idolatry] of the nations of the land to seek YHVH the God of Israel" (Ezra 6:21). Here in Isa 56:2, 4, 6, as noted, Sabbath observance, while by no means the only legal obligation imposed on foreigners and eunuchs, is diagnostically more significant than circumcision.

A text from about this time speaks of a second election of Israel, which will include proselytes (Isa 14:1), and another prophet from sometime in the Achaemenid period holds out the prospect that "many nations shall associate themselves with YHVH on that day, and shall be my people." (Zech 2:15[11]). The same expectation inspired the exilic Isaian prophet to expand the promise of Abraham to include outsiders:

> This one will say, "I belong to YHVH,"
> another will take the name Jacob,
> yet another will write YHVH's name on the hand,
> and add the name Israel to his own. (Isa 44:5)

And, indeed, it would be difficult if not impossible to explain the remarkable demographic expansion of the Jewish people throughout the Second Temple period without taking account of proselytism. Here, and elsewhere in biblical texts, the attitude toward proselytes is positive, but the prophetic voice we are hearing in Isa 56:1–8 is not the only voice to be heard in these chapters.

The complaint of the other class of people, the eunuchs (*sārîsîm*), is that they are doomed to be without descendants, but we will see that their status as community members is also in jeopardy. Apart from the book of Esther and possibly Daniel, this is one of the few places where we can be sure that *sārîs* refers to a sexually-mutilated male rather than a court official. Nehemiah the cupbearer was not a eunuch (Blenkinsopp 1988a, 212–13), but the Ethiopian *ʾîš sārîs* called Ebed-melech probably was (Jer 38:7). As far as we know, castration was not practiced in Israel, either for court and harem officials or as a judicial punishment (as in the Middle Assyrian laws, *ANET*, 181); and it is even less likely that cultic self-mutilation was practiced. The *sārîsîm* in need of reassurance were therefore also, in all probability, of non-Jewish origin, hence a subcategory of the *běnê hannēkār*.

We would like to know who was threatening these people with exclusion from the community, for what reasons, and on what basis. We may assume in general terms that the threat came from a more rigorist, integrationist, and ritualistic source within the community, of a kind that has left traces in the literature extant from the Second Temple period, including Isa 56–66. In the Ezekielan law of the temple (Ezek 44:4–9), no "foreigner uncircumcised in heart and flesh" is to be admitted to the temple or, a fortiori, is to occupy any position of responsibility on the temple staff. While we cannot attach a date to this measure, it is in line with restrictive cultic stipulations in the Priestly laws—for example, the prohibition of accepting sacrificial animals from foreigners (Lev 22:25). Whether the law was ever implemented and, if so, to what extent is another matter.

Nehemiah expelled Tobiah from the Jerusalem temple, but his action was probably directed against a commercial concession in the temple precincts granted to this Ammonite (Neh 13:4–9). To judge by the kinds of names it contains, the census of Ezra 2 (= Neh 7) lists several nationalities among the temple servants—Arab, Babylonian, Egyptian, Edomite, and possibly others (Ezra 2:43–54)—but the prohibition of foreigners in Ezek 44:4–9, if it was then in force, may not have applied to such low-status individuals as the temple servants listed in Ezra and Nehemiah.

A more promising source for the threatened expulsion is the so-called law of the community (qĕhāl YHVH, LXX ekklēsia tou theou) in Deut 23:2–9[1–8]. It excludes three categories of people: the sexually mutilated; the mamzērîm; and four ethnic groups: Ammonites and Moabites in perpetuity, Edomites and Egyptians to the third generation. The first prohibition, specifying those whose testicles are crushed or whose penis is cut off, appears to be an extension to the people as a whole of the Levitical rules governing the priesthood (cf. Lev 21:17–23). The identity of the mamzērîm (a word, usually rendered "bastards," appearing only here and in Zech 9:6) is the subject of a long-standing debate that need not concern us. The mainline rabbinic interpretation is anyone born of incest (e.g., m. Yebam. 4:13), but many modern scholars argue that it refers to people of mixed race. This Deuteronomic law gives historical reasons for the exclusion of foreigners (Deut 23:5–9[4–8]), but we may suspect that it was more a case of what has been called "ritualized ethnicity" (Fishbane 1985, 114).

While there is no consensus on the date of this particular stipulation of law, we at least know that it could be appealed to by the mid–fifth century (Neh 13:1–3); and Isa 56:1–8 could hardly have been written much before the completion of the temple and the resumption of the cult—and it may have been quite some time later (see, for example, Marti 1900, 362; Volz 1932, 202–3). This being the case, we can compare this halaka with the rigorist interpretation of Neh 13:1–3. But the example of the proselyte Ruth from Moab and the conversion to the Jewish faith of Achior from Ammon (Jdt 14:10) will suffice to remind us that laws do not always find universal acceptance or meet with universal compliance.

The assurance addressed to the eunuchs (vv 4–5) comes with three conditions attached: Sabbath observance, choosing what is pleasing to YHVH, and holding fast to the covenant. The second of these is couched in language characteristic of what we will identify as the minority and opposition position represented in chs. 56–66 (65:12; 66:4; see also 55:11b). It thereby provides us with a small but significant clue to the underlying religious dynamics in the early Second Temple Judean polity. What the eunuchs are promised is encapsulated in the hendiadys *yād vāšēm*, the name familiar from the Holocaust Memorial in Jerusalem, literally, "a hand/memorial/monument and a name." On the basis of Deut 23:13[12] (*vĕyād tihyeh lĕkâ*), and in keeping with the Targum paraphrase (*'ătār*), Ibn Ezra took *yād* to mean "place," but "monument" as the secondary meaning of *yād*, "hand," is more appropriate (for a discussion of the semantic issues, see Ackroyd 1986).

Saul set up a *yād* for himself at Carmel (1 Sam 15:12), and Absalom did the same in the King's Valley:

> In his lifetime Absalom had taken and set up for himself the stele (*maṣṣēbâ*) that is in the King's Valley, for he thought, "I have no son to keep my name in remembrance." So he called the stele by his own name. To this day it is called "Absalom's monument." (2 Sam 18:18)

We see here the belief that something of one's presence and personality will endure only through children on whom falls the responsibility to bury and care for parents when they die; and that in the absence of children, some substitute must be found.

There is also an underlying *lusus verborum*, since a tertiary meaning of *yād* is "penis" (Isa 57:8, 10; Cant 5:4–5; cf. *raglayim*, "feet," for the genitals, Isa 6:2; 7:20; 1 Sam 24:4); so the eunuch is promised a *yād* that will not be cut off (*'ăšer lo' yikkārēt*). Combined with this is the stock expression "to cut off the name" (cf. Isa 14:22; 48:19), equivalent to obliterating the memory of someone. This seems to have been thought of as the real and final death, since the name and descendants (*zera'*, "seed") are inseparable (cf. Isa 66:22 "your seed and your name").

But the assurance given to the eunuchs carries weight only because their memory will live on "in my house and within my walls." What this implies is membership in good standing in the Jerusalem cult community ("in my house"), with which civic status—that is, status "within the walls," meaning, in the city—was at that time inseparably united.

One example must suffice: the account of the plenary assembly summoned by Ezra to deal with the crisis of the intermarriage of Judeo-Babylonian men and local women. The meeting took place in the open space in front of the temple, and those who did not answer the call were threatened with confiscation of their property to the temple and expulsion from the *qĕhal haggôlâ*, the Judeo-Babylonian assembly (Ezra 10:8). It is implied that participation in and support of the Jerusalem cultus were inseparably related to civic status and even title to property; a situation comparable in some respects to the practice of *atimia*, loss of civic rights, in Athens of that same period. In this regard, the long-lasting name that will not be cut off (*'ǎšer lo' yikkārēt*) echoes the *kārēt* or excommunication formula abundantly in evidence in the Priestly texts (e.g., Lev 20:8 *nikrětû miqqereb 'ammām*, literally, "they will be cut off from the midst of their people").

Toward the end of the section we will come across another formulation, where the *ḥǎrēdîm*, those who tremble at God's word, are hated (i.e., shunned) and banished by their brethren (66:5, *niddāh* Piel, only here and Amos 6:3; with the meaning "excommunicate," as in Mishnaic Hebrew). In Ezra–Nehemiah the same process is expressed in terms of separating (*bdl* Hiphil and Niphal, Ezra 6:21; Neh 13:3).

The assurance given to individuals of foreign descent (vv 6–7) also stipulates Sabbath observance and holding fast to the covenant. Ministering to the God of Israel, loving his Name, and being his servants are not further stipulations but profile what is implied in being members of the community, as the speaker understands it. "To minister" (verbal stem *šrt*) can imply secular service of one kind or another—so Abishag ministered to David (1 Kgs 1:4, 15) and a prophet is ministered to by his acolyte (1 Kgs 19:21)—but by the time of this writing, the minister (*měšārēt*) was essentially the priest (e.g., Isa 61:6; Joel 1:9, 13; 2:17; Neh 10:37, 40). This verb and the corresponding substantive are also used exclusively of priests and their activities in the Priestly source (Exod 28:35, 43 etc.), Ezekiel (Ezek 40:46 etc.), and Deuteronomy (Deut 10:8; 17:12; 18:5, 7; 21:5), though Levites are sometimes said to minister in a secondary capacity to priests (Num 1:50; Ezek 44:11 etc.).

The conclusion is unavoidable that people of foreign descent are considered by the prophetic author to be eligible for the priestly office, and therefore the sacrifices mentioned are sacrifices they may offer as priests. Confirmation is at hand in one of the last sayings in the book, affirming that YHVH will take some of those gathered in from Gentile nations to be priests and Levites (66:21). These affirmations at the beginning and end of the section must have been highly controversial, and we may be sure that they would not have been acceptable to the temple authorities at any time after the restoration of the Jerusalem cult. They are not, however, entirely isolated. Texts from the early Persian period speak of a pure offering (*minḥâ ṭěhôrâ*) to YHVH's name among the nations (Mal 1:11), and there are Gentiles who, in reality or in aspiration, call on his name, serve him, and make offerings (Zeph 3:9–10). It will be seen that reverence for the divine Name is a characteristic feature of post-disaster piety, well attested in Isa 56–66.

The holy mountain (*har qodšî*, also 11:9; 57:13; 65:11, 25; 66:20), to which those of foreign descent have access, is the Jerusalem temple. Whereas the city was the focal point in chs. 49–55, in this last section, chs. 56–66, concern converges from different quarters on the temple. Once the temple was completed and the cult resumed—according to Ezra 6:15 on the 23d of Adar in the 6th year of Darius I, therefore about March 12, 515 B.C.E—control of the operation of the temple emerged as a, perhaps *the*, vital issue.

There was also a division of opinion concerning the political and social role of the temple and the nature of cultic activity in general. This first statement clearly accepts sacrifice as legitimate and necessary but emphasizes the role of prayer: the temple is to be "a house of prayer for all peoples" (*bêt-tĕpillâ . . . lĕkol-hā'ammîm*). This, too, is a notable shift of emphasis from the situation during the time of the kingdoms. The essential role of the priest had always been to sacrifice rather than to pray. Intercessory prayer (*tĕpillâ*) was a prophetic not a priestly function, except insofar as certain types of hymns or psalms accompanied corresponding types of sacrifice. Solomon's prayer at the dedication of the First Temple, certainly composed during the time of the Second Temple, captures some of the essential features of contemporary piety and bears comparison with Isa 56:1–8:

> Likewise, when a foreigner (*nokrî*), who is not of your people Israel, comes from a far land on account of your name . . . and prays towards this house, then hear in heaven, the place where you dwell, and fulfill all the foreigner's requests; so that all the peoples of the earth may acknowledge your name and revere you, as do your people Israel. (1 Kgs 8:41–43)

In the final verse (56:8) the designation *nĕ'um* ("oracle, utterance, declaration"), exceptionally at the beginning rather than the end of a prophetic declaration, introduces a brief saying that can stand by itself but, as we have seen, follows the words addressed to foreigners. The superscription consists of the *nĕ'um* and a relative clause identifying the Sovereign Lord YHVH as the one who gathers in the dispersed of Israel (v 8a). This description of YHVH as the Ingatherer is heard frequently in texts from that time, often formulated in practically identical terms (Deut 30:4; Mic 4:6; Zeph 3:19; Ps 147:2), and later taken up in the tenth petition of *Shemoneh Esreh* (The Eighteen Benedictions).

The saying itself (8b) goes beyond this common topos to make a further point of great import, and it does so in the form of a comment on and expansion of an existing Isaiah text:

> He will raise a signal for the nations,
> and gather the dispersed men of Israel,
> he will assemble the scattered women of Judah
> from the four corners of the earth. (Isa 11:12)

The most natural explanation of this declaration, when read in its context, is that the nations are being alerted that the time is right for them to see to the repatriation of diaspora Jews (cf. Isa 14:2; 60:8–9). In the first of many instances of intertextuality in these chapters, the author of 56:8b reinterprets and reformulates this statement and takes it further (as noted by Ibn Ezra) by extending the ingathering process to proselytes, namely, to Gentiles who aspire to embrace the Jewish faith. This is certainly a more attractive option than assigning Gentiles the task of repatriating Jews. We shall find the same point made, if somewhat less clearly, at the end of the section (66:18–19, 21). In this way 56:8 sums up the essence of the preceding words of reassurance.

It has been common practice in the modern exegetical *catena* to read 56:1–8 as polemic directed against the rigorist measures of Ezra, Nehemiah, and their supporters. Like most scholarly generalizations, however, this one calls for close scrutiny. Assuming the historicity of the first- and third-person narratives in Ezra–Nehemiah, or at least assuming that they represent religious views held in fifth century B.C.E. Jewish communities, we can conclude that outsiders could celebrate Passover, thus indicating membership in good standing in a Jewish community, on condition of separating themselves from "abominations", a code word for idolatry (Ezra 6:21).

The operative term is "separation" (verbal stem *bdl*, Ezra 6:21; 9:1; Neh 9:2; 13:3 cf. Isa 56:3), in other words, making a clean break with one's previous religious practice. The same specifically religious issue, the fear of idolatry, lies behind the account of the marriage crisis and the measures taken to resolve it (Ezra 9–10). The Ezra narrative is therefore as open to the recruitment of foreigners as the author of Isa 56:1–8, but both stipulate the full observance of the Jewish law as an essential condition for membership.

Understood in this way, the author of Isa 56:1–8 could have been no less insistent on the law than Ezra. But in fact the only point at which legal rigorism, in the sense of either going further than the law or basing one's actions on a rigorist interpretation of laws, enters into play is the attempt, by Ezra and his supporters, to coerce men who had married women from outside their group to divorce them. This was to be done "according to the law" (Ezra 10:3), but there is no law corresponding to this requirement. In Ezra 9–10 we are therefore dealing with a rigorist interpretation of a law forbidding marriage with native women—perhaps Deut 7:3—and one that, not surprisingly, proved unenforceable.

In the Nehemiah narratives we hear the same insistence on separation (Neh 9:1; 13:3) but nothing more on the subject of coercive divorce. The marked emphasis on strict enforcement of the Sabbath law (Neh 10:32; 13:15–22) in fact aligns Nehemiah rather closely with the author of Isa 56:1–8. Nor should too much weight be given to the law of the *qāhāl* (Deut 23:2–9) as referred to in Neh 13:1–3, the same law that the prophetic author of Isa 56:1–8 appears to have abrogated. The passage in Nehemiah alludes only to excluding Ammonites and Moabites from the community because they hired the prophet Balaam against Israel. It therefore functions as justification for Nehemiah's expulsion of the Ammonite Tobiah from the temple, the account of which immediately follows (Neh 13:4–9). This is the Tobiah who, together with his associates, had hired (the same verb *śkr*) a prophet against Nehemiah (Neh 6:10–14).

There is therefore no necessary close link between Isa 56:1–8 and measures enacted by Ezra and Nehemiah. Commentators who claim to find evidence of serial composition in the passage (e.g., Elliger, Koenen, Sekine) obviously need a broader chronological spread than those who do not, but most agree on the restoration of temple worship in Jerusalem as a terminus a quo—therefore ca. 520 B.C.E.

For Steck (1991a, 34–44, especially 39 n. 116) 56:1–8 together with 63:7–66:24 is part of the final stage in the editorial history of the book with the exception of Isa 19:18–25 and 25:6–8. He dates this stage rather precisely to the early Hellenistic period, a few years after Ptolemy I's occupation of Jerusalem 302/301 B.C.E. Apart from the fact that the date of the composition of a passage is not necessarily identical with that of its editorial manipulation, there is nothing in 56:1–8 that requires so late a date. In any case, Steck is relying more on the community lament in Isa 63:7–64:12, which speaks of the temple as being burned and the cities of Judah devastated. We know that this is what happened in 586 and that something like it seems to have happened shortly before 445, the year of Nehemiah's mission to Jerusalem (Neh 1:3–4 cf. Josephus, *Ant.* 11.159–63), but we have no reason to believe that anything like it happened in 302/301. There is also nothing in either the language or the content of 56:1–8 to suggest the date assigned to the passage by Steck

What is important is that we have here a case, from some time in the first century of the Persian control of Judah, of the abrogation of a point of law on prophetic authority and within an eschatological perspective. This set a precedent of potentially enormous importance and bears directly on the central issue of the formation of dissident groups within Second Temple Judaism. For further discussion of this issue of abrogation, see Donner (1985, 81–95), and for legal hermeneutics in general, Fishbane (1985, 91–277).

The perspective of the writer is still the message of chs. 40–48 and the discipleship of the prophetic Servant of chs. 49–55, but with three important differences. The first is that concern now focuses not on Israel vis-à-vis the nations but on tensions and divisions within Israel. Within this perspective, the delay in the fulfillment of the promises is causing serious stress within Jewish communities and making it more difficult for prophetic preachers to persuade their public. Finally, salvation is no longer presented as unconditional but is contingent on a level of moral performance and the removal of social abuses in the community. This is indicated right at the outset by the injunction to maintain justice and do what is right.

CORRUPT LEADERS INVITE DISASTER (56:9–12)

(Beuken 1986a, 48–64; Brongers 1975a, 791–92; Koenen 1990, 239–40; Polan 1986, 109–19; Sommer 1998, 54–57; Steck 1991a, 175,183)

TRANSLATION

56 [9]All you wild animals,[a] come[b] and devour,
    all you animals of the forest!

^{10}Israel's watchmen^c are blind, one and all,
they have no understanding.^{d}
They are all dumb dogs,
dogs that cannot bark;
panting,^{e} stretched out on the ground,
they love to slumber.
^{11}The dogs have a mighty appetite,
they never have enough.
[They are shepherds.]^f
They all go their own way,
to their own gain, one and all.^{g}
^{12}"Come," says one, "I'll get the wine.^{h}
Let's drink strong drink to satiety.
Tomorrow will be like today,
or even better still!"

NOTES

a   *ḥayĕtô* with archaic case ending, cf. *bĕnô bĕ'or*, Num 24:8, 15 (GKC §90o); 1QIsa^a simplifies with *ḥāyyôt* pl.

b   *'ĕtāyû* → Aram. verb *'ātāh*, pl. imperative (GKC §76d) only here, 56:12, and 21:12.

c   Literally, "his watchmen," with Q and 1QIsa^a *ṣōpâv* for K *ṣōpāv*.

d   *lo' yādā'û*, "they do not know," can stand by itself (see Brongers 1975a, who cites Isa 44:18 and 45:20), but it normally requires an object, which most LXX MSS provide with *phronēsai*, "to think"; however, the threefold occurrence of the same phrase in this short passage (see 11a, 11b) is suspicious; I therefore propose that *lo' yādĕ'û hābîn* 11b belongs here, the cause of the confusion being the insertion of the gloss in the same verse, on which see below.

e   MT *hozîm* → *hāzāh* hapax, on the basis of a rather dubious Arab. cognate is taken to mean "rave," "talk irrationally," which is not right for dogs; Ibn Ezra prefers *hōzîm* hapax = *kĕlābîm*, "dogs," which is unsupported; LXX has *enupniazomenoi*, "dreaming"; 1QIsa^a reads *ḥozîm*, "seers," supported by Vulg. *videntes vana* and Symm. The rare word may have been chosen on account of close similarity with *ḥozîm*, "seers"; see Comments.

f   I take *vĕhēmmâ rō'îm*, "and they are shepherds," to be a gloss identifying the nonbarking dogs as community leaders; cf. the *rō'îm* in the parallel text, Jer 12:9–10, and the gloss at Isa 9:14, which identifies the elders and those of high station as the head and the prophets as the tail (of the dog?). LXX and Syr. read *rā'îm*, "evil," and Tg. paraphrases with *mb'šyn*, "doing evil."

g   *miqqāṣēhû*, literally, "from its end," idiomatic for "without exception"; cf. Gen 19:4, *kol-hā'ām miqqāṣēhû*, "all the people[of Sodom] without exception."

ᵸ 1QIsaiahᵃ and Tg. read pl., but MT sing. (with 1QIsaᵇ) is acceptable. Verse 12 is missing from LXX.

COMMENTS

The abrupt transition between 56:1–8 and 56:9–12 led the Targumist to introduce a linking verse with a catchword hooking the two together: "All the kings of the peoples who gather together (*knś* cf. *qbṣ* three times in v 8) to oppress you, Jerusalem . . . will be food for the wild animals." The link had the further advantage of redirecting the opprobrious language in vv 9–12 to Gentiles who have "wandered off, each on his own way, to prey on Israel's wealth" (*mmvnyh dyśr'l*). Ibn Ezra is more to the point: "The idea connecting the following with the preceding verses is that the righteous Israelites and the proselytes will return, but those who persevere in the worship of idols will not." Setting aside the question whether Ibn Ezra has correctly identified the situation envisaged here, the common rhetorical device of alternating positive words of assurance and promise with denunciation and threat appears to be a feature of these chapters, as a reading of the following in sequence demonstrates: 56:1–8; 56:9–12; 57:1–2; 57:3–13; 57:14–21; and 58:1–14.

Verbal markers of a kind that make it relatively easy to identify sayings in early prophetic texts are not abundant in these chapters, and their appearance in the initial or final position in sayings is mostly limited to the beginning and end of 56–66. The following prophetic *incipits* and *excipits* of sayings appear in these chapters:

koh 'āmar YHVH	56:1; 65:8, 13; 66:1, 12
'āmar YHVH	57:14?; 65:24; 66:9, 21, 23
nĕ'um YHVH	56:8; 59:20; 66:17
others	58:14; 66:5

The distribution appears to confirm the opinion stated earlier and shared by many commentators (e.g., Westermann 1969, 305–6) that 56:1–8 and much if not all of the final chapter were added as bookends to the rest of the material.

Isaiah 56:9–12 is not set off with an incipit and excipit, which has made it easier to read it as part of a larger unit. This larger unit would include 56:1–8, preceding it, according to Beuken (1986a); and following it, 57:1–21, according to Steck (1991a), or 57:1–13, according to Beuken (1986a; 1989a, 45–48), or at least 57:1–2, according to Bonnard (1972, 353) and Hanson (1975, 186). For Muilenburg (1956, 660), 56:9–12 constitutes the first two strophes of a nine-strophe poem that ends at 57:13. However, the subject matter and tone of 56:9–12 set it apart rather decisively from both 56:1–8 and 57:1–2. It is also self-enclosed, beginning with an invitation to eat and ending with an invitation to drink, using the same rare aramaicizing form *'ētāyû*, "come." It will still be important to determine the function of this brief diatribe within the larger unit of chs. 56–66, but we should first acknowledge its distinctive character.

The proposal of Volz (1932, 208), taken up by Westermann (1969, 317), that 56:9–12 is preexilic, depends on the unsustainable argument that only under the monarchy was Israel threatened by invasion and devastation by foreign nations, an argument that a cursory reading of Ezra–Nehemiah will suffice to dispel. If, moreover, 56:9–12 is dependent on Jer 12:9–10, as I will argue, a pre-exilic date would be ruled out. Precision is out of the question, but the situation as described would be consistent with a date in the early part of the reign of Darius I, that is, shortly before or after 520 B.C.E. This time frame would be consistent with the description of hazardous social and political conditions in Zech 7–8 and Ezra 1–6, referring to that period.

The denunciation exploits the familiar biblical metaphor of a flock of sheep or goats vulnerable to attack by wild animals and therefore in need of protection by shepherds assisted by guard dogs (e.g., Ezek 34:1–10). The invitation to the wild animals (external enemies) to come and make a meal of the flock (a Jewish community) points to dereliction of duty on the part of those whose task it was to guard the flock. Pace Hanson (1975, 196), there is no indication that the watchmen are antieschatological Zadokite priests. That the civic and religious leadership is intended (McKenzie 1968, 154; Westermann 1969, 317; Whybray 1975, 200) may be accepted in a general sense. The metaphor of shepherd and shepherding had been applied to rulers for centuries in the Near East, it is so used in biblical texts from the later period (e.g., Jer 12:10; Ezek 34:1–10), and this may have been the idea behind the gloss in v 11 (vĕhēmmāh rōʿîm), which identifies the nonbarking dogs as "shepherds" in this sense.

It is possible in this instance, however, to be more precise. The term "watch-man" or "sentinel" (ṣōpeh) was by the time of writing a well-established synonym for "prophet" (nābîʾ). Ezekiel was appointed as a ṣōpeh to warn and admonish (Ezek 3:16–21), and the function of the prophet-sentinel is further described in the context of threat from war or wild animals, as here (Ezek 33:1–9 cf. 14:12–20; Jer 6:17).

An Isaian text from the Neo-Babylonian period provides a rare insight into the soliciting of an oracle by the prophet-sentinel (here mĕṣappeh), who is stationed on the wall to look and to listen hard, very hard. The text continues:

> Then the seer cried out,
> "On the watchtower, O Lord, I stand
> all the day long;
> at my post I take my station
> night after night." (Isa 2:8)

The vigil is rewarded with the announcement "Fallen, fallen, is Babylon" (Isa 21:6–9). The situation is no different in Habakkuk, where the prophet-sentinel takes up a position at the lookout post and waits patiently (ṣph Piel) for a revelation (Hab 2:1). And not too distant in time from 56:9–12 are references to sentinels on the walls of Jerusalem—whether in reality or metaphorically—whose task is the prophetic one of offering round-the-clock intercessory prayer for the city (Isa 62:6–7). The prophet, in short, served as the antenna for the community, a kind of early warning system.

That it is a prophet taking prophetic colleagues to task will help to explain the acrimony of the language in Isa 56:9–12. Some of the accusations are part of the stock-in-trade of verbal abuse dealt out reciprocally and freely in priestly and prophetic circles, especially lack of spiritual perception, laziness, heavy drinking, and gluttony (e.g., Mic 2:11; 3:5; Jer 14:18). The only accusation lacking here is sexual transgression (as in Jer 23:9–15). Comparing prophets to guard dogs was a particularly gross insult, especially dogs incapable of or unwilling to do the one thing that guard dogs are supposed to do: bark at the approach of danger.

This antiprophetic diatribe agrees with what appears to have been a remarkable loss of esteem for the institution of prophecy in the early Second Temple period. A late gloss on an Isaian text ("YHVH cut off from Israel both head and tail," Isa 9:13) identifies the head as the civic authorities and the tail (of the dog?) as prophets who teach lies (9:14). An especially ferocious attack links prophets with idols and unclean spirits (Zech 13:2–6), and Nehemiah has some hard things to say about the political intrigues in which prophets, male and female, engaged during his governorship (Neh 6:7, 10–14).

If the otherwise unattested word *hōzîm* (v 10c) was chosen to recall *ḥōzîm*, "visionaries," the point would be even clearer; see the Note on this word.

The indications are that, beginning in the Neo-Babylonian period, the approved kind of prophecy was becoming increasingly an activity of taking over, editing, commenting on, and updating existing prophecies. Prophecy became, in other words, more scribal and exegetical, more a matter of inspired appropriation and interpretation of existing prophetic words deemed to be still authoritative and valid than a matter of direct prophetic inspiration. The phenomenon is more clearly in evidence in the first part of the book, where we find numerous addenda, often of an eschatologizing kind.

We saw an example in the previous passage: 56:8 appropriates Isa 11:12 and expands its scope, but 11:12 is itself an expansion on a saying about the diaspora in Isa 11:10–11. Likewise, the long anti-Moabite saying (Isa 15:1–16:11) receives a later comment (Isa 16:12), and the scope of 16:12 is, in its turn, extended further into the future. In this last instance, the procedure is quite explicit: "This is the saying YHVH addressed to Moab a long time ago; but now YHVH says . . ."—and the updated saying in 16:13–14 follows.

In this third section of the book of Isaiah, the process is more difficult to detect and often obscured by the problem of establishing chronological priority. The alleged dependence of 56:9–12 on Jer 12:7–13 is a case in point. The Jeremiah text is a lament of YHVH in *oratio recta*. YHVH has abandoned his house (household? temple?) and his inheritance (*naḥălâ*), delivered his people over to their enemies, and his land has been turned into a hyena's den (Jer 12:7–9). The text continues:

^{9b}*Come, all you wild animals,*
come and devour!
¹⁰Many *shepherds* have ruined my vineyard,
they have trampled down my plot of land;
they have turned my fine plot of land
into a desolate wilderness.
¹¹They have made it a desolation,
a desolation that mourns to me.
The entire land is desolate,
but no one takes it to heart.
¹²On all the bare heights in the wilderness,
plunderers have come;
for YHVH's sword devours the land
from one end to the other.
There is no peace for any living thing. (Jer 12:9b–12)

The italic phrases have clear echoes in Isa 56–66: 9b in 56:9, 10a in 56:11b, 11b in 57:1a, 12b in 57:21. This is sometimes represented as a case of innerbiblical intertextuality (recently Sommer 1998, 54–56) but, assuming that Jer 12:7–13 comes from Jeremiah or at least from the time of Jeremiah, it seems to be a more casual matter of picking up phrases and motifs from this and other prophetic texts rather than a deliberate taking over and rereading (*relecture, Fortschreibung*) of an earlier prophetic text, as we saw was the case with 56:8 vis-à-vis 11:12. On the other hand, we cannot exclude the possibility that the Jeremian text comes from a time when Isa chs. 56–57 were already formed more or less as we have them.

Isaiah 56:9–12 ends with the *gaudeamus igitur* theme common in times ancient and modern. It lacks the bitter undertones of Isa 22:13 quoted in 1 Cor 15:32, and of Wis 2:1–9, and while hardly a drinking song (Muilenburg 1956, 663; Bonnard 1972, 356; Whybray 1975, 201), it communicates very well the impression of thoughtless and directionless insouciance that the writer wished to convey.

LAMENT FOR THE DEAD PROPHET AND HIS DISCIPLES (57:1–2)

(Beuken 1989a, 53–56; Renaud 1977, 3–21; Smart 1965, 240–41; Torrey 1928, 433)

TRANSLATION

57   ^{1a}The Righteous One has perished,^b
and no one takes it to heart;
the devout are swept away,

and no one gives a thought.
ᶜIt was on account of evilᵈ
that the Righteous One was swept away.
²[He enters into peace.ᵉ
They repose in their last resting places.ᶠ
He is upright in his conduct.]ᵍ

NOTES

ᵃ   LXX starts out with "see" (*idete*) cf. Syr. *hā*; 1QIsaᵃ adds the conjunction, also before *yābô'* and *yānûḥû* v 2.

ᵇ   Cf. LXX *apōleto*; 1QIsaᵃ has participle *'ōbēd*.

ᶜ   *kî* is probably secondary and in any case does not introduce either a noun clause or a clause of purpose.

ᵈ   The compound preposition *mippĕnê* could be translated either "from the presence of evil" (cf. Isa 20:6; 30:11 and Vulg. *a facie malitiae*) or "on account of evil"; the latter is required here by the meaning given to the verb *'sp*.

ᵉ   LXX has *estai en eirēnē hē taphē autou*, "his burial will be in peace"; 1QIsaᵇ seems to have read pl.

ᶠ   Literally, "couches"; see Comments; 1QIsaᵃ has 3d-person masc. sing. suffix *mškbvtyv*.

ᵍ   It seems that the LXX translator could make neither head nor tail of this last part and simply substituted "he is removed from the midst" (*ērtai ek tou mesou*); supplying a preposition before *nĕkoḥô* is normal (cf. *šōkĕbê qeber*, "they that lie in the grave," Ps 88:6; see GKC §116h).

COMMENTS

The ancient versions did what they could to wrest some meaning from this short passage which, apparently by design, creates a marked contrast with the vitriolic diatribe that follows. The Targum provides a good example of creative reconstruction:

> The righteous [*ṣdyqy'*, pl.] die, and there is no one who takes my fear to heart; and those who do works of mercy are gathered [i.e., perish], and they do not consider that the righteous [pl.] perish from before the prospect of the evil that is to come. They shall go in peace, those who observe His law shall rest on their beds.

Ibn Ezra takes more or less the same line: no one considers the old problem why the wicked remain alive while the righteous perish; the prophetic answer is that the latter are removed from the scene so as not to experience the evils that are to overtake Israel and Jerusalem. With varying degrees of ingenuity, more recent exegetes have extracted a consecutive meaning of some kind out of the second verse.

The first verse is coherent and calls for no emendation: it speaks of the fate of a group bracketed by the fate of an individual (thus a-b-a) and begins and ends with the word *haṣṣadîq* ("the righteous one"). I take the second verse to be an ensemble of three glosses arranged in the same way: individual—group—individual (also a-b-a). What we are left with, therefore, is a brief lament to which scribal glosses have been appended.

When we read 57:1–2 in context, we see that it fits a pattern in the second half of the book of alternating assurance with condemnation, the fate of the righteous with that of the reprobate. This is a well-known feature of Israelite didacticism, of which Isa 3:9b–11 provides an example, but it is also much in evidence in a certain type of psalm. Comparison with Pss 34 and 37, both alphabetic acrostics, is instructive. A typical couplet may be cited:

> The eyes of YHVH are on the righteous,
> his ears are attentive to their cry.
> The face of YHVH is against evildoers,
> to cut off their memory from the earth. (Ps 34:16–17)

The contrast is repeated redundantly throughout both psalms in language often reminiscent of Isa 56–66. As in Isa 57:1–2, people favored by YHVH are righteous (*ṣaddîqîm*, Ps 34:16; 37:17, 29, 39; also in the singular collective Ps 34:20, 22; 37:12, 16, 21, 25, 30, 32). They are those who take refuge in YHVH (*ḥōsîm bô*, Ps 34:9, 23; 37:40), with which compare the word of assurance at the end of the diatribe in Isa 57:3–13a, addressed to those who take refuge in YHVH (57:13b). The promise to the latter is that they will possess the land and inherit the holy mountain, that is, the temple. The promise of land inheritance, a major concern in the early Achaemenid period, is moreover a central theme of Ps 37 (vv 9, 11, 22, 29). Other synonyms for the *ṣaddîqîm* in these psalms are *nišbĕrê-lēb* ("the broken in spirit"), *dakkĕ'ê-rûaḥ* ("the crushed in spirit"—only in Ps 34:19, Isa 61:1, and 57:15), and, not least, *'ăbādîm* ("servants"), appearing in Ps 34:23 and often in Isa 65.

It is tempting to disregard the alternation between singular and plural in Isa 57:1–2 and read the one legible and intelligible verse as a lament that the devout members of the community have perished, that their passing has gone unlamented, and that only the reprobate (exemplified in the passages immediately preceding and following) are left alive. Parallels come readily to mind:

> Save, O YHVH, for the devout one has passed away,
> for the faithful have disappeared from among humanity. (Ps 12:2[1])

> The devout one has perished from the land,
> there is no longer one who is upright among humanity. (Mic 7:2)

However, the emphasis on the *ṣaddîq* (the righteous or innocent one) in the singular, together with the location of this term at the beginning and end of the lament, suggests a covert reference to the death of a particular *ṣaddîq*; and if this is so, the reference is very likely to the Servant of ch. 53 who, by his teaching and example, will render the many righteous (*ṣaddîqîm*, 53:11). To my knowledge, Smart (1965, 240–41) is the only commentator in the modern period to have explicitly made this connection. If the designation *ṣaddîq* in 53:11 has been added, as several exegetes conclude (see Volume 2, pp. 348–49), the addition may well have been due to reading 57:1 in this way. The complaint that no one has taken his death to heart (57:1) then brings to mind the sad observation of a disciple that the Servant was despised and held of no account (53:3).

The term used in 57:1 to describe people associated with the *ṣaddîq*— namely, *'anšê-ḥesed* ("the devout")—appears only here (cf. *'îš ḥesed* Prov 11:17 and *malkê ḥesed*, 1 Kgs 20:31, but is the equivalent of *ḥāsîdîm*; compare Ps 116:15, "Precious in YHVH's sight is the death of his *ḥāsîdîm*." The *'îš ḥesed* is the one who performs good deeds (*ḥāsîdîm*, 2 Chr 32:32; Neh 13:14). It may go beyond the evidence to claim these *'anšê ḥesed* as the ancestors of the Hasidim (*asidaioi*) of Maccabean times, as Muilenburg (1956, 664) rightly points out, but there must at least be some link with the Servants (*'ăbādîm*) and those who tremble at God's word (*ḥărēdîm*) of the last two chapters of the book. And in fact, the terms *ḥasîd* and *'ebed* appear as synonyms in psalm contexts (Pss 79:1; 116:15–16).

In Classical Hebrew "to be gathered" (*'sp* Niphal) is one of several euphemisms for dying, an abbreviated form of being "gathered to one's people" or, less succinctly, being aggregated to the totality of the clan (Gen 25:8, 17; 35:29 etc.). Here, too, the brief notice about the circumstances under which the was "gathered" points to the fate of the Suffering Servant of Isa 53, where the verb used (*lqḥ* Pual) has the same meaning as *'sp* Niphal:

> By oppressive acts of judgment he was led away,
> and who gives a thought to his fate? (53:8a)

If I am correct in identifying three glosses in v 2, we would expect them to comment on the death of the righteous in v 1. With the conspicuous exception of Torrey (1928, 433), who reads v 2 as the righteous man leaving Jerusalem because he would feel more comfortable somewhere else, most recent exegetes have agreed that this is so.

The first gloss (*yābô' šālôm*), here translated "he enters into peace," perhaps short for "he goes to his ancestors in peace" (Gen 15:15), would then imply that the Righteous One is removed by death from the suffering and contumely inflicted on him during his lifetime. This meaning would also link up with the debate on the destiny of the Servant, who "after his painful life will see light and be satisfied" (53:11a). The gloss is too abridged to permit us to go much further—for example, to read a belief in the immortality of the soul into these two words (Renaud 1977, 3–21; Muilenburg 1956, 665 speaks of "intimations of immortality"). The fairly clear echoes of this part of Isaiah in the Wisdom of

Solomon are nevertheless worth noting. The righteous are taken away from evil and are at peace (Wis 3:3; 4:11, 14), and their passing is not taken to heart (4:14).

The translation of the second gloss, *yānûḥû ʿal-miškĕbôtām* ("they repose in their last resting places"), reflects the semantic range of the word *miškāb* which, in addition to "bed" or "couch" and the sexual connotation evident in the following section (57:7–8), can also refer to the bier on which the body is placed (2 Chr 16:14) or the grave in which it is laid (Ezek 32:25). The state of the dead is one of rest (e.g., Isa 14:8, 18; Job 3:13). The dead are supposed to rest; we recall that Saul's disturbance of Samuel's rest provided one more reason for condemnation (1 Sam 28:15). In one of M. R. James's ghost stories, *Count Magnus*, we hear that the unquiet dead should be resting not walking.

The third gloss, *hōlēk nĕkoḥô* ("he is upright in his conduct," literally, "he walks uprightly"), is the most enigmatic. If it is about the dead *ṣaddîq*, the verb must be in the past tense, perhaps with reference to undeserved abuse and suffering during his lifetime. But the entire verse remains one of the most obscure in these 11 chapters.

DENUNCIATION OF THE SORCERESS AND HER CHILDREN (57:3–13)

(Ackerman 1990, 38–44; Beuken 1986, 48–64; Biddle 1995, 124–39; Blenkinsopp 2000a, 391–95; 2000b, 472–83; Dahood 1971, 343–44; Day 1989; 2000, 209–16; Delcor 1967, 238–40; G. R. Driver 1935, 294; 1967, 54–55; Greenfield 1961, 226–28; Hanson 1975, 186–202; Heider 1985, 379–81; 1992, 895–98; 1999, 581–85; Irwin 1967, 31–40; Kennedy 1989, 47–52; Koenen 1988a, 46–53; 1990, 37–46; Lewis 1989, 49–51, 151–54; Loretz 1989, 241–46; B. B. Schmidt 1994, 210–20, 254–59; Weise 1960, 25–32)

TRANSLATION

i

57 ³As for you, draw near, children of the sorceress,
offspring of an adulterer and a whore![a]
⁴Of whom are you making fun?
At whom are you making faces
and sticking out your tongue?
Sinful brood,[b] treacherous offspring!
⁵You who seek consolation with the shades of the dead[c]
under every green tree;
sacrificing children in the valleys,
under the clefts of the rocks.
Faced with all this, should I relent?[d]

ii

⁶As for you, woman,[e]
with the dead of the valley[f] is your destiny,

it is they who are your portion;[g]
to them you have poured out a libation,
you have made a cereal offering.
[7]On a high and lofty mountain
you have set up your bed;
there too you have gone up
to offer sacrifice.[h]
[8]Beside the door and the doorpost
you have put up your sign;
for when I was absent you disrobed,
you lay down, made room in your bed[i]
for those with whom you made bargains[j]
for the pleasure of sleeping with them.
You gazed on them naked.[k]
[9]You journeyed[l] to Molek[m] with oil,
you put on a lot of perfume;
you dispatched your envoys far afield,[n]
you sent them down even to Sheol.
[10]You were worn out with all your journeying,[o]
but you never said "It is in vain";
you found your vigor renewed,[p]
and so you did not weaken.

iii

[11]Whom did you dread and fear[q]
that you proved so false?
It was not me you kept in mind,
you never gave me a thought.[r]
Did I not stay silent and avert my gaze[s]
while you did not fear me?
[12]I will proclaim your conquests, all your doings,[t]
but they will profit you nothing.
[13]When you cry out for help,
may your "gathered ones"[u] come to your rescue.
The wind will carry them all off,
a breath of air will bear them away.

But the one who takes refuge in me will inherit the land,
will possess my holy mountain.

NOTES

[a] MT *vāttizneh* could be retained as finite verb following a noun in construct (GKC §130d cf. Isa 29:1, *qiryat ḥānāh dāvid*), but emend to *vĕzōnâ* with LXX (*kai pornēs*), Syr., Symm., and Vulg. (*semen adulteri et fornicariae*).

b   MT *yildê-pešaʿ*, literally "children of iniquity"; *yildê* a dissimilated or weakened form of *yaldê*.

c   "Shades of the dead" for MT *ʾēlîm*; for the meaning of this disputed term see the Comments; the participle *hannēḥāmîm* is derived, following Syr. and Vulg., from *nḥm*, "be consoled," "seek consolation," rather than from *ḥmm*, "to be/get warm"; LXX "you who invoke the idols" (*hoi parakalountes ta eidōla*); Tg. "you who serve idols" (*dplḥyn ltʿvtʾ*).

d   Transposed from v 6c, where it appears out of place; *ʾennāḥēm* → *nḥm* I belongs with *hannēḥāmîm* (v 5a) → *nḥm* II.

e   Added to indicate that beginning here the *ʿōněnâ* ("sorceress") is addressed.

f   For this meaning of the phrase *ḥallěqê-naḥal*, see Comments.

g   LXX "That is your portion, that is your lot"; 1QIsaᵃ has *šmh ḥmh gvrlkh*, "there they are your lot," but MT is supported by 4QIsa.ⁱ

h   LXX has an abbreviated and censored version: "there was your couch (*koitē*) and there you brought up sacrifices"; cf. Tg. *ʾtr byt mšrk*, "the place of your dwelling," for MT "your bed."

i   Isaiah 57:8bc is disjointed and may have been scrambled in transmission: "when I was absent" translates *mēʾittî*, a compound preposition, literally, "from [being] with me"; "you lay down" translates *vattaʾălî*, an idiomatic term for getting into bed, (cf. 2 Kgs 1:4, 6, 16) but perhaps with a *double entendre* referring to summoning up the spirits of the dead; "made room in your bed," literally, "made wide your bed." The LXX offers a bowdlerized version: "you thought that if you were to rebel against me you would gain an advantage"; cf. Tg., "You resembled a woman who is loved by her husband but goes astray after strangers; you opened up the place of your dwelling." The Vulg. is closer: *quia iuxta me discooperuisti et suscepisti adulterum dilatasti cubile tuum* ("because while with me you uncovered yourself and accepted an adulterer; you made wide your bed"). For another way of reading this verse, see Comments.

j   The verbal form *vattikrāt*, masc., should probably be emended to fem. in keeping with the context; cf. 1QIsaᵃ *vtkrvty*, but see GKC §47k; "those men" represents an attempt to express the partitive sense of *mēhem* (GKC §119w).

k   *yād ḥāzît* literally, "You gazed on a penis," for *yād* = penis; cf. Isa 56:5; 57:10 (?); Cant 5:4–5; 1QS 7:13; 1QIsaᵃ 65:3.

l   *vattāšurî* has been variously explained: (1) → *šûr* = "look at," which leaves *baššemen* unexplained; (2) the verbal form otherwise unattested corresponding to *těšûrâ*, "gift" (1 Sam 9:7); (3) → *šrr* Arab. cognate meaning "to be abundant"; cf. "you drenched your tresses in oil, blended with many perfumes," NEB and G. R. Driver 1967, 54–55, reading *lammelek* as from *mēl*, "hair," unattested in Classical Hebrew; (4) → *šûr* = "travel," "journey" cf. Cant 4:8, *tāšûrî mēroʾš ʾămānâ*, "journey from the peak of Amana"; probably also Ezek 27:25. This meaning seems to fit the context best.

^m   MT *lammelek*, "to the king." See Comments.

ⁿ   MT *mērāḥoq*, normally, "from afar;" perhaps read *merḥāq*.

^o   1QIsaiah^a and LXX have pl.; *derek*, "way," also "sexual vigor"; see Comments.

^p   *ḥayyat yādēk*, literally, "the life/the animal of your hand," is an idiomatic expression of uncertain meaning; in the context *yād* cannot have the same meaning as in 8c, but the more general sense of "strength," "vigor"; emending to *dê ḥayyātēk*, "(you found) sufficient livelihood" (BHS), is not helpful; for other suggestions, see Delcor 1967:234–35.

^q   1QIsaiah^a *vtyr'yny*, "and you feared me"; 4QIsa^d and LXX are same as MT.

^r   With LXX; MT and 4QIsa^d, "you never gave a thought"; 1QIsa^a, "you never gave these things a thought."

^s   Reading *ma'ĕlīm* Hiphil participle → *'lm* for MT *mē'ôlām*; cf. Vulg. *quasi non videns*, "as if not seeing."

^t   Taking *ṣidqātēk* in the same sense as 56:1b and as hendiadys with *ma'ăśayik*, perhaps in the sarcastic sense of proclaiming the woman's "conquests"; other possibilities: "I will proclaim your righteous deeds," sarcastic; "I shall expose your conduct that you think so righteous" (NEB).

^u   This meaning of *qibbûṣîm* is based on the parallel with *rp'm*, "Rephaim, shades of the dead," in Ugarit (CTA 15.3:3–4, 14–15; see Heider 1985, 381; Lewis 1989, 151–52).

COMMENTS

In this instance, as in others in the second half of the book, continuity is by way of contrast, indicated here by the initial *vě'attem*, "as for you . . ." Contrast also marks the conclusion of the passage, with its reference to those who take refuge in YHVH (57:13). Occasional objurgations appear in chs. 40–55, including complaints that the hearers are spiritually imperceptive (42:18–20; 43:8), stubborn (46:12–13), rebellious (48:8), and indifferent to the cult of YHVH (43:22–28), but idolatry is mentioned only as a recurrent temptation, not as a present reality (48:3–5). The virulence of the diatribe in the present passage presupposes a polarization and schism within the community of a kind that is only hinted at in the comments on the fate of the prophetic Servant in 50:10–11 and 53:1–11a. This point will call for further elaboration, but it is consistent with my interpretation of the preceding passage (57:1–2).

There seems to be no compelling reason for a preexilic origin either for this passage or for 56:9–57:13 (Westermann 1969, 321–25, after Volz 1932, 208, 210, 212; Duhm 1922, 423). There are likewise no grounds for reading 57:3–13 as a reworking of a pre-destruction prophetic diatribe. It is also difficult to follow Childs's argument that the passage was part of Trito-Isaiah's strategy of shaping the entire book of Isaiah into a unity by means of intertextual linkage with First Isaiah. In support of this thesis, Childs (2000, 462–67) can cite only Isa 1:28–31 and 2:2, neither of which is particularly close or even, according to most critical commentators, attributable to First Isaiah.

The target of vituperation is a woman who combines sorcery with sexual transgression, together with her children who follow her example. The children are addressed first (vv 3–5), and then the sorceress (vv 6–13). The unattractive family group is completed with an adulterous father (*mĕnā'ēp*) about whom, however, the author says nothing.

This literary figure of a corrupt and dysfunctional family has biblical precedent in Hosea's marriage to Gomer, and the couple's three children with the names of ill omen (Hos 1–3). But a close reading of Ezekiel chs. 16 and 23, which condemn Jerusalem by use of the figure of YHVH's faithless and dissolute bride, and do so in even more explicit, violent, and pornographic language, will reveal a major source of inspiration for the author of our passage. According to Ezekiel, the bride's father was an Amorite, her mother a Hittite (Ezek 16:3), and this tainted descent explains the child's unbridled sexual appetite and addiction to foreign cults ("like mother, like daughter," 16:44–45).

The conduct of the sorceress and her children is also modeled on that of YHVH's bride-to-be in Ezekiel: sexual acts committed in open places in connection with deviant cults (Ezek 16:24, 31 cf. 23:17: *miškab dōdîm*, "the couch of love-making"), display of sexually explicit images (23:14, 20), child sacrifice (16:20–21, 37, 39), dispatching messengers to her lovers (23:16, 40) and, in general, the disquieting association between sexual deviance and mortuary cults.

It follows that the invective in Isa 57:3–13 targets Jerusalem (the woman) and the city's inhabitants (her children) or, more likely, the civic and religious functionaries who are in control of city and temple, following the opening denunciation in 56:9–12. The contrast with the personification of Zion/Jerusalem in 40–55 as a bride once abandoned but now reunited with her husband and surrounded by numerous children could hardly be greater (e.g., 49:14–26; 54:1–17).

The passage only remotely resembles the classical prophetic judgment saying, with vv 3–10 serving as the indictment and vv 11–13 as the verdict. After on has read chs. 40–55, it becomes apparent that these *Gattungen*, studied in great detail by the form critics, have to a considerable extent disintegrated into longer and less-structured discourses.

The invitation addressed to the children to approach (*qirĕbû hēnnâ*, v 3) probably carries the same forensic undertones as the trial speeches in 40–48 (41:1, 5; 48:16)—namely, an invitation to the children to come forward, as if in a court of law, and defend their conduct. Volz (1932, 210) compares the invitation to Amos 4:12, "Prepare to meet your God!" Their response to the summons may be heard in a similar context near the end of section 56–66: *qĕrab 'ēlêkâ* (65:5), literally, "approach yourself," in effect, an insolent and vulgar dismissal of the invitation, rather like the vernacular expression "get lost!"

Contempt is notoriously easy to convey through facial expressions—by the eyes (Isa 37:23) or by the mouth (Ps 22:8; 35:21; Lam 2:16). The Targum interprets the wide-open mouth as scornful speech, uttering great things, but the combination of opening wide the mouth and sticking out the tongue suggests rather a grimace of disgust and a gesture of contempt. Unlike Isa 5:14, this text provides no occasion for introducing Mot, who opens wide his mouth to swallow Baal in the Ugaritic text CTA 5.2:2–4 (Lewis 1989, 152–53).

The mockery is directed not at the righteous (as Whybray 1975, 203; Childs 2000, 466) but directly at YHVH, and is reminiscent of an earlier Isaiah's reply to Sennacherib:

> Whom have you mocked and abused?
> Against whom have you raised your voice?
> You have looked down on the Holy One of Israel! (Isa 37:23)

The first accusation against the children (i.e., *hannēḥāmîm bāʾēlîm*, "seeking consolation with the shades of the dead," v 5) contains several ambiguities and obscurities, in part deliberate. The only biblically attested meaning of *ʾēlîm* is "deities," and so it was understood in LXX (*hoi parakalountes ta eidōla*, "you who invoke the idols"), cf. Vulg. (*qui consolamini in diis*, "you who console yourselves with the gods"), as well as Syr. and the Targum.

But the further suggestion has been made that in this and other contexts *ʾēlîm* can have the same connotation as is attested for *ilm* in Ugarit and *ilāni* in certain Akkadian texts: that is, deified ancestors to whom cult was offered (see, among others, Weise 1960, 25–32; Lewis 1989, 49–51; rejected by B. B. Schmidt 1994, 210–20). This is possible, especially in view of the mortuary associations to be noted in due course, and it is well established that at least *ʾĕlōhîm* is attested with the meaning "spirits, shades, ghosts of the dead" (1 Sam 28:13; Isa 8:19–20b; Num 25:1–12 cf. Ps 106:28; perhaps 2 Sam 12:16). In ancient thinking in general the boundary between the divine and human was more fluid and permeable than we represent it to be.

But *ʾēlîm* could also be read as an alternative plural of *ʾayil*, a species of large tree, perhaps the equivalent of *ʾallôn* or *ʾēlôn*, "oak," or the plural of *ʾēlâ*, "terebinth" (?), attested elsewhere only in the singular. The affinity of such trees with gods and especially with goddesses is well known, and names such as *ʾallôn bākût*, "The Oak of (ritual) Weeping" (Gen 35:8), and *ʾēlôn mĕʿônĕnîm*, "The Oak of the Diviners or Answerers" (Judg 9:37) would also suggest an association with mortuary practices and cults. Hosea complains about people who engage in divinatory practices, "whoring" after and sacrificing to alien deities under oaks and terebinths (Hos 4:12–13). The Deuteronomic law forbids planting a tree as an Asherah—that is, a tree representing the goddess of that name (Deut 16:21). Perhaps, then, *ʾēlîm* is the first of several deliberate ambiguities in the passage.

No less ambiguous is the verbal form *hannēḥāmîm*, a Niphal participle from either *ḥmm*, "to be/grow warm," or from *nḥm*, "to be consoled," or "to seek consolation." Choosing the former, for example, "you who burn with lust" (RSV and NEB), has the disadvantage that this is the only instance of *ḥmm* in the Niphal and the only occurrence of the verb with reference to lust. Its meaning in the context would also be unclear, however the *ʾēlîm* are understood. We would expect a form deriving from *nḥm* to be followed by the preposition *ʿal* (as in 57:6c), but the thought of seeking consolation *by means of* the deities in question (*beth instrumentalis*) and the sequence *b . . . taḥat*, which is repeated in the following line, could explain this usage.

We are not told with any precision where this activity was going on. "Under every green tree" is a stereotypical way of naming the location of these open-air cults, apparently of Deuteronomic origin (Deut 12:2; 1 Kgs 14:23; 2 Kgs 16:4; Jer 2:20; 3:6,13). Matching passages at the beginning and end of the book speak of oaks and gardens (1:29; 65:3), about which more will be said in due course, but here we are to think either of dried river beds and the caves and hollows, difficult of access, in the surrounding hills or the Kidron and Hinnom Valleys, east and south of Jerusalem, respectively. The similar tirade in 65:1–7 (v 4) speaks of night vigils passed in "tombs" (*baqqĕbārîm*) and "secret places" (*bannĕṣûrîm*) or, alternatively, "between the rocks" (*bên ṣûrîm*), perhaps a special kind of incubation ritual to solicit communication with the dead. Something of the same seems to be implied in 57:5–6.

Why, beginning with v 6, the woman is addressed directly will be apparent from the familiar association between deviant (i.e., non-Yahvistic) cults and *female* sexual transgression. It will suffice to mention the "many whoredoms and sorceries" attributed to Jezebel (2 Kgs 9:22). The diatribe in vv 6–13 is full of intentional ambiguity and double or triple meanings, often of a sexual nature, beginning with the first accusation, delivered like a series of hammer blows:

bĕḥallĕqê-naḥal ḥelqēk hēm hēm gôrālēk

with the dead of the valley is your destiny,
it is they who are your portion.

The verb *ḥlq* in the opening phrase can denote smoothness and therefore refer to the stones in the wadi basin smoothed by the elements, but in ancient as in modern times "smoothness" can also signify falseness and hypocrisy (e.g., Ezek 12:24, *miqsam ḥālāq*, "smooth i.e., flattering divination"; also Ps 12:3 and Prov 26:23). Note in particular how often the "outsider woman" (*'iššâ zārâ*) of Prov 1–9 is said to speak smooth words with a smooth tongue (Prov 2:16; 5:3; 6:24; 7:5,21; see Excursus 1).

Another meaning of the root *ḥlq*, unattested elsewhere in Biblical Hebrew but suggested by cognates in other Semitic languages (Akk. *ḥalāqu*, "perish," Eth. *ḥalqa* with the same meaning, Ug. *ḥlq* used in parallelism with *mt*, "dead"), gives the phrase the meaning "the dead of the valley" (Irwin 1967, 31–40; Lewis 1989, 147–49). This meaning fits well with the context. Thus, the woman's destiny (*ḥēleq*, from the same root) is to be not with YHVH, God of the living, but with those buried in rock tombs, perhaps in the Kidron Valley (cf. 2 Kgs 23:6; Jer 31:40) or the Hinnom, where child sacrifice to Molech was carried out (2 Kgs 23:10).

The "dead of the valley" could refer to the sacrificed children of the previous verse, but it does not seem likely that those whom the prophet is condemning would sacrifice children and then offer libations and cereal offerings to them as part of the same cultic act. A libation (*nēsek*), usually of wine, accompanied the cereal offering (*minḥâ*) according to priestly orthopraxy (Exod 29:40–41; Lev 23:13; Num 6:15; Joel 1:9, 13 etc.). But libations also accompanied the setting up of a stele representing a male or female deity (Gen 35:14), and they were offered to deities other than YHVH, including "the Queen of Heaven," either Asherah or Astarte (Jer 7:18; 19:13; 44:17–19 etc.). In one text, admittedly somewhat obscure, we hear of a blood libation offered to unnamed deities (Ps 16:4).

Beginning with v 7, the scene changes from the valleys to a high and lofty mountain. The expression (*har-gāboah vĕniśśā'*) sends back a faint echo of the throne raised up on high (*rām vĕniśśā'*) in Isaiah's vision (6:1), but the reader would in any case be led to think of Jerusalem, Mount Zion, and, in the context of these last chapters of the book, more specifically of the temple, God's holy mountain (56:7; 57:13; 65:11, 26; 66:20).

At this point, however, we encounter yet another ambiguity. The sacrifice of children took place in the Valley of the Sons of Hinnom, south of the city, on a natural or artificial platform or "high place" (*bāmâ*, Jer 7:31; 19:4–6; 32:35). But it seems that this cult offered to the god Molech also involved ceremonies in the temple. We read about participants' entering the temple on the same day that they had sacrificed to Molech (Ezek 23:39) and, by doing so, desecrating it (Lev 20:3; Jer 7:30; 32:34; Ezek 23:37). It is therefore unclear whether we are being told that the sorceress sets up her bed and goes about her business in Hinnom or in the temple precincts.

I noted above the mortuary associations of this term *miškāb* (57:2 cf. 2 Chr 16:14, where it refers to a bier or catafalque). Less arcane are its sexual connotations, including both bed and intercourse (Num 31:18, 35; Judg 21:11–12; Ezek 23:17; 32:25—in keeping with the corresponding verb *škb*, "lie"). A certain parallelism between the sacrificial high place in Hinnom and the high and lofty temple mound is therefore insinuated. Making due allowance for homiletic hyperbole, we may read this as indicating a continuation of the *official* cult of the late Judean monarchy into the post-destruction period.

Jeremiah attests to the prevalence and popularity of the worship of the Queen of Heaven (Jer 7:18; 44:17–19, 25), has much to say about child sacrifice in Hinnom (1:34; 7:31; 19:4–6; 32:35), and denounces "abominations" going on in the Jerusalem temple (7:30; 11:15; 23:11; 32:34). On the subject of these temple "abominations," Ezekiel is more specific. The statue of the goddess, probably Asherah, was set up near the north gate of the inner courtyard, certainly as the object of cult. It is described as *sēmel haqqin'â hammaqneh* (Ezek 8:3: "the lustful image that provokes lust"). Cult was also offered to deities represented by theriomorphic images, and the temple precincts were the site of the worship of Thammuz or Adonis (cf. Isa 17:10) and a sun deity (Ezek 8:3, 9–12, 14–17).

In keeping with the line of thought established in the previous verse, the woman's sacrifices are offered to alien, probably chthonic deities. The association of ideas can be illustrated by the incident of Baal Peor (Num 25:1–12).

Israelites took part in sacrificial cult offered to the local deities (*zibḥê 'ĕlo-hêhen*, 25:2), they shared in a communal meal, and engaged in sexual relations with the local women. Remarkably, these acts were atoned for by what appears to be a ritual human sacrifice—the perpetrators were impaled "before YHVH," that is, in a cultic act, in the open air where the deed had taken place (25:4). In referring to this incident, Ps 106:28 refers to "sacrifices to the dead" (*zibḥê mētîm*)—"they yoked themselves to Baal Peor and ate the sacrifices (offered) to the dead," once again, therefore, the association between sexual transgression and the cult of the dead.

The scene of sexual excess continues in v 8 in the manner of Ezekiel's long and lurid description of the depraved conduct of the two sisters Oholah and Oholibah (Ezek 16:1–52; 23:1–49). The choice of the word *zikkārôn* for the sign set up to identify the house as a bordello (cf. the crimson cord of the prostitute Rahab at Jericho, Josh 2:18) was no doubt chosen because of the double entendre with *zākār*, "male"; compare the male images (*ṣalmê zākār*) of YHVH's bride-to-be in Ezek 16:17 (cf. 23:14). The effect is intensified by mention of the sign on the doorpost (*mĕzûzâ*), which would bring to mind Passover night (Exod 12:7, 22–23), the *šĕma'* (Deut 6:9; 11:20), and the holy phylacteries.

We find a similar contrast between the house of the Woman Wisdom, with its door and doorposts and its open invitation to enter (Prov 8:34), and the open door of the Outsider Woman's house, with its invitation of a different nature (Prov 5:8; 7:6–8; 9:14). Contrast with the violated covenant with YHVH is also implied in the sorceress's "cutting" deals with her male clients, probably with the same implication as the wayward bride of Ezek 16 who, rather than receiving payment for her services, herself pays her clients (vv 31, 33–34).

Isaiah 57:8 is obscure enough to permit more than one reading, especially in view of the constant *lusus verborum* throughout this passage. In 8b, *gillît vatta'ălî*, translated above "you disrobed, you lay down," could also be translated "you uncovered secrets, you summoned up (spirits)." For this use of *glh* Piel, see Job 12:22; Prov 11:13; 25:9; and for *'lh* Hiphil, 1 Sam 28:8, 11, describing the summoning up of Samuel's ghost by the mistress of the spirits (*ba'ălat 'ôb*) at Endor.

To judge by the very incomplete biblical record, ritual infanticide began to be practiced in Judah in the eighth century B.C.E. (2 Kgs 16:3), was promoted as part of the royal cult by Manasseh (2 Kgs 21:6), proscribed by Deuteronomic-Josianic orthodoxy (Deut 18:10; 2 Kgs 23:10), as also in the Levitical legislation (Lev 18:21; 20:5), but continued on well after the disasters of the early sixth century (Jer 7:30–32; 19:5–6; 32:34–35; Ezek 20:31).

Though much still remains uncertain, the Molech cult has been well studied in recent years (Heider 1985; 1992; 1999; Day 1989; 2000, 209–16), and some progress has been made. Only a brief summary of generally accepted conclusions need be given. Molech was the name of a Canaanite-Israelite chthonic deity, not a type of sacrifice; children were really killed, not just dedicated to the god; the royal Judean cult was carried out in the Valley of Hinnom southeast of Jerusalem on a raised platform, earthwork, or "high place" called the Topheth; it may have involved sexual activity of some kind, though the sexualization of the cult may be due at least in part to the polemic of the biblical authors.

As vocalized, the name of the deity appears to be a dysphemism formed with the vowels of the word *bōšet*, "shame," similar in that respect to Ashtoreth and Tophet. Since Molech is a god of the underworld, the realm of the dead, the sorceress must travel and send envoys in order to encounter him. Unfortunately, we do not know whether this descent into the underworld was enacted in the cult or, if so, how it was done.

One of the more subtle of the many double meanings in this passage is *běrōb darkēk* in v 10 ("with all your journeying"). In addition to the common meaning of the word *derek*, "way," the meaning "strength," "vigor," inclusive of "sexual vigor," is attested in Ugaritic (*drkt*) and residually in Hebrew. The much-discussed *derek bě'ēr šeba'* of Amos 8:14 must, in the context, refer to a deity, probably an early attestation of Derketo associated with Ashkelon in the Hellenistic period. Of more immediate relevance is the following:

> Do not give your strength (*ḥêlekā*) to women,
> nor your sexual vigor (*děrākêkā*) to those who destroy kings. (Prov 31:3)

Thematically even closer to our passage is the following, addressed to a female personification of Israel:

> You have showered your favors (*děrākayik*) on strangers under every green tree. (Jer 3:13)

This passage is particularly interesting on account of the many parallels between Isa 57:3–13 and the early chapters of Jeremiah. In Jer 2:18–37 Israel is addressed as a young bride (2:2) who prostitutes herself on every high hill and under every green tree (2:20), who says "it is in vain" (*nô'āš* cf. Isa 57:10), who venerates a tree as a symbol of ancestors (2:27), and who expends her *derek* in the valley (2:23, 33). Both passages end with an ironic invitation to look to these alien gods for salvation (2:28 cf. Isa 57:13).

The diatribe that begins with Isa 57:3 concludes with a complaint or *improperium* (vv 11–13) of a kind heard often in chs. 56–66. The key to understanding the contrast between those who engage in falsehood (*těkazzēbî* → *kzb* Piel, v 11) and those who take refuge in YHVH (v 13b) can be found in the Isaian account of Judah's covenant with death in the context of the crisis of 701 B.C.E., when invasion by Sennacherib was imminent (Isa 28:14–22). Those who, in that desperate situation, entered into a covenant with Death (Mot) and Sheol—in other words with underworld deities—claimed that "we have made a lie (*kāzāb*) our shelter (*maḥsēnû*), in falsehood we have taken refuge" (28:15d). The language, which needless to say is not language they would have actually used, is reminiscent of the finale to our passage. It is also reflected in the covenanting with the underworld powers attributed to the sorceress (57:8c), the mortuary associations of bed and bed covering (28:20 cf. 57:7–8), and the scoffing at YHVH (28:1, 22 cf. 57:3; Blenkinsopp 2000a, 391–95; 2000b, 472–83).

Isaiah 57:3–13, then, is a passage of remarkable linguistic, thematic, and intertextual density. It is not a rehash of old prophecies or an old prophetic text written up in the post-destruction period, but it has made selective and effective use of existing prophetic material, including Jer 2–3, Ezek 16 and 23, and Isa 28:14–22. Allowing for polemical hyperbole on a rather massive scale, what little we know of the situation in Judah in the late Neo-Babylonian and early Persian period is consistent with, or at least not inconsistent with, the scenes depicted in this passage.

The concluding assurance, that those who take refuge in YHVH will possess the land and inherit his holy mountain, raises issues that were of immediate and practical importance at that time. Title to land must have been one of these issues after Judeo-Babylonians claiming descent from former Judean landowners began to trickle back after the Persian conquest. The argument that the latter had been expelled from the Yahwistic cult community and therefore had lost title to their lands (Ezek 11:15) would not have "cut ice" with these early ʿôlîm any more than the claim that the indigenous population had inherited the Abrahamic promise of land (Ezek 33:24).

During the years prior to and immediately following the rebuilding of the Jerusalem temple, the resolution of this and similar issues would have been seen to depend on who controlled the temple together with its considerable assets. The indications are that participation in and support of the temple cult was an essential prerequisite for civic status and title to immovable property; hence the connection between land ownership and temple in this final verse, which parallels the promise of a monument and a name to the eunuch "in my house and within my walls" (56:5). This issue will emerge more clearly as we proceed.

EXCURSUS 1: DOUBLE MEANINGS IN ISAIAH 57:3–13

5a, bc	*hannēḥāmim*	ḥmm heated (with lust); nḥm seeking consolation
	ʾēlîm	deities, spirits of the dead; sacred trees
6a	*ḥālāq*	smooth; smooth (deceitful); dead, departed (cf. Akk. *ḥālāqa*; Ug. *ḥlq* // mt) cf. portion *ḥēleq*
7a, 8b, c	*mĭškāb*	bed, couch; grave, tomb; intercourse

8a	*zikkārôn*	sign
		cf. *zākār* = male
8b	*gîllît*	you undressed;
		you uncovered secret things
	taʿălî	you went up (to your bed);
		you raised up spirits
8c	*yād*	hand;
		monument;
		penis
9a	*melek*	king;
		the god Molech
10a	*derek*	way, conduct;
		strength, sexual vigor
12a	*ṣĕdāqâ*	righteousness;
		victory, conquest
12b	*qibbûṣ*	a collection (of idols);
		"gathered ones" i.e., dead
		ancestors (cf. Ugaritic)

EXCURSUS 2: THE SORCERESS OF ISAIAH 57:3–13

Modern versions of the Bible reveal a fair amount of indeterminacy in translating the list of seven religious specialists whose activities are prohibited in Deut 18:10b–11. One of these is the *mĕʿōnēn* (vv 10, 14) which NRSV translates "soothsayers" here and Mic 5:11, but "diviners" in Judg 9:37. A variant form of the same specialization is *ʿōnēn* (Isa 2:6; Jer 27:9), feminine *ʿōnĕnâ* (Isa 57:3 hapax). The corresponding verb *ʿnn* (Polel) appears in connection with divination (*nḥš*), child sacrifice, and eating non-kosher meat (Lev 19:26; 2 Kgs 21:6). On the basis of an Arabic cognate, the meaning "to cause to appear" has been assigned to *ʿnn*, with reference to the summoning up of a ghost from the realm of death (for other meanings, see Lewis 1989, 146–47 and the dictionaries). Hence, the *ʿōnĕnâ* of Isa 57:3–13 is a female practitioner of the necromantic arts, and therefore in the same order of activity as the *baʿălat ʾôb* ("mistress of the spirits") consulted by Saul in 1 Sam 28.

We deduce from the designations in the biblical texts that these activities were not exclusively male or female. With the exception of the male priesthoods, religious intermediaries and mediums were not as a rule gender-specific in the ancient Near East and Levant. There is ample evidence for male practitioners in Mesopotamia but also for the female ecstatic (*muḫḫutum*), the one who gives answers (*apiltum*), the female shaman (*kaššaptu* cf. the Hebrew *mĕkaššēpâ*, who is subject to the death penalty, Exod 22:17). In the Kingdom of Mari in the eighteenth century B.C.E., most of the lay ecstatic intermediaries were female. Among the Hittites, a mediumistic person called "the old woman" (*hašawaš*) played an important role. In Israel, in addition to female prophets (Exod 15:20; Judg 4:4; 2 Kgs 22:14; Isa 8:3; Neh 6:14) and the "mistress of the spirits" already mentioned, there were the women who were denounced by Ezekiel for casting spells and practicing divination, women who were believed capable of inflicting physical and psychic harm (Ezek 13:17–23).

The *'ôbôt vĕyiddĕ'ōnîm* (ghosts and spirits or their handlers, depending one the context), denounced on numerous occasions (Lev 19:31; 20:6; 2 Kgs 21:6; 23:24; Isa 8:19; 19:3), were also understood to be female and male necromancers, respectively (see Hoffer 1974). It seems that in Israel communication with the dead and the spirit world came to be seen as predominantly a female domain. In the so-called Covenant Code, only the female practitioner is threatened with the death penalty (Exod 22:17), and Saul sought out and was immediately able to locate, a female medium to summon up Samuel from the underworld (1 Sam 28:7).

The activities with which the *'ōnĕnâ* was charged in Isa 57:3–13, to which we can add the activities listed in 65:3–7, include taking part in deviant, open-air cults in gardens and under sacred trees; sacrificing children to Molech; offering libations, incense, and sacrifices to the dead, presumably dead ancestors; incubation in tombs with a view to receiving communications from the dead; eating unclean food; and sexual rites. Since this is religious polemic of the most vitriolic kind, the author is not interested in exploring the purpose and point of these activities for those who participated in them. The literary and archaeological evidence for mortuary cults throughout the history of Israel is uneven, but there is enough to establish that mortuary cults—and not just funerary rites—were a significant feature of the communal life of the household and clan. (Lewis 1989, 99–170; Bloch-Smith 1992; van der Toorn 1996, 181–372). These cults seem to have achieved a special prominence during the last critical decades of the Kingdom of Judah, and the allusions to them in these last chapters of Isaiah (57:3–13; 65:3–4) suggest that they continued on into the early Persian period at least. Some commentators take Isa 8:19–22, which rejects the advice to "consult the spirits of the dead who chirp and mutter," to be an editorial addendum from the post-destruction period. With this text we can compare Isa 29:4, which speaks of a voice issuing from the underworld and whispering in the dust.

The combination of heterodox cults, and especially necromancy, with sexual transgression was a well-established feature of prophetic polemic by the time our text was written. Hosea's marriage to and begetting of children with the sexually promiscuous Gomer may have been suggested by the common idiomatic expression *bĕnê yiśrā'ēl* ("children of Israel") which, taken literally, could be represented by three children with ominous names. These names could then be spelled out in a chronological sequence of progressive decline leading to total alienation from YHVH. The metaphor is complex but transparent: Hosea himself, as the father, represents YHVH; Gomer stands for the land (*'ereṣ* fem.), as is made clear in the second chapter. Gomer looks to indigenous and no doubt also chthonic deities to promote fertility. This was the normal pattern in that kind of society that called for no moralizing, but in the context of prophetic thought it represented marital (i.e., covenantal) infidelity, and therefore Gomer is ʾēšet zĕnûnîm, and her children yaldê zĕnûnîm (NRSV, "a wife of whoredom," "children of whoredom," Hos 1:2; 2:6[4]). This way of representing religious deviance entered the prophetic mainstream (Jer 2:20; 3:1–2, 6–10; Ezek 16:1–52; 23:1–49; Isa 50:1). It also made a natural if regrettable alliance with the fear of women as possessing occult powers. Hence the Historian's condemnation (through the mouth of Jehu, hardly a credible witness) of Jezebel's "whoredoms and sorceries" (2 Kgs 9:22).

Since cities were conventionally and grammatically feminine, the same combination of reprehensible qualities could be employed as a polemical weapon, whether the target was Nineveh (Nah 3:4), Babylon (Isa 47:9–13), or Jerusalem (Ezek 16:1–52; 23:1–49; Isa 57:3–13).

We come closer to grasping the polemic of Isa 57:3–13 with the figure of the "outsider woman" (ʾiššâ nokriyyâ/ʾiššâ zārâ of Prov 1–9), which most scholars would agree is roughly contemporaneous with the Isaiah passage. This female personification is the dark shadow of the Woman Wisdom (ḥokmâ), who uses prophetic forms of speech familiar from Isa 56–66. How close the language is can be seen in the pattern of calling out and response or (more commonly) the refusal to respond (Prov 1:24, 28 cf. Isa 58:9; 65:1–2a; 66:4), the invitation to a banquet (Prov 9:1–6 cf. Isa 65:11), and the description of the reprobates (Prov 1:10–19 cf. Isa 58:3–4; 59:1–15). In some instances (e.g., Prov 1:16; Isa 59:7a) the wording is practically identical.

The "Outsider Woman" (Prov 2:16–19; 5:3–23; 7:5–27; 9:13–18) is the negation of all the qualities of the Woman Wisdom in Prov 1–9. She is lascivious, her speech is smooth (Prov 2:16; 5:3; 7:5, 21), her pitch is on a high place (Prov 9:14 cf. Isa 57:7), she has her own house (Prov 5:8; 7:6, 27) in which the most important piece of furniture is the bed (Prov 7:16–17 cf. Isa 57:8), she offers sacrifice (Prov 7:14 cf. Isa 57:7), and she is associated with the underworld and the Rephaim, the spirits of the dead (Prov 2:18; 5:5; 7:27). These characteristics suggest a degree of influence from a goddess cult of the kind that was an important component of both popular religion and the state and royal cult under the monarchy in both kingdoms. That a goddess cult continued into the Neo-Babylonian and Persian periods is clearly attested (e.g., Ezek 8:5; Jer 44:15–19; Zech 5:5–11 and has doubtless influenced both Prov 1–9 and Isa 57:3–13. (For the biblical and archaeological evidence with bibliography, see most recently Day 2000 passim.)

Proverbs 1–9 is presented as a moral exhortation by Solomon, drawing on his own experience of foreign or outsider women (nāšîm nokriyyôt) and the fact that his addiction to them led him to adopt alien cults (1 Kgs 11:1–13). For the Historian, this meant that Solomon was in violation of the law forbidding intermarriage with women outside of the Israelite cult community (Deut 7:1–4 cf. Deut 17:17, the law forbidding the king to accumulate women). Solomon's bad example is also appealed to in Neh 13:23–27; and marriage with non-Israelite women or, more precisely, with women from outside the dominant

Judeo-Babylonian elite, in also an important issue for Ezra. (The designation *nāšîm nokriyyôt* is used seven times in the account of the marriage crisis in Ezra 9–10.)

It seems reasonable to conclude that both the depiction of the "outsider woman" in Prov 1–9 and the even more lurid description of the sorceress in Isa 57:3–13 reflect concerns about the religious consequences of exogamous marriage during the early stages of the reestablishment of a religiopolitical polity in Judah after the collapse of the Babylonian Empire. But, as is so often the case, the concerns are not exclusively and purely religious. Exogamous marriage could have undesirable social and economic implications, including alienation of household property. Both the levirate law (Deut 25:5–10) and the dispositions concerning inheritance of property by the daughters of Zelophahad (Num 27:1–11; Josh 17:3–6) reflect anxiety about the alienation of paternal domain both before and after the fall of Jerusalem.

We recall that failure to attend the assembly of the *běnê haggôlâ* convoked by Ezra to resolve the marriage crisis resulted in exclusion from the group and confiscation of property, presumably including real estate (Ezra 10:8). Religious infidelity could also undermine the economic basis of the temple cult operated by a large number of almost certainly tax-free personnel.

These side-effects are more in evidence in Prov 1–9 than in Isa 56–66. The young man who succumbs to the outsider woman's wiles will lose his property to strangers and will end up in all sorts of trouble in the *qāhāl* (Prov 5:7–14). The author of Isa 57:3–13 comes at the issue from a more radical and exigently religious perspective and from a different location in Judean society, but for both authors the social and economic implications of their religious commitments are unavoidable.

A CALL FOR A NEW BEGINNING (57:14–21)

(Bergmeier 1969, 93–97; Beuken 1989a, 79–98; Cannon 1934, 75–77; Dahood 1968, 362; 1969, 347; Koenen 1990, 46–58; Kselman 1981, 539–42; Odeberg 1931, 14–20, 100–18; Pauritsch 1971, 66–73; Polan 1986, 147–72; Steck 1991a, 69–86, 192–214; Weinfeld 1995, 22–38; Westermann 1997, 590–602; Zimmerli 1950, 110–22 = 1963, 217–33)

TRANSLATION

57 [14]He said:[a]
    "Build up, build up the road[b] and clear the way,
    remove every obstacle from my people's path."
    [15]For thus says the Exalted One,
    who dwells in an eternal place,
    whose name is holy:
    "I dwell[c] in a high and holy place[d]
    and with the contrite and humble in spirit,

to revive the spirits of the humble,
to revive the hearts of the contrite.
[16]I will not be forever accusing,
nor will I always be angry;
apart from me[e] the spirit weakens,
for it was I made all creatures that breathe.
[17]I was angry at their[f] sinful avarice;[g]
I struck them,[h] and in my anger I stayed hidden;
yet they kept turning back to their own devices.
[18]Though I note their conduct, I will heal them,
give them respite,[i] repay them with comfort,
[19]putting words of praise on the lips[j]
of those among them that mourn.[k]

Peace, peace, for those far off and those that are near,
YHVH affirms it; yes, I will heal them.[l]
[20]But the wicked are like the driven sea
that never can be still.
[Its waters dredge up slime and mud.][m]
[21]There is no peace, says my God, for the wicked.

NOTES

[a] For MT *vě'āmar*, 1QIsa[a] has *vyv'mr*, "and he said"; LXX *kai erousin*, "and they will say"; Vulg. *et dicam*, "and I will say"; YHVH discourse would not be expected here in view of v 15, *koh 'āmar rām věniśśā'*; its insertion may have been suggested by 40:6 (Marti 1900, 370), but deleting it is unwarranted; it stands on its own and is therefore not vav consecutive following *věyîraš*, as 1QIsa[a] seems to have understood it.

[b] 1QIsaiah[a] but not 4QIsa[d] adds *hamměsillâ*, "highway," after *sollû sollû*.

[c] Both 1QIsa[a] and 4QIsa[d] have 3d-person *yškn* cf. LXX *en hagiois anapauomenos*, "resting among the holy ones"; Vulg. *in sancto habitans*, "dwelling in the holy [place]"; Tg. *brvm' šry*, "he dwells in the height"; but the context seems to require 1st person.

[d] For MT *mārôm věqādôš*, 1QIsa[a] has *běmārôm ûběqōdeš*, "on high and in the sanctuary."

[e] For this translation of *millěpānay* cf. Gen 4:16 *vayyēṣē' qayin millipnê YHVH*, "and Cain went out from the presence of YHVH." The LXX (*pneuma gar par'emou exelousetai*), Vulg. (*spiritus a facie mea egredietur*), and Syr. understand the verb *'ṭp* as "go out." Targum reads the resurrection of the dead into this verse: "I am about to restore the spirits of the dead and the souls I have made."

[f] Plural for MT sing. to indicate reference to Israelites.

[g] Taking *ba'ǎvôn biṣ'ô* as construct formation cf. Vulg. *propter iniquitatem avaritiae eius* and Tg. *bhvby mmvnhvn*, "on account of the iniquities of

their wealth"; therefore, no need to emend either *ba'ăvôn* to *ba'ăvônô* or *biṣ'ô* to *beṣa'*, "a little while" (cf. LXX *brachu ti*).

h   Read *vā'akkēhû*, vav consecutive.

i   *va'ănihēhû* → *nûaḥ* seems to fit the context ("heal," "comfort") better than → *nḥḥ*, "guide," and is supported by LXX (*kai parekalesa auton*) and Tg. (*v'rḥym 'lyhvn*); but see J. Kselman 1981.

j   Literally, "creating the fruit of the lips," on which, see the Comments. Read with Q and 1QIsa[a] but not 4QIsa[d], *nîb*, for K *nûb*.

k   Literally, "and for his [Israel's] mourners." The punctuation and metric arrangement appears to be confused; 1QIsa[a] and 4QIsa[d] are not helpful, since they are not written stichometrically, and LXX omits the reference to the mourners. The meter is a regular 3–3 from 15b until it stumbles at 17b. I suggest the following line division:

> *dĕrākâv rā'îtî vĕ'erpā'ēhû*
> *vĕ'anhēhû va'ăsallēm niḥumîm lô*
> *vĕla'ăbēlâv bôrē' nîb sĕpātāyim*

l   *'āmar YHVH* is usually in the final position (59:20; 65:25; 66:9, 17, 21, 23), occasionally internal to a saying (57:21; 59:21; 65:7; 66:2).

m   Probably a gloss on *nigrāš* 20a, identifying the opponents as "mud" (*ṭîṭ*) and "scum" (*repeš* hapax cf. Akk. *rupuštu*).

COMMENTS

The core of this passage is a saying, offering the prospect of relief and well-being—in conventional terms, a salvation oracle (15b–19). In an adaptation of the usual prophetic *incipit*, the speaker is identified as the Enthroned One of the vision narrative in Isa 6 (*rām vĕniśśā'*, "raised up on high," 6:1), while the conclusion is signaled by the phrase "YHVH affirms it" near the end. On this reading, the concluding vv 20–21 about the fate of the reprobate would be an addendum in keeping with the positive-negative alternation in the second part of the book, noted earlier. Compare the similar conclusion to chs. 40–48 (48:22) and the final reprobation with which the book concludes (66:24).

At first sight, "he said" (v 14a; see Notes) looks like a conventional phrase linking 57:14–21 with the preceding passage (Westermann 1969, 327–28). But 57:14 is a paraphrase of 40:3 ("clear in the wilderness a way for YHVH; level in the desert a highway for our God") and therefore refers back to Isa 40:3 together with 40:6 (reading *vĕ'āmar* 3d person) as a prophetic word spoken in the past. We would then have a valuable clue to the meaning of the saying that follows as an interpretative expansion of 40:3–8, which begins as follows:

A voice proclaims:
"Clear in the wilderness
a way for YHVH;

level in the desert
a highway for our God!"

The rather unusual opening phrase ("He said") may therefore be one of the
few points in chs. 40–66 where the authorial voice is heard. It will be heard
again at the end of this first section, chs. 56–59, where a promise is addressed
to a prophet and his "seed"—that is, his disciples (59:21; see also the Comments on 58:1).

The intent to keep alive and contemporize the message of the prophetic author of 40–55 is apparent in the choice of language—*pannû derek*, "clear the
road"; *sollû, sollû*, "build up, build up the road"; the verb is related to the substantive *mĕsillâ*, "highway" (40:3; 62:10). Repetition is also characteristic of the
rhetorically emphatic style of 40–55, beginning with the opening injunction
"Comfort, O comfort my people" (40:1).

Bringing out the contemporary relevance of this word spoken in the past also
implies that the road-building is no longer meant to be a highway through the
wilderness. The author of 57:14–21 is speaking out of a different experience.
Babylon has fallen, but Cyrus has not lived up to the expectations or fulfilled
the charge laid on him by the prophetic author of chs. 40–48. Since the word
of God does not return to God empty but accomplishes what it purposes (Isa
55:11), the reason for nonfulfillment must lie with the people whose sins have
created an "obstacle, stumbling block" (*mikšôl*, 14b). The "way" (*derek*), therefore, loses the particular reference it had in 40:3 and assumes a broader and
less specific meaning—not just a way of life in general but a way of life in conformity with prophetic example and teaching and, in the context of Isa 40–66,
the example and teaching of the Servant-prophet of ch. 53. To that extent, I
agree with Zimmerli's "ethical interpretation" of *derek*, "the way" (1963 [1950],
217–33), against the objections of Oswalt (1998, 486–87) and Childs (2000, 470).

The full import of this exegetical procedure only emerges, however, in juxtaposition with the previous passage. We have had occasion to note more than
once the deliberate alternation of judgment and reassurance in these chapters.
In this instance the contrast is between the children of the sorceress of 57:3–13a
and the contrite and humble faithful of 57:15. While the people addressed—
"my people" (*'ammî*)—is ideally the community as a whole, as in 40:1 ("Comfort, O comfort my people"), it is already becoming clear that there is a price to
pay for belonging to God's people and that the privilege can be forfeited.

The consolation offered in 40:1 is therefore not unconditional. The point is
made and the theme laid out in the opening statement of this last section of the
book (56:1), where the author sets the tone by enjoining the practice of justice
and righteousness *in view of* a turning point that still lies in the future (56:1).
We might also mention the mysterious passage in which the disciples hear the
voice of their teacher from behind them, that is, from beyond the grave: "This
is the way (*zeh hadderek*); keep to it" (30:21).

As is often the case in prophetic preaching, especially in Ezekiel (Ezek 7:19;
14:3–4, 7; 44:12), the obstacle that must be removed is a sinful way of life and

especially a sinful addiction to alien cults of a kind graphically illustrated in the previous passage. The author is not concerned to clarify to whom the injunction to build up and clear the road is addressed, but we can at least rule out, both here and in 40:3, members of the heavenly court (Childs 2000, 470 and others). Both here and at 58:1, the expression "my people" (v 14b) refers to the community or nation as a whole, as we have just seen, but polarization in the community, already well underway, will result in a situation in which the people of YHVH, "my people," will be explicitly limited to the elect among them (65:22), those who mourn (57:9; 61:2–3; 66:10), and those who seek after their God (65:10).

Dependence on existing Isaianic material, in evidence throughout the passage, suggests that the author, faced with the challenge of a new and problematic situation, is creating new Isaianic prophecy out of old. The superscription (v 15a) identifies the speaker of the saying as the Enthroned One of Isaiah's vision (6:1), whose holiness is proclaimed in the liturgy of the seraphim (6:3), and whose essence is enshrined in the title "The Holy One of Israel" (qědôš yiśrā'ēl), an expression appearing in all sections of the book.

Holiness signifies apartness, transcendence, and therefore raises the question of location, the place where God resides. The simple answer is that gods, like people, live in their houses, and that therefore YHVH lives in his house in Jerusalem on Mount Zion. But simple answers rarely satisfy, and since this way of thinking could (and did) lead to crass anthropomorphic representations, and could be (and was) manipulated to their own ends by the personnel who controlled the temple, more sophisticated views evolved among the learned. The Deuteronomists elaborated what von Rad called a Name theology: YHVH has placed his Name (Deut 12:5), or caused it to dwell (Deut 12:11; 14:23 etc.), in the sanctuary, with the implication that divine presence is realized and may be experienced in the invocation of the Name in worship. This is the origin of the idea of the divine Name as a kind of hypostasis of and circumlocution for God (as in bārûk haššēm, "Blessed be the Name").

Other priestly and scribal circles came up with the theologoumenon of the divine glory or effulgence (kābôd; Greek doxa) as a way of expressing presence and activity without sacrificing transcendence. In the wilderness narratives, the kābôd is represented in the familiar theophanic language of fire, cloud, and smoke, especially in association with the wilderness sanctuary (e.g., Exod 24:16; 25:18). The concept is well developed in Ezekiel and was certainly familiar to the prophetic authors of Isa 40–66 (40:5; 58:8; 59:19; 60:1–2; 66:18–19; see Weinfeld 1995; Westermann 1997).

The cluster of terms at the beginning of this short discourse creates a strong impression of transcendence through the temporal dimension of time without end and the spatial dimension of height. The latter—God's dwelling in highest heaven, in a high and holy place—echoes the language of liturgical hymns (Pss 7:8; 56:3; 102:20; 150:1; including the psalm-like passage Isa 33:5). The expression "a high and holy place" is a hendiadys composed of mārôm (also Isa 33:5, 16; 58:4) and qādôš (also Ps 150:1), both substantives indicating location. There is not only no mention of the temple (whether already in existence or not) but the earthly counterpart to the heavenly location is the divine presence among the contrite and humble, meaning also the poor and the oppressed. With this we may compare 66:1–2:

> Heaven is my throne, the earth is my footstool.
> What kind of house could you build for me?
> What kind of place for my abode?
> Did not my hand make all of these,
> and all these things came to be?
> But on these I look with favor:
> the poor, the afflicted in spirit, and those who tremble at my word.

A similar expression of the inadequacy of any place of worship is heard in Solomon's prayer at the dedication of the first temple, composed at roughly the same time as these chapters in Isaiah:

> Will God indeed dwell on earth? Even heaven and the highest heaven cannot contain you, much less this house that I have built. (2 Kgs 8:27)

Since Solomon's prayer occurs in the context of the dedication of the temple, it can hardly be interpreted as an outright rejection of the idea of divine presence in a temple. Yet it would be wrong to minimize the force and originality of the prophetic redefinition of religious priorities, according to which ceremony, and even the sacrificial cult, take second place to the option for the poor and oppressed. We will return to this theme in the Comments on the last chapter of the book.

The promise to foreswear anger and to bring healing (vv 16–19) follows. Whybray (1975, 208) has the interesting suggestion that this and similar promises of salvation in chs. 40–66 are in response to corporate cultic lamentations in which the psalmist complains of God's anger or inattention. He cites Pss 44:23–24; 74:1; and 79:5, and to these we add Ps 85, which has many parallels with Isa 56–66. The psalmist asks God whether he will be angry forever, prolonging his wrath from one generation to the next, and prays for him to revive his people. The petition ends with the assurance that God will speak peace to his people and that his salvation is near for those who fear him (*qārôb lîrē'âv yiš'ô*). Even closer is the parallel between Isa 57:16a and Ps 103:9:

> *kî lo' lĕ'ôlām 'ārîb / vĕlo' lāneṣaḥ 'eqṣôp* (Isa 57:16a)

> For I will not be forever accusing,
> nor will I be always angry.

> *lo' lāneṣaḥ yārîb / vĕlo' lĕ'ôlām yiṭṭôr* (Ps 103:9)

> He will not be always accusing,
> nor will he keep up his anger forever.

Why God should restrain his anger is explained (16b) with reference to the creation of humanity, according to which God blew the breath of life (něšāmâ ḥayyim) into the first man's nostrils (Gen 2:7). The point seems to be that indefinite exposure to the divine anger would reduce that divinely originating essence, resulting in weakness and eventually death.

There follows (17) one of the summary accounts of Israel's history as a history of religious and moral failure, summarized here rather surprisingly in the accusation of avarice (beṣaʿ). Such back-references are characteristic of the second half of the book, using allusions (familiar from psalms) to the divine anger (cf. 42:25; 48:9; 51:17, 20, 22), abandonment (54:7), and the hiddenness, silence, or sleep of God (40:27; 42:14; 54:8). In fact, 57:17 looks much like a restatement of the consoling word spoken to Zion in 54:7–8:

For a brief space of time I forsook you,
but with love overflowing I will bring you back.
In an outburst of anger I hid my face from you for a while,
but with love never failing I have pitied you.

The brief discourse ends with words of promise (57:18–19). The God of Israel is a God who strikes but also heals the blows he inflicts: he kills and gives life, he wounds and heals (Deut 32:39 cf. Isa 6:10; 19:22; 30:26). That he is also a comforting God is one of the major themes of Isa 40–66 (40:1; 49:13; 51:3, 12, 19; 52:9), and it includes the image of the mother comforting her child (66:13). Among those to be comforted are the mourners (ʾăbēlîm, miṯʾabbēlîm: 61:2–3; 66:10), mentioned also here.

The only parallel to the curious phrase "fruit of the lips" (nîb śĕpātayim) is the even more curious "the bullocks of our lips" (pārîm śĕpātēnû) in Hos 14:2. The reference is clearly to hymns of praise that either accompany or, more likely, substitute for animal sacrifice, which is one of several indications in these chapters of a certain reserve with respect to the sacrificial system and the temple cult in general. As in ordinary funerary rites, mourning has a fixed terminus (60:20). So the day will come when those who now mourn will have songs of praise and thanksgiving on their lips, a conviction expressed toward the end of the book in the form of eschatological reversal: my servants will rejoice and sing while you (their opponents) will be shamed and lament (65:13–14). The same reversal is expressed in pure Isaianic terms in the Gospel Beatitudes: "Blessed are those who mourn, for they will be comforted" (Matt 5:4 cf. Luke 6:21).

The final statement (vv 20–21) looks like an addition with the purpose of excluding the reprobate in the community from the promise of well-being addressed to all and sundry, those near and those far off, in the previous verse. If so, it would have been added at a time when the lines between different parties were more sharply drawn. In this respect, it resembles the dark finale of the book (66:24), which has the effect of excluding the reprobate from the eschatological worship offered in Jerusalem (66:22–23). Perhaps the same scribe added the practically identical finale to chs. 40–48 (48:22), where its relevance is not so obvious. In that case, it could have served as a structural marker dividing chs.40–66 into three sections of nine chapters each, a suggestion first made, as far as I have been able to determine, by Bernhard Duhm.

In conclusion: This brief prophetic discourse provides the first clear indications of dependence on both the first (chs. 1–39) and the second section of the book (40–55). The command to prepare the way of YHVH (40:3) is now attributed to the Enthroned One of Isaiah's vision (6:1) but is issued with different wording and different emphases to apply to a new situation, that of the early, uncertain decades of Iranian control of Judah. The message is still one of comfort (57:18 cf. 40:1) following the termination of hostility between YHVH and his people (57:16–18 cf. 40:2). The difference now is that God's people can no longer simply be identified with the people as a whole. The question of the identity of the true Israel of God will be raised in an increasingly sharp and confrontational manner throughout these last chapters of the book.

TRUE FASTING, TRUE PIETY (58:1–14)

(Barré 1985, 94–97; Barrick 1982, 481–503; Brongers 1975b, 212–16; Dahood 1976, 105; Daris 1978, 106–9; Diebner 1998, 139–56; G. R. Driver 1934b, 53–54; Hoppe 1983, 44–47; Hurowitz 1997, 43–52; Koenen 1988b, 564–65; 1989a, 255–58; Kosmala 1967, 69–81; Lau 1994, 240–61; Podella 1989; Polan 1986, 173–242; Schottroff 1997, 263–78; Zwickel 1991, 37–40)

TRANSLATION

i

58   ¹Shout it out loud, do not hold back,
    raise your voice like a trumpet!
    Proclaim to my people their transgression,[a]
    to the household of Jacob their sins.
    ²Yet they seek guidance from me day after day
    and take pleasure in knowing my ways,
    like a nation that does what is right,
    that has not abandoned the justice of its god.
    They ask of me just decisions,
    they take pleasure in approaching God.

ii

    ³"Why should we fast," they say,[b] "when you take no notice?
    Why should we afflict ourselves when you do not acknowledge it?"
    "Look, on your fast days you pursue your own interests,[c]
    you oppress all your workers.[d]
    ⁴Look, your fasting leads only to disputes and quarrels
    and striking with vicious fists.

The fast you are keeping today
will not give you a hearing on high.

iii

5Is the fast that I favor
a day for humble self-affliction of this kind,[e]
for bowing down the head[f] like a bulrush,[g]
making one's bed of sackcloth and ashes?
Is this what you call a fast,
a day acceptable to YHVH?
6Is not this the fasting[h] that I favor:
to free those unjustly detained,
to loosen the straps of the yoke,
to release the oppressed into freedom,
pulling off every yoke?
7Is it not sharing your bread with the hungry,
bringing into your home the homeless,[i]
clothing the one you see naked,[j]
not hiding yourself from your neighbor?[k]
8Then your light will break out like the dawn,
your wound will quickly be healed;[l]
your vindication will precede you,
the glory of YHVH will be your rearguard.
9Then when you call, YHVH will answer;
when you cry out he will say, 'Here I am.' "

iv

"If you banish perverse conduct[m] from among you,
pointing the finger, and malicious talk,
10if you offer[n] your substance[o] to the hungry
and satisfy the appetite of the afflicted,
your light will shine in the darkness,
your darkness will become like the noonday light.
11YHVH will always be your guide,
he will see to your needs in an arid land,[p]
he will strengthen your bones.[q]
You will be like a well-watered garden,
like a spring whose water never fails.
12Some of you will rebuild[r] the ancient ruins,
you will build again on foundations laid long ago;
you will be called repairer of the breach,
restorer of ruined dwellings.[s]

v

13If you refrain from travel on the Sabbath,
from engaging in business[t] on my holy day;

if you call the Sabbath a delight,
this holy day of YHVH most esteemed —
if you honor it, not following your inclinations,
or pursuing your own affairs
or engaging in idle talk[u] —
[14]then you will take delight in YHVH.
I shall set you[v] astride on the heights of the earth,
I shall give you[v] the heritage of your ancestor Jacob to enjoy."
This is what YHVH has spoken.

NOTES

4QIsaiah[d] has a few words from vv 1–3, 5–7, and 4QIsa[n] some words from vv 13–14.

[a] 1QIsaiah[a] has pl., but MT should be retained.

[b] Added with LXX (*legontes*), Symm., Theod., Tg. (*'mryn*); Tg. also omits negatives in 3a, no doubt *reverentiae causa*.

[c] *ḥepeṣ* understood as in v 13 and Qoh 3:1, 17 etc. Both LXX (*ta thelēmata*) and Vulg. (*voluntas vestra*) take the alternative meaning, "pleasure."

[d] The BHS proposal, *'ōbĕtêkem*, "your debtors," is unnecessary because *ngś* refers to oppression of various kinds, not just exacting payment for debts; cf. LXX *hupocheirious humōn*, "those under your control;" Syr. understands "your idols" → *'aṣabbêkem*.

[e] Literally, "a day for a person to afflict his soul."

[f] 1QIsaiah[b] has *r'šk*, "your head."

[g] LXX, curiously, "not even if you twist your neck like a ring (*hōs krikon*)"; cf. Job 40:26, where *'agmon*, "the ring," perhaps made out of twisted bulrushes, is in Leviathan's snout; cf. Vulg. *quasi circulum*.

[h] 1QIsaiah[a] adds the relative pronoun: "which I favor."

[i] MT adds *'ăniyyim*, "afflicted," absent from Syr., probably an explanatory gloss on the rarer *mĕrûdîm* (only here and Lam 1:7; 3:19); see G. R. Driver 1937.

[j] 1QIsaiah[a] adds *beged*, "[with a] garment."

[k] Literally, "your flesh" (*bĕśārĕkâ*), that is, "fellow human beings," rather than "hide none of your meat (*bāśār*) for yourself" (Dahood 1976, 105).

[l] Literally, "your healing (*'ărukātĕkâ*) will quickly spring up," with reference to the formation of a new layer of skin over a wound.

[m] Reading *muṭṭâ* (cf. Ezek 9:9) for MT *môṭâ*, "yoke"; cf. Tg. *'styvt dyn*, "perversions of judgment."

[n] Read *tāpîq* Hiphil → *pûq*; for the meaning, see Ps 140:9; 144:13.

[o] MT *napšekâ*, "your soul, yourself"; LXX paraphrases *ton arton sou ek psuchēs sou*, "your bread from your soul." On the basis of Akk. *napāšu* = "to be spacious, abundant," G. R. Driver (1934b, 53–54) translates the first *nepeš* "plenty, "abundance"; *nepeš* therefore would have two different meanings in the same line.

p   MT ṣaḥṣaḥôt → ṣḥḥ connotes whiteness or bareness; cf. Lam 4:7; Ezek
    24:7–8; 26:4,14; Neh 4:7; Ps 68:7. REB "in the bare desert" corrects NEB "in
    the shimmering heat," which is preferable to "vorzügliche Speisen" (Koenen
    1988b, 564–65).
q   1QIsaiahᵃ and 1QIsaᵇ have pl. *yhlysv,* "your bones will be strengthened."
r   LXX *oikodomēthēsontai* and Vulg. *aedificabuntur,* "they will be rebuilt,"
    presuppose Qal Passive (*ûbūnû*) or Pual (*ûbunnû*) for MT *ûbūnû* Active.
s   MT "paths for dwelling" does not make good sense, pace Duhm 1922, 439:
    "Wiederhersteller der Strassen zum Wohnen" = "Restorer of the streets for
    living"); and *nĕtîbâ,* "path," is almost exclusively used metaphorically; read
    nĕtîṣôt, "ruins," for MT *nĕtîbôt.*
t   MT *ḥăpāṣêkâ* pl. is unusual; cf. sing. 13c; 1QIsaᵇ also has sing.
u   MT *vĕdabbēr dābār,* "or speaking a word," literally; LXX adds "in anger."
v   1QIsaiahᵃ, 1QIsaᵇ, LXX, Syr., and Tg. All have 3d person in 14a, likewise
    (with the exception of 1QIsaᵇ⁾ in 14b; but YHVH occurs frequently in *ora-
    tio recta* of YHVH, as in 2c, 5c, 8b, and 9a.

COMMENTS

In contrast to what precedes and follows, chs. 58–59 have a consistency of subject matter, approach, and tone that sets them apart as a distinct section. They
also begin with a command to a prophet to do what prophets traditionally do
(58:1) and end with a rare intrusion of the prophetic-authorial voice (59:21).
This first passage, 58:1–14, is, in addition, clearly distinguished from what precedes it by *'āmar 'ĕlohay* ("says my God," 57:21), and the conclusion is equally
clearly delineated by "this is what YHVH has spoken" (58:14). The mention of
Jacob at the beginning and end of both 58 and 58–59, rare in chs. 56–66 (elsewhere only 60:16; 65:9), forms a kind of inclusion or bracketing.

There are nonetheless some rough transitions in ch. 58. The injunction to
the prophet to proclaim the sin of the people is somewhat unexpectedly followed by a flattering reference to their positive religious outlook, one that does
not seem to be ironic (vv 1–2). Then we hear a complaint of a kind that must
have been common in those first difficult and uncertain decades of Persian
rule (3a cf. Isa 63:7–64:12; Mal 3:14–15), and indeed on many occasions since:
we pray, we fast, we sacrifice; why doesn't it *work?* To this complaint there are
three answers, vv 3b–4, 5–9a, and 9b–12, which most critical commentators
have found difficult to explain without a theory of serial composition or the
successive expansion of an original core (for Michel 1965–1966, 213–30, consisting in vv 1–3a + 5–9a). That 5a originally followed immediately after 3a is
suggested by the quite different and less radical kind of objection to the people's
fasting in vv 3b–4. Furthermore, the question about fasting and self-affliction
in v 3a is taken up in the same terms only in v 5a. Then again, the reply to the
complaint appears to conclude with the call-response statement in v 9a (compare 65:12, 24; 66:4; Zech 7:13) but is followed by a new set of injunctions in
9b–12. Finally (a point of no great importance) vv 13–14 deal with the quite dif-

ferent subject of Sabbath observance (cf. 56:2, 4, 6) and have therefore more often than not been considered either an addendum (e.g., Duhm 1922, 440) or a separate saying (e.g., Volz 1932, 228–29.)

The fact that the injunction to proclaim *bĕgārôn*, literally, "with the throat," and blow the trumpet or ram's horn (*šôpār*) is addressed to a prophet is explicitly if superfluously stated in the Targum. This is what the prophets of old did all the time. When the people broke the covenant, Hosea was commanded to put the trumpet to his lips (Hos 8:1). The prophet is a sentinel (*ṣōpeh*) who must warn the people by doing the same (Ezek 33:1–9). The trumpet blast warns of danger: "Is a trumpet blown in the city and the people are not afraid?" (Amos 3:6a). The public denunciation of sin, *social sin* in the first place, is the primary and essential prophetic function:

> As for me, I am filled with power,
> with YHVH's spirit,
> to proclaim to Jacob his transgression,
> to Israel his sin. (Mic 3:8)

The injunction in 58:1 is simply the Micah text restated, one of many indications of the rereading (*relecture*), reassimilation, and taking further (*Fortschreibung*) of older prophecy going on in Jewish communities in this period.

The statement about the religious life of the particular community addressed is succinct and well rounded, beginning and ending with their seeking guidance of God (*drš, š'l*) and taking pleasure (*ḥēpeṣ*) in religious exercises. Traditionally, religious guidance was available through the recognized channels of the priesthood and officially designated prophets—for example, on matters of clean and unclean (Hag 2:10–14) or on when and how to fast (Zech 7:1–14). The priest in particular was responsible for religious teaching (*tôrâ*) and handing down authoritative rulings (*mišpĕṭê-ṣedeq*). But the most important and paradigmatic form of "approach to God" (*qirbat 'ĕlohîm*) was through sacrifice, by "bringing near" (*hiqrîb*) a victim—so much so that, even as the sacrificial system declined in prestige throughout the Second Temple period, the language of sacrifice could be used to articulate other forms of religious expression. We saw one example in the preceding passage (57:19 with Note). Qumranic and early Christian writings present many illustrations of the same phenomenon, such as Paul's use of the term *prosagōgē*, "access [to God]" (Rom 5:2), a term taken from the sacrificial cult vocabulary, corresponding to *qirbat 'ĕlohîm*, used here.

The complaint of these religious people that follows (3a) is easy to understand and perhaps even sympathize with. The common perception was, and is, that religious activities such as fasting are designed to have beneficial results for their practitioners. The miserable social conditions obtaining during the first century of Persian rule, to which several biblical texts attest (Hag 1:6, 9–11; 2:16–19; Zech 8:10; Neh 5:1–5), suggest that this was not happening. Also, past disasters continued to cast a long and dark shadow. Hence, the prevalence of communal laments and complaints in the temple liturgy and private devotion during the Second Temple period (Isa 63:7–64:12; Ezra 9:5–15; Neh 9:6–37; Dan 9:4–19; 4Q504 etc.).

It is interesting that the people addressed had complained about the inefficacy of fasting rather than of other religious exercises, for example, prayer and sacrifice. Fasting and mourning as a response to extreme crisis were distinctive features of religious life in the post-disaster period (see Excursus 3). For example, they are attested in the account of the delegates from the north to a temple of YHVH, who found themselves in the wrong place at the wrong time and were slaughtered by Ishmael in Mizpah (Jer 41:4–8). The fact that their clothes were torn, their bodies gashed, and their beards shaved off suggests that they were also fasting.

Even closer is the account of a later delegation (early winter 518 B.C.E.) sent to inquire about the fasts of the fifth and seventh months. These fasts commemorated the sequence of disasters from the burning of the Jerusalem temple to the assassination of Gedaliah (Zech 7:1–3 cf. 2 Kgs 25:8, 25). The prophetic rejection of this practice as disingenuous and self- interested (Zech 7:4–14) seems to have served as a model for both Isa 58:3b–4 and 58:5–9a.

These holy days had become occasions for pursuing the people's own interests (Zech 7:5–6, they fast only for themselves). What they should have been doing was practicing true justice (mišpaṭ 'ĕmet, Zech 7:9a cf. mišpĕṭê-ṣedeq, Isa 58:2c) and looking after the needs of widows, orphans, resident aliens, and the poor, a message that is restated in more concrete terms in Isa 58:6–7. It is implied that in the absence of outreach to those in need there can be no genuine piety. Both discourses (Zech 7:4–14; Isa 58:1–14), finally, feature the call-response statement referred to above (Zech 7:13; Isa 58:9a).

Isaiah 58:1–14 provides one more example of the assimilation of the older prophetic social ethic and the forms of speech in which it was expressed to a more discursive and sustained kind of discourse. Volz described chs. 56–66, and ch. 58 in particular, as the work more of a preacher, pastor, or synagogue leader than a prophet, one whose reliance on existing prophecies known to his hearers, which he reapplied to the situation of the community of his own day, was meant to demonstrate that he stood in the prophetic tradition (1932, 197, 223). Such a role and such a setting would be particularly appropriate with respect to 58:1–14, which is much closer to the genre of sermon than of prophetic oracle. Even though it scans in a fairly regular tricola meter, it could be written out in prose as a highly interactive sermon. What we are witnessing, then, is the transformation of prophet to preacher and the beginnings of what can be called ecclesiastical literature.

The miserable social conditions that Nehemiah claims to have rectified (Neh 5:1–13) led some commentators to read Isa 58:3b–4 as an addendum from that time (mid–fifth century B.C.E), but conditions in the early years of Persian rule could have been as bad or worse—given the drought, bad harvests, lack of employment, inflation, and social unrest (cf. Hag 1:5–6, 10–11; 2:16–17; Zech 8:10).

The second response to the complaint (vv 5–9a) goes further than a criticism of the abuses to which all forms of religious piety are potentially subject. It appears to reject the activity as then understood and practiced and to do so in a manner reminiscent of what earlier prophets had to say about sacrifice (Amos 5:21–25; Isa 1:12–17; Mic 6:6–8). It is unlikely, however, that the preacher is rejecting fasting out of hand. Detailed allusion to the epiphenomena of fasting—hanging the head, sleeping on the ground, sackcloth and ashes—suggests otherwise, and the preacher goes on to identify a very different set of actions as an acceptable form of fasting.

The Christian reader will inevitably be reminded of what Jesus says in the Sermon on the Mount (Matt 6:16–18) about genuine and disingenuous ways of fasting. The common denominator seems to be the equal or greater degree of self-abnegation required in order to alleviate the sufferings of others. It is more acceptable in the sight of God, and certainly more difficult and costly, to direct one's energy toward this end rather than to expend it in the kind of self-dramatization involved in the practice of fasting, as described. In the event, commemorative and penitential fasting did not disappear, though Zech 8:18–19 declares that the former will in the future provide occasions for rejoicing rather than sadness.

In the alternative form of fasting recommended, the primacy is given to releasing people under some form of constraint, judicial or otherwise. The language has a high level of specificity: loosening the bonds of wickedness (*ḥarṣubbôt rešaʿ*, epexegetical genitive); untying the straps of the yoke, with the verb *ntr* Hiphil, used elsewhere of setting prisoners free (Ps 105:20; 146:7); releasing the oppressed, in which the idiom *šallaḥ ḥopšî* is used elsewhere of the manumission of slaves (Exod 21:26–27; Deut 15:12–13,18; Jer 34:8–16); getting rid of physical constraint—the yoke around the neck or the bonds and shackles around the arms or legs (cf. Jer 2:20; 5:5; 30:8). Freedom is the first and indispensable requisite.

In the context of this place and time, we may find here a reference to indentured service resulting from insolvency. The conditions to which the relevant biblical texts refer can easily be imagined: a succession of bad harvests, creating an immediate crisis for a subsistence agrarian economy; the individual small farmer forced to borrow at exorbitant rates (up to 75 percent in Mesopotamia; no comparable data available for Syria–Palestine) to pay for seed for the next harvest; indentured service of members of the household as a result of failing to amortize the debt; loss of the plot of land on which survival depended; the breakup of the household, whose members then go to swell the population of casual laborers, the homeless, and down-and-outs.

To practice true fasting is therefore to work to undo the conditions, morally corrupt and corrupting as they are, underlying such situations. Whether the preacher also had in mind political liberation (Westermann 1969, 337, referring to Isa 61:1–2) is less certain, though it is quite possible that the message of Isa 40–55 resulted in a new and enhanced value being attached to the freedom of the individual. But freedom without the means to sustain a decent existence is a hollow promise, then as now. For this reason the texts presents the need to feed (literally, "break bread with") the hungry, house the homeless (literally, "the wanderers"), clothe the naked, and not hide oneself from one's own flesh and blood, that is, one's fellow–human beings.

As the same wording in the Deuteronomic law makes clear (Deut 22:1–4), "hiding oneself" means pretending that these people are not there, persuading oneself that someone else will take care of them, or just wishing they would go away. The final judgment scene in Matt 25:31–46, which may have this Isaianic text in mind, makes the fulfillment of this true "fasting" the *exclusive* criterion for salvation or reprobation.

The assurance contingent on the performance of true fasting with which this second response ends (vv 8–9) reveals the true nature of the complaint. We find the same language at the beginning of the eschatological core of Isa 56–66 addressed to Jerusalem, the people personified:

> Arise, shine forth, for your light (*'ôrek*) has come,
> the glory of YHVH (*kĕbôd YHVH*) has dawned (*zārāḥ*) over you! (60:1)

In later Isaianic passages, and in Jewish end-time imagery in general, "light" stands for the consummation, the fulfillment of the people's aspirations. The promise that "I will turn their darkness into light" (42:16) has obviously not been fulfilled, and now they are being told why not. The same point is made by a subtle use of language in the next statement, that "your wound will quickly be healed" or, more literally, "your new layer of skin [covering the wound] will quickly spring up." The unexpected, and in the context anomalous, use of this verb "spring up" (*ṣāmāḥ*) can be explained with reference to the "springing up" of the new events (*ḥădāšôt*) predicted by the prophetic author of 40–55 (42:9; 43:19). Hence, the promised healing is the coming into existence of a new situation—and in the near future; compare "in an instant I will bring about my victory, my deliverance goes forth" (*qārôb ṣidqî yāṣā' yišʿî*, 51:5). Another indication of the author's starting point in the expectations aroused by the publication (in whatever form) of Isa 40–55 is the allusion to the glory of YHVH as their rearguard, drawing on 52:12, itself recalling the angel of YHVH and the cloud that formed Israel's rearguard at the Papyrus Sea (Exod 14:19–20).

If, as proposed, vv 3b–4 and 5–9a were originally distinct responses to the complaint, they must have been combined before vv 9b–12 were added. With the exception of v 12, spoken to the community as a whole in spite of the suffixes in the singular, this additional reply is a conditional promise addressed to the individual. Westermann (1969, 339) finds an instructive parallel in Job 11:13–20 in which, if evil conduct is avoided,

> your life will shine brighter than the noonday,
> its darkness will be like the morning. (11:17)

Compare:

your light will shine in the darkness,
your darkness will become like the noonday light. (Isa 58:10b)

Avoidance of false accusations (if this is the meaning of "pointing the finger") and defamatory speech (v 9b) are of the same order as the accusations in vv 3b–4, while concern for the hungry (v 10a) is in line with the injunctions in v 7a. The promises contingent on performing these works of justice and mercy (8–9, 11) also run parallel. The concluding verse, referring to ancient ruins, the rebuilding of which still lay in the future, suggests a date several generations after the Babylonian conquest.

Fasting is no longer the issue after vv 3b–9a, but the urgent need to explain in moralistic terms the unsatisfactory situation in which those addressed find themselves is still felt. The final segment (vv 13–14) is generally taken to be an addendum (we might call it a minisermon on Sabbath observance), and its distinctive character is acknowledged in 1QIsaᵃ by an almost entirely blank line preceding it. The first conditional clause is unclear and the translation uncertain. The rare idiom *hēšîb regel min* (literally, "turning the foot away from [something]") must imply turning away from something reprehensible (cf. Prov 4:27, *hāsēr raglĕkâ mērā'*, "turning away from doing evil") but may, in addition, have been chosen to indicate the prohibition of travel on Sabbath (literally, "turn the foot away from the Sabbath"). There is, at any rate, no longer a concern for the humanitarian or philanthropic aspect of the Sabbath rest, comparable to the accusation of exploiting the fast days in 3b–4, and in agreement with the Deuteronomic formulation of the Sabbath command (Deut 5:12–15). Sabbath observance is considered exclusively an act of obedience and devotion to God.

It was only after the fall of Jerusalem and the deportations that the Sabbath achieved confessional status together with circumcision and the purity laws — neither of which, however, is mentioned in chs. 56–66. The celebration of the Sabbath and new moon festival is attested in both biblical and nonbiblical texts for the time of the Kingdoms. It was an occasion for visiting a "man of God" (2 Kgs 4:23) and for the changing of the palace guard (2 Kgs 11:5–9). It was subject to abuse, as were other festivals (Hos 2:13[11]), but it does not seem to have had any great prominence or diagnostic significance.

According to the Priestly theology, Sabbath was instituted at Sinai as a perpetual covenant (Exod 31:12–17; 35:2–3) though its observance, together with its first violation, was anticipated during the journey through the wilderness (Exod 16:22–30). The Sabbath of God on the seventh day of the Priestly creation recital (Gen 2:2–3) provided ultimate validation for its celebration by locating it within the created order. Not to celebrate the Sabbath is to be out of synchronism with that order.

The confessional status of the Sabbath is clear from the reassurance given to marginal individuals in the community in 56:1–8. For the first time there existed a situation in which the issue of membership was no longer ascriptive and unproblematic. Membership therefore called for recognizable distinguishing characteristics. With the destruction of the temple, the need for set times for liturgical gathering, prayer, and religious instruction would have been felt, though the origins of the synagogue and synagogue service remain obscure. The theological elaborations on the Sabbath by the Priestly-scribal class, an early stage of which is reflected in Ezekiel (20:12–24; 22:8, 26; 23:38; 44:24), could also have had an impact. The increasing prominence of the Sabbath is also apparent in the incidence of the personal name Shabbetai in Babylon, Elephantine (three), Syene (two), and Judah (Ezra 10:15; Neh 8:7; 11:16).

At the time of the composition of Isa 58:13–14, what was forbidden and permitted on Sabbath was still indeterminate. This was at the beginning of the process that would lead to the 39 categories of prohibited activities in *m. Šabb.*7:2, and our passage is too imprecise to provide much guidance in this respect. The earlier prohibition against selling (Amos 8:5) was, by the time of Nehemiah (Neh 10:32[31]; 13:16), broadened to include buying, even buying from foreigners, and to this was added a general prohibition of engaging in trade (Neh 13:15). A special concern for the sanctity of Jerusalem can be detected in the emphasis on avoiding going in and out of the city on Sabbath with the purpose of trading (Neh 13:19–22; Jer 17:19–27). We have no information from that time on the ʿerub, the maximum distance for travel (2000 cubits by the Roman period; Josephus, *Ant.* 12.8.4; Acts 1:12; CD 13:20–21; *m. ʿErub.* 4–5).

The promises, the fulfillment of which is to be contingent on Sabbath observance, are formulated on the basis of familiar and unspecific expressions of reassurance. "You will take delight in YHVH" is reminiscent of Job 22:26, and "I shall set you astride on the heights of the earth" is taken almost verbatim from the Song of Moses (Deut 32:13a), which also suggests the promise about Jacob's heritage (Deut 32:9,13a). The finale, "this is what YHVH has spoken," is borrowed from Isa 40:5 in order to confer the character of a prophetic pronouncement on what is, in effect, a very brief homiletic admonition.

It is noteworthy that, in contrast to the unconditional promises in chs. 40–55, promises are now conditional on genuine religious observance. We hear no more about an imminent decisive change in Israel's situation as a result of epoch-making international events, and the assurance of a return from the diaspora seems to have receded into the background.

EXCURSUS 3: FASTING IN ISAIAH 58:1–14

Fasting, the deliberate, temporary abstention from the consumption of food and perhaps also drink, is phenomenologically similar to dieting but distinguished from it by the ends it is meant to serve. It is not to our purpose to pursue the matter on a comparativist basis. Suffice it to say that these ends could include personal asceticism or purification, preparation for receiving a vision or participating in a ritual, and influencing the Deity or spirit to intervene—for example, in an economic or political crisis or in a healing or exorcism. In the early period in Israel, fasting could be part of a private ritual of mourning, for example, the seven-day fast for the dead Saul (1 Sam 31:13), but one also fasted during sickness, as David did for his mortally sick child (2 Sam 12:15–23) and the psalmist claimed to have done for his enemies (Ps 35:13).

Fasting was intended to influence the Deity and perhaps at the same time served an apotropaic function at critical moments of public life—when, for example, drought or military disaster threatened or could be anticipated (e.g., 1 Kgs 21:27–29; Jer 14:12; 36:6, 9; 2 Chr 20:3). The parallel 40-day fasts of Moses on the mountain (Deut 9:9) and Elijah on the way to the mountain (1 Kgs 19:8) have been variously explained, but probably served, in the manner of hagiography, to illustrate the preternatural stature of these heroic figures and divine providence in their regard.

All of these instances were occasional or ad hoc; it was only after the fall of Jerusalem and destruction of the temple that fast days became a regular feature on the liturgical calendar, though a critical situation (e.g., a plague of locusts, a drought) could still call for "sanctifying a fast, convoking a liturgical assembly" (Joel 1:14; 2:15; *m. Taʿanit* 1:4). The first scheduled fasts, in the fourth, fifth, seventh, and tenth months of the year, commemorated successive stages in the Babylonian conquest, from the beginning of the siege to the assassination of the Babylonian appointee Gedaliah (2 Kgs 25:1, 3, 8, 25). In the course of time only the fast of Yom Kippur survived (Lev 16:29 etc.), though pietistic communities and sects followed their own practice (e.g., Pharisees every Monday and Thursday, Luke 18:12; *Did.* 8:1).

The brief sermon on fasting in Isa 58 provides incidental information on the morphology of fasting and, to some extent, what it meant for those who fasted at that time. A first clue is the synonymous expression "to afflict oneself" (ʿin-nāh nepeš), used in connection with the Yom Kippur fast (Lev 16:29, 31; 23:27, 32; Num 29:7), which suggests a deliberate diminution of vital energies in the pursuit of personal catharsis or ascesis. The preacher-prophet also shows little appreciation for the bowing of the head (cf. Ps 35:14), the posture of mourning that can have the same import.

Wearing sackcloth, a rough kind of burlap, symbolized the shroud in which the corpse was laid out, and ashes placed on the head, the earth in which the body of the deceased was laid (e.g., 1 Kgs 21:27; Jer 36:9; Joel 1:13; Jonah 3:5–10; Esth 4:2–3). Making one's bed of sackcloth is a reference to the practice of lying prone on the ground during a ritual of fasting (David in 2 Sam 12:15; Ahab in 1 Kgs 21:27; cf. *m.Taʿanit* 4:7); this also could simulate the laying out of the dead. The verb used here, *yṣʿ* Hiphil, appears elsewhere in a mortuary context: a psalmist speaks of making his bed in Sheol (Ps 139:8), and maggots form a bed (*yuṣṣaʿ*) in the underworld for the king of Babylon (Isa 14:11).

Tearing one's clothes, finally, is a ritualized stripping naked (1 Kgs 21:27–29; Esth 4:2–3). So Job, in his extremity, tears his robe, falls to the ground, and says, "Naked I came from my mother's womb, and naked I shall return there" (Job 1:20–21). The three "friends" likewise tear their robes, throw dust on their heads, and sit on the ground with him seven days and nights (Job 2:12–13). In other words, though Job is still alive, they perform the prescribed ritual mourning for the dead, a kind of *Kaddish*.

WHY GOD REMAINS INACTIVE
AND SILENT (59:1–8)

(Kendall 1984, 391–405; Kessler 1956, 335–58; Pauritsch 1971, 87–103; Polan 1986, 243–75; Sekine 1989, 136–39; Steck 1991a, 169–86, 203–9; Weissert 1967, 315–22; Wernberg-Møller 1954, 322–25)

TRANSLATION

59   [1]YHVH's arm is not so short that he cannot save,
     nor his hearing so dull[a] that he cannot hear.[b]
     [2]Your iniquities have created the rift
     between you and your God;
     your sins have concealed the Face from you[c]
     so that he does not hear.[d]
     [3]Your hands are stained[e] with blood,
     your fingers with iniquity;
     your lips utter what is false,[f]
     your tongue mutters what is perverse.
     [4]No one issues a summons justly,
     no one goes to law[g] honestly.
     Relying on worthless and fraudulent arguments,
     they conceive trouble and bring forth iniquity.[h]
     [5]They hatch vipers' eggs,[i]
     they spin spiders' webs;
     [if you eat their eggs you die.[j]
     The cracked egg[k] hatches out as a poisonous snake.][l]
     [6]Their webs will not serve for clothing,
     [they will not be able to clothe themselves with what they produce.][m]
     Their works are evil,
     they perpetrate deeds of violence.
     [7]Their feet run to evil,
     they hasten to shed innocent[n] blood.
     Their scheming is all perverse,
     bringing ruin and destruction[o] in its wake.
     [8]They are ignorant of the way of peace;
     justice does not guide their conduct.
     They have made their paths crooked for themselves;
     none who walks in them knows peace.

NOTES

[a]   1QIsaiah[a] has pl., "his ears are not so heavy."
[b]   LXX formulates v 1 as two questions.

^c Targum, Syr., Vulg., LXX have "his face"; LXX: "on account of your sins, he turned away his face from you." While *pānîm* may not be a technical term like *haššēm*, "the Name," the fact that it occurs elsewhere without the possessive adjective (Isa 53:3; Job 34:29) suggests that the omission here was deliberate.

^d Targum adds "your prayer" (*slvtkvn*).

^e MT *něgoʾǎlû* appears to be a compound of Niphal Perfect (*nigʾǎlû*) and Pual Perfect (*goʾǎlû*); see GKC §51h.

^f This half-verse is absent from 1QIsa^a but not from 1QIsa^b.

^g The probable sense of *špṭ*, Niphal, expressing reciprocity with respect to plaintiff and defendant (cf. Isa 43:26).

^h The four infinitive absolutes in 4b (*bātôaḥ, dabbēr, hārô, hôlêd*) express continuous action or a persistent pattern of behavior; this usage fell into desuetude in the postbiblical period and is replaced in 1QIsa^a and, with the exception of the third, in 1QIsa^b with the Perfect.

ⁱ MT sing. is collective; 1QIsa^a and LXX: pl.

^j Literally, "the one who eats [some of] their eggs will die"; LXX, more curiously: "The one about to eat their eggs, when he breaks one [of them], he finds wind and, in it, a basilisk"; Vulg. *quod confotum est erumpet in regulum*, "the one that is pierced hatches out as a serpent."

^k MT *hazzûreh* could be a rare weakened form of the fem. *hazzûrâ* cf. 1 Sam 28:15; Prov 24:14 (GKC §27u), agreeing with *bêṣâ*, "egg," fem. This is a fem. participle → *zûr* = "crush, squeeze, crack open"; cf. Judg 6:38 (Gideon's fleece), Job 39:15 (ostrich eggs trampled on); this meaning suits the context better than → *zûr* "stink," as in Job 19:17, *rûḥî zārāh lěʾištî*, "my breath stinks to my wife"; see Wernberg-Møller 1954: "a stinking egg hatches out as a serpent."

^l Verse 5b appears to be a gloss that interrupts the train of thought.

^m This, too, looks like a gloss; literally, "they will not cover themselves with their deeds": in MT and 1QIsa^b the verb is Hithpael *yitkassû*; 1QIsa^a has *yksv*, the more common Piel, but MT need not be emended; *maʿǎśêhem*, "their deeds, what they produce" may conceal a double meaning with *ʿśh* III = "cover, protect," cf. Ezek 17:17 and Ps 104:13 (*maʿǎśeh* = cloud?).

ⁿ Absent from LXX.

^o 1QIsaiah^a adds *vḥms*, "and violence."

COMMENTS

There is a clear association in style, mood, and substance between the previous chapter and the series of connected passages beginning at this point. A state of collective depression fed by disappointed hopes has led to the collapse of confidence in traditional religious resources, including prayer and fasting. The lament, or rather complaint, was voiced explicitly in 58:3a, whereas now (59:1) it is implicit in the preacher's response to it.

The present chapter goes further in presenting a sort of confession of sin in vv 9–15a, though God is addressed directly only in v 12. This leads at last to the positive response of YHVH promised in the previous chapter (58:9a) but now only affecting the penitent minority: *šābê pešaʿ bĕyiśrāʾēl*, "those who turn from transgression in Israel" (vv 15b–20), those who do "the true turning" (*tĕšûbâ*). The breaking up of the text into pericopes of manageable length demanded by commentary writing must not lead us to overlook these continuities. Torrey's summary of the chapter as a single composition (Torrey 1928, 439) is worth quoting:

> This great poem *de profundis* stands alone in the collection as a picture of sin and misery. The prevailing impression, through most of its extent, is of *darkness*. Sin has separated the people from their God (verse 2), his face is hidden from them. Thus the light is gone; they have become as blind men, staggering in the dark, groping for support, stumbling at noon as in twilight.

This first section (vv 1–8) exonerates YHVH of responsibility for the breakdown in communication and puts the blame squarely on barriers created by the community itself, resulting in an indictment of a kind common in older prophetic writings. There is a change of address from the second to the third person, beginning with v 5 and continuing through v 8, and some rather outré imagery in vv 5–6, which seemed to some scholars to justify setting off either vv 5–8 (Marti 1900, 376–77; Pauritsch 1971, 89) or vv 4–8 (Elliger 1928, 15–20; Volz 1932, 233) as a *Zusatz* (addition). Volz also thought that the language in this insertion must have been addressed to the reprobates in the community rather than to the community as a whole. These questions are generally impossible to decide with any assurance. It seems better to read 59:1–20 on the assumption that it constitutes a literary unity of some kind (with Westermann 1969, 344; Beuken 1989a, 124–30), though not necessarily composed at one time and by one author. For the presence of expansive or explanatory glosses in v 5b and the second half of v 6a, see the Notes.

In reviewing the various attempts to describe either this present subsection or 58:1–20 as a whole, form-critically, we may find it worthwhile to remember that we are not dealing with a transcript either of a liturgy (as Muilenburg 1956, 686–87) or a sermon (Kessler 1956, 337–38; Whybray 1975, 221, who calls it a "hell-fire sermon"). Kendall (1984, 391–405) neatly organizes the chapter around the ambivalent term *mišpāṭ*: it has the meaning "justice" in vv 1–8, and its absence is being decried; it carries the meaning "vindication" or "salvation" in 9–15a, and its absence is lamented by the people being addressed; and it at last comes into sight with God's intervention to judge and to save in 15b–20. Isaiah 58:1–20 is, in any case, a *literary* work that makes eclectic use of familiar resources from both the prophetic and the didactic traditions, together with familiar literary schemata.

As in so much of Isa 40–66, its tone is basically homiletic, and it is much closer to a sermon, or a brief abstract of a sermon, than to a prophetic saying.

It reflects the pervasive influence of the "new prophecy," decidedly homiletic in character, of the Deuteronomistic Levites, examples of which can be found in Deuteronomy, Jeremiah (note, for example, the small "sermon" on the Sabbath in Jer 17:19–27), and Zech 7–8. Since it is difficult to visualize socially disembodied individuals composing this kind of material for their own private edification or delectation, we conceive of it as presupposing some kind of synagogal or protosynagogal system, however rudimentary, during the early decades of Persian rule.

The derivative nature of the language and motifs is evident in the opening reference to the arm of YHVH, which paraphrases an earlier text:

Is my reach [arm] too short to rescue?
Do I lack the strength to deliver? (50:2)

In both texts the arm evokes the collective memory of the Exodus from Egypt, accomplished by God's "outstretched arm" (*bizrôaʿ nĕṭûyâ*, Exod 6:6; 15:16; Deut 4:34; 2 Kgs 17:36 etc.). The arm as the symbol of the power to save is also a common topos in the second part of the book (48:14; 51:5, 9–11; 52:10; 53:1; 59:16; 62:8).

Another familiar motif is the willful making dull ("making heavy") of the faculty of hearing. We recall the injunction addressed to Isaiah in the course of his vision: "Make this people dull of perception, hard of hearing, sight impaired, lest they see with their eyes, hear with their ears, and grasp with their mind, and then change their ways and be healed" (6:10). The same figure occurs in the homily in Zech 7:8–14: "The people made their ears dull [heavy] so that they could not hear" (7:11). Incidentally, Zech 7:8–14 has much in common with Isa 58–59, beginning with the pattern: injunction of the preacher–reaction of the congregation–positive result.

The arm, therefore, represents the ability and the ear the willingness to intervene on the plaintiff's behalf. The rupture in relationship is not YHVH's doing but the effect of the plaintiff's conduct, and to describe this a bewildering variety of terms is marshaled in this brief indictment: *ʿāvôn*, "iniquity," *ḥaṭṭaʾâ*, "sin," *šeqer*, "falsity," *ʿāvlâ*, "perversity," *tōhû*, "worthlessness," *šāvʾ*, "fraud," *ʿāmāl*, "trouble," *ʾāven*, "evil, deception," *ḥāmās*, "violence," *raʿ*, "evil." The effect is to create distance and to conceal the face of God.

YHVH does not himself hide his Face, an expression equivalent to withdrawing or averting the gaze in anger or disgust (8:17; 54:8; 64:6 and cf. 53:3). If this happens, some other factor must be involved. God's Face (*pānîm*) is God's presence, in some contexts serving as a kind of hypostasis, comparable to the divine *kābôd* ("glory, effulgence") or the *malʾāk* ("angel, messenger"), as in the narrative theme of guidance through the wilderness (Exod 33:14–15; Deut 4:37; Isa 63:9). This kind of language can be traced back to ancient Near Eastern court protocol. To see the face of the king is to be granted an audience and therefore to enjoy the royal favor. In one of the Amarna letters to the Egyptian court in the early fourteenth century B.C.E., Abimilku, ruler of Tyre, asks:

"When shall I see the face of my lord the king?" (*ANET*, 484). Transferred to the religious sphere, seeing the face of god (Akk.: *amāru pānī ili*) means participating in cult offered to the god, language encountered often in the biblical psalms in which the one who prays expresses the desire for an experience of the divine presence in worship (e.g., "When shall I come and behold the face of God?" Ps 42:3). The impression is, therefore, that the people addressed in 59:1–8 are taking part in religious activities, including fasting already mentioned, but without experiencing any of their beneficial effects.

There follows a more specific indictment of immoral, even criminal, activity. Being stained with blood (verbal stem *g'l*) connotes the polluting, miasmic effect of shedding innocent blood, whether on the hands or on the earth (e.g., Isa 1:15; 26:21). Abel's blood, which the ground received, cried out for vengeance, with the result that Cain was hidden from God's face, that is, presence (Gen 4:14). That murder is specifically indicated in Isa 58:3 is suggested by the reference later on (vv 6–7) to deeds of violence and the shedding of innocent blood.

This indictment, "their feet run to evil, they hasten to shed innocent blood" (7a), occurs in practically identical form in Prov 1:16 and 6:18 in connection with false testimony, one of several ways in which the judicial process could be undermined. We find the same association here, since the false and perverse utterance can be understood in a forensic sense as bringing false charges or as the issuance of an unwarranted summons or subpoena (e.g., Job 5:1; 9:16; 13:22; 31:35 cf. the technical Latin expression *in ius vocare*). The terminology (e.g., *špṭ* Hiphil cf. 43:26; 66:16) is explicitly forensic. The corruption of the judicial system, one of the principal targets of eighth-century prophetic diatribe, was (and is) one of the worst crimes of all, since it removed (removes) the last appeal for the victims of social injustice.

We are unfortunately in no position to decide whether the situation obtaining at that time and in that place actually warranted this extreme denunciation. To repeat, this is a kind of literary construct for which models were available. Several examples of a generally brief moral catechesis show up in prophetic books and in psalms, some of which include shedding innocent blood and oppressing the marginal elements in society (Isa 33:15; Jer 7:6; 22:3; Ps 15). We have just seen that v 7a is identical with Prov 1:16 (with the omission of *nāqî*, "innocent"), and the association of lying and treachery with the tongue and lips is commonplace in aphoristic writings (*lěšôn šeqer*, "a lying tongue," Prov 6:17; 12:19; 21:6; 26:28; *śiptê šeqer*, "lying lips," Prov 10:18; 12:12; 17:7).

The influence of the didactic tradition is also apparent in the multiplication of metaphors for the moral life that cluster around the *derek šālôm*, "the way of peace," in vv 7–8: *měsillâ*, "highway": Prov 16:17; *ma'gāl*, "cart track": Prov 2:9, 15, 18; 4:11, 26; 5:6, 21; *nětîbâ*, "path" : Prov 1:15; 3:17; 7:25; 8:2, 20; 12:28. With these metaphors, finally, the verb *'qš*, "pervert," "make crooked" (Isa 59:8b) and the corresponding adjective *'iqqēš* are often associated (Prov 2:15; 10:9; 22:5; 28:6).

Another indication of affinity with the didactic tradition is the metaphor of conception and birth introduced in v 4b and developed in rather strange fashion in vv 5–6a. While similar expressions, of uncertain provenance, appear elsewhere in Isaiah—bringing forth nothing but wind (26:18), conceiving chaff and bringing forth stubble (33:11)—the closest parallels are the practically identical statement in Job 15:35, which refers to the company of the godless; and Ps 7:15, which is addressed to the unrepentant: "They conceive trouble and bring forth deceit."

The familiar metaphor has suggested to the preacher a restatement in terms that may reflect popular folklore then familiar but now unknown. The species *ṣip'ônî* (*ṣepa'*)—known as a reptile whose bite is poisonous (Isa 11:8; 14:29; Jer 8:17; Prov 23:32), probably *vipera palastinensis* though both Vulg. and LXX translate "asp"—lays eggs that hatch out as an *'ep'eh*. One would suppose this to be a young viper, but the ancient versions are uncertain, and LXX identifies it as a basilisk, a legendary reptile, whose breath and glance were presumed to be fatal. The image of spiders' webs as inadequate clothing is odd indeed, and may have been introduced to show how the moral evils denounced by the author are responsible for the lack of the necessities of life, that is, food and clothing.

The indictment concludes with a longer restatement of an earlier finale, "There is no peace for the wicked" (57:21 cf. 48:22).

A COMMUNITY COMPLAINT (59:9–15a)

(Baldacci 1980, 237–42; Cheyne 1905, 172; Hanson 1975, 119–34; Kendall 1984, 391–405; Koenen 1988b, 565–67; Meinhold 1922, 156–57)

TRANSLATION

59 [9]Therefore, vindication remains far from us,
     deliverance is not in our grasp.[a]
     We wait for daylight, and there is only darkness,
     for light to dawn, and we walk in dark places.[b]
     [10]We grope[c] like the blind along a wall,
     we feel our way like the sightless;
     we stumble at midday as at twilight,
     like the walking dead among the healthy.[d]
     [11]We all growl like bears,
     like doves we keep on moaning.[e]
     We wait for vindication, but there is none,
     for salvation, but it is far from us.
     [12]Our transgressions against you are many,
     our sins bear witness[f] against us.
     Our transgressions are present to us,
     we know only too well our iniquities.

¹³We have transgressed,ᵍ we have disavowed YHVH,
we have turned away from our God.
We utter threatening and rebellious words,
 we mutter lies conceived in the heart.ʰ
¹⁴Justice is turned around,ⁱ
righteousness stays at a distance;
honesty stumbles in the street,
probity finds no entry.
¹⁵ᵃHonesty is nowhere to be found,ʲ
and whoever renounces evil is despoiled.ᵏ

NOTES

ᵃ   For the meaning of *mišpāṭ* and *ṣĕdāqâ*, see Notes and Comments on 56:1.
    The LXX, more than usually paraphrastic in this passage, has vv 9–11a and
    14b–15a in 3d-person pl.

ᵇ   Conjunction added with Syr., Vulg., Tg.; 1QIsaᵃ has sing. *b'plh* for MT
    pl., *bā'āpēlôt*, which I read as an intensive pl.

ᶜ   With 1QIsaᵃ, *ngšš* for MT *nĕgaššĕšāh*, 1st-person pl. Cohortative.

ᵈ   MT *bā'ašmannîm kāmmētîm* (1QIsaᵃ *b'šmvnym*) is obscure because *'ašman*
    is hapax, and the ancient versions are not helpful: LXX (cf. Syr.) "They shall
    groan like dying men" sounds like guesswork, while Tg., "The world is shut
    in our faces just as the graves are shut on the faces of the dead," is impres-
    sive but enigmatic; Vulg. *in caliginosis quasi mortui*, "like the dead in dark
    places," makes a good parallel to "at midday" cf. NEB "in the desolate under-
    world"; Meinhold's (1922) emendation to *bā'atnû šĕmāmâ kāmmētîm*,
    "destruction comes over us like the dead," is speculative, as also is Bal-
    dacci's (1980) allusion to the deities Eshmun and Mot; for other options,
    see Koenen (1988b); my translation assumes → *šmn*, "to be fat," "to be
    healthy," cf. *mr'* with similar meaning.

ᵉ   LXX "Like a bear and a dove they will go together"; in Tg. the bears are
    transformed into the enemies of Israel.

ᶠ   1QIsaiahᵃ has pl. *'nv'* correctly as against MT with pl. noun governing sing.
    verb *'ānĕtāh*; LXX *antestēsan*, "stand up," meaning standing up to testify.

ᵍ   *pāšoa'* is the first of six infinitive absolutes in this verse, giving a sense of
    continuous and unremitting activity and a regular pattern of behavior; in
    1QIsaᵃ *pšv'v*, the scribe inserted the vav superscript to emend to infinitive
    absolute but forgot to omit the final vav.

ʰ   Literally, "conceiving and meditating from the heart false things"; 1QIsaᵃ
    omits *hōrô* ("conceiving," more properly *hārô*), probably correctly, since its
    omission preserves metrical regularity and appropriate parallelism.

ⁱ   1QIsaiahᵃ has *v'syg*, "I will turn back," for MT *hussag* Pual, but MT is surely
    correct.

ʲ   Literally, "is lacking"; Tg. substitutes categories of people for the abstracts
    in 14–15a.

ᵏ   LXX "They have turned their mind from understanding" fits the context of vv 14–15a better than MT but is unsupported.

COMMENTS

Even if the initial "therefore" (*'al-kēn*)is an editorial link, vv 9–15a belong in style and substance with 1–8. Much of the language is derivative, as we shall see, giving the appearance more of a work of literary *bricolage* than a distinctive genre in the manner of classical form criticism. It is certainly not a community lament since, in spite of prolonged dwelling on the sad situation being experienced, God is addressed only in v 12. There is also no appeal for divine assistance and no assurance of a positive outcome—though the addition of vv 15b–20 might fill this lack (Volz 1932, 235–36). It is certainly not a lament by the prophetic party over the corruption of the "cult community," which has caused the delay in divine intervention (Hanson 1975, 119–34). The speaker clearly identifies with the community or congregation as a whole in this confession of spiritual disorientation and failure.

The confession in v 12 marks the point at which description of the condition in which the people find themselves (9–11 with inclusio) gives way to acknowledgment of the cause—namely, the low level of public and personal morality (vv 12–15a). The language throughout is vocative and homiletic. The prosodic question, whether this material is to be classed as poetry or prose, can be illustrated by presenting a reading without the familiar stichometric layout of our Hebrew Bible, as follows:

A Brief Sermon (Isaiah 59:1–15a)

YHVH's arm is not so short that he cannot save, nor is his hearing so dull that he cannot hear. It is, rather, your iniquities that have made a rift between you and your God; it is your sins that have concealed the Face from you, with the result that he does not hear. Your hands are stained with blood, your fingers with iniquity! Your lips utter what is false, your tongue mutters what is perverse! No one issues a summons justly, no one goes to law honestly. Relying on worthless and fraudulent arguments, they conceive trouble and bring forth iniquity. They hatch vipers' eggs, they spin spiders' webs, but their webs will not serve for clothing. Their works are evil, they perpetuate deeds of violence. Their feet run to evil, they hasten to shed innocent blood. Their scheming is all perverse, bringing ruin and destruction in its wake. They are ignorant of the way of peace, nor does justice guide their conduct. The paths they pursue are crooked; no one who walks in them knows peace.

Therefore, vindication remains far from us, deliverance is not in our grasp. We wait for daylight, and there is only darkness; for light to dawn, and we walk in dark places. We grope like the blind along a wall, we feel our way like the sightless. We stumble at midday as at twilight, like the walking dead among the healthy. We all growl like bears, and like doves we keep on moaning. We wait for vindication, but there is none; for salvation, but it is far from us. Our transgressions against you are many, our sins bear witness against us. Our transgressions are present to us, and we know only too well our iniquities. We have transgressed, we have disavowed YHVH, we have turned away from our God. We utter threatening and rebellious words, we mutter lies conceived in the heart. Justice is turned around, righteousness stays at a distance; honesty stumbles in the street, probity finds no entry. Honesty is nowhere to be found, and whoever renounces evil is despoiled.

In the manner of a preacher, the writer is attempting to convince his public that their unsatisfactory situation is due, not to a lack of either ability or will on the part of their God to intervene, but to their own behavior (vv 1–8). This now evokes a response on the part of the audience consisting in an acknowledgment of their responsibility (9–15a), which will at last elicit a response from God (15b–20). It is worth noting that there is no attempt to present any of this as prophetic discourse until we come to the laconic *nĕ'um YHVH* ("a pronouncement of YHVH") at the conclusion.

The basic situation is the absence of *mišpāṭ* ("vindication"), *ṣĕdāqâ* ("deliverance"), and *yĕšû'â* ("salvation"), an absence affirmed at the beginning (9a), in the middle (11b), and at the end (14a). The absence of *mišpāṭ* (*'ên mišpāṭ*, "there is no *mišpāṭ*") also skillfully links vv 9–15a with what precedes and follows (vv 8a, 15b). The author exploits the dual meaning of the twinned terms *mišpāṭ* and *ṣĕdāqâ*. In v 14a the context makes it clear that they function as a hendiadys to express in a comprehensive way a social order based on an ethical foundation of justice—one of the fundamental demands of the great eighth century prophets (Amos 5:24; 6:12; Mic 3:1, 8–9; 6:8; Isa 1:17, 21; 5:7, 16; 10:2). In the course of time, the basic judicial connotation of *mišpāṭ* evolved into a connotation of a definitive divine act of judgment, implying both condemnation of the reprobate and vindication for the righteous (Isa 3:14; 4:4; 28:6; 34:5; 41:1). A similar transformation led to *ṣĕdāqâ* having the sense of deliverance from an unjust sentence for the innocent (*ṣaddîqîm*), a meaning much in evidence throughout the second section of the book (51:6, 8; 56:1; 59:9, 16–17; 61:10–11; 63:1).

In the self-enclosed section, vv 9–11, we are hearing what life is like when promises and predictions remain unfulfilled. This theme of a promised deliverance that remains far off was anticipated in the previous section of the book:

> Listen to me, you stubborn people,
> far removed from deliverance as you are:
> "I bring my deliverance near, it is not far off;
> my salvation will not be delayed." (46:12–13)

Other passages in 40–55 reflect a similar reaction of discouragement following the disconfirmation of expectations aroused by prophetic predictions. Whether these passages constitute a fairly extensive layer in this section (see the *qārôb*

Schicht of Hermisson 1998, 139–41, 155) or just the occasional editorial expansion from the same hand as in ch. 59, they help to explain the situation described in the present chapter—darkness, blindness, groping, stumbling, sounds of desperation.

The contrast between light and darkness that follows (v 9b) points us in the same direction. It is not difficult to detect here an allusion to the old prophetic motif of the Day of YHVH (*yôm YHVH*):

> Woe to you who desire the Day of YHVH!
> Why would you want the Day of YHVH?
> It is darkness, not light! (Amos 5:18)

It was perhaps inevitable that the Day of YHVH, understood as a decisive future intervention on behalf of Israel, would be identified with fulfillment of the optimistic predictions by the author of Isa 40–55 (or the core of these chapters) of a "new thing"—a divine intervention that would effect a transformation in the situation of Jewish communities. By the time of writing, these expectations no longer focused on Cyrus but on Judah's relations with its immediate neighbors, which is to say enemies, which were first of all the Edomites.

It is generally and correctly recognized that chs. 60–62 form a distinct block of material, and thus the military language in which the promised *mišpāṭ* and *ṣĕdāqâ* are proclaimed in vv 15b–20 (the arm of YHVH, breastplate, helmet, military garments) creates the right kind of link with the horrific description of the destruction of Edom in 63:1–6.

The complaint continues with the image of a people groping in the dark, stumbling, and finding no sure footing (59:10). Blindness appears as an obvious but expressive metaphor in this second section of the book (42:19; 43:8; 56:10); but the people addressed in 59:9–10 are not blind, but in the dark, and therefore groping. We can compare Zeph 1:17, which speaks of people who walk like the blind because they have sinned; or Lam 4:14, in which people wander blindly, stained with blood, through the streets. Closer still to our passage is one of the covenant curses, which threatens a similar fate: "You will grope about at noon as the blind grope in darkness" (Deut 28:29, with the verb *mšš* rather than *gšš*, which occurs only here in Isa 59:10).

"Stumbling" (verbal stem *kšl*) is also a way of describing the effect of sin in prophetic preaching (e.g., Hos 5:5; 14:2[1], 10[9]; Isa 3:8; Jer 6:15, 21). Growling like bears could denote aggression (cf. Ps 59:7, 15 dogs) but is used in psalms as an expression of disquietude (Pss 42:6, 12; 43:5). Moaning like doves is a more common expression of lamentation. In an Assyrian lament addressed to the goddess Ishtar, the suppliant mourns like a dove day and night (*ANET*, 384), and the same figure appears elsewhere in prophetic texts (Isa 38:14; Ezek 7:6; Nah 2:8).

The confession of sin (v 12) is couched in familiar liturgical form, as in Ps 51:5[3], *kî-pĕšāʿay ʾănî ʾēdā*, "I acknowledge my transgressions" (cf. Ps 5:11; Lam 1:5; Jer 5:6). Communal confession of sin is a religious expression characteristic of the Second Temple period, either in the direct liturgical form of prayer (Isa 63:7–64:12; Ezra 9:6–15; Neh 9:6–37; Dan 9:3–19; 1QS 1:4–2:1; 4QDibHam[a]) or in derived homiletic mode (e.g., Zech 1, 7–8 and frequently in these chapters of Isaiah).

The passage draws to a close with what sounds like a reflective comment or expansion of the confession (vv 13–15a). The writer employs the full vocabulary of sin, making use of 14 more or less synonymous terms. Transgression includes repudiation of the God of Israel as a result of skepticism about his ability or willingness to stand behind the optimistic predictions of his prophets. Collapse of confidence in the traditional religious resources, involving the loss of religious bearings, can have an impact on the moral quality of life, both personal and social, as the final statement in vv 14–15a makes clear. The point is made by restating what has been said by way of personifying moral qualities: *mišpāṭ* (now "justice") and *ṣĕdāqâ* (now "righteousness") are distant (cf. v 9a), while *'ĕmet* ("honesty," "truth") and *nĕkōḥâ* ("probity") stumble and fall behind (cf. 10). These people are living in a moral wilderness.

FINALLY, A REPLY (59:15b-20)

(Dietrich 1976, 450–72; Gosse 1994, 303–6; H. Gross 1967, 97–109, 619–31; Harding 1914, 213–17; Kendall 1984, 391–405; Kruger 1997, 268–78; Pauritsch 1971, 97–103; Peels 1995; Polan 1986, 292–319; Rofé 1989, 407–10; Rubinstein 1963, 52–55; Scullion 1971, 335–48; Steck 1987b, 51–56 = 1991a, 187–91)

TRANSLATION

59   [15b]When YHVH saw it, he was displeased
that no retribution was in sight.[a]
[16]He saw that there was no one else,
he was appalled that there was none to intervene.
So his own arm won him victory,
his triumphant power[b] sustained him.
[17]He donned triumph like a coat of mail,
with the helmet of salvation on his head.
He clothed himself with garments of vengeance,[c]
wrapped himself in rage like a robe.
[18]As their deserts are, so will he requite them,[d]
wrath to his adversaries, requital[e] to his enemies.
[To the coastlands and islands he will make requital.][f]
[19]They will fear[g] the name of YHVH from the west,
from the rising of the sun, his glory.
He will come like a pent-up torrent,[h]
driven on by YHVH's breath.
[20]He will come to Zion as Redeemer
for those in Israel who turn from transgression.[i]
A saying of YHVH.

NOTES

a 4QIsaiah[e] has *k'yn* (*kĕ'ēn*), as in Isa 40:17 and 41:11, 12, which, however, makes little sense in the context; 1QIsa[a] supports MT.

b An attempt to translate *ṣĕdāqâ*, a word with a wide range of meanings cf. 17a; 1:27; 56:1; Rubinstein's emendation of *ṣidqātô* to *'ammātô* ("his forearm") is unsupported and unwarranted.

c *tilbōšet*, "clothing," seems unnecessary after *vayyilbaš*; it is omitted by LXX, Syr., and Vulg. but supported by 1QIsa[a].

d Targum substitutes *gml'*, "retribution," for the second *kĕ'al*, but the repetition is syntactically correct (GKC §118s n. 2) and is supported by 1QIsa[a]. LXX, Syr., and Tg. are paraphrastic.

e LXX *oneidos* = *ḥerpâ* or another synonym for *ḥēmâ*, "wrath, fury," but MT is supported by 1QIsa[a] and should not be emended.

f This half-line may have been added to identify the enemies more explicitly as foreigners; see Comments.

g Some medieval MSS read *vĕyir'û* → *r'h*, "see," probably because the expression "to fear YHVH's glory" is somewhat unfamiliar, on which see Comments; 1QIsa[a] *vyyr'v* is identical with MT cf. LXX *phobēthēsontai*, "they will fear."

h The MT pointing (*kannāhār ṣār*) indicates that the Masoretes read it as "an adversary will come like a torrent," which is grammatically possible, but it seems better to repoint as *kĕnāhār ṣār*, on account of the similar expressions in 48:18 and 66:12; perhaps with a view to deemphasizing the violence of the eschatological imagery, Tg. reads, "When oppressors come like the flooding of the river Euphrates, they will be plundered by the Memra of YHVH"; 1QIsa[a] has *knhr ṣvr*.

i LXX seems to have misunderstood *šābê pešaʿ*, translating, "he will turn away impiety from Jacob."

COMMENTS

The impression one has on first reading this brief passage—that YHVH suddenly noticed the situation, reacted initially with dismay, and then went immediately into action—is probably a function of the way the section of the book to which it belongs (chs. 56–59) was put together. There are plenty of indications that 56:9–59:20 constitutes a literary unity *in some sense* and that 59:15b–20 serves as a response to the complaint immediately preceding. Linkage with the preceding passage is also established by repetition of the key words *mišpāṭ* and *ṣĕdāqâ*, exploiting their ambivalent meanings (vv 9, 14, 15b–16).

But we do not get the impression that section 56:9–59:20 was put together at one time and by one hand. It has some features in common with psalms of communal lament but not enough to justify classifying it as a liturgy (Muilenburg 1956, 686; Westermann 1969, 344–520, with qualifications). The prophetic voice is heard clearly at the beginning (56:1–8) and end (59:21), and one feature that it has in common with chs. 49–55 is the alternation of words of reproach and comfort.

The dominant theme throughout is the importance of ethical behavior as a precondition for salvific divine intervention. The moral failure of the community, or certain elements in the community including the leadership, explains why the promised intervention has been delayed and states what might be done about it. All of this notwithstanding, transition from one unit to the next is far from smooth and the tone and temper throughout far from even.

This account of chs. 56–59 as a more or less coherent unit would today be widely accepted, with variations from one interpreter to the next. According to one of the more thorough investigations, that of Steck (1991a, 177–86), the literary unit 56:9–59:21 belongs (with the exception of 58:13–14) to the penultimate redactional layer of Third Isaiah and was inserted between chs. 1–55 and 60–62. It is therefore to be interpreted in the context of what Steck calls the *Grossjesajabuch* already in existence and is related to and contemporaneous with such passages in the first section of the book as 30:27–28, 34:1–8, and 35:4. The unit Isa 56:9–59:21 was composed a few years before the final redactional stage (56:1–8; 63:7–66:24) which Steck believes reflects the capture of Jerusalem by Ptolemy I. The date of composition would therefore be between 311 and 302/301 B.C.E. (see especially Steck 1991a, 39 n. 116). The date is based on indications that Steck claims to find in the lament of 63:7–64:12 (63:18; 64:10–11), though there is no evidence that Ptolemy burned the Jerusalem temple and devastated the cities of Judah, and there is nothing in 63:7–64:12 suggestive of a Hellenistic background. The lament is much more reminiscent of the book of Lamentations and other allusions to the great disaster of the early sixth century.

An important element in the interpretation of 59:15b–20 is its close linkage with 63:1–6, describing vengeance visited on Edom, a point emphasized by Steck, for whom both passages belong to the same redactional layer, even though Edom is not mentioned in 59:15b–20. The parallels can be briefly set out as follows:

- YHVH will come to Zion as Redeemer (*ûbā' lĕṣiyyôn gō'ēl*, 59:20); who is this that comes from Edom? (*mî-zeh bā' mē'ĕdôm*, 63:1)
- YHVH dons military attire (59:17); YHVH is splendidly attired, his clothes bloodstained (63:1–2)
- YHVH is presented as vindicator (*ṣĕdāqâ hî' sĕmākātĕhû, yilbaš ṣĕdāqâ*, 59:16–17); I announce vindication/triumph, mighty to save (*'ănî mĕdabbēr biṣĕdāqâ rab lĕhôšîa'*, 63:1)
- He saw that there was no one (*vayyar' kî-'ên 'îš*, 59:16); I trod the winepress alone (*lĕbaddî*), and . . . there was no one with me (*'ên-'îš 'ittî*, 63:3)
- YHVH's action has the dual purpose of redemption (*gō'ēl*, 59:20; *šĕnat gĕ'ûlay*, 63:1) and vengeance (*bigdê nāqām*, 59:17; *yôm nāqām*, 63:4)

The clearest indication of affinity is that 63:5 is in effect a variant of 59:16. Together, the two verses tell how YHVH goes to war on behalf of his city, devastates Edom, and then comes to Zion as its vindicator and redeemer. As both the biblical and archaeological data attest, Edom rivaled Babylon as Israel's public enemy number one from the last decades of the Kingdom of Judah, and hostility continued to come from that quarter in the Persian period in the person of Geshem (Gashmu) and the expansionist Kedarite Kingdom (Neh 2:19; 4:1[7]; 6:1). Later still, Edom came to serve as a code name for an oppressive foreign power, especially for Rome, as in the early midrashim.

That the adversaries (*ṣārîm*) and enemies (*'oyĕbîm*) of YHVH in 59:18 are external to Israel is also indicated by the effect of violent divine action in the east, the west, the distant coastal areas, and beyond. This is no more than we would expect, since, in epic compositions deemed to be ancient, YHVH the warrior takes up arms against the enemies of his people, not against his own people (e.g., Exod 15:3; Judg 5:4–5). But there is in 59:15b–20 a qualification absent from other texts featuring YHVH as warrior. The final verse, the force of which is strengthened by the asseveration formula with which it ends, states in effect that the promised redemption is limited to Israelites who turn from transgression (*šābê pešaʿ*, 59:20). This does not appear to imply that Edom in 63:1–6 stands for reprobate Israelites (Whybray 1975, 226; Berges 1998, 254), but it does bring the description of the ideal and eschatological Zion in chs. 60–62 to bear on the moral realism and disillusionment about the experiential Israel that run throughout the previous four chapters.

The necessity of "turning" (*tĕšûbâ*) is often emphasized throughout Isaiah (6:10; 9:12; 19:22; 31:6; 44:22; 55:7), one of several indications of affinity with the Deuteronomist preachers active during the post-disaster years (Deut 4:30; 30:1–3, with explicit reference to that time). The distinction between those who have undergone the true "turning," the *šābîm*, and those who have not is brought out most strongly in the final chapters of the book (65–66) and in the recapitulatory passage with the same message at the beginning:

Zion will be saved in the judgment,
her penitents (*šābêhā*) din the retribution,
but rebels and sinners will be destroyed together,
those forsaking YHVH will be consumed. (1:27–28)

This distinction, which draws a line running through the community, is absent from 60–62 in which the people addressed are deemed to be all righteous, God's holy and redeemed people (60:21; 62:12).

This passage (59:15b–17) begins in the past tense by stating that the turning point has already come about—not, however, through the agency of great figures on the international scene such as Cyrus but by direct divine intervention. (The Targum, followed by Ibn Ezra, translates, "there was none to intercede," perhaps with the Servant in mind cf. 53:12c.) This may be an example of the prophetic Perfect, a prediction uttered with such certainty that it is as if it had already taken place.

In describing divine action in terms of warfare and YHVH as warrior, the author was drawing on a long tradition nourished by cosmogonic combat myths and traditions about "the wars of YHVH" (Num 21:14–15; Exod 14:16) commemorated in heroic verse (Exod 15:3–4; Deut 33:2–3; Judg 5:4–5; Ps 68:8–9, 18; Hab 3:3–15). The description includes the violent psychological transformation induced by the anticipation or experience of combat, reminiscent of the Norse berserkers or the Turkish Janissaries: "he clothed himself with garments of vengeance, wrapped himself in rage like a robe."

The author may have had in mind an earlier description of YHVH's sudden irruption into action:

YHVH goes forth as a hero,
as a warrior he fires up his fury;
raising the battle cry, he shouts aloud;
he prevails over his enemies. (Isa 42:13)

The coat of mail (*širyôn*), metal strips held together with thongs, and the helmet (*kôba'*), presumably of bronze (cf. 1 Sam 17:5), sufficed to sketch in the image of the warrior. There is no mention of YHVH's sword (*ḥereb*), so much in evidence elsewhere in Isaiah (e.g., 27:1; 31:8; 34:5–6; 66:16). In the second half of the book, the dominant metaphor for divine power is the arm of YHVH (40:10; 48:14; 51:5 ,9; 52:10; 53:1; 62:8; 63:5). We find a close linguistic and thematic parallel in one of the hymns celebrating YHVH's military prowess:

His right hand and his holy arm
have won him victory (*hôšî'āh lô*);
YHVH has proclaimed his victory (*yěšû'ātô*),
in the sight of the nations he has revealed his vindication (*ṣidqātô*).
(Ps 98:1–2)

In Judaism of late antiquity and early Christianity, the military metaphor–field was reapplied to the moral life of the believer, probably under Stoic influence. It was expanded to include other items of equipment, including the sword, shield, belt, and footwear (Wis 5:17–20; Eph 6:13–17; 1 Thess 5:8).

The description of the outcome of the intervention (59:18–20) presents problems of interpretation that call for a further and final comment. What is being said here is the simple but often overlooked point that salvation and judgment are inseparable. This idea often comes to expression in the (chronologically) later sections of the book. For example:

Behold your God!
Vengeance is at hand,
fearsome retribution;
it is he who comes to save you. (35:4)

Emphasis on retribution (*gěmûl, gěmūlîm*) and vengeance (*nāqām*) may offend our modern liberal sensitivities, and it is certainly subject to misunderstanding and abuse, but the basic idea seems to be a setting right of what has been skewed and distorted by sin, an affirmation that injustice will not ultimately prevail. Hence, people far beyond the traditional jurisdiction of Israel's God will fear (not "revere") his name and his glory. The idea of the fear of God's Name was familiar from Deuteronomy (28:58) and liturgical compositions— Ps 102:15, practically identical with Isa 59:19a, and Ps 86:11, for example. Fear is less commonly associated with the divine glory or effulgence (*kābôd*), but in several incidents in the wilderness narratives the appearance of the *kābôd* signaled divine displeasure and judgment (Exod 16:10; Num 14:10; 16:19).

The last two verses (vv 19b–20) have given rise to much discussion and have been understood in a wide variety of ways. As is often the case where the Hebrew *Vorlage* is obscure, LXX 19b is paraphrastic: "For anger will come like a rushing river from the Lord; it will come with wrath."

The Targum version softens the strong apocalyptic tone, perhaps out of political prudence. The Euphrates is introduced by courtesy of the definite article (*hannāhar*), since in biblical texts the Euphrates is *the* river (Isa 8:7; 11:15; 27:12): "When oppressors come like the flooding of the river Euphrates, they will be despoiled by the Memra of YHVH." The Jewish medieval exegetical tradition tended to derive the verbal form *nōsĕsāh* from *nss*, a denominative verb from *nēs*, "standard," which permitted the rendering, "the spirit of the Lord shall lift up a standard against them [i.e., the enemies]" (identical with AV). Ibn Ezra has his own variation on this tradition, according to which *nss* takes its meaning from *nēs* = "miracle," as in Mishnaic Hebrew; therefore: "The spirit of the Lord will wonderfully act thereon." The Vulgate is the closest to the translation offered above: *Cum venerit quasi fluvius violentus quem spiritus Domini cogit* ("When he comes like a turbulent river that the Spirit of the Lord drives on").

Among the numerous modern interpretations of the bicolon, I mention the interpretation of Kruger (1997, 268–78) who introduces the mythological river deity Nahar, and Rofé (1989, 407–10,) who conjures up from the text an envoy (*ṣîr* for MT *ṣār*) who will come like light (alternative meaning of *nāhār*) and whom YHVH will wave like a flag (verb *nss*); ingenious but unconvincing. The NEB uses the more sober option of taking *kĕbôdô*, "his glory," as the antecedent of the verb *yābô*: therefore, "His glory will come like a swift river." The translation I have offered must be considered tentative, but it has at least the advantage of making a good fit with the context.

THE GIFT OF PROPHECY (59:21)

(Gosse 1989, 116–18; Kellermann 1991, 46–82; Rofé 1993, 78–85)

TRANSLATION

59 [21]As for me,[a] this is my covenant with them,[b] declares YHVH: my spirit[c] that rests upon you and my words that I have put in your mouth will not be absent from your mouth or from the mouths of your descendants or from those of the descendants of your descendants,[d] declares YHVH, from this time forward and forever more.

NOTES

[a] For this construction, a personal pronoun as subject (*va'ānî*) followed by independent noun clause, see GKC §143a.

[b] Read *'ittām* with several medieval MSS and 1QIsa[a] (cf. Tg., Vulg.) for MT *'ôtām*.

[c] 1QIsaiah[a] adds conjunction; Tg. "my holy spirit" (*rvḥ qdšy*).

[d] LXX omitted "or from those of the descendants of your descendants," probably because it was thought to be too cumbersome.

COMMENTS

It will not do to dismiss this brief passage, apparently in prose, as totally isolated (Volz 1932, 238) or as a simple addendum to the liturgy (e.g., Muilenburg 1956, 696) or as having migrated from its original place in the last chapter of the book (Westermann 1969, 352, 427), at least not without raising the question of its place in the overall arrangement of Isa 40–66. It could have served to round off chs. 56–59, since the prophetic voice is heard clearly at the beginning (56:1–8) as it is here at the end, marked by the use of traditional prophetic formulas (56:1, 4, 8; *'āmar YHVH* repeated in 59:21), otherwise rare in these chapters. The other alternative is to read it as an introduction to chs. 60–62 (Pauritsch 1971, 94; Sekine 1989, 135; Stuhlmueller 1990, 345), or as linking these two sections together (Lau 1994, 225–26). Further clarification will depend on the interpretation of the statement itself and how and to what extent it corresponds with views expressed throughout this section of the book.

Isaiah 59:21 is identified explicitly as an asseveration of YHVH addressed to an individual prophet but dealing with a plurality (*'ittām*, "with them"). It seems to have little in common with the preceding passage, 59:15b–20, but the link may be the identification of the beneficiaries of the covenant (*bĕrît*) mentioned here as the *šābîm*, those who have turned away from transgression, in the previous verse. The covenant promised would in that case be restricted to one section of the people—the group that emerges with increasing clarity as we read on through these chapters.

Some commentators (e.g., Whybray 1975, 228) find another link with the preceding passage in the catchword *rûaḥ* in v 19b, though bearing a different meaning from its appearance in v 21, a situation comparable, therefore, to *mišpaṭ* as catchword in the link between 59:1–15a and 59:15b–20. Possibly so, but not every repetition calls for an explanation of this kind. The location of the verse can, on the whole, be best explained as a prose colophon to chs. 56–59, serving not only as an authentication what has been written as genuine prophetic discourse but also as the signature of the prophetic author of the discourse.

The simple fact that the people with whom the covenant is to be made are distinct from the person addressed creates a major problem for the many commentators (e.g., Bonnard 1972, 395; Whybray 1975, 229; Lau 1994, 225–26; Oswalt 1998, 531–32) who read the passage as the gift of prophecy with which all God's people are to be endowed, comparable therefore to Joel 2:28–29 ("I will pour out my spirit on all flesh . . ."). This understanding of the statement as referring to Israel as a "prophet-nation" (NJPSV) accords with the standard Jewish interpretation as represented by Ibn Ezra. That the spirit of God is poured out on all the people is indeed an idea expressed in all sections of the book (32:15; 44:3; 63:11), but what we do not find elsewhere is the combination *in one place* of spirit endowment and putting words in the mouth. This points unmistakably to an individual prophetic figure and excludes the idea of the prophetic endowment of the people as a whole—a point already made by Volz (1932, 238–39).

The phrase "my spirit that rests upon you" (*rûḥî ʾăšer ʿalêkā*) is a type of phrase that indicates an individual in the first of Duhm's *Dichtungen* (42:1). More significantly, it occurs with reference to an individual who is indubitably a prophetic figure in 61:1 (*rûaḥ ʾădonay YHVH ʾālāy*, "The spirit of the Sovereign Lord YHVH is upon me"). The presence of other lexical parallels between 59:21 and chs. 60–61 (especially *běrît, zeraʿ*; see Sekine 1989, 135) supports the conclusion of a close connection between the statement addressed to an individual prophet here in 59:21 and the personal prophetic testimony of 61:1–4, on which more will be said later.

The other aspect of prophetic endowment—"my words that I have put in your mouth" (*děbāray ʾăšer-śamtî běpîkā*)—reproduces the formula of prophetic endowment in Jeremiah's commissioning (Jer 1:9), a figure of speech that is characteristically Deuteronomic. The words of YHVH will be put into the mouth of "the prophet like Moses" who is to be raised up (Deut 18:18). Isaiah 59:21 is particularly close to this seminal statement about prophecy, since Deut 18:15–18 is the promise of continued prophetic presence in the community in response to the people's request to Moses at Horeb. Association with this Deuteronomic text also brings to the fore the frequently expressed affinity between the prophetic and the legal *dābār*, between prophecy and law.

In language reminiscent of our passage we read, for example, that the book of the (Deuteronomic) law is not to depart out of Joshua's mouth (Josh 1:8 with the verb *mûš*, as in Isa 59:21). This language seems to have been chosen deliberately to identify the prophetic tradition within which the speaker stands with the "prophet like Moses" of Deut 18:15–18, understood as the continuators of the mission of Moses, the protoprophet.

If, then, the gift of the spirit and the gift of communicating the will of God in human speech are bestowed by covenant on an individual prophet, it follows that the descendants (*zeraʿ*, literally, "seed") are the prophet's disciples. It is true that this term is used overwhelmingly with reference to the people of Israel, or the surviving remnant of the people, especially in the post-destruction period when the issue was that of ethnic survival (41:8; 43:5; 44:3; 45:19, 25;

48:18; 54:3; 61:9; 65:23; 66:22; see also the late gloss describing the remnant as zera' qodeš, "the holy seed," Isa 6:13). But the Servant whose suffering and death are described in ch. 53 is also promised posterity: "He will see posterity (zera'), he will prolong his days," 53:10b. On the assumption that the promised vindication is to be realized after the death of the Servant, this must refer to disciples (see Vol. 2, p. 355). Since chs. 56–66 are linked thematically with 40–55, it would be reasonable to find in 59:21 and the closely related 61:1–4 evidence of continuity in discipleship originating with the Isaianic Servant of ch. 53.

While the identity of prophet and disciples will probably always elude us, the second major section of the book provides a few clues, apart from 59:21, to their hidden presence. At the outset (40:1–8), the six imperatives in the plural and one in the singular attest to a mission confided to an individual prophet together with a prophetic plurality. To the question "What shall I proclaim?" (40:6) the chapters that follow provide the answer. This opening scene concludes with a statement affirming the permanence of prophetic witness, similar therefore to 59:21: "the word of our God stands firm forever" (40:8), and the word is the prophetic word.

We pick up the individual prophetic voice again in the fragmentary 48:16c ("And now the Sovereign Lord YHVH has sent me, and his spirit . . ."), and the affirmation of the permanence of the word is repeated at the end of this major section (55:10–11). The "words in the mouth" motif is found expressed in different ways in both "Servant" passages in which an individual prophetic voice is heard (49:1–6; 50:4–9). Far from being an isolated intrusion or addendum, Isa 59:21 therefore provides a valuable clue to an underlying consistency and continuity in Isa 40–66. In its context, it serves as a kind of colophon to chs. 56–59, a summation and legitimation of the prophetic witness, claiming descent from the Servant of chapter 53, and giving assurance that it will continue.

It remains to be noted that this assurance is put under the rubric of a promissory covenant offered to the righteous among the people. The formulation is reminiscent of the style of the Priestly source in the Pentateuch:

> As for me, I am setting up my covenant with you and your descendants after you. (Gen 9:9)

> As for me, this is my covenant with you. (Gen 17:4)

The former is the covenant made with the new creation after the deluge, the bĕrît šālôm also referred to in Isa 54:10. Both are called bĕrît 'ôlām, "everlasting covenant," meaning a covenant that, unlike political pacts and treaties, does not require periodic renewal and revalidation. This expression, "everlasting covenant," is also familiar to Isaian authors (55:3; 61:8). The close association between covenant and Sabbath in the opening statement of 56–66 (56:4, 6) is another Priestly characteristic, as we saw at that point of the Commentary. But, since there is no observable connection between this view of covenant and prophecy, the influence of the Priestly source (P) on our passage seems to be purely formal.

If the prophetic author addressed in 59:21 belonged to the discipleship of the Isaianic Servant (or, more broadly, the *Jesaja-Tradentenkreis*, Steck 1991a, 29 n. 70), it would be relevant to recall that the prophetic Servant was described as a "covenant to the people" (*běrît ʿām*, 49:8). We suspect that behind this association between covenant and prophecy in Isaiah lies the "prophet like Moses" of Deut 18:15–18. According to the Deuteronomic view, prophecy was the answer to the people's request for mediation made at Horeb during the covenant-making ceremony (Deut 18:16–17). The prophet is to communicate the words of God: "I will put my words in his mouth" (*věnātattî děbāray běpîv*, 18:18) compare this with "my words that I have put in your mouth" (*děbāray ʾăšer śamtî běpîkā*, Isa 59:21). The Deuteronomists are also familiar with the idea of prophecy as endowment with the spirit (Deut 34:9–10).

To what extent these traditions (digested in modern scholarship under the sigla P and D) were formalized in writing by the time 59:21 was written we do not know. In whatever form they existed, they contributed to giving this summarizing statement at the conclusion of Isa 56–59 an impressive depth and resonance.

AN APOSTROPHE TO ZION (60:1–22)

(Brayley 1960, 275–86; Causse 1939, 739–50; Clements 1997, 441–54; Grelot 1957, 319–21; Junker 1962, 29–35; Koenen 1990, 137–57; Langer 1989; Lau 1994, 22–66; de Moor 1997, 325–46; Ollenburger 1987; Pauritsch 1971, 119–27, 134–37; von Rad 1966, 232–42; Ruszkowski 2000, 22–27; Schneider and Berke 1995, 86–90; Sekine 1989, 68–74; P. A. Smith 1995, 26–49; Steck 1985a, 29–34 = 1991a, 101–5; 1985b, 1279–94 = 1991a, 80–96; 1986a, 261–96 = 1991a, 49–79; 1986c, 275–77 = 1991a, 97–100; 1991a, 119–40; Zimmerli 1950, 110–22 = 1963, 217–33)

TRANSLATION

i

60 ¹Rise up, shine forth,[a] for your light has come,
The glory of YHVH has dawned over you!
²Though darkness[b] covers the earth
and deep gloom the nations,
YHVH shines over you like the dawn,
his glory appears over you.
³Nations will come to your light,
and kings to the radiance of your dawn.[c]

ii

⁴Lift up your eyes, look about you:
they are all assembling, they are coming to you!
Your sons will come from afar,
your daughters will be held on the hip.[d]

5When you see it, you will be radiant,[e]
your heart will thrill and dilate;
the sea's abundance will be lavished on you,
they will bring you[f] the wealth of nations;
6Countless camels will cover your land,[g]
young camels from Midian and Ephah,
all those from Sheba will come
bearing gifts of gold and incense,
proclaiming the praise[h] of YHVH.
7All Kedar's flocks will be herded for you,
all Nebaioth's rams will be at your disposal;
they will be acceptable for offering on my altar,[i]
and I will enhance the splendor of my house.

iii

8Who are these that fly like the clouds,
like doves to their dovecotes?[j]
9The vessels from the coastlands are waiting,[k]
ships of Tarshish in the lead,
to bring your sons[l] from afar,
together with their silver and gold
for the name of YHVH your God,
for the Holy One of Israel;
for it is he has made you glorious.

iv

10Foreigners will build your walls,
their kings will minister to you.
In my wrath I struck you down,
but in my good pleasure I had compassion on you.
11Your gates will always stay open,[m]
day and night they will never be shut,
so they can bring you the wealth of nations,
with their kings leading the way.[n]

[12For the nation or kingdom that will not serve you shall perish, and the nations shall be utterly destroyed.][o]

13The glory of Lebanon[p] will come to you,
cypress, fir tree, and box,
to adorn the place of my sanctuary;
I will honor the place where my feet rest.[q]
14The children of those who oppress you
will come to you bending low,[r]
and all who despise you
will do homage at the soles of your feet.
They will address you as YHVH's City,
the Holy One of Israel's Zion.[s]

¹⁵Instead of being abandoned and hated,
unheeded by those passing by,
I will make you an object of pride forever,
a joy for all generations.
¹⁶You will suck the milk of nations,
you will be suckled at the breast of royalty.
Then you will acknowledge
that I am YHVH your Savior,
your Redeemer, the Strong One of Jacob.

v

¹⁷In place of bronze, I bring gold;
in place of iron, I bring silver;
bronze in place of wood, iron in place of stone.
I assign Peace as your overseer,
Righteousness as your taskmaster.
¹⁸Never again will the sound of violence
be heard in your land;
there will be neither devastation nor destruction
within your borders;
you will name your walls Salvation,
Praise^t you will name your gates.
¹⁹No longer will the sun be your light in the daytime,
nor the moon give you light in the nighttime,^u
for YHVH will be your light everlasting,
your God will be your splendor.
²⁰Your sun will no longer^v go down,
your moon will not set,
for YHVH will be your light everlasting,
and your days of mourning will be ended.

vi

²¹Your people, righteous one and all,
will possess the land forever,
the shoot that I myself planted,^w
the work of my hands^x so that I might be glorified.
²²The least will become a thousand,
the youngest a numerous nation.
I am YHVH!
At its appointed time,
swiftly will I bring it about.

NOTES

[a]   LXX, Tg., Vulg. add "Jerusalem"; Tg. also adds "Jerusalem" in vv 4a and 12;
LXX repeats "shine forth" (*phōtizou, phōtizou*).

^b   The article (*haḥōšek*) in MT and 1QIsa^a is the result of dittography with the
final *he* of the preceding word, *hinnēh*.

^c   LXX omits this final clause by haplography; 1QIsa^a *lngd zrḥk*, "in the pres-
ence of your dawn," probably a slip (*lngd* for *lngh*).

^d   For MT *tē'āmanāh* (for the form, see GKC §51m) → *'mn*; 1QIsa^b has
tnśynn, "carried," perhaps influenced by 49:22 and/or 66:12; the proposed
alternative reading of BHS is unnecessary; Ibn Ezra derived the form from
'mn = "nurse, take care of," cf. Esth 2:7.

^e   MT *věnāhart* → *nhr* II, as in Ps 34:6[5] and perhaps Jer 31:12, not *nhr* I,
"flow," as in Vulg. *adflues*.

^f   Reading *yābî'û* Hiphil for MT *yābō'û*; if in Qal, the verb should be in sing.,
as in 1QIsa^b. MT Qal could be retained, as in 6b (therefore reading "The
wealth of nations will come to you"), by assuming metathesis (*yābô'* for
yābî'û).

^g   Literally, "will cover you."

^h   Both MT and 1QIsa^a write *thlt* defectively, though the Masoretes vocalized
it as a pl.; read *těhillat*.

ⁱ   MT *ya'ălû 'al-rāṣôn mizbĕḥî*, literally, "They shall go up at the pleasure of
my altar"; 1QIsa^a *vy'lv lrṣvn 'l mzbḥy*, "and they will be offered in acceptance
on my altar," reads more smoothly cf. Syr. and Tg.; LXX "and acceptable
sacrifices will be offered on my altar" renders the sense.

^j   *'ărubbâ*, often translated "window" (e.g., Vulg. *ad fenestras*; Qoh12:3, met-
aphorical for "eye socket"), but clearly inappropriate here, means a hole,
for example, in the sky for rain to come through (Gen 7:11 etc.) or in the
roof to allow smoke to pass.

^k   I read *kĕlê'iyyîm* (for *kĕlî* = "vessel" i.e., ship, see Isa 18:2) for MT *kî-lî* ("for
for me . . . waiting") to balance *'oniyyôt taršîš*, "ships of Tarshish"; Duhm's
proposed reading (1922, 449) *kî-lî ṣiyyîm yiqqāvû*, "Ja, mir sammeln sich
die Seefahrer" ("Yes, the seafarers gather to me") has the disadvantage of
making YHVH the speaker; there may also be an echo in this verse from
51:5, "the islands (coastlands) wait for me."

^l   1QIsaiah^a has *bny*, "my sons," but Jerusalem is not the speaker.

^m   There is no need to emend *pittěhû* Piel (Active) to Niphal (Passive); 3d-
person pl. can have Passive sense, and Piel can be intransitive, for example,
lo'-pittěhāh 'oznekâ, "your ear was not opened," on which see GKC §52k
where, however, the authors recommend emending Isa 48:8 and 60:9 to
the Niphal.

ⁿ   MT and 1QIsa^a *něhûgîm*, "led," "escorted," is possible but oddly elliptical,
though it seems to be implied in Tg. *zqyqyn*, "in chains"; Duhm's pro-
posal (1922, 450; also Westermann 1969, 354; Whybray 1975, 234) to read
nōhăgîm, Active participle, fits the context, in the sense that the kings are
reduced to leading the pack animals.

^o   A scribal insertion in prose; Hanson's attempt (1975, 51, 56–57) to make it
render a 3:3 meter by dint of arbitrary emendation is not persuasive.

^p   1QIsaiah^a adds *ntn lk*, "is given to you," cf. 35:2b.

q   Literally, "the place of my feet"; LXX omits this half-verse.
r   *sĕhôah*, Infinitive absolute used adverbially; see GKC §113h. 1QIsaiah[a] adds *kvl* before *mʿnyk* ("all those who oppress you"); there is a substantial omission in the major MSS, restored in Hexaplaric MSS (D. N. Freedman).
s   The phrase *ṣiyyôn qĕdôš yiśrāʾēl* raises the issue of a proper noun (*ṣiyyôn*) in a construct chain; GKC §125h argues that in such cases we must posit ellipsis of a common noun that really governs the genitive; perhaps so, but similar cases are attested, for example, YHVH *ṣĕbāʾôt* and *ʾûr kāṣdîm*, perhaps also YHVH *šmrn* ("YHVH of Samaria") from Kuntillet ʿAjrud; hence, the BHS proposed emendation to *ṣiyyûn*, "sign," "monument," should not be accepted.
t   LXX *glumma*, "sculpture," "carved work," perhaps a corruption of *agalma* or *agalliama*, "rejoicing."
u   Literally, "And for brightness the moon will not shine for you"; 1QIsa[a] adds *blylh*, "at night," after *hayyārēah*, "the moon," and LXX adds *tēn nukta* ("The moon will not light up the night for you").
v   1QIsaiah[a] omits *ʿvd*, reading, "Your sun will not set."
w   Reading Q *nēṣer mattāʿy*, literally, "the shoot of my planting," in preference to K "his planting" with Syr., Tg., Vulg.; 1QIsa[a] *nṣr mtʿy* YHVH, "the shoot of YHVH's planting," favors K, while 1QIsa[b] has *mtʿyv*, "his plantings"; LXX takes a quite different approach with *phulassōn to phuteuma*, "guarding the plant(ation)," with reference to YHVH as "Guardian of his plantation" (see Brayley 1960, 275–86).
x   1QIsaiah[a] and 1QIsa[b] have *ydyv*, "his hands" in keeping with their respective readings in the previous phrase.

COMMENTS

The place of ch. 60 in chs. 56–66 and the book of Isaiah as a literary whole has been a major issue in discussions of the formation of this final segment of the book. With the exception of the few scholars who still maintain (following Duhm, Torrey, and Elliger) that 56–66 is the product of one author, the thesis that chs. 60–62 form the core of "Trito-Isaiah" has come to be widely accepted. Unlike the other major sections in chs. 56–66—that is, 56–59 and 65–66—these chapters speak exclusively of salvation. There are no denunciations and comminations; no conditions are laid down for access to the salvation on offer, except the willingness to accept it; and, with the possible exception of those who mourn over Zion and the promised day of vindication (61:2–3), there are no overt signs of division between the elect and the reprobates of the kind much in evidence in chs. 65–66. That chs. 60–62 have particularly close thematic and linguistic links with chs. 40–55 has also created a presumption in favor of their basic status and therefore their earlier dating.

The hypothesis that chs. 60–62 form the original Trito-Isaianic core, and are therefore closest thematically to Deutero-Isaiah is certainly arguable and probably correct, but not as unproblematic as some commentators have assumed.

The euphoric and upbeat tone of 60–62 is not entirely consonant with the note of disillusionment and skepticism about prophetic assurances that we hear from time to time in 40–55, especially in 49–55, and it may seem strange that the fate of the prophetic Servant finds no clear and unambiguous echo in 60–62. We would also have to ask why chs. 60–62 are located in the center of this final segment of the book, preceded and followed by passages dealing with the actual, empirical, and largely unsatisfactory situation of the Jewish community addressed.

The question has been raised from time to time whether these three chapters forming the Trito-Isaianic core are in their original order. Duhm (1922, 454) speculated that Trito-Isaiah was originally divided into two halves of equal length, 61–66 and 56–60, the order of which was reversed, perhaps accidentally. Volz (1932, 254–55) thought that 61 (with the exception of vv 5–6), which speaks of YHVH's day of vindication (*nāqām*) and is concerned with those of low social status (*'ănāvîm*) who are still in mourning was quite different from 60 and 62. He therefore proposed this original order: 60, 62, 61. More recently, Pauritsch (1971, 103–6) reconstructed the sayings in the order 61, 62, 60 with 62:10 introducing 60:1–22 and 62:11–12 serving as the finale to the entire unit, added by a redactor.

One rather basic problem with reconstructive attempts such as that of Pauritisch is that they lack inevitability. It is generally possible to think of several ways in which a text *could* be arranged differently, but in doing so the principal task, that of explaining the text as it is, in the order in which it is present to the reader, is often neglected. Volz had correctly noted some special features of ch. 61 that set it apart from 60 and 62, but he failed to note the principal difference: namely, 60 and 62 are both apostrophes to Zion/Jerusalem, and 61 is not. We can then conclude that 60–62 as a unit replicates the same envelope schema (a-b-a) according to which chs. 56–66 as a whole are organized: 56–59, 60–62, 63–66.

We can take this further and suggest that the highly distinctive declaration of an anonymous prophet about his prophetic credentials and assignment in 61:1–3b has been placed deliberately in the center of 60–62—there are 44 verses (i.e., lines) preceding and 45 following this passage, or, to be more precise, there are 295 words preceding and 296 following it (I owe this calculation to D. N. Freedman). This gives us another a-b-a pattern within the larger scheme. As I noted in the Introduction, 63:1–3b can be read as the signature of the prophetic author of 60–62, who is recommending the good news announced to Zion in this section as endowed with the highest authority. That 61:1–3b has been spliced into this lengthy apostrophe to Zion is suggested by the fact that 61:3c–7 continues 60:1–22 and, more specifically, that 61:3c ("They will be called strong and sturdy oaks / that YHVH has planted for his glory") belongs with 60:21: *'êlê haṣṣedeq* cf. *ṣaddîqîm, maṭṭa' YHVH lĕhitpā'ēr* cf. *nēṣer maṭṭ'ay . . . lĕhitpā'ēr* .

There are, needless to say, exceptions to the quasi consensus on 60–62 as the Trito-Isaianic core, especially among scholars addicted to redactional investigation at the microtextual level. It would take up too much space and test the patience of the reader unduly to attempt an exhaustive review of scholarly opinion on the subject, but one or two examples from recent decades may be given. Practically all commentators agree that 60:12 is a scribal addition, and there are others who doubt that 60:19–20, read as a rather literalistic reinterpretation of vv 1–3 on the theme of light, was originally part of the poem (P. A. Smith 1995, 24–25). Steck argued for the dependence on chs. 40–55 of individual passages and even minute units of text in these three chapters, as distinct from other passages that also betray dependence on 1–39 and that he therefore judged to be secondary and redactional. With the help of this distinction, he then built up an elaborate theory of the formation of his *Grossjesajabuch*. The implication for ch. 60 was that it must have passed through at least three stages of formation before arriving at its present form. He assigned vv 1–9, 13–16 to the mid-fifth century B.C.E., vv 10–11 to the time of Nehemiah, and vv 17–22 to the Hellenistic period (see especially Steck 1991a, 14–19).

Applying similar criteria, Vermeylen (1978, 471–78) read the original nucleus of the poem in ch. 60 as reflecting the euphoria of the first return to Judah in the final decades of the sixth century. But themes that he judged to be incompatible with this scenario, or verses that he read as *relectures* of earlier material, were assigned to a secondary redactional level. These include vv 14–18, constituting a *relecture* of the original Trito-Isaianic poem, and parts of vv 4 and 9, which introduce the theme of Gentiles' repatriating Jews, which Vermeylen took to be a distinct and later idea. For Koenen (1990, 137–57), "proclaiming the praises of YHVH" (from 6b), the similar allusion in 9b, and divine speech in 10b and 13b betray editorial activity, and v 21 was inserted to bind chs. 60 and 61 together.

Since biblical texts such as ch. 60 were not copyrighted and had not yet attained canonical immunity from later intrusion, it would not be surprising if they contained scribal expansions and explanatory glossing. It would not be unreasonable, for example, to speculate that the poem originally ended at v 16 ("your Redeemer, the Strong One of Jacob") or v 20 ("your days of mourning will be ended"), but these speculations only rarely move beyond mere possibilities. It seems, then, on the whole, advisable to assume the substantial integrity of a text such as 60:1–22, in the absence of unmistakably clear indications to the contrary.

The situation with respect to chs. 60–62 as a unit one and indivisible, the core of Trito-Isaiah, is however not so clear. Following 60:1–22, the community is referred to in the third person (61:1–4). A speaker then addresses the community directly (61:5–6 or 61:5–7), followed by speech in divine *oratio recta* (61:8–9) and rounded off with a hymn (61:10–11). The apostrophe to Zion that follows (62:1–9) and the section as a whole are brought to a close with a summons to prepare the way for salvation, one of several such calls that constitute one of the clearest structural markers in chs. 40–66 (40:1–3; 48:20–22; 52:11–12; 62:10–12).

It seems, then, that chs. 60–62 constitute an assemblage of different types of material, though all bearing in one way or another on the central theme of

God's decisive intervention on behalf of Jerusalem and the faithful core of the people. Whether the result is a compilation from different authors or the work of one alone cannot be determined, but in either case a unifying intent is indicated. In the first place, chs. 60–62 begin and end with the coming of the saving God to Zion (60:1–3; 62:11). The presentation of YHVH as warrior-God before and after these three chapters (59:15b–19; 63:1–6) provides a literary inclusion or envelope and a vision of final judgment corresponding to the salvation presented in 60–62. In Isaiah, salvation and judgment always come together. Isaiah 63:1–6 should not, therefore, be considered part of the core section, contra P. A. Smith (1995, 38–44).

The poem in 60:1–22 is prosodically fairly regular, set out in the usual bicola and tricola. Since there are no clearly delimited strophes, commentators divide the poem in different ways. Muilenburg (1956, 697) has ten strophes divided into an introduction (1–3) and three sections (4–9, 10–16, 17–22), each with three strophes of roughly equal length. The division into six adopted in this translation corresponds with Muilenburg's main divisions, but how one divides the poem is not a matter of great importance. While the passage seems to be introduced quite abruptly, there is a connection with the preceding material in that the light and glory coming over Zion give vivid expression to the coming of YHVH as Judge and Redeemer in 59:19–20. As an "apostrophe to Zion," it belongs very clearly to the same category as similar poems in chs. 49–54: namely, 49:14–26; 51:17–23; 52:1–2, 7–10; and 54:1–17.

The first stanza (vv 1–3) is elegantly structured. Jerusalem is the center and the rest of the world the periphery, but the motif of the earth and its population out there in the dark is enveloped and contained by the familiar topos of Zion as a central zone of light. The key word 'ôr ("light"), the corresponding verb (vv 1, 3a), zāraḥ ("to dawn") and its corresponding noun (vv 1, 2b, 3), and kābôd ("glory," 1, 2b) contrast with ḥōšek ("darkness") and 'ărāpel ("deep gloom") in the middle (2a). We may catch a faint echo here of the ninth Egyptian plague: "There was deep darkness on all the land of Egypt . . . , but for all the Israelites there was light" (Exod 10:22–23). The same echo can be heard more strongly in Ezekiel's mock-lament over an Egyptian ruler: "I will put darkness on your land" (Ezek 32:8: 'ereṣ, "land" can also mean "earth"); one of several indications that the plague narrative owes a debt to prophetic preaching.

The summons to Zion to rise up and shine forth is a further extension of a theme often repeated in chs. 49–54, especially in the apostrophes to Zion that have preceded this one (49:14–26; 51:17–23; 52:1–2, 7–10; 54:1–17). In these very similar poems, the Woman Zion is urged to rouse herself (hit'ôrĕrî, 'ûrî, 51:17; 52:1–2), to rejoice (rānnî, piṣḥî rinnâ, ṣahălî, 54:1), and to rise up (qûmî, 51:17; 52:2a). The God who comes, whose coming is announced throughout chs. 56–66, is the source of the light. The poet is therefore thinking of Zion as reflecting the light, somewhat like the shining face of Moses at Sinai (Exod 34:29–35). The verb translated "dawn" (zāraḥ) is the normal term for sunrise (e.g., Qoh 1:5), but it also belongs to the language of theophany, the coming of God:

YHVH came from Sinai
and dawned from Seir upon us. (Deut 33:2)

The promise of light, and therefore enlightenment, with the coming of God, is a theme of frequent occurrence in hymns, no doubt with reference to intense liturgical experience (Ps 27:1; 36:10). The contrast between light and darkness is also Trito-Isaianic (58:10; 59:9), and perhaps can be traced back to the old idea of the "Day of YHVH." ("What is the Day of YHVH to you? It is darkness and not light!" Amos 5:18b.) The eschatological vision of both foreigners and Israelites going up to Jerusalem to "walk in the light of YHVH" in Isa 2:2–5 (= Mic 4:1–5) is also thematically close to ch. 60, though perhaps somewhat earlier because it contains no hint of compulsion (Lau 1994, 34).

Light is often associated with the glory of God (*kĕbôd YHVH*), and in this respect 60:1–3 is the fulfillment of the promise made at the beginning of the second major section of the book: "the glory of YHVH will be revealed," 40:5. There is in the Isaianic tradition an understanding of the key term *kĕbôd YHVH* ("the glory of YHVH") that is rather different from that of Ezekiel, who represents the *kābôd* as abandoning the temple shortly before its destruction and sees in vision its future return (Ezek 9:3; 10:18–19; 11:22–25; 43:2–5; 44:4). The prophet Isaiah's vision of the *kābôd* during a heavenly liturgy in the presence of "the king, YHVH of the hosts" (Isa 6:3–5), points in a somewhat different direction—namely, that of YHVH's glory revealed when his kingdom is established and his kingship proclaimed in Zion. We hear unmistakable echoes of our poem in an eschatological addendum to a late liturgical passage in the first major section of the book:

The moon will be put to shame and the sun abashed when YHVH of the hosts inaugurates his reign on Mount Zion and in Jerusalem, revealing his glory in the presence of his elders. (24:23)

This in its turn links with the hymns celebrating the kingship of YHVH (Pss 93, 95–99) that take up old, familiar myths of combat, the subduing of the chaotic waters, creation, and temple-building (von Rad). These enthronement psalms speak of the coming of God in salvation and judgment (Ps 96:13; 98:9), they describe how he sets up his throne and, with it, his footstool in Jerusalem (Ps 93:2; 97:2; 99:1), his "holy mountain" (Ps 99:9), and how this will be an occasion for Zion to rejoice (Ps 97:8) and for all people to see his glory (Ps 97:6). This is what the poem in ch. 60 is about, and it leads us to think of this first stanza as in essence proclaiming the inauguration of the kingship of YHVH in Jerusalem, specifically in the temple rebuilt or to be rebuilt. In this respect, the "message" is similar to that of Haggai, for whom the rebuilding of the temple was an essential precondition for the manifestation of the glory of YHVH of the hosts (Hag 1:8). (This designation, *YHVH ṣĕbā'ôt*, connected with the kingship of YHVH, occurs 11 times in this brief prophecy.) The principal difference is that, unlike the author of Isa 60:1–22, Haggai believed that YHVH's kingship would be exercised through a human agent.

The next stanza (Isa 60:4–7) takes over and develops one of the major themes of chs. 40–55, namely, the repatriation of diaspora Jews. With this idea is linked the theme of rich tribute, arriving by sea—therefore from the west; and on the backs of camels serving as pack animals, "the ships of the desert"— therefore from the east. The natural assumption is that this is tribute brought by the nations and kings mentioned in v 3 and that the occasion is the proclamation of the universal kingship of YHVH and the inauguration of his reign in Jerusalem. It is therefore natural that the tribute should include animals for sacrifice in the temple, either already functioning or to be built.

That the author is recapitulating and developing themes from his prophetic predecessor, at times practically verbatim, becomes apparent when we compare v 4 with the following:

> Look, these are coming from afar,
> look, these others from the north and the west,
> and yet others from the land of Syene. . . .
> Lift up your eyes, look about you;
> they are all assembled, to you they come. . . .
> I lift up a signal for the peoples;
> they will carry your sons in their laps,
> your daughters will be borne on their shoulders. (49:12, 18, 22)

The repatriation theme is well represented in both chs. 1–39 and chs. 40–55, where diaspora centers in Mesopotamia, Egypt, Ethiopia (Sudan), and north Syria are mentioned (11:11; 27:12–13, where "Assyria" and "Egypt" could stand for regions in the Seleucid and Ptolemaic Empires, respectively; 43:5–7; 45:14; 49:12). More often than not, the task of repatriating diaspora Jews is entrusted to Gentiles (11:12; 14:1–2; 45:13; 49:22–23), whose lot thereafter is to serve as slaves or as a dependent serf population.

These themes are well developed in chs. 60–62 but almost entirely absent from 56–59 and 63–66 which, all allowance being made for difference of genres, reflect the quite different mind-set and concerns of a later generation and are more concerned with present problems than with fantasies of the future. It should be painfully clear that the perspective of the author of this poem is far removed from a religiously universalistic world view of a kind expressed, for example, in Isa 19:25: "Blessed be my people Egypt, Assyria the work of my hands, Israel my possession."

This vision of the establishment of God's kingdom in Jerusalem, a worldwide empire on which the sun never sets, draws on the polemic of the author of chs. 40–48 preceding the fall of Babylon (e.g., 40:15; 45:14). It can be read as a reaction to the collapse of confidence in solutions attained by action on the international scene, solutions that could be expected to arise within the flow of historical events under the providential guidance of the God of Israel. The impression now is that the change in fortune will come about suddenly, by direct divine intervention, and the effect on the Woman Zion (v 5a) is psychologically realistic, as of something totally unexpected, like winning the lottery. The sudden onset of disaster is a common Isaianic theme (29:5; 30:13; 47:9, 11), but the good news of salvation can also come suddenly (48:3).

Interestingly enough, in this poem the wealth of nations (the origin of George Adam Smith's famous title) derives entirely from established Arabian trade partners. The Midianites, and Ephah their leading tribe, were situated east of the Gulf of Aqaba and in southern Transjordan. Sheba (Saba) was in southwest Arabia, and both traded in incense and other aromata (Jer 6:20), gems (Ezek 27:22), and gold (Ezek 27:22; 38:13; Ps 72:15). The Kedarite Arabs, whose ruler Geshem (Gashmu) was to give Nehemiah a lot of trouble (Neh 2:19; 6:1–2, 16), and Nebaioth in the Edomite region traded in livestock (Ezek 27:21). Additional sites and commodities are mentioned elsewhere in Isaiah and other prophetic texts (Isa 18:7; 23:18; 45:15; Hag 2:8; Zech 14:14).

In the next strophe (vv 8–9) the poet takes up the theme of repatriation from v 4. Introducing something unfamiliar, unknown, or unexpected by means of a question, as in 63:1 ("Who is this that comes from Edom?"), is an effective stylistic device reminiscent of the rhetorical questions that appear frequently in chs. 40–55. The return from the diaspora is likened to clouds (*'āb* collective) flying through the sky on a windy day or a flock of homing pigeons.

The following verse raises some intriguing questions. The first half-verse of 9a is almost identical with the first half-verse of 51:5b:

> *kî-lî 'iyyîm yĕqavvû* (60:9a unemended text)
> *'ēlay 'iyyîm yĕqavvû* (51:5b)

Both could be translated "for me the coastlands/islands wait," but it seems that 60:5b has been accomodated to 51:5b and that the original reading was "the vessels from (of) the coastlands/islands are gathering" (*kĕlê* for *kî-lî* and *qvh* II = "gather" for *qvh* I = "wait"; see Notes). Likewise, 60:9c is almost identical with 55:5b:

> *lĕšēm YHVH 'ĕlohayik*
> *vĕliqĕdôš yiśrā'ēl*
> *kî pē'ărāk*

For the name of YHVH your God,
for the Holy One of Israel;
for it is he has made you glorious. (60:9c)

> *lĕma'an YHVH 'ĕlohayik*
> *vĕliqĕdôš yiśrā'ēl kî pē'ărāk*

For the sake of YHVH your God,
the Holy One of Israel who made you glorious. (55:5b)

The slight alteration from *lĕmaʿan YHVH* ("for the sake of YHVH") to *lĕšēm YHVH* ("for the name of YHVH") may have been triggered by a recollection of Jer 3:17: "At that time they will call Jerusalem 'the throne of YHVH' and all the nations will be gathered (*niqqĕvvû*) to it, to Jerusalem, for the name of YHVH (*lĕšēm YHVH*)." The verse (Isa 60:9) may then be taken as a small-scale example of how new prophecy could be generated out of existing prophetic texts to fit a different situation. This process seems to have involved memory more than recourse to written texts, though there is no reason to doubt that prophetic texts were then available in written form.

That foreigners will be charged with the repatriation of Jews in the dispersion is a theme repeated at intervals through Isaiah (11:12; 14:1–2; 45:13–14; 49:22–23; 66:20). It derives from the more integrationist and xenophobic elements in the post-disaster Judean community and is at the furthest remove from the views expressed at the beginning and end of chs. 56–66 (56:1–8 and 66:18–19, 21).

Tarshish ships were large oceangoing vessels that, to judge by the name, originally plied between the Phoenician ports and Phoenician colonies in the western Mediterranean (Isa 23:1–14; Ezek 27:12–25). The place called Tarshish is variously located in Tartessos in southern Spain, in Malta, Sardinia, or (according to *Vetus Latina*) Carthage, and it is quite possible that the author was as uncertain of its precise location as we are. In addition to silver and gold mentioned here, the Tarshish vessels carried iron, tin, lead, ivory, apes, and peacocks (1 Kgs 10:22; 22:49; 2 Chr 9:21; Jer 10:9; Ezek 27:12).

The following stanza (60:10–16) returns to the theme of reversal of fortune with regard to the condition of the city after the return, and in the first place the walls and the gates. In the context of 60–62 as a unit, there are discrepancies here that make it difficult to sustain unity of authorship, for here the city wall will be rebuilt by foreign work gangs, in 61:4 the inhabitants themselves will rebuild it, while from 62:6 we learn that the wall is standing. According to the view represented here and elsewhere in the book, foreigners, including their rulers, will serve the Israel of the future as slaves and serfs, whether as child-minders (49:23), shepherds, and vinedressers (61:5) or, as here, in labor gangs engaged in rebuilding the walls formerly destroyed by foreigners. This total reversal of the political situation corresponds to a change from the time of divine anger (*qesep*) to favor and compassion (v 10b). There is therefore no need to explain this verse (which paraphrases Isa 54:7–8, using some of the same language) as due to editorial intrusion.

City gates that remain open are either a sign that resistance has come to an end, as with the cities conquered by Cyrus (45:1, *loʾ yissāgērû*, "they will not be shut," cf. 60:11a), or an indication of complete security (54:14–17). The city gate has a religious significance as the point of entry for the procession that will end in the temple (62:10), through which "the King of glory" will pass (Ps 24:7–10). This is perhaps the point of the liturgical-sounding name Tehillah ("Praise") for the gates in the age to come (60:18). But, in keeping with one of his main themes, the author has a more mundane purpose in mind for wide-open gates, namely, to allow the steady flow of merchandise into the city. While the verb *nhg* is used of leading away captives (Isa 20:4), in most instances it refers to driving animals. It seems likely, then, that the caravan of pack animals loaded with goods has in its turn conjured up the image of foreign rulers leading animals into the city like common drovers.

The prose gloss (v 12), referring back to the *gôyyîm* and their kings in the previous verse, embodies a more polarized and intransigent idea of judgment. It is of a kind found throughout the prophetic corpus; one could compare it with similar glosses in the judgment poem in Isa 2:6–22 (see Vol. 1, 192–94) or with the Aramaic gloss in Jer 10:11 that passes final judgment on foreign gods: "The gods who did not make the heavens and the earth will perish from the earth and from under the heavens."

After the walls and the gates, it was time to turn to the rebuilding and refurbishing of the temple, promised earlier in the poem (7b). The verb *pā'ēr* ("glorify," "make splendid," "adorn") appears with reference to the temple only in this poem (vv 7b, 13b) and in Ezra 7:27, *lĕpā'ēr 'et bêt YHVH* ("to adorn YHVH's house"), which helps us to situate the poem and, at the same, emphasizes the contrast between the ideal and the real situation. The Ezra narrative mentions only stone and timber as building materials for the temple (Ezra 5:8), and the timber seems to have been harvested from the wooded hills surrounding Jerusalem (Hag 1:8). With the building of the Solomonic temple in mind, the poet speaks of the "glory of Lebanon" (cf. 35:2)—that is, the cedar wood for which Solomon made a pact with the Phoenicians (1 Kgs 5:5–12) and, for good measure, added the last three of the seven species of trees listed in 41:19. There is some uncertainty about the identity of the three species in question (*bĕrôš, tidhār, tĕ'aššûr*), but of the seven mentioned in 41:19 they seem to be the ones most suitable for construction.

Where the Solomonic temple is referred to, YHVH's footstool is the ark originally located in Shiloh and then transferred to Jerusalem (Ps 132:7; 1 Chr 28:2). With the destruction of the first temple, the disappearance of the ark from the scene (Jer 3:15–18), and increasing emphasis on divine transcendence, God's residence is relocated in the heavens and the temple becomes his footstool (66:1; Ezek 43:7). It is there that the descendants of the foreigners who oppressed Israel will do homage (v 14).

The theme of eschatological reversal is expressed in many different forms in chs. 56–66. At this point, the train of thought is dictated by the predictions in 49:22–23, which also conclude with an acknowledgment of YHVH as the one who brings the change about (49:23c; 60:16b). Jerusalem once carried names of ill omen—it was Azubah (the Abandoned One, 54:6 cf.49:14) and Aqarah (the Barren One, 54:1). It was hated (the verb *śn'* is a technical term for marital repudiation) and no one passed by (*'br*), that it, took any notice of it (cf. Ezek 16:6, 8, 15, 25).

The aspect of the transformation that the author chooses to mention is, once again, adapted from the 40–55 prophetic corpus and dictated by one of the major themes of the poem:

kings will look after your children,
their queens will serve you as nurses . . .
then all flesh will know that I, YHVH, am your Savior,
your Redeemer, the Strong One of Jacob. (49:23a,26b)

Picking up the idea of female royalty serving as wet nurses, intended literally in 49:23a, the author turns it into a metaphor for "milking" the resources of the Gentiles and their rulers, even risking the (to us) absurd image of suckling at the breast of kings. The intent is to convey the idea of rich and satisfying prosperity, perhaps with the kind of mythological undertone expressed in a Late Bronze Age poem from Ugarit:

She shall bear Yassib the lad,
who shall draw the milk of Asherah,
suck the breasts of the maiden Anath,
the two wet-nurses of the gods. (*ANET*, 146)

Here, too, as in the figure of light and darkness, we may suspect an allusion to Exodus traditions. The theme of the despoiling of the Egyptians (Exod 3:21–22; 11:2; 12:35–36) also underlies the requirement in the Cyrus Diktat that the local population had to hand over silver, gold, livestock, and other goods to those about to leave Babylon for Judah (Ezra 1:4).

The poem moves on to specify the materials for the rebuilding of the city and the symbolic names to be assigned to its walls and gates upon their completion and dedication (vv 17–18). Since the splendor of the Second Temple is to surpass that of the First (Hag 2:9), gold, silver, bronze, and iron are to replace bronze, iron, wood, and stone respectively, though for the author of Chronicles the more precious materials in the series beginning, with gold and ending with iron, were stored up by David for the Solomonic temple (1 Chr 29:1–5). The Historian also goes on to note that gold, silver, and cedarwood were abundant during the reign of Solomon (1 Kgs 10:21, 27). This inventory of building materials compares with a promise in an earlier apostrophe to Zion that the gates and walls of the city would be encrusted with precious stones (54:12). In describing the heavenly Jerusalem made of gold, with its walls covered in gemstones and its gates always open, the author of the earliest Christian apocalypse (Rev 21:1–21) has drawn copiously on these Isaian texts.

The terms *pĕqūdâ* (perhaps an abbreviation of *'anšê pĕqūdâ*, "the men charged with overseeing," as Ibn Ezra suggested) and *nōgĕśîm*, "taskmasters," the latter in particular carrying strong negative connotations (Isa 3:12; 9:3[4]; 14:2, 4), contrast sharply with the designations Peace and Righteousness. Ibn Ezra emphasized this negative aspect by identifying them as revenue officials. The point may simply be that there will be no more oppression from forces external or internal, no more coercion, and no more corvée labor. This would be in keeping with other Isaianic allusions to the eschatological horizon of the abolition of war in a nonviolent, harmonious environment (2:2–5; 9:1–6[2–7]; 32:17; and 11:6–9 taken up in 65:25).

But in spite of the previous assertion that foreigners would build the walls (v 10), the author may also have had in mind work leading up to the dedication of the walls and gates, which would have called for overseers and taskmasters. The symbolic names could have been given at a ceremony of consecration with a solemn procession around the walls, as described in Neh 12:27–43. Gates were and are of course named, and we know of ten such names from the account of Nehemiah's reconstruction of the city wall (Neh 3:1–32). But instead of mundane names such as the Dung Gate, the Fish Gate, or the Second City Gate, in the glorious city of the future all the gates will bear the name Tehillah, "Praise."

Return to the theme of light radiating from a divine source (vv 19–20 cf. vv 1–2) looks like an inclusio and has therefore suggested to some commentators that the following two verses (21–22) have been added to the poem. Koenen (1990, 156), for example, takes v 21 to be a redactional link between chs. 60 and 61 and relegates v 22 to a later glossator. Commentators have also noticed that v 20, stating that there will be no more sunsets or settings of the moon, in effect restates v 19, and in both verses YHVH is described as *'ôr 'ôlām*, "everlasting light." There seems therefore to have been some duplication.

If, however, we simply take the text as it is, we can read it as a variation on a common apocalyptic theme. According to one version, the sun and moon, regarded and worshiped as celestial powers or deities (e.g., Deut 4:19; 17:3; Jer 8:2; 19:3; Zeph 1:5), will be punished with imprisonment and eventual extinction when the Kingdom of God is established in Jerusalem (Isa 24:23). This theme will undergo further and sometimes strange developments in post-biblical texts (e.g., *1 En.* 18:11–19:3) and in early Christian writings (2 Pet 2:4; Jude 13). At the other extreme is the version that the last age will witness a sevenfold increase in intensity from the light of both the sun and moon. The effect is seen to be beneficial, and it would perhaps be too literal-minded to ask whether the writer has considered what effect a corresponding increase in temperature would have (Isa 30:26). In the poem under consideration, YHVH God, as the ultimate source of light, will substitute for the sun and moon in the city. It is this variation that is taken up by the author of the book of Revelation: "The city has no need for the sun or the moon to shine on it, for the glory of God is its light" (Rev 21:23; see also 22:5).

The poem ends with its own nuanced restatement of the Abrahamic promise of land and nationhood (vv 21–22). In these verses the promise is addressed to Zion's people: YHVH's planting and the work of his hands. The shoot planted by YHVH does not allude to the Davidic dynast (11:1) but is an ideal projection of the people of Israel as they were intended by God to be from the beginning (cf. 61:3, where the same language is used).

The promise of land cannot be construed (as it often has been construed) in a straightforward way as legitimating a political claim to territory centuries later. In the first place, this would imply factoring out the overriding moral dimension of prophetic discourse (justice and righteousness as absolutely indispensable) and some important qualifications. The promise is not unconditional, and those to whom the promise is addressed in this section of the book are the servants and elect of YHVH (65:9). Possession of "my holy mountain" is not promised to all, only to those who take refuge in the God of Israel (57:13).

The alphabetic Ps 37, on which the author of Isa 60:1–22 may have drawn, has as its main theme the promise of land, but the promise is made to the lowly and humble ('ănāvîm)—to those who trust in God and wait for him, who are blessed by him and (as in Isa 60:21) are acknowledged as righteous (ṣaddîqîm). It should also not be overlooked that in v 21 and throughout Ps 37 the word "land" ('ereṣ) occurs without the article. Hence, as several commentators have pointed out (e.g., Fohrer 1964, 232), there is here an underlying issue of setting to right social wrongs in evidence at the time of writing, probably about the mid–fifth century B.C.E.: expropriations, enclosure of peasant land, and unjust taxation leading to forfeiture of the plot of land on which one's survival depended. This promise of land may also have been the original sense of the blessing on the "meek" (praeis → 'ănāvîm) in the Beatitudes (Matt 5:5).

The promise of posterity made to Abraham and the other ancestors (gôy 'āṣûm, "a numerous nation," here and in Gen 18:18) became a major theme in Deuteronomy and related writings (Deut 9:14; 26:5). In the context of the poem's original production, the promise recapitulates the demographic theme often expressed in these chapters (43:5–7; 44:3–5; 49:19–21; 51:1–2; 54:1–3; 65:9).

Volz (1932, 249) was probably correct in reading the last verse (22b) as the finale to the entire poem. All that has been described will indeed come about, it is guaranteed by the simple self-declaration "I am YHVH," but it will come about in God's good time, meaning at its appointed and predestined time (bě-'ittî). Only God knows the day and the hour. This is the only answer to the dismay and perplexity of people at that time, and at other times, faced with the "delay of the parousia" and the silence and absence of God in the troubled affairs of humanity.

THE PROPHETIC DISCIPLE'S MISSION (61:1–7)

(Ausin 1999, 97–124; Beuken 1989b, 411–26; Cannon 1929, 284–88; Collins 1997, 225–40; Everson 1978, 69–73; Gerstenberger 2001; Gowan 1981, 404–9; Grelot 1990, 414–31; Jüngling 1993:199–219; Kellermann 1991, 46–82; Koenen 1990, 103–12; Lau 1994, 66–80; Neirynck 1997, 27–64; Sanders 1975, 75–106; 1982, 144–55; J. J. Schmitt 1980, 97–108; Steck 1986b, 323–38 = 1991a, 106–18; Zimmerli 1963[1950], 226–28)

i

61   ¹The spirit of the Sovereign Lord YHVHª is upon me,
       because YHVH has anointed me.
       He has sent me to announce good news to the poor,
       to bind up the wounds of those broken in spirit;
       to proclaim freedom to captives,
       releaseᵇ to those in prison;

[2]to proclaim the year of YHVH's good pleasure,
a day of vindication for our God;
to comfort all those who mourn,
[3]to give to those who mourn over Zion[c]
a turban in place of ashes,
festive oil in place of a mournful appearance,
a splendid garment in place of a drooping spirit.

ii

They will be called[d] strong and sturdy oaks[e]
that YHVH has planted for his glory.
[4]They will rebuild the ancient ruins,
restore the places long desolate,
repair the ruined cities
desolate for ages past.[f]
[5]Foreigners will serve as shepherds of your flocks,
aliens will farm your land and dress your vines;
[6]but you will be called the priests of YHVH,
you will be addressed as the ministers of our God.
You will live off the wealth of nations,
you will revel[g] in their riches.
[7]Instead of shame,[h] they will have a double portion,
instead of disgrace they will exult in their lot,[i]
they will possess a double portion in their land,
everlasting joy will be theirs.

NOTES

[a]   1QIsaiah[a] omits *'ădōnāy*, but this fuller title appears elsewhere when the prophet speaks in his own name (48:16; 50:4–9).

[b]   This word, *pĕqaḥ-qôaḥ*, is hapax; 1QIsa[a] writes it as one word, *pqḥqvḥ*, but MT is supported by 4QIsa[m]; GKC §84[b]n takes it to be a case of reduplicated second and third radicals (*qĕtaltal* form), but it could be an error for *pĕqôaḥ*; LXX (also Luke 4:18) substitutes "recovery of sight for the blind," for "release," perhaps because the verb *pqḥ* refers, with one exception (Isa 42:20), to opening eyes.

[c]   This verse (3a) is overloaded with two infinitives, but *la'ăbēlê ṣiyyôn*, also in LXX, Vulg., and 1QIsa[a], should not be omitted; if LXX *dothēnai* translates *lāśûm (lāśîm)* there is nothing corresponding to *lātēt lāhem* ("to give them"), though *autois* ("to them") precedes *doxan* in LXX[ℵ] and LXX[B]; there is still nothing corresponding to the second infinite; I therefore conclude tentatively that *lātēt lāhem* is an alternative phrasing that has found its way into the text.

[d]   1QIsaiah[a] has active *vqr'v*, "they will call them," but LXX (*klēthēsontai*) and Vulg. (*vocabuntur*) support MT.

^e An attempt to render the sense of MT *'êlê haṣṣedeq*, cf. Vulg. *fortes iustitiae*
     ("strong ones of justice") and Aqu., Symm., Theod. *ischuroi tou dikaiou*
     ("strong ones of the Just One") cf. Scullion 1982, 178, "the oaks of the Just
     One." See Comments.

^f 1QIsaiah^a repeats the verb *yqvmmv* from the end of v 4a, a simple case of
     dittography.

^g MT *tityammārû* apparently → *ymr* Hithpael hapax cf. LXX *thaumasthēsest-*
     hai, "[in their wealth] you will be an object of wonder," presumably → *tmh*
     Hithpael "to be astonished" (e.g., Hab 1:5); others propose a derivation
     from *môr*, "exchange," e.g., NEB "[You will] succeed to their riches";
     1QIsa^a *tty'mrv* cf. Ps 94:4 *yit'ammĕrû* → *'mr* II "boast" has strong support
     in the Jewish exegetical tradition (Ibn Ezra, Radaq, et al.), Vulg. *super-*
     bietis, Syr., Theod., Symm.; further discussion in Barthélemy 1986, 422–23.

^h Literally, "your shame," with 2d-person pl. suffix (*boštĕkem*); the change
     from 2d to 3d person in this verse is somewhat unusual.

ⁱ This entire verse, 7a, is very elliptical; literally "instead of your shame,
     [you will have] a double portion, [instead of] disgrace, they will exult [in]
     their lot"; *taḥat* = "instead of," is preferable to *taḥat* = "because," since
     (1) the latter requires *taḥat kî* (cf. Prov 1:29; perhaps Deut 4:37); and
     (2) this construction with the meaning "instead of" is attested in the same
     section (60:15, 17) and in the passage immediately preceding (61:3).

COMMENTS

In Isa 61:1–7 we are hearing a different voice, one that conveys a sense of strong
individuality. The reference to anointing has led to the view that this is the
high priest speaking of his consecration (Grelot 1990, 414–31), but the mission
is not really consistent with high priestly responsibilities, and the verb "anoint"
is used metaphorically as well as in the literal sense. It is equally difficult to understand how the speaker could be the Servant (Torrey 1928, 453) or the Servant as Israel (Smart 1965, 259–60) or as "la communauté des justes," since the
community would then have a mission directed at itself (Vermeylen 1978,
478–81). For similar reasons, the voice is not the collective voice of Hanson's
visionary-prophetic-Levitical minority (Hanson 1975, 65–70; Achtemeier 1982,
88). Arguing for the speaker as the Messiah-Servant (Oswalt 1998, 562–63) fa-
cilitates a straightforward identification with Jesus, who applied Isa 61:1–2a
(quoted according to LXX) to himself in the synagogue at Nazareth (Luke 4:18–
19). We may accept this in a general sense, but it does not relieve us of the necessity to seek an answer in the context of the place and time of composition.

The language in which the speaker's endowment is described sends back
an echo of the investiture of Cyrus as YHVH's servant (42:1–4), reinforced by
his appointment as YHVH's *māšîaḥ*, "anointed one." The resemblance is readily
understandable on the supposition that the mission laid on Cyrus passed, by
default, to the Servant and his disciples and that, in consequence, what was
said about Cyrus in 42:1–4 was reinterpreted to apply to the Servant. More-

over, no one could credibly have made Cyrus an instrument of vindication "for our God" (v 2).

With relatively few exceptions, interpreters have followed the Targum in identifying the speaker in 61:1–3 as an individual prophet, for the simple reason that the language indicates *prophetic* commissioning. At intervals throughout chs. 40–66, the prophetic-authorial voice is heard, beginning with the brief dialogue at the outset:

> A voice says, "Proclaim!"
> I replied, "What shall I proclaim?" (40:6)

The giving of the spirit and sending on a mission is anticipated in the fragmentary saying in 48:16 ("and now the Sovereign Lord YHVH has sent me, and his spirit . . ."). There the voice trails away, but it comes through loud and clear in the Servant's declarations in 49:1–6 and 50:4–9. Finally, there is the promise in 59:21 that the mission to utter spirit-inspired prophecy will be carried on into the future by the disciples of the seer who is here addressed. The language of spirit possession combined with that of mission, both in Isaiah (cf. 6:8; 9:7; 42:19; 48:16) and elsewhere (Exod 3:13–15; 1 Sam 15:1; 2 Kgs 2:4; Jer 25:17; 26:12–15), points to a prophetic profile.

The wording of the account of investiture and mission is also reminiscent of language dealing with the same phenomena in chs. 40–55, especially Duhm's *Ebedlieder* (42:1–4 with the comment in vv 5–9; 49:1–6; 50:4–11; 52:13–53:12). This can be seen by comparing the way the mission is described in 61:1–3 with two of these passages that contain a similar series of clauses of purpose introduced with the infinitive (42:7; 49:5–6). Endowment with the spirit of God recalls 42:1 (*nātattî rûḥî ʿālâv*, "I have put my spirit upon him"), and announcing good news (verb *bśr*) is the heart and soul of the prophetic commission in chs. 40–55 (40:9; 41:27; 52:7). It may also be significant that the fuller title "the Sovereign Lord YHVH" appears in passages in which the prophet speaks in his own name (48:16; 50:4–9) and rarely elsewhere. A necessary clarification is in order — namely, that the original attribution of the first of the Servant passages to Cyrus (argued in Volume 2, pp. 207–12) is not a problem, since it is hardly possible that the passage would have been preserved without reinterpretation once Cyrus, having failed to live up to expectations, had passed from the scene.

The view that 61:1–3 (or, according to others, 61:1–4) is a displaced "Servant song" was advocated in the early twentieth century by some scholars of note (Rudolph, Procksch, Caspari; see also Cannon 1929, 284–88) but is rarely heard today. If we assume some degree of continuity of tradition within the second half of the book, the similarities and the differences of chs. 56–66 vis-à-vis chs. 40–55 (which will be pointed out as we proceed) can best be explained on the supposition that the voice we are hearing in 61:1–3 is that of a disciple of the Servant and therefore one of the "Servants of YHVH" of whom we hear in chs. 65–66.

There is some uncertainty regarding the extent of this prophetic declaration and the way it relates to the remainder of ch. 61. According to Beuken (1989b,

414), vv 1–7 are the prophet's statement about his mission, 8–9 contain divine confirmation of the same, and 10–11 present the prophet's own song of thanksgiving. This is an attractive reading not only because of its integrative character but also because a parallel is available in the words of assurance followed by a hymn immediately after Duhm's second Servant passage (49:8–13). There is also a hymn of praise and thanksgiving following the first "Servant song" (42:10–13), and we shall note in due course that the hymn uses terminology similar to the commissioning. But 61:8–9 cannot be construed as a confirmation of the prophet's mission, and vv 3b–7 (set out in a separate stanza in my translation), which predict the community's future well-being, read like a continuation of the preceding passage 60:10–16, but have no essential relationship with the prophet's assignment in vv 1–3a.

The speaker justifies the good news for Jerusalem proclaimed in chs. 60–62 by his endowment with the spirit of God. The term corresponding to "spirit" (rûaḥ), has a broad semantic range, including wind; breath; psychic energy manifested in different ways, including, for example, jealousy (Num 5:14, 30), depression (1 Sam 16:14–16), and states of extraordinary excitation (Judg 14:6, 19; 15:14). In accounts of prophetic phenomena in the early history of Israel, charismatic leaders and warlords (e.g., Samson and the other "judges," and, preeminently, Saul) are endowed with the spirit of God. Spirit-possession is, however, associated in a special way with ecstatic prophecy, especially of the communal kind, inducing transformed states of consciousness, whether spontaneous or solicited, and with or without the use of psychotropic agents. It has often been noted that this kind of phenomenon and the corresponding vocabulary are relatively rare in classical prophecy, beginning in the eighth century B.C.E., but reappear in sometimes strange and disturbing ways in Ezekiel (3:12, 14; 8:3; 11:1 etc.).

By the time our texts were being spoken or written, spirit-possession was seen to be a permanent rather than sporadic endowment, one linked with rites and institutions. This change is evident if we compare Deut 34:9 — in which Joshua is full of the spirit as a result of the rite of laying on of hands — with Num 27:18 — in which Joshua is Moses' successor by virtue of being antecedently "a man in whom is the spirit." It seems that succession to the prophetic leader, the passing on of charisma, is modeled on the succession of Elisha to the prophetic office of Elijah (2 Kgs 2:9–15). As Max Weber has shown, succession in office after the death or retirement of the founder or leader is the crucial event that decides whether charismatic authority can continue as a force within the group of disciples, a point that has often been verified throughout history. We can detect the influence of the prophetic Elijah–Elisha paradigm in the account of the taking up of Jesus and coming of the Holy Spirit on the disciples (Acts 1:6–11: the looking up to heaven, being clothed with power, endowment with the leader's spirit, and the subsequent working of miracles).

In the case of the anonymous prophet of Isa 61:1, the routinization of prophetic charisma is connected with anointing. Anointing is a rite associated with priests (Exod 28:41; 29:7; 30:30 etc.) and kings (Judg 9:8, 15; 1 Sam 9:16;

2 Sam 2:4 etc.) but not with prophets. Here, therefore, the anointing is metaphorical, conveying the idea of full and permanent authorization to carry out the prophet's God-given assignment.

It bears repeating that, when this statement is read in the context of chs. 40–66 as a whole, it adds another sliver of evidence in favor of an ongoing discipleship that owed allegiance to the prophetic Servant whose witness, we are told, would be continued after his death by his "seed" (*zera'*)—that is, his disciples (53:10). The spirit and the mission are mentioned in the fragment of discourse in 48:16b and again, more fully, in 59:21 which, together with our passage, forms an inclusion or envelope for the apostrophe in 60:1–22 (see Comments on 59:21).

In this statement (59:21) addressed to a disciple, the essence of prophecy is expressed in the association of spirit-endowment with a mission to speak, using the Deuteronomic idiom of putting words in the mouth (Deut 18:18; Jer 1:9). The idiom is not used in 61:1–3a, but it is clear that the assignment has to do essentially with speaking (proclaiming, announcing, comforting). As stated, the mission is fivefold, but these five charges coalesce in one undertaking. As one who is sent to announce good news (verb *bśr* cf. 40:9; 41:27; and LXX *euangelisasthai*, "to gospel"), the speaker takes over and continues the role of thè *měbaśśēr* of Isa 52:7–8, whose message is that YHVH is about to return to Zion and inaugurate his rule.

To whom is this good news addressed? Most scholars now take the term *'ānāv* (always in the pl., *'ănāvîm*, with the exception of Num 12:3) as a variant form of the more common *'ānî*, both derived from the verb *'nh* II, "to be destitute, miserable, oppressed." Both the contexts in which these words appear and the terms denoting poverty and destitution with which they are associated (*'ebyôn, dal, rāš*) lead to the conclusion that the socioeconomic connotation is the basic one. So, for example, the legislation forbids charging interest to a fellow–Hebrew debtor who is *'ānî* (Exod 22:24[25]), the poor day-laborer must be paid his wages promptly (Deut 24:14–15), and gleaning rights for the poor are part of a kind of social security system required by law (Lev 19:10; 23:22). Some of the fiercest invective of the great eighth-century B.C.E. prophets is reserved for those who oppress the *'ănāvîm* and deprive them of their legal rights—a class that also includes widows, orphans, and displaced persons (Amos 2:7 cf. Isa 3:14; 10:2). This prophetic "preferential option for the poor" is perhaps the most significant contribution of the Hebrew prophets to the moral tradition of Judaism and Christianity.

The creation in Judah of a peasant underclass detached from the basic securities of household and land can be traced back to the consolidation of the state apparatus in the eighth century B.C.E. The state needed land to support its operations and reward its retainers. Because the state also came to control the judicial system, it could pass "wicked decrees and oppressive regulations" (Isa 10:1), resulting in enclosure of peasant land, heavy taxation, forfeiture of property as a result of insolvency, and the formation of latifundia for the benefit of the Judean *nouveaux riches*. The resulting situation was exacerbated by the

Babylonian conquest and occupation and by social conflict following the immigration of Judeo-Babylonians in the early Persian period.

We have seen a passing allusion to this situation in the sermon on true fasting, which refers to the imprisoned, the hungry, and the homeless (Isa 58:6–7). The Nehemiah Memoir gives us a more substantial and detailed picture:

There arose a great outcry of the common people and their wives against their fellow Jews. Some were saying, "We are putting up our sons and daughters as surety to buy grain in order to stay alive," while others were saying, "We are mortgaging our fields, vineyards and houses in order to get grain during the famine." Others again were saying, "We have borrowed money against our fields and vineyards to pay the king's tax. Our bodies are no different from the bodies of our fellows, and our children are no different from theirs; yet here we are, at the point of forcing our sons and daughters to become slaves. Indeed, some of our daughters have already been forced into that condition, but there is nothing we can do, since our fields and vineyards belong to others." (Neh 5:1–5)

The fact that the poor are associated with people whose spirit has been broken by affliction (nišběrê-lēb, literally, "the brokenhearted") anticipates the declaration in 66:2 that those whom God regards with favor are the poor ('ānî) and the afflicted in spirit (někēh-rûaḥ). It is relevant to note that whenever the poor, needy, or oppressed are mentioned in the liturgical hymns the context is always religious. The poor are the righteous (ṣaddîqîm, Ps 109:16, 22), God's own people (Ps 72:2, 4, 12), and their opponents are the proud, impious, and godless (Ps 10:2, 9; 35:10; 147:6). The poor are, above all, those who seek YHVH (Ps 22:27; 69:33), and to seek God is, in these texts, the essence of true religion.

By the time of writing, therefore, the terms in question ('ǎnāvîm, 'āniyyîm) had acquired a broader and specifically religious connotation without losing their basic sense of economic deprivation, marginalization, and exploitation. Some scholars have argued that the 'ǎnāvîm, whom we hear of occasionally in psalms (e.g., Ps 10:17–18), addressed God collectively as a distinct community or party, an anticipation therefore of encratic sects in early Christianity, including the Ebionites (i.e., "The Poor") and, eventually, monasticism and religious orders. If this is so, it is doubtful that it came about as the result of embracing voluntary poverty. As exploited subjects of an imperial power (the Babylonians and then the Persians) the people as a whole would have merited being called "the poor of YHVH." Control of the temple with its considerable assets would have translated into a great deal of social control, including the power to excommunicate, with the resulting loss of social status and property (Ezra 10:8); hence, the complaint of those who "tremble at God's word" that they have been cast out for his Name's sake (Isa 66:5).

In keeping with the good news of the removal of economic and social disabilities, the prophet is to proclaim freedom for individuals sold into indentured service for the kinds of reasons exemplified in the Nehemiah Memoir. That debt or poverty was the primary if not necessarily exclusive reason for captivity and prison can be deduced from the language. The expression *liqrō᾽ děrôr* ("proclaim freedom") is a technical term for the solemn proclamation of the *šěmiṭṭâ* (Jer 34:17), the seventh year "release," when fellow-Israelites who had been sold into indentured service were to be set free and their outstanding debts forgiven (Exod 21:2; Deut 15:1–11; Jer 34:8–22). "The year of YHVH's good pleasure" (*šěnat rāṣôn laYHVH*) probably refers to the same social institution, one we suspect that was more honored in the breach than the observance.

Linking the year of divine favor with the day of vindication (*yôm nāqām*, "the day of vengeance," in RSV) is surprising at first sight because this Trito-Isaianic core (chs. 60–62) appears to focus exclusively on the positive aspects of Zion's future. Steck (1991a, 114–17), therefore, removed the problem by the simple expedient of emending *nāqām* to *yěšû῾â* ("salvation"), arguing that the idea of vengeance was introduced by the editor of the *Grossjesajabuch* with reference to punishment on Babylon (cf. 47:3). Others (e.g., Westermann 1969, 367; Beuken 1989b, 421–22) have taken the less drastic option of interpreting *nāqām* in the positive sense of "restoration" or "restitution." This seems to be going too far since, following biblical usage, punitive action against YHVH's enemies seems to be an essential feature of the end-time scenario (Lev 26:25; Deut 32:35, 41, 43; Ps 58:11; Prov 6:34), not least in Isaiah (34:8; 35:4; 47:3; 59:17; 63:4). In this sense, "the day of vindication" signifies an aspect of the "Day of YHVH," familiar from prophetic texts (with Westermann 1969, 367; Lau 1994, 75–76; for further discussion of the issue, see Koenen 1990, 118–19).

In keeping with the original commissioning of prophets in 40:1 ("Comfort, O comfort my people"), this prophetic disciple must also address words of comfort to those who mourn. Mourning is the spiritual and psychological condition appropriate to a time of fasting, in the present context fasting that commemorated the destruction of Jerusalem and its temple (58:1–12; Zech 7:1–7; 8:18–19). It seems that the devout, including the disciples of the prophetic Servant, went beyond the scheduled fasts to make this attitude of mourning into a characteristic feature of their piety; hence, "mourners," *᾽ăbēlîm, mit᾽abbělîm* (57:18; 61:2–3; 66:10), became a familiar designation analogous to "Servants of YHVH" (*῾abdê YHVH*) and "Tremblers" (*ḥărēdîm*). We can compare them with those mentioned in Mal 3:14 who went about as mourners (*qědōrannît*) and appear to have formed a distinctive group.

One of the most characteristic themes of chs. 56–66 is the assurance that the present unsatisfactory situation will be reversed by a divine intervention in the affairs of the Jewish community that will bring history as we know it to an end. At this point the reversal is from mourning to comfort, and assurance of its ultimate fulfillment is continued from the prophetic witness in chs. 40–55 (40:1; 49:13; 51:3, 12, 19; 52:9) and will reappear in the Matthean Beatitudes (Matt 5:4).

Reversal is also rendered by means of the traditional behavior associated with fasting. Instead of the uncovered head (Ezek 24:17, 23) on which ashes are sprinkled (2 Sam 13:19; Ezek 27:30), there will be a turban; instead of an unwashed and disheveled aspect, a body treated with oil; and instead of a mournful posture ("bowing the head like a bulrush," 58:5), reinforced no doubt by torn garments (2 Sam 13:19; Jer 41:5), a festive robe (maʿătēh hapax). The point is also made by the reversal of consonants and sound in the first of the three images: pĕʾēr taḥat ʾēper, "a turban instead of ashes."

The remainder of this passage (vv 3c–7) is attached to the prophetic commissioning but is in reality, as we proposed earlier, the continuation of the interrupted apostrophe in the preceding chapter. Exegetes ancient and modern have had a lot of trouble with the description of the "mourners" as ʾêlê haṣṣedeq, literally, "oaks of righteousness." This genitival phrase could be translated "righteous oaks" (as in Duhm 1922, 455), but an alternative meaning of ṣedeq is shown by its parallelism with yĕšûʿâ or yešaʿ, "salvation" (45:8; 51:5; 62:1), and kābôd, "glory" (58:8; 62:2), which gives a more satisfactory sense — Eichen des Heils ("oaks of salvation") (Volz 1932, 253; Fohrer 1964, 233; Westermann 1969, 364). Even more satisfactory is Volz's suggestion, in his commentary, that in this context ṣedeq implies Echtheit, "authenticity" — namely, that the oaks are Eichen wie sie sein sollen, "oaks as oaks ought to be." This is what I have tried to convey in translating the expression "strong and sturdy oaks."

If the statement about the work of repair, restoration, and rebuilding (v 4) is read in context, it contradicts the earlier statement that the walls would be built by foreigners (60:10). It may have been known at the time of writing that foreigners did not in fact build or repair the walls, or this may have been considered an inappropriate assignment for foreigners, in consequence of which they were given more menial tasks. The wall rebuilt under Nehemiah's leadership (Neh 3:1–32) may have been damaged shortly before his arrival in 445 B.C.E. under circumstances unknown to us; we do not know whether any work on the wall had been carried out prior to this time. But if, as suggested above, the location of vv 1–3b was the result of a deliberate editorial decision, the rebuilders, restorers, and repairers could still be foreigners. It should be noted that the "ruins and desolate places" (ḥorbôt, šōmĕmôt, a stereotypical combination, Isa 49:19; Ezek 29:10) had been there for a long time. This would be consistent with a date near the middle of the fifth century, some one hundred thirty years after the destruction of Jerusalem.

That the people addressed — in the immediate context, Judeans responsive to prophetic preaching — will be regarded as priests and ministers (kōhănîm, mĕšārētîm, terms practically synonymous at the time of writing) does not imply "an astonishing democratization of the formerly exclusive sacerdotal office" (Hanson 1975, 68). The immediate sequel provides a less recondite meaning: these Judeans will be to Gentiles as priests are to laity, who therefore are obliged to support the priests with material resources; hence, a more vivid restatement of the "despoiling of the Egyptians" theme often heard in these chapters, most recently in 60:5–7, 16.

The passage ends with the promise of a double portion in their land (this last phrase unaccountably omitted from NRSV) and the promise of everlasting joy. The assurance of a double portion (mišneh) of land echoes the double punishment (kiplayim) inflicted on Israel for its sins (40:2) and perhaps also the double disaster, famine, and sword inflicted on Jerusalem (51:19; see Vol. 2, p. 181). It is, in its turn, echoed in later prophecy (Zech 9:12). This kind of language brings to mind the sufferings of Job and how the account ended with his receiving double (*lĕmišneh*, Job 42:10): twice as many sons and twice as much property. The correspondence between Job's situation and that of Israel and between the land of Uz and the land of Judah comes into clearer focus when we read, in the same verse in Job, that YHVH restored his fortunes (*šāb 'et-šĕbût*), since this is the standard phrase for return from exile and post-destruction restoration in Deuteronomy (30:3) and prophetic texts (Jer 29:14; 30:3, 18; Ezek 39:25; Amos 9:14; Zeph 3:20 etc.). These and other parallels prompt a reading of the book of Job as a different way of coming to terms with the disasters of the sixth century B.C.E.

COVENANT OF BLESSING AND A HYMN OF THANKSGIVING (61:8–11)

(Beuken 1989b, 411–42; Elliger 1928, 24–26; Gowen 1981, 404–9; Koenen 1990, 115–22; de Moor 1997, 325–46)

TRANSLATION

i

61   [8]I, YHVH, love justice,
    I hate rapine and wrongdoing.[a]
    I will give them[b] a sure reward[c]
    and make with them a perpetual covenant.
    [9]Their descendants will be known[d] among the nations,
    their offspring in the midst of the peoples;
    all who see them will acknowledge
    that they are a race blessed by YHVH.

ii

    [10e]I will rejoice in YHVH with all my heart,
    my whole being will delight in my God,
    for he has clothed me in the garments of triumph,[f]
    wrapped[g] me in the robe of victory,
    as a bridegroom puts on a turban like a priest,[h]
    or a bride adorns herself with her finery.
    [11]As the earth brings forth its growth,
    as a garden causes its plants to flourish,
    so will the Sovereign Lord God[i] make victory and renown
    to flourish before all the nations.[j]

NOTES

a   MT *gāzēl bĕʿôlâ*, "rapine accompanied by a burnt offering," supported by Vulg. *in holocausto*, possible but unlikely; *ʿôlâ* is a rare variant of the more common *ʿavlâ*, "wrongdoing," as in 1QIsaᵃ; Ps 58:3[2] and 64:7[6] cf. LXX *ex adikias*, "from injustice."

b   1QIsaiahᵃ has 2d-person pl. suffixes down to 9a, inclusive.

c   *pĕʿullâ*, "reward" or "just wage," 40:10; 49:4; 62:11; 65:7. LXX *kai dōsō to mochthon autōn tois dikaiois*, "I will give the righteous their labor," and Vulg. *opus eorum*, "their work," based on a misunderstanding of the verb *pʿl*.

d   Targum *ytrbvn*, "they will be brought up [among the nations]," a more explicit reference to the diaspora.

e   Targum "Jerusalem has said, 'I will rejoice . . .'"; LXX *euphranthēsontai*, "they will rejoice."

f   LXX *himation sōtēriou*, "the cloak of salvation."

g   For MT *yĕʿāṭānî*, apparently Perfect → *yʿṭ* (unattested); BHS proposes *yaʿāṭēnî* 3d-person sing. Imperfect Hiphil *ʿṭh*, "cover," put on."

h   The verb *yĕkahēn* is denominative → *khn* "to function as, or act like a priest (*kōhēn*)"; no need to emend to *yākîn* (BHS), "place firmly," which is not very appropriate in the context; cf. 1QIsaᵃ *kkvhn*, "like a priest," and Tg. "who is happy in his bridal chamber, and as the high priest adorned with his vestments."

i   1QIsaiahᵃ omits *ʾădōnay*, reading YHVH *ʾlvhym* instead.

j   Targum ends "So will YHVH God reveal the righteousness and glory of Jerusalem before all the peoples."

COMMENTS

The core passage of chs. 56–66 continues with a declaration or self-predication of YHVH (61:8–9) followed by a hymn that, although based on the thanksgiving psalms, was created ad hoc for this situation (10–11). One result of the prophetic conviction of speaking in the Name of God is that it is not always possible to distinguish the prophetic from the divine first person. This going back and forth between third and first person with reference to YHVH is attested throughout chs. 60–62 and is not always indicative of a division in the text. The only exceptions are 61:1–3b, where the prophet speaks in his own name; 62:8, which is a direct citation; and 61:8–9, where YHVH is also explicitly identified as speaker.

This first passage (61:8–9) should be read as affirming the truth and authority of the prophetic prediction in vv 1–3b rather than confirming the prophet's credentials. Read in context, it would be a declaration in favor of those who mourn over Zion (vv 2–3), but as a distinct statement it is a declaration in favor of Israel *tout court* vis-à-vis foreign nations. Hence the need to reject the alternative reading of the second half of v 8a ("I hate rapine together with a burnt offering"; see Notes). The idea is that, since YHVH is a God of justice (cf. Ps 37:28), he opposes the rapine and wrongdoing from which Israel has suffered for so long. The twin concepts of reward (*pĕ'ullâ*) and retribution (*gĕmûl*) play an important role in Isa 40–66. The positive term (*pĕ'ullâ*) connotes giving people what is their due, and it is therefore found parallel with "justice" (*mišpāṭ*, 49:4) and "wages" (*śākār*, 40:10; 62:10; cf. Lev 19:13). The idea is introduced at the very beginning of 40–66 (Israel's servitude is over, her debt has been paid, 40:2) and serves to make connection with the "double portion" in the passage immediately preceding (61:7). In one instance only (65:7), *pĕ'ullâ* has the same negative force as *gĕmûl* (35:4; 59:18; 66:6), with the sense of paying someone back for wrongs committed.

The perpetual covenant (*bĕrît 'ôlām*) is more a declaration of intent than a bilateral agreement, and in this sense it appears in the Priestly history in the Pentateuch in connection with the postdiluvian dispensation (Gen 9:16) and the institution of circumcision (Gen 17:7, 13, 19). A perpetual covenant is one that, unlike other covenants and treaties between parties equal or unequal, does not require reconfirmation or reratification at intervals—or example at the death of a ruler. Use of the expression at this point may have been prompted by the perpetual Davidic covenant mentioned at 55:3–5, which gave him pre-eminence among the nations. This is precisely what is promised for Israel as a whole in 61:8–9.

Since no one at the time of writing was concerned with identifying distinct sources in the Pentateuch, there would have been no problem in applying the Priestly concept of a *bĕrît 'ôlām* to the Abrahamic promises. Without subscribing to Torrey's identification of the Servant figure with Abraham (Torrey 1928, 310–13 and passim), we can say that the Abrahamic traditions, in whatever form they existed at that time, constitute an important subplot throughout chs. 40–66. Anxiety about demographic survival and land tenure, for understandable reasons acute in the early Persian period, are reflected in the Abraham narrative cycle.

In Isa 40–66, wherever the great nation theme (44:1–5; 48:19; 51:2; 54:1; 60:21–22) or secure tenure of land (49:19–21; 60:21) in an issue, the figure of Abraham will be somewhere in the background. Likewise, the shadowy figure of the initially infertile Sarah, who is mentioned once (51:2), can be discerned behind that of the woman Zion (54:1–8). The clearest statement is 60:21–22:

> Your people, righteous one and all,
> will possess the land forever,
> the shoot that I myself planted,
> the work of my hands that I might be glorified.
> The least will become a thousand,
> the youngest a numerous nation.
> I am YHVH!
> At its appointed time,
> swiftly will I bring it about.

The people will be righteous like Abraham (Gen 15:6), they will inherit land (Gen 15:7), they will become a great nation (*gôy gādôl*, Gen 12:2), and all of this is confirmed by a strong asseveration comparable to an oath (Gen 15:18–21).

The linked promises of land and nationhood are encapsulated in the blessing on Abraham and his descendants with which vv 8–9 conclude. Invocation of the blessing on Abraham is repeated practically verbatim in 65:23b: "they will be a race blessed by YHVH, / they and their offspring with them," using the same paired terms, *zeraʿ*, "race," literally "seed"; and *ṣeʾĕṣāʾîm*, "offspring" (see also 44:3 and 48:19).

There is a rather abrupt passage from vv 8–9, spoken by YHVH, to v 10, which is a thanksgiving hymn addressed to YHVH, though similar eschatological psalms of praise are present throughout the second major segment of the book (42:10–13; 44:23; 45:8; 49:13 cf. also 12:1–6). Many commentators restrict the hymn to v 10 on the grounds that it interrupts the continuity between v 9 and v 11 and has therefore been inserted at this point (Marti 1900, 387–88; Duhm 1922, 458; Fohrer 1964, 254; Pauritsch 1971, 106; Westermann 1969, 370–71; Vermeylen 1978, 482–83).

There is reason to believe that v 11 has been appended to v 10 since the transition from investiture and bridal attire in v 10 to the organic metaphor in v 11 is somewhat jarring. But the similarity between 9 and 11 is not striking, and v 11 reads more like a concluding reflection on the ineluctability of the divine plan, comparable to 55:10–11. Both passages use similar metaphors, organic growth and rainfall, and deploy them in the same manner (*kaʾăšer . . . kēn*, "Just as X . . . so Y"). Above all, the two passages are similar in function, in providing a final assurance that what God promises through the words of his prophet will come about as surely as the processes of growth and regeneration in nature will continue to take place.

For the same reason, 61:11 or 61:10–11 should not be attached to the following chapter. Kissane (1960, 281), for example, read 61:10–11 as the first stanza in a poem (61:10–62:9), and de Moor reached the same conclusion on purely stichometric grounds, dividing this extended composition into twelve strophes and six canticles (1997, 325–46). However, the language of this brief psalm and the concluding verse have closer links with 61:1–3 than with ch. 62. The following similarities may be noted:

> *šôś ʾāśîś* (10a) – *šemen śāśôn* (3b)
> *yaʿăṭēnî* (10b) – *maʿaṭeh* (3b)
> *pĕʾēr* (10c) – *pĕʾēr* (3a), *lĕhitpāʾēr* (3c)
> *tĕhillâ* (11b) – *tĕhillâ* (3b)

In addition, the title *ʾădonay YHVH* ("the Sovereign Lord YHVH") is used in both and is absent from ch. 62.

Who is the speaker who rejoices in v 10? Since this brief hymn is modeled on the liturgical thanksgiving psalms (e.g., 9:2–5; 30:2; 35:9–10), the simple answer is this: regardless of who composed the psalm in question, the words are put into the mouth of the anonymous worshiper who has received benefits from YHVH. But, since the psalm was created expressly for this situation, the beneficiaries must be the mourners over Zion (61:2–3), who constitute the holy remnant and who are referred to elsewhere as the Servants of YHVH. Though the language is unspecific in regard to gender, the Targum was not wrong in identifying the speaker explicitly as Jerusalem, since in chs. 56–66 Jerusalem represents the community of the last age, now present proleptically in the community of the faithful. Writers who hold that the speaker is the prophet (e.g., Volz 1932, 260; Sekine 1989, 87; Lau 1994, 86–87) may be correct in terms of authorship. However, the language of this brief psalm is eminently appropriate for Jerusalem as the central symbolic entity in 56–66, but not for a prophet.

Our best clue to decoding the symbolism of investiture is found in the following chapter, which combines the images of royalty (the royal crown and diadem) and the bridal couple and focuses them on Zion/Jerusalem (62:3–5). The age-old rite of the investiture of a monarch gives visual expression to the supreme status of the office. The garments are the garments of triumph and the robe of victory. This ancient royal rite also influenced the investiture of the priest in Israel (Exod 28:1–43; 39:1–31) and is reflected in the Isa 61 psalm, which alludes to the robe (*mĕ'îl*) and the turban (*pĕ'ēr*), which were also part of the sacerdotal wardrobe (Exod 39:28; Ezek 44:18; 1 Chr 15:27). The priestly allusion is the reason for the anomalous use of the verb *khn* (Piel, normally "to function as a priest"), which should not be emended (see Note h).

In the concluding verse rounding off the hymn, the verb *ṣmḥ* (Hiphil, "blossom," "spring up") is used twice, together with the corresponding substantive *ṣemaḥ* ("growth," "shoot"). This raises an interesting issue, because *ṣemaḥ* seems to have become a code name for the Davidic dynast in the post-destruction period. Jeremiah 23:5 and 33:15 anticipate the coming of a righteous or legitimate ruler (*ṣemaḥ ṣaddîq*), and other texts speak symbolically of the raising up of the horn of David (Ezek 29:21; Ps 132:17) or the fallen booth of David (Amos 9:11), clearly referring to the restoration of the national dynasty. During the great crisis at the beginning of the reign of Darius I (521–520), prophetic groups in Judah and possibly in the diaspora were supporting the restoration of the Judean royal house in the person of Zerubbabel, grandson of Jehoiachin, second-last king of Judah. As ruler designate, he is referred to as "my servant *ṣemaḥ*" (Zech 3:8; 6:12), and it is predicted that he will "spring up in his place" (*mittaḥtâv yiṣmaḥ*, Zech 6:12). For these groups, the triumph of Israel would come about under the leadership of a restored dynasty.

By the time Isa 61:10–11 came to be written, Zerubbabel had long disappeared from the scene. There were probably still those who cherished the dynastic hope, but for the Isaianic Servant and his disciples the future lay with a purified Israel as the instrument of God's own unmediated work within human affairs. We see that the organic metaphor of a plant or shoot rising from the ground is still in use but has been reapplied to new events and situations (*ḥǎdāšôt*, Isa 42:9; 43:19) and to the nucleus of a new people envisaged in this prophetic tradition (Isa 44:4; 4:2).

THE NEW JERUSALEM (62:1–5)

(T. D. Anderson 1986, 75–80; Koenen 1990, 122–28; Lau 1994, 90–102; McCarter 1999, 940–41; Schmitt 1985, 557–69)

TRANSLATION

62 [1]For Zion's sake I will not be silent,[a]
for Jerusalem's sake I will not be still
till her vindication[b] breaks out like the morning light,
her salvation[b] burns bright like a flaming torch.
[2]Then nations will see your vindication,
all kings will witness your glory;
you will be called[c] by a new name
that YHVH himself will bestow;[d]
[3]you will be a splendid crown in YHVH's hand,
a royal diadem in the palm of God's hand.
[4]Nevermore will you be called "the Forsaken One,"
never more will your land be called "the Desolate One";[e]
but you will be called[f] "I delight in her,"
and your land will be called "Espoused,"
for YHVH will take delight in you,
and your land will indeed be espoused.
[5]As a young man weds[g] a young woman,
so will your children be united with you;[h]
as the bridegroom rejoices over the bride,
so will your God rejoice over you.

NOTES

[a]   For MT *'eḥĕšeh* → *ḥšh*, 1QIsa[a] has *'ḥryš* → *ḥrš* Hiphil but with the same meaning.

[b]   LXX has the alternative meaning of "righteousness" (*hē dikaiosunē mou*); Vulg. finds a messianic meaning in vv 1–2: *donec egredietur ut splendor iustus eius et salvator eius ut lampas accendatur . . . et videbunt gentes iustum tuum* ("until her Just One proceeds like spendor and her Savior is lit like a lamp . . . and the nations will see your Just One."

[c]   For MT and 1QIsa[b] *qōrā'* Pual (Passive), 1QIsa[a] has *vqr'v lk*, 3d-masc. pl. Active: "and they will call you."

[d]   The verb *nqb* = "pierce," "mark," "designate," but, since designation is by naming (e.g., Num 1:17; Ezra 8:20), "bestow" seems appropriate; Dahood 1977, 527–28 proposed a derivation from *qb'* parallel with *qr'*, "call"; this verb is attested in Ugaritic but not in Biblical Hebrew.

[e]   "The Desolate One" follows 1QIsa[a] *švmmh* (*šômāmâ* fem. participle), supported by Syr. (*sdyt'*) and Vulg. (*desolata*), over MT *šĕmāmâ*, "a desolation,"

supported by LXX (*erēmos*), because it is more in keeping with the context and dependent on Isa 54:1b (pace Barthélemy 1986, 426); see Comments.

f   Here too 1QIsaᵃ has 3d-person pl., as in v 2b.

g   1QIsaiahᵃ has *kbʿvl*, expressing comparison explicitly ("like the marrying of . . ."), as do also the ancient versions; but the comparison is implicit in MT.

h   Since MT *yibʿālûk bānāyik*, "your sons will marry you" seems unacceptable, many commentators and modern versions (e.g., NRSV, NEB) accept Bishop Lowth's emendation to *bōnēk*, "your Builder," that is, God (as in Ps 147:2, *bōnēh yĕrûšālayim* YHVH); see Lowth 1833 (10th ed.), 118: "For as a young man weddeth a virgin, So shall thy restorer wed thee"; but the ancient versions support MT, and the infelicitous suggestion of sons marrying their mother is removed if we assume that MT is playing on the double meaning of the verb *bʿl*, "marry," and "master, possess"; my translation attempts to preserve the basic meaning of the original while avoiding language that for most readers would be insensitive.

COMMENTS

Chapter 62 quickly becomes an apostrophe to Jerusalem, after a brief introduction by the speaker (vv 1–5). Verses 6–9 are an address, citing the direct speech of YHVH and concluding with an invitation or injunction to prepare for the final coming of salvation (10–12). The first question to arise concerns the identity of the speaker in 1–5, who refuses to remain silent. Of course the speaker throughout is the prophet, so the question is really whether the prophet is here speaking in his own name or as the mouthpiece of YHVH. A strong argument in favor of the latter option is the theme of the silence of God repeated poignantly and often in post-destruction prophecies and hymns (Isa 42:14; 57:11; 64:11[12]; 65:6; Ps 28:1; 83:2). The prophet's speaking as the mouthpiece of YHVH is the view of some modern commentators, for example, Bonnard 1972, 425 and Whybray 1975, 246–47. Whybray reads v 1 as a brief oracle of salvation in *oratio recta* by YHVH and vv 2–5 as a prophetic comment on it.

If, however, we read the chapter as an integrated unit, we must take into account the parallel between what the speaker says in v 1 ("I will not be silent") and the task of the "sentinels" in v 6, who will not be silent (using the same verb, *ḥšh*, as in v 1). Since these "sentinels" are to bring Jerusalem to YHVH's mind or, better, to keep Jerusalem in his mind—in other words, to engage in intercessory prayer—they perform a prophetic function, which would be in keeping with a prophetic declaration of purpose at the beginning of the chapter. Most commentators have accepted that in v 1 the prophet (presumed to be "Trito-Isaiah") is speaking in his own name (Marti 1900, 388; Duhm 1922, 458; Volz 1932, 251; Fohrer 1964, 240; Westermann 1969, 374 et al.). The fact that this is self-referential prophetic speech is an important clue regarding the anxiety about the nonfulfilment of the prophecies and the need for reinforcement of eschatological faith that the chapter reflects—the thematic equivalent of the cry "how long, O Lord?" heard often in the psalms of communal lamentation (Westermann 1969, 375).

If chs. 60–62 form a unity of some kind, how does ch. 62 fit in to it? Some scholars argue that the three chapters are not in their original order; one version is that 60 and 62 belong together and that 61, which is different metrically and thematically, served as a kind of *Beischrift* to 60 + 62 (Elliger 1928, 90; Volz 1932, 239–41 and, much more recently, Lau 1994, 90–102). Duhm (1922, 454), on the other hand, speculated that 61:1 originally stood at the beginning of Trito-Isaiah and that the order of the two major sections into which he divides Trito-Isaiah, 56–60 and 61–66, was somehow reversed. None of the arguments for a different sequence of these three chapters is apodictic, and it is also possible that 61 was deliberately placed between the other two chapters precisely on account of its special character.

In any case, the linkage between 62 and 61 is much more clearly in evidence than the one between 62 and 60, a point noted by Koenen, for whom the hymn in 61:10–11 was intended to serve as the nexus with ch. 62 (Koenen 1990, 156–57). There is an impressive overlap of vocabulary between 61:10–11 and 62:1–5: *ṣedeq/ṣĕdāqâ, yĕšû'â/yeša* ("vindication, salvation"), 61:10b, 62:1b; *mĕśôś, śôś* ("rejoicing"), 61:10a,62:5b; and, most distinctively, *ḥātān, kallâ* ("bridegroom, bride"), 61:10c, 62:5b. A final point: the concluding passage of ch. 62 (62:10–12)—which is similar in type to 48:20–21 and 52:11–12, which conclude major sections of chs. 40–55—serves appropriately as the conclusion to chs. 60–62 as a whole.

The meter of this first passage (vv 1–5) begins with a regular 3–3 pattern (vv 1–2) and ends regularly (5b) but falls apart in the middle. This is fairly characteristic in chs. 56–66, and emendations based uniquely or primarily on prosodic grounds should be treated with suspicion. The notion of relegating v 2b to the status of a gloss correcting the name-giving in v 4 (Duhm 1922, 459; Marti 1900, 388) should be treated with suspicion—on which more will be said in due course.

The disciple of the Servant-prophet, therefore, affirms his intention to continue his campaign of preaching and intercessory prayer on behalf of Jerusalem without intermission. The nature of this activity can be more closely defined by referring to the *šōmĕrîm* ("watchmen, sentinels, lookouts"), posted on the walls of Jerusalem, who are mentioned in the following passage (62:6–7). They are to give no rest either to themselves or to God and are further described as *mazkîrîm 'et-YHVH*. If the verb (*zkr* Hiphil) is taken literally, their task is, so to speak, to activate God's memory, but the more common meaning is to intercede on someone's behalf, as Joseph asked Pharaoh's cupbearer to intercede for him (Gen 40:14), and to invoke the name of God in a liturgical act (Exod 20:24; 23:13; 1 Chr 16:4; Isa 12:4; 26:13; 48:1).

Intercessory prayer is associated with the prophetic rather than the priestly office. We may refer in corroboration to the *ṣōpîm* ("watchmen") who, together with their nonbarking watchdogs, are taken to task in Isa 56:9–12. The fact that this term *ṣōpeh* is a metaphor for *nābî'* ("prophet") is clear (Ezek 3:17; 33:2, 6–7; Jer 6:17), and it indicates the social responsibility inherent in the predictive and admonitory roles of the prophet. One aspect of the role is exemplified in the *měṣappeh* ("lookout") in Isa 21:6–9, who keeps his *mišmeret* ("watch") day and night on the *miṣpeh* ("watchtower"), until he hears, in some form of prophetic communication, of the fall of Babylon (cf. Hab 2:1–2).

The terms in which the future state of Jerusalem is expressed in 1b and 2a are recurrent in the Deutero-Isaianic prophetic tradition, beginning with the Jerusalem-Zion onomastic duality (40:9; 41:27; 52:1). The passage from the ethical to the eschatological connotation of *ṣedeq* (here translated "vindication") and its variant *ṣědāqâ* corresponds to the passage from the forensic sense of vindication of innocence in a court of law to an ultimate vindication. Often paired, as here, with *yěšû'â* ("salvation"), *ṣedeq/ṣědāqâ* is a central concept in this prophetic tradition (41:2, 10; 45:8, 13; 51:5, 6, 8; 58:8; 59:17). Also developed on the basis of the Deutero-Isaianic deposit (beginning with 40:3) is the idea that foreign nations and their rulers will see the glory of God (*kěbôd YHVH*, 58:8; 59:19; 60:3).

All of this eschatological scenario is suffused with light (cf. 60:3, 19). Throughout these chapters, light is the dominant metaphor for salvation. On the basis of rabbinic descriptions of the celebration of Sukkoth during the time when the temple yet stood, with the temple courts lit up with flaming torches, Paul Volz (1932, 244–45, 251) concluded that chs. 60–62 were composed to be sung or recited during this festival. The coincidence of Sukkoth with the New Year festival also brought with it immemorial themes of renewal of creation and restoration of a lost order. Volz recalls that it was with reference to the same festival that Jesus proclaimed himself to be the light of the world (John 7:2; 8:12). This hypothesis goes beyond the evidence, as most commentators agree, but is interesting and provocative nevertheless.

It is worth noting, finally, that both sources of light mentioned here—*nōgah* ("the morning light") and *lappîd* ("a flaming torch")—appear elsewhere in the context of visionary experiences (Gen 15:17; Ezek 1:4, 13, 27–28; 10:4; Dan 10:6).

When it happens in real time, the acquisition of a new name implies a new status. This is what happened when Laish was conquered by the Danites (Judg 18:29) and when two of the last kings of Judah were renamed as vassals of the Egyptians and Babylonians, respectively (2 Kgs 23:34; 24:17). New names thus acquired need not have any symbolic content, though both persons and places may be given names that embody certain expectations or aspirations. One thinks, for example, of personal names taken from *Pilgrim's Progress* by Puritans and of places such as Petaḥ Tikva in Israel, taken from Hos 2:17 and meaning "a door of hope." We recall also Ruth's mother-in-law, who invited the people of Bethlehem to call her Mara ("Bitter") rather than Naomi ("Pleasant"). There are many examples in the prophetic literature of a type of name-giving functioning as a literary device with no suggestion that the names in question would ever be given to people or places. This is the case with the name-giving in Isa 1:26, ʿîr haṣṣedeq ("City of Righteousness") and qiryâ neʾĕmānâ ("Loyal Town"); Jer 33:16, YHVH ṣidqēnû ("YHVH Our Righteousness"); and Zech 8:3, ʿîr hāʾĕmet ("Faithful City").

In much the same way, name-changing in chs.60–62 is another way of expressing the theme of eschatological reversal with respect to Jerusalem. In v 4 the change from Azubah ("Forsaken") to Hephzibah ("I Delight in Her") happens to correspond with the names of the mothers of Kings Jehoshaphat and Manasseh, respectively (1 Kgs 22:42; 2 Kgs 21:1), though we must suppose that in this case Azubah had a less ominous meaning than it has here. The same point is being made with the names dĕrûšâ ("Sought Out") and ʿîr loʾ neʿĕzābâ ("City Not Forsaken") in v 12, which summarize the whole point and purpose of chs. 60–62. The new name promised in v 2, like the different name promised to YHVH's Servants (65:15), and the new name of the faithful inhabitants of the city in the book of Revelation (Rev 3:12), is a name to be revealed only in the end time and therefore of a quite different kind from the names elsewhere in 60–62. So there is no need to read v 2b as a gloss added to correct v 4 (as does Duhm 1922, 459 et al., on which, see Sekine 1989, 96–97).

The image of a city as the crown or diadem for its patron deity is exemplified in a prayer to be recited by the urigallu-priest during the Mesopotamian New Year festival. The prayer is addressed to Bel (Marduk), who is reminded that "your dwelling is the city of Babylon, your tiara is the city of Borsippa" (ANET, 331). The language in both texts implies acknowledgment of the kingship of the deity which, for the biblical writer, goes with an apparently complete lack of interest in the restoration of the native dynasty. Both ʿăṭeret ("crown") and sĕnîp ("diadem") could be used metaphorically (e.g., Prov 4:9; 12:4; 16:31; Job 29:14; 31:36), and ʿăṭeret tipʾeret ("a splendid crown") seems to have been a common metaphor (Prov 4:19; 16:31; Jer 13:18; Ezek 16:12; 23:42). But the choice of this language indicates what is implied but rarely stated in these chapters: the establishment of the effective rule of God in Israel and in the world, encapsulated in the expression "the Kingdom of God."

Some commentators have found it puzzling that the crown or diadem is held in the hand rather than placed on the head. Ibn Ezra took the term ʿăṭeret to be an ornament for the hand rather than the head, and David Kimḥi understood "in YHVH's hand" to mean simply "in YHVH's keeping." In using this language, the writer may have had in mind the perimeter wall of the city, an image that would be out of place, metaphorically speaking, on the head. Or, alternatively, the placing on the head could, like the giving of a new name, be reserved for the last age. In the meantime, the city is in God's hands.

A somewhat different interpretation emerges when we focus on the linking of the themes of renaming, crowning, and espousals or marriage. In the Canticles (3:11) the women of Zion are invited to look at the crown (ʿăṭārâ) with which King Solomon's mother crowned him on the day of his wedding. According to rabbinic testimony, while the temple still stood, the bride and bridegroom wore crowns during the wedding ceremony. The bride was addressed as "the queen" and the bridegroom as "the king" (ḥātān dômeh lĕmelek, "the bridegroom is like a king," *Pirqe R. El.* 16). This may be the missing link in the association of ideas between the acquisition of a new name, the crowning ceremony, and the wedding symbolism.

This complex image is not in all respects internally self-consistent. YHVH is bridegroom (cf. 50:1; 54:6–8) but also officiant at the wedding. Another complication is the land (*'ereṣ*, fem.), whose name is changed from *šōmēmâ*, "Desolate," to *bě'ûlâ* ("Espoused"). While the woman Zion continues to be addressed after the espousal of the land is mentioned, we have the impression that city and land are somehow conflated in the writer's mind. Then we are surprised to hear that the sons of Zion are the prospective marriage partners. In the writer's principal source we hear a great deal about these sons. They are brought from the ends of the earth (41:9), from its four quarters (43:5–6); they include children born after the destruction of Jerusalem (49:20–21); and foreigners are charged with repatriating those scattered abroad (49:22). The same source has suggested the imagery in 62:4–5: "The children of the *šōmēmâ* will be more numerous than the children of the *bě'ûlâ*, 54:1"). It seems that the writer has also borrowed the play on the words *bānîm/bōnîm* ("children/builders") from 49:17: "Those who build you up [*bōnayik*; read also *bānayik*, "your sons"] work faster than those who tore you down." It was clearly important to include, even at the risk of introducing the incongruous image of incestuous union, the repopulation of both city and land.

PROPHETS, GUARDIANS OF THE CITY (62:6–9)

(J. Maier 1979, 126; Nebe 1978, 106–11)

62   [6]Upon your walls, O Jerusalem, I have posted watchmen;
they will never[a] be silent, by day or by night.
O you who invoke YHVH's name, take no rest,
[7]and give no rest to YHVH,[b]
until he establish Jerusalem solid and firm[c]
and spread her renown throughout the earth.[d]

ii

[8]YHVH has sworn with his own right hand,[e]
with his strong arm:
"Nevermore will I give your grain[f] to feed your foes,
nor shall foreigners drink the wine
that you have toiled to produce;
[9]but[g] those who harvest the grain shall eat it
and give praise to YHVH;[h]
and those who gather the grapes shall drink the wine
within my sacred courts."[i]

NOTES

[a]   1QIsaiah[a] and 1QIsa[b] omit *tāmîd*, but MT is represented in LXX and Vulg.

[b]   1QIsaiah[b], LXX, Syr. have 2d-person pl. "you," "yourselves," perhaps out of reverence; LXX *ouk estin gar humin homoios*, "for you do not have one like [him]," understands MT *domî* as → *dmh* I = "resemble."

[c]   Following 1QIsa[a], which has *'d ykyn v'd ykvnn*, "until he sets up and establishes"; 1QIsa[b] and LXX support MT, but MT *'ad yĕkônēn* is more easily explained by haplography (*'d ykyn v'd ykvnn*), and the longer version fits the meter better (communication with D. N. Freedman).

[d]   Literally, "Until he place Jerusalem [as] a praise in the earth."

[e]   LXX "by his glory"; *doxēs*, a probable corruption of *dexias*, "right hand."

[f]   LXX *ton siton sou kai ta brōmata sou*, "your grain and your meats"; 1QIsa[a] and 1QIsa[b] have a slightly different word order, which does not affect the sense.

[g]   1QIsaiah[a] *kî 'im*, "but rather," for MT *kî*, perhaps to establish that meaning rather than "because."

[h]   1QIsaiah[a] has "give praise to YHVH's name," but MT is supported by 1QIsa[b] and LXX.

[i]   1QIsaiah[a] rounds off the passage with *'mr 'lvhyk*, "says your God"; not in MT, 1QIsa[b], or LXX.

COMMENTS

Continuity with 62:1–5 is established by repetition of the refusal to be silent (v 1, *lo' 'eḥĕšeh*; v 6, *lo' yeḥĕšû*). In fact, 1–5 and 6–9 are variations on the same theme. Commentators have experienced the same problem in identifying the speaker in v 6 as in v 1, and there has been a similar spread of opinion here as there. With the *angelus interpres* of Zech 1:12 in mind, Duhm (1922, 460) opted for angelic beings, those whose task as *mazkîrîm* was to keep reminding God about Jerusalem, and other scholars followed suit (e.g., Marti 1900, 389; Whitehouse 1908, 298). Cheyne (1882, 97) took this further by linking the speaker with the "watchers" (*'îrîm*) of Dan 4:10[13]; and 1 En. 1:5 and passim; and even the Paraclete of the Gospel of John. But the idea of angelic beings stationed on the walls is unusual, to say the least, and even if we translate *'al-ḥômōtayik* as "concerning your walls" (Dillmann 1890, 515; Whybray 1975, 249), the parallel between 1–5 and 6–9 would tell against it.

I take it, then, that here as in v 1 the speaker is the disciple of the Servant who, as the leader of a prophetic group, is stating what the group takes its collective responsibility to be. The language is metaphorical, not literal (pace Watts 1987, 313, who has in mind Nehemiah's defense of the city under Artaxerxes I), and therefore is not relevant for establishing a precise date for the passage on the assumption that the city wall was already in existence. The term "watchman" (*šōmēr*) can signify the bodyguard responsible for protecting the person of the ruler (1 Sam 28:2), a palace guard (2 Kgs 11:5), a military scout

(Judg 1:24), or the keeper of the royal wardrobe (2 Kgs 22:14). The term is also used of temple personnel, principally Levites (*šōmērê mišmeret haqqōdeš*, Num 3:32; Ezek 44:14 etc.) and the priest-guardians of the threshold (*hakkōhănîm šōmērê hassap*, 2 Kgs 12:10; 22:4 etc.). But the primary function indicated by the term is that of the lookout on the city wall or tower (Judg 7:19; Jer 51:12; Ps 127:1).

As was noted earlier, *ṣōpeh* ("lookout", "sentinel": 1 Sam 14:16; 2 Sam 13:34; 18:24–27; 2 Kgs 9:17) is a synonym used explicitly with reference to the prophet: "I have made you a lookout for the house of Israel; whenever you hear a word from my mouth, you must give them warning from me" (Ezek 3:17; also 33:1–9 and perhaps Jer 6:17). A variant formed from the Piel of the same verb, *ṣph*, (i.e., *mĕṣappeh*), has a similar connotation of prophetic visionary in Isa 21:1–10, a valuable account of the solicitation and reception of a vision in which the fall of Babylon is announced (cf. Hab 2:1–3). It is worth noting that the Dumah oracle (21:11–12), in which a person from Edom asks the *šōmēr* a mysterious question and gets an even more mysterious answer, immediately follows this account of the "watchman's" vision.

We would have to assume that the unflattering comparison of Israel's pampered and self-indulgent prophetic watchmen with watchdogs in 56:9–12 comes from another source or another period, and perhaps refers to a different category of prophets—of the kind referred to in Nehemiah (6:7, 14) and Zechariah (13:2–6; see Comments on 56:9–12). On the other hand, the scene in which Jerusalem's "watchmen" (*ṣōpîm*) see YHVH returning to Zion and sing for joy (52:8) depicts the desired outcome of the initiative described in 62:6 and may in fact have suggested it.

The watchmen on the walls are further described as *mazkîrîm 'et-YHVH*, that is, keeping YHVH in remembrance of Jerusalem. While the functions attached to the state office of *mazkîr* are still not entirely clear, they seem to have included the writing and preserving of official records (2 Sam 8:16; 20:24; 1 Kgs 4:3; 2 Kgs 8:18, 37 = Isa 36:3, 22). The term could be translated somewhat literally as "remembrancer" (→ *zkr*, "remember"), and if we are to believe Herodotus (5.105), the Persian king Darius I had a servant whose task was to keep repeating to him, after the disastrous defeat at Marathon, "Master, remember the Athenians." We might then say that the "remembrancers" of Isa 62:6 are performing the standard prophetic task of intercession, following the example of Abraham and Moses as paradigmatic prophetic figures (Gen 20:7; Exod 5:22–23; 8:8; 32:11–14).

It would be natural to think that the oath sworn by YHVH (v 8) is a response to the round-the-clock intercessory prayer of the prophetic lookouts, even though what is promised falls somewhat short of the glowing picture presented elsewhere in 60–62. The solemn, public pronouncement of an oath followed a more or less fixed formula and was accompanied by significant gestures. One of the latter, by no means confined to ancient Israel and in fact still in use in courts of law, was the raising of the right hand (Deut 32:4; Dan 12:7 cf. Rev 10:5–6, where the angel straddling the land and the sea raises his right hand to heaven). The conventional nature of the gesture can be deduced from the reference to people "whose right hands are false" (Ps 144:8)—in other words, those who swear false oaths. Some commentators note the Islamic custom of swearing "by the right hand of Allah," but its relevance to 62:8a is doubtful. The point seems to be that YHVH swears with his right hand (upraised), to which is added, by a natural association, the "strong arm" (*zĕrôaʿ ʿuzzô* cf. Ps 89:11[10]) and the Exodus formula of redemption by means of God's "mighty hand and outstretched arm."

The form of words in which oaths were expressed was also more or less fixed. The most common formulation is exemplified in Job's oath of clearance, probably corresponding to a last recourse of the defendant in a court of law and possibly based on the structure according to which case laws were formulated:

If I have raised my hand against the orphan . . . ,
then let my shoulder blade fall from my shoulder
and let my arm be wrenched from its socket. (Job 31:21–22)

The structure is conditional or counterfactual, consisting in protasis ("If I have done X") and apodosis ("then may Y happen to me") or, more elaborately, "may YHVH do Y to me, and yet more" (1 Sam 3:17; 14:44; 1 Kgs 2:23; 19:2; Ruth 1:17). It became common in the course of time to omit the apodosis either because of its fearful implications or simply as a common way of making strong asseverations even in the absence of a judicial context. Hence v 8b, literally translated, reads, "If I ever give your grain to feed your foes. . . ."

The divine asseveration assures the entire community of immunity not only from foreign occupation but also from taxation and tribute on agricultural produce at a confiscatory level, exemplified by Nehemiah's complaint about his predecessors (Neh 5:15). The fate of having worked hard to grow wheat and grapes (the *dāgān* and *tîrôš* of traditional descriptions of Israel's land) only to witness their being taken and eaten by strangers, features as a curse in covenant formulations (Deut 28:30, 33) and as a threat in prophetic diatribe (Amos 5:11; Mic 6:15).

Not only will this curse be removed in the new age (65:21–22), but it is predicted that the foreigners who formerly lived off Israel's agricultural labor will be obliged to raise crops and tend vines on behalf of God's chosen people (61:5). The prophetic author of 62:6–9 does not go this far but contents himself with the satisfying vision of the Judean farmer's productive labor reaching a satisfying conclusion in the offering of the firstfruits of the land at the temple (Deut 12:17–18; 14:22–27; 16:9–17; 26:1–3; Neh 10:40; 13:5, 12).

THE PROCESSIONAL WAY (62:10–12)

(Koenen 1990, 131–37; Lau 1994, 108–15; P. A. Smith 1995, 33–38; Steck 1985c, 65–68; 1989a, 379–86; 1991a, 143–66)

TRANSLATION

62 ¹⁰Pass through, pass through the gates!ᵃ
Clear a way for the people;
build up the highway, build it up,ᵇ
clear away the stones,ᶜ
raise a signal over the peoples!ᵈ
¹¹See, YHVH has proclaimed
from one end of the earth to the other:ᵉ
"Tell daughter Zion,
See, your salvationᶠ comes;
see, his reward is with him,
his recompenseᵍ precedes him."
¹²They will call themʰ "the Holy People,"
"the Redeemed of YHVH,"
but you will be calledⁱ "Sought Out,"
"City No Longer Forsaken."

NOTES

ᵃ   1QIsaiahᵃ marks 62:10–12 as a distinct passage by leaving a gap of almost an entire line between vv 9 and 10 and a half-line between v 12 and 63:1; 1QIsaᵃ has *ʿbvrv* only once (cf. LXX *poreuesthe*); Kutscher 1974, 554 states that 1QIsaᵃ often avoids repetition of words, but in chs. 40–66 the only instances are 57:19 and this one.

ᵇ   This half-verse is omitted in LXX, either on account of haplography or confusion about the meaning to be assigned to the two verbs *sollû* and *saqqĕlû*.

ᶜ   1QIsaiahᵃ has *mʾbn hngp*, "(Clear it) of the stone of stumbling . . . ," perhaps influenced by Isa 8:14 and/or 57:14. 1QIsaiahᵇ and LXX follow MT.

ᵈ   1QIsaiahᵃ *ʾmvrv bʿmym*, "say among the peoples"; 1QIsaᵇ and LXX follow MT.

ᵉ   MT (*qĕṣēh hāʾāreṣ*), 1QIsaᵇ, and LXX have sing.; 1QIsaᵃ *qṣvy* pl.

ᶠ   The ancient versions have "Savior": LXX *ho sōtēr*, Vulg. *salvator*, Tg. *prqyk*, "your Savior."

ᵍ   1QIsaiahᵃ has pl.; LXX *kai to ergon pro prosōpou autou*, "and his work before his face"; cf. Vulg. *opus eius coram illo*, "his work in his presence."

ʰ   LXX *kalesei auton*, "he will call it. . . ."

ⁱ   1QIsaiahᵃ *yqrʾv*, "they will call (you)."

COMMENTS

Isaiah 62:10–12 rounds off ch. 62 by providing the answer to the prayer with which the chapter begins (v 1) and by bringing the naming theme to completion (v 12 cf. vv 2, 4). Steck (1989a, 374; 1991a, 143–66) accumulated arguments designed to prove that these three verses were added by a redactor to serve as the finale for his *Grossjesajabuch*: that is, a compilation consisting in 40–55 + 60–62 + the core of 1–39. It was therefore necessary for him to demonstrate a lack of connection between vv 10–12 and vv 8–9 or vv 1–9. But abrupt transitions are common throughout 40–66 and cannot be taken without further ado to indicate difference of authorship. While impressed by this same abrupt transition, Lau (1994, 108) chose the less radical option of designating vv 8–9 as an *Einschub* ("insertion"), which at least had the advantage of bringing v 10 into immediate connection with v 7, thereby making it abundantly clear to which gates the writer is referring. This may be a correct if unnecessary hypothesis, but there is no way of knowing for sure.

Since we have seen that there is no good reason to suppose that chs. 60–62 were originally in a different sequence, we can say that 62:10–12 also concludes the Trito-Isaianic core (60–62), again by giving a more specific content to the opening phrase "your light has come" (*bā' 'ôrēk*, 60:1) by means of "your salvation comes" (*yiš'ēk bā'*, 62:11). The recapitulatory intent can be observed in other ways: the naming theme (60:14); redemption (60:16); salvation (61:10; 62:1); and the negating of negatives—"there is no one passing by" (*'ên 'ōbēr*, 60:15); "pass through, pass through" (*'ibrû, 'ibrû*, 62:1).

For the author of chs. 60–62, prophecy is the outcome of reflection on earlier prophecies, principally those contained in 40–55, and their adaptation to an evolving situation within the Judean community and in its relation to external forces. It is therefore not surprising that dependence on chs. 40–55 is abundantly in evidence in this final recapitulation. Clearing the way and building up the highway take us back to the opening injunction:

Clear in the wilderness
a way for YHVH;
level in the desert
a highway for our God! (40:3)

It is repeated again in 57:14, "Build up, build up the road and clear the way," using the same language. That 40:3 has been adapted to a different situation is apparent from the fact that the way must now be prepared for the people. Furthermore, the key concept of "the way" (*derek*) is no longer limited to the way back from the Babylonian diaspora, or even to the diaspora in general; it has been transformed into an eschatological concept. The way that must be built up in 57:14 represents a yet later stage, with strong ethnical implications, as is apparent from the pronouncement of the "High and Holy One" that follows (57:14–21).

The signal (*nēs*) raised over the nations of the world recalls 49:22, possibly also 11:11–12, where it serves to alert Gentiles to begin repatriating the Jewish diaspora. Neither the change from *'el* to *'al* nor the context justifies translating v 10c "Raise a signal *against* the peoples" (against Steck 1991a, 150–51). While the idea that the repatriation of Jews is a task assigned to Gentiles may not have been left behind, the signal now indicates the beginning of the great eschatological procession to the city and the temple. The proclamation of YHVH (with the verb *hišmîaʿ*, literally, "cause to be heard") brings to a point of definition and closure many proclamations—of former things, new things, well-being, saving events—in 40–55 (42:9; 43:12; 44:8; 45:21; 48:3, 5, 6; 52:7).

The repetition verbatim of 40:10b in 62:11c is the clearest pointer to the context in which this brief final utterance was meant to be understood:

> Climb to the top of a mountain,
> Zion, herald of good news;
> lift up your voice with power,
> Jerusalem, herald of good news;
> lift it up without fear.
> Say to the cities of Judah:
> "See, here is your God!"
> See, YHVH is coming with power,
> his strong arm affirms his rule;
> see, his reward is with him,
> his recompense precedes him. (40:9–10)

The repeated verse (emphasized) provides a clue to the direction in which the writer's thoughts were moving. There is an assurance that what was then spoken will be fulfilled, all obstacles notwithstanding.

Taking in the entire corpus of chs. 40–66, this invitation to pass through the gates is the last of three similar passages that impose a certain structure, and therefore a certain overall meaning, on this segment of the book. The first concludes chs. 40–48:

> Get out of Babylon, get away from the Chaldeans!
> With a shout of joy declare this out loud,
> send forth the message to the ends of the earth;
> tell them: "YHVH has redeemed his servant Jacob!" (48:20)

The similarity in form and wording with 62:10–12 is apparent, but in 48:20 the message of good news is the limited salvation of return from the diaspora. The second passage concludes 49:1–52:12 and immediately precedes the threnody on the suffering and death of the Servant:

> Away! away! Go thence,
> touch nothing unclean;
> purify yourselves as you depart,
> you who bear the vessels of YHVH;
> for you shall not leave in haste,
> nor shall you depart in flight,
> for YHVH goes on before you;
> the God of Israel is your rearguard. (52:11–12)

Return from the diaspora is still the theme, but it is overlaid with and transformed by other intimations. The way of return is now a processional way, and its goal is the sanctuary.

In much the same way, "the Song at the Papyrus Sea" in Exod 15 re-presents the trek through the wilderness as a procession to "the mountain of your possession," "the place you have made your abode," "the sanctuary your hands have established," where God's rule in the world will finally be realized: "YHVH will reign forever and ever" (Exod 15:17–18). Without giving up on the specific goals of return from the diaspora, temple worship, and land tenure, 62:10–12 therefore has broadened the understanding of "the way" (derek) by infusing it with the idea of spiritual and moral transformation, in keeping with the thrust of chs. 56–66 as a whole.

What is described in 62:10 is analogous to a parousia type-scene from the Hellenistic and Roman periods. The term parousia, meaning "presence" and, by implication, "advent" leading to presence, was used of the visit of a ruler to a city or of a theophany, for example, of Dionysus, to an individual or group. The visit of the emperor to a provincial city was an extraordinary event, requiring careful preparation on the part of the citizens and calling for a delegation to meet the distinguished visitor, exchange gifts, and escort him back into the city. The gates mentioned here are therefore the city gates, and it may reasonably be surmised that those who are to pass through them in leaving the city are the prophetic acolytes who, earlier (v 6), had been stationed on the city wall. To this extent there is agreement with the Targumist, who identifies the hearers as prophets, though he sees them as passing in and out of the city gates.

The task assigned to the prophetic discipleship, which follows a divine proclamation (11a) and prepares for the parousia, is set out in five imperatives. The disciples are to level the processional way (pannû), build up the highway (sollû), clear it of boulders (saqqĕlû), raise a signal for proceedings to commence (hārîmû nēs), and explain the significance of the event to people in the city ('imrû). The parallelism with the prophetic plurality associated with an individual prophetic figure addressed at the beginning of chs. 40–66 (40:1–11) is unmistakable (see Volume 2, pp. 185–86) and is further reinforced by the verbatim repetition of 40:10: "his reward is with him / his recompense precedes him." These terms—śākar, pĕ'ullâ—should not be taken literally, in the sense that Zion and its people had earned this salvation, that they were now being paid their wages. They connote rather the reversal of fortune bestowed as a gift, the gift of divine presence. If we take in the scene as a whole, we could read it as an eschatologized version of the processional hymns in which the gates of righteousness (in this instance, the temple gates) are addressed directly and through which a righteous people enter with thanksgiving (Pss 24:7–10; 100:4; 118:19–20).

The passage ends with the bestowal of the new names promised in 62:2b. The honorific title 'am-haqqōdeš ("the Holy People"), elsewhere in Isaiah only in the community lament (63:18) but comparable to "the holy seed" (zera' qōdeš, 6:13), corresponds to 'îr haqqōdeš ("the Holy City" cf. Arab. al quds). The basic meaning is that of dedication to God and the service of God, as is said elsewhere of the Sabbath (53:13) and of more pedestrian matters (e.g., Tyrian merchandise, 23:18). The other title, *gĕʾullîm*, "the Redeemed," is reminiscent of the "Redeemed" for whom alone the holy way, the *via sacra* (*derek haqqōdeš*), was laid down, according to 35:8–9. The names for the city—*dĕrûšâ* ("Sought Out," "Sought After") and *ʿîr loʾ neʿĕzābâ* ("City not Abandoned")—represent one application of the theme of eschatological reversal to Jerusalem (cf. the name *ʿăzûbâ*, "Abandoned," 62:4).

A BLOODBATH IN EDOM (63:1–6)

(Bartlett 1989; Blenkinsopp 2000a, 447–54; Cresson 1972, 125–48; Gordon and Young 1951, 54; Gosse 1990a, 105–10; Grelot 1963, 371–80; Harding 1914, 213–17; Holmgren 1974, 133–48; Koehler 1921, 316; Koenen 1990, 76–87; Lau 1994, 279–86; Lipiński 1999, 1–9; de Moor 1997, 325–46; Myers 1971, 377–92; Olley 1983, 446–53; Pauritsch 1971, 138–44; Peels 1995; Ringgren 1963, 107–13; Rubinstein 1963, 52–55; Sekine 1989, 140–47; P. A. Smith 1995, 38–49; Steck 1986b, 323–38 = 1991a, 106–18; Webster 1990, 89–102; Zimmerli 1970, 321–32)

TRANSLATION

63 [1]Who is this that comes from Edom,
with glistening[a] garments from Bosrah,[b]
this person splendidly attired,
striding[c] in the fullness of his power?

It is I who speak what is right,
who contend in order to save.[d]

[2]Why is your clothing all red,[e]
your garments like those of the one
who treads grapes in the winepress?

[3]I have trod the wine vat[f] alone,
no one from all the peoples[g] was with me;
I tread[h] them down in my anger,
I trample them in my fury.
Their lifeblood[i] spatters my garments,
I have stained[j] all my clothing.
[4]A day for vengeance is on my mind,
my year of redemption has arrived;
[5]I look for a helper, but there is none,[k]
I am aggrieved that there is no one to sustain me;
so my own arm won me the victory,
my fury it was that sustained me.
[6]I trample peoples in my anger,
I make them drunk[l] with my fury,
I pour out their lifeblood on the ground.

NOTES

[a] The probable meaning of the adjective *ḥāmûṣ*, which is hapax.

[b] Lagarde's 1878 emendation of *mē'ĕdôm*, "from Edom," to *mē'ŏddām*, "rot gefärbt (red colored)," and from *mibboṣrâ*, "from Bosrah," to *mibbōṣēr*, "mehr als ein *Winzer* (more than that of a grape gatherer)," taken up by Duhm (1922, 464) and several of the older commentaries, is ingenious and attractive, especially since Isa 56–66 does not mention specific nations elsewhere, and we hear nothing more of Edom in this poem; however, it is unsupported by the ancient versions, and a *bōṣēr* ("grape harvester") is not the same as a *dōrēk bĕgat* ("one who treads the grapes in the wine vat"); see further on this point Sekine 1989, 146.

[c] MT *ṣō'eh*, "bending," "bowing down," "cowering," elsewhere Isa 51:14 and Jer 48:12 (the latter with the meaning of tipping or decanting a bottle), is supported by 1QIsa[a] and 1QIsa[b] but does not make good sense in the context; the BHS emendation to *ṣō'ēd*,"marching," "striding" (cf. Judg 5:4 with reference to YHVH), traceable to Bishop Lowth, is supported by Symm. (*bainōn*) and Vulg. (*gradiens*); see also Barthélemy 1986, 429–30.

[d] This meaning of *ṣĕdāqâ* with *beth instrumentalis* (cf. Jer 4:2, *vĕnišba'tâ* . . . *biṣĕdāqâ*, "If you swear an oath righteously, i.e., in the proper manner") seems preferable to the alternative, "vindication" cf. 56:1; for MT *rab*, "great," e.g., NRSV "mighty to save," repunctate *rāb* → *rîb*, "contend in law" cf. Vulg. *propugnator*.

[e] *lilĕbûšekā* need not be emended to *lĕbûšekā* (BHS after LXX, Syr., Vulg.), since the first lamed is possessive and *'ādom* can be a substantive as well as an adjective (Gen 25:30); in this way the point is made that red is not the color of the clothes.

[f] The precise meaning of *pûrâ* here and in Hag 2:16 is uncertain but presumably more or less synonymous with *gat* (Judg 6:11; Lam 1:15; Joel 4:13; Neh 13:15).

[g] 1QIsaiah[a] has *'my* (*'ammî*), "my people," probably an intentional alteration due to the difficulty of accepting that YHVH would look to Gentiles for assistance.

[h] Beginning with *vĕ'edrĕkēm*, "I tread," MT has all the remaining verbs except *vattôša'*, "won [me] victory," in the Imperfect (i.e., present or future time), probably for more vivid narrative style; v 5 remains in past time because it is a variant of 59:16.

[i] *nēṣaḥ* here and in v 6 = "juice," i.e., "blood" → either *nṣḥ* I = "to be bright, splendid" or *nṣḥ* II = "sprinkle."

[j] MT *'g'āltî* is anomalous, having both an Imperfect 1st-person preformative and a Perfect 1st-person ending; rather than a genuine ancient mixed form (Gordon and Young 1951, 54), it is either an Aramaizing form of Hiphil or rare Aphel Causative form (Dahood 1957, 70) or is simply a scribal error (GKC §53p).

[k] 1QIsaiah[a] has *'ên 'îš* for MT *'ên 'ōzēr*.

¹ An impressive number of Hebrew MSS have *vā'ăšabbĕrēm*, "and I shattered them," for MT *vā'ăšakkĕrēm* (see de Rossi 1786, 3:58), but MT is supported by 1QIsaª and Vulg. (*inebriavi*) and fits the context of treading out the grapes; LXX omits.

COMMENTS

There follows a carefully constructed poem, exceptionally regular in meter, with eight of the twelve verses set out in tricola. Beginning with Duhm (1922, 463), several commentators have suspected that at least a half-verse is missing at the end (v 6b), but the short final verse is stylistically right and not at all uncommon. The structure is quite simple. A first question and answer (1ab, 1c) is followed by a second (2, 3–6), the latter including an explanation about the state of the speaker's clothing (4–6). Nowhere is there any clear indication of glosses or additions.

The question-and-answer format is not antiphonal in the manner of Ps 24 (question v 3, answer v 4; question and answer v 8), and it is not comparable to the dialogue in the Canticle (Cant 3:6; 6:10; 8:5), which is more reminiscent of the chorus in Greek drama. A closer parallel is the brief and enigmatic dialogue between the watchman (*šōmēr*) and a passerby in Isa 21:11–12, the more intriguing since this one too involves Edom (Duma, Seir):

Someone is calling me from Seir,
"Sentinel, how much of the night is left?
Sentinel, how much of the night is left?"
The sentinel replied,
"The morning is coming, though it is still nighttime;
if you wish to ask you may do so,
come back once again."

Westermann (1969, 381) passes on Herder's genial comparison of the above questions with the questions that the warrior in the border ballads was plied with on his return—such as, for example, "Why is your sword so red with blood, Edward, Edward?" But such questions did not really call for a reply (e.g., "I have been killing a few more Scots") any more than did the questions asked by Sisera's mother and her ladies-in-waiting after the battle by the Wadi Kishon (Judg 5:28–30).

Challenge and questioning by a lookout or sentry is a realistic enough model since, in that by the time the second question is asked, the one approaching is close enough for the condition of his clothing to be noted and commented on. On the other hand, as Duhm wryly observed, if the sentry knew where he was coming from, he should have known who he was.

The poem has also been described as an apocalyptic vision. In this respect, comparison with Isa 21:6–9, in which the fall of Babylon is revealed, comes to mind. But in this latter case we are told explicitly that the visual experience of the lookout (*mĕṣappeh*, v 6), that is, the seer, was indeed a vision (*ḥazût*, v 2), and in other cases indications to this effect are generally provided. Since such indications are lacking in 63:1–6, we should be content with considering it a literary work composed with a view to its place in the larger Isaianic scheme of things and in Isa 56–66 in particular.

What, then, is the place of 63:1–6 in this larger context? It is clearly discontinuous with and from a different source than chs. 60–62 (pace P. A. Smith). The thematic links of this poem with 59:15b–20 were noted earlier: principally, YHVH's advent as Redeemer in the guise of warrior (59:17, 20), the coupling of redemption and vengeance on enemies (59:16), and the absence of human agency (59:16). Similarity does not, however, imply a unity or continuity at some point broken by the insertion of chs. 60–62. These three chapters, the core of the last section of the book, were already in place at the center. The persistent attempt to demonstrate that the rest of the material was arranged in a chiasm around these chapters, for example, by Bonnard (1972, 318) and Polan (1986, 14–16), has helped to emphasize certain structural parallels (especially 56:1–8 with 66:18–24 and 59:15b–20 with 63:1–6) but lacks enough linguistic and structural specificity to persuade, a common problem with chiasms, the more so as one moves away from the central panel in chs. 60–62.

The two brief poems about redemption and vengeance, but especially vengeance, in 59:15b–20 and 63:1–6 were deliberately placed on either side of 60–62 as a redactional framework for these chapters (with Koenen 1990, 84), and we may suppose that the purpose was to fill out the apocalyptic scenario in which Jerusalem was to play a central role.

The deliberate location of 60–62 at the center of chs. 56–66 rather than at their conclusion also allowed for the juxtaposition of the empirical with the ideal Israel of the future and for the introduction of important qualifications to this idealized vision of an elect people and city set out in glowing colors in chs. 60–62. An ethical criterion for participation in the eschatological drama and survival of judgment, entirely absent from 60–62, introduced the possibility of failure and rendered inevitable a division within the community, a situation most clearly in evidence in the final two chapters of the book. In some respects, it also blurred the distinction between those inside and those outside. In 59:20 redemption is restricted to those in the household of Jacob who turn away from transgression, while in 63:1–6 YHVH looks in vain for support from the peoples, not just from his own people.

The location of 59:15b–20 and 63:1–6, the one immediately before, the other immediately after 60–62, is therefore part of a deliberate and meaningful arrangement of the material in 56–66. The one theme uniting these two passages with 60–62 is vengeance (*nāqām*), or the day of vengeance (*yôm nāqām*, 59:17b; 61:2; 63:4), a kind of mirror image of the old prophetic idea of the "day of YHVH" (*yôm YHVH*, Amos 5:18–20). The same theme is central to the horrific description of the systematic, total destruction of Edom in 34:1–17 (*yôm nāqām*, 34:8). It would be natural to think of some structural linkage between this passage and 63:1–6, especially if one accepts Steck's view that 63:1–6, together with 56–59 as a whole, was added in the early Hellenistic period to a "Greater Isaiah" book already in place (Steck 1991a, 30–34 and often elsewhere). But it has proved difficult to establish what the relationship between these two passages might be, and it cannot simply be assumed that 63:1–6 was composed with 34:1–17 in mind, or even that 34:1–17 was the earlier composition of the two.

In Isa 34:1–4, the destruction of Edom takes place in the context of international and even cosmic disintegration and ruin, and likewise the bloodbath in Edom described in 63:1–16 is not restricted to the inhabitants of that country. In fact, Edom is introduced not as the victim of the violence described, not exclusively at any rate, but as the *scene* of the apocalyptic scenario, the final, annihilating judgment. At the same time, 63:1–6 has nothing of the blow by blow description in 34:1–17, which is in language and detail closer to 66:15–16, 22–24: YHVH's sword (34:5–6; 66:16), abandoned and rotting corpses (34:3; 66:24), judgment by unquenchable fire (34:5, 10; 66:15–16, 24), and convulsions in the heavens (34:4; 66:22).

We have seen that the one who asks the two questions—in effect: Who are you? Why are you covered in blood? (vv 1–2)—is the city guard (*šōmēr* cf. 21:11–12; 62:6) or lookout (*mĕṣappeh*, 21:6–9). As noted earlier, it is not presented as a vision report (Whybray 1975, 252), though we do begin to note a degree of interactivity in vision reports in the exilic and postexilic periods (Ezek 8:1–11:22; Zech 1:7–6:8). The questioner is not Megabyzus, satrap of the province Across-the-River under Xerxes and Artaxerxes I, who as far as we know never campaigned in Edom and could never have said what is recorded here (Watts 1987, 317–19). We infer from the questions and answers not that Edom has just been devastated, as in 34:1–17, but that Edom was the site of a final, annihilating action against hostile nations. The choice of Edom is dictated by the paradigmatic status of Edom as neighbor, related by kinship, yet unremittingly hostile, and also by the fact that traditionally, in heroic poetry, Edom is where YHVH first came from:

YHVH came from Sinai,
he shone forth from Seir upon us. (Deut 33:2)

YHVH, when you went out from Seir,
when you strode forth from the land of Edom. . . . (Judg 5:4)

God comes from Teman,
the Holy One from Mount Paran. (Hab 3:2)

(Seir is another name for Edom; Teman also stands for Edom or a part of that country [cf. Amos 1:12, where Teman is parallel with Bozrah]; Paran is in the direction of Edom.)

The image presented is of the return of the warrior from battle, not necessarily from single combat (Westermann 1969, 382), bringing news of victory or defeat. At first sighting, within hailing distance, the lookout makes out something puzzling about the warrior's attire which, as he comes closer, turns out to be blood. "Blood" (*dām*) is the dominant motif in this poem. The language is given resonance by means of the punning allusion to Edom, *'ĕdôm*, meaning "Red Land," a *lusus verborum* which (literally) adds color to the story of the two brothers, Jacob and Esau (Gen 25:25, 30), and to the campaign of the three kings in Edom (2 Kgs 3:8, 23: "This is blood!"). The fact that Edom, like its northern neighbor Moab, was well known as a center of viniculture (cf. Isa 16:8–10) may also have contributed to the rather ghastly metaphor of treading people like grapes into pulp in the wine press.

What is emphasized in the reply to the second question (v 3) is that in executing judgment YHVH acted alone. The same point is made, in practically the same language, in the matching passage, 59:15b–19. This statement, repeated before and after the panorama of Jerusalem's future laid out in chs. 60–62, marks an important juncture. We can understand why the 1QIsa^a scribe altered the text from *'ammîm* ("the peoples") to *'ammî* ("my people"; see Notes), but the emendation misses the point, which is that the author has definitively abandoned the expectations placed on Cyrus in Isa 40–48. The statement therefore marks a turning away from the historical arena and international affairs in the search for intimations of a change in fortune for Israel and therefore comes a step closer to embracing an apocalyptic world view.

The second half of the poem (vv 4–6) can be read as an explanation of the second answer. It also contains much repetition, but we should resist the temptation to speak of additions and expansions (6a cf. 3b; 6b cf. 3c; 5a cf. 3a; and, in addition, 5 as a variant of 59:16). It seems to be saying that the day of vengeance and the year of redemption predicted by the "Zionist" prophet of 61:1–4 are now at hand. The idea of vengeance looms large in Isaianic compositions of the post-destruction period (34:8; 35:4; 47:3; 59:17; 61:2), and here and elsewhere it is accompanied by such violent and lurid images as to repel the reader of even mildly liberal instincts. We recall that reading or rereading Isaiah 63:1–6 was the point at which Friedrich Delitzsch, in his *Zweiter Vortrag über Babel und Bibel* (1903), gave up on the Old Testament.

There is an important issue here to which we shall return, but in the meantime we can at least try to reduce the cultural distance between what the word "vengeance" connotes to us today and what the full semantic range of the word *nāqām* (here "vengeance") was in that place and at that time. To execute vengeance was a way of obtaining redress, of righting a lost balance and restoring the damaged integrity of the kinship group. It can therefore be seen as an application of the *lex talionis*. As a prescription governing the moral life, the "eye for an eye, tooth for a tooth" formula does not have much appeal today, but in societies without effective means of detecting and bringing to justice the criminal, it was a way of applying the principle of equity in situations of damaged social relations. We might try rephrasing it as: "*Only* an eye for an eye, *only* a tooth for a tooth."

Viewed in this social context, the execution of vengeance, blood vengeance (*niqmat dam*, Ps 79:10), was not optional. It was a contractual obligation, as the most effective means for protecting people who could not act on their own behalf in claiming the rights that custom and law assigned to them. This is the point at which the intimate link between vengeance and redemption comes into sight, because the redeemer (*gō'ēl*) was the person among one's kin (*bĕnê 'ammĕkā*, Lev 19:18) who assumed the role of protector and vindicator by executing vengeance.

The "year of redemption" (*šĕnat gĕ'ûlay*, taking the plural as an abstract term, rather than "my redeemed ones"), continues the same association of ideas and is also dependent on 61:1–4, where the year of redemption is "the year of YHVH's good pleasure" (*šĕnat-rāṣôn laYHVH*, 61:2a). Behind these ideas is the institution of the Jubilee Year, setting aside the undecided question about whether Lev 25 is describing real stipulations of customary law or setting out a utopian program that was never implemented. Fundamental to the ideology of the Jubilee are the associated ideas of freedom (*dĕrôr*, Lev 25:10 cf. Isa 61:1c) and return to one's ancestral land (Lev 25:8–12). The freedom in question is release from the burden of debt-slavery during the Jubilee (Lev 25:39–46; cf. the manumission of slaves during the sabbatical year, Exod 21:1–7; Deut 15:12–18), but it would have been easy to make the transition to political freedom, freedom from subjection to a foreign power.

Likewise, the law of return held out the prospect of recovering patrimonial domain, but for the contemporaries of these Isaianic authors the idea of return to the ancestral land from the diaspora would not have been far away. If we re-read this entire section of the book (chs. 40–66) with these ideas in mind, we see that the prophetic pronouncement of 61:1–4 states explicitly what is there from the beginning but only occasionally comes to the surface. I note only the assurance at the beginning of this major section that Jerusalem's indentured service is over and her debt has been amortized (40:2), the insistence on the release of individuals imprisoned or in servitude (42:7; 49:9), repossession of land (49:8; 54:3), and, not least, the numerous references to the redemption of Israel and Israel's God as Redeemer.

A COMMUNITY LAMENTS (63:7–64:11[12])

(Aejmelaeus 1995, 31–50; Beek 1973, 23–30; Blank 1952, 149–54; Clifford 1989, 93–102; D. Conrad 1968, 332–34; E. W. Conrad 1988, 382–93; Ferris 1992: Fischer 1989; Hanson 1975, 81–100; Hoass 1997, 138–59; Kellas 1907, 384; Koenen 1990, 159–61; Kuntzmann 1977, 22–39; Lau 1994, 286–315; Lipiński 1969; Morgenstern 1950, 187–203; Mowinckel 1962; Newman 1999; Pauritsch 1971, 144–71; Plöger 1957, 35–49; Sekine 1989, 148–64; Steck 1991a, 229–65; Veijola 1985, 286–307; Webster 1990, 89–102; Werline 1998; Westermann 1981; Williamson 1990a; 1990b)

TRANSLATION

i

63 ⁷I will recite the benevolent acts of YHVH,
    his deeds worthy of praise,

for all the favors he has shown us,
his abundant goodness[a] to the household of Israel;[b]
the favors he bestowed on them[c] in his compassion
and in the abundance of his benevolence.
[8]He thought, "Surely they are my people,
children who will not play me false,"
so he became for them a savior.
[9]In all their afflictions he too was afflicted,
and the angel of his presence saved them.[d]
In his love and his pity,
he himself redeemed them;
he lifted them up and carried them
for all the days of old.

ii

[10]Yet they rebelled and grieved his holy spirit,[e]
so he turned against them and became their enemy;
he himself made war against them.
[11]Then they recalled[f] the days of old:
[Moses, his people][g]
Where is the one who brought them up[h] from the sea
together with the shepherd[i] of his flock?
Where is the one who placed within him[j]
his holy spirit;
[12]the one who sent his splendid power
to go at the right hand of Moses;[k]
who divided the waters before them
to win himself a name everlasting;
[13]who led them through the watery depths
like horses through the desert without stumbling?
[14]Like cattle going down into the valley,
the spirit of YHVH gave them respite.[l]
Thus did you lead your people
to win yourself a glorious name.

iii

[15]Look down from heaven and see,
from your holy, glorious, and exalted dwelling![m]
Where is your zeal, your power,[n]
your abundant, tender compassion?
Do not stand aloof, [16]for you are our Father![o]
Were Abraham not to know us,
Israel not to acknowledge us,[p]
yet you, YHVH, are our Father,
our Redeemer from old is your name.

[17]YHVH, why do you let us stray from your paths,
why harden our hearts, so that we do not revere you?
Return for the sake of your servants,
the tribes you have inherited.
[18]Why have the reprobates made light of your holy place?[q]
Our adversaries have trampled down your sanctuary.
[19a]We have long been like those over whom you do not rule,
as though we no longer bore your name.

iv

[19b]Would that you might rend the heavens and come down,
that the mountains might quake[r] in your presence,

64 [1][like fire that ignites the kindling,
like fire that makes the water boil][s]
to make your name known to your adversaries;
so that nations will tremble before you
[2]when you do awesome deeds we could not hope for.[t]
[When you came down, the mountains quaked in your presence.][u]
[3]From ages past no ear had ever heard or heeded,[v]
no eye had ever seen any god but you,
who acts on behalf of those who wait for him.
[4]You come to meet those who rejoice to do what is right,[w]
those who keep you in mind by observing your ways.[x]
But when you grew angry, we sinned,
when you hid yourself, we transgressed.[y]
[5]We have become like a thing unclean,
all our righteous acts like a filthy rag;
we all shrivel up[z] like a leaf,
our iniquities bear us off[aa] like the wind.
[6]There is none who invokes your name,
who bestirs himself to hold on to you;
for you have hidden your face from us
and handed us over[bb] to our iniquities.

v

[7]Yet[cc] you, O YHVH, are our Father;
we are the clay, you are the one that shaped us;
we are all the work of your hand.
[8]Do not then be angry beyond measure,
nor forever bear iniquity in mind.
Consider, we are all your people!
[9]Your holy cities[dd] are a wilderness,
Zion, too, has become a wilderness,
Jerusalem a place of desolation.
[10]Our holy house, our pride and joy,

where our ancestors sang your praise,
has been consumed by fire;
our most precious possession[ee] has been turned into a shambles.
[11]In view of all this, will you stand aloof, O YHVH?
Will you keep silent and afflict us beyond measure?

NOTES

4QIsaiah[b] has some words from 64:5–11, but with no variants.

[a] LXX *kritēs agathos*, "a good judge," presupposes a reading *rāb* (→ *rîb*) cf. Isa 19:20: *vayyišlaḥ lāhem môšîaʿ vārāb*, "and he sent to them a savior and defender"; Vulg. *(super) multitudinem bonorum* is closer to MT, which is intelligible without change of punctuation.

[b] BHS suggests that *lĕbêt yiśrāʾēl*, "to the household of Israel" has been added, since it disturbs the *qînâ*, or "limping measure" (3:2), but the meter is not always regular.

[c] LXX *epagei hēmin* reads 1st-person pl. common suffix for MT 3d-person suffix *gĕmālām*, but emendation is not justified.

[d] The problem with this verse is indicated by the (medieval) verse division. LXX reads 8b and 9a as one verse: *kai egeneto autois eis sōterian ek pasēs thlipseōs / ou presbeis oude angelos all'autos Kurios esōsen autous* = "and he became their salvation from every affliction / it was no messenger and no angel, but the Lord himself who saved them"; this version requires reading *ṣîr* = "messenger" for *ṣār* = "afflicted" and K *loʾ* negative particle for Q *lô*, "to him," the latter also (apparently) in 1QIsaᵃ (*lvʾ*); the LXX reading is occasionally accepted in the commentaries, but it is unsupported by other ancient versions and results in a very irregular meter and dubious syntax; the translation offered reads *ṣār lô* ("he was afflicted") with Q.

[e] 1QIsaiahᵃ *rvḥ qvdšyv*, "the spirit of his holy ones," cf. v 11c *rvḥ qvdšv*, a mixed form; perhaps the scribe was thinking of angels (Ps 89:6, 8) or devout Israelites (Pss 16:3; 34:10). Vulg. *adflixerunt spiritum sancti eius*, "They afflicted the spirit of his holy one," appears to be a messianic reference.

[f] MT and all ancient versions, have the sing., which could refer either to YHVH or the people; the latter makes better sense.

[g] *mōšeh ʿammô* or, with Vulg., *mōšeh vĕʿammô*, "Moses and his people," omitted in LXX and paraphrased in Tg. (probably), with Gesenius (GKC §128c), a gloss either on *yĕmê ʿôlām*, "days of old" or, more likely, on *rōʿeh* (for MT pl., with LXX and Tg.) *ṣōʾnô*, "the shepherd of his flock" (see Cheyne 1882, 105).

[h] 1QIsaiahᵃ lacks the suffix: therefore, "Where is the one who brought up from the sea the shepherds of his flock?"; LXX: *ho anabibasas ek gēs ton poimena tōn probatōn*, "The one who brought up from the land the shepherd of the sheep," with reference to Egypt (cf. Exod 6:1; 20:2).

[i] Reading sing., see Note g.

j With reference to Moses, with Syr. but not LXX and Tg.; suggested by the immediate context and the pl. suffixes elsewhere in vv 7–14 with reference to the people.

k Literally, "Who caused his splendid arm to walk at Moses' right hand."

l LXX *ēgages* ("you led"), Vulg. *spiritus Domini ductor eius fuit* ("the spirit of the Lord was their leader"), and Tg. *dbrynvn* ("you led them") presuppose the verb *nāḥāh*, "lead, guide," but MT *tĕnîḥennû* → *nûaḥ*, "rest," stands as *lectio difficilior*; the corresponding substantive *mĕnûḥâ*, "rest," is the Deuteronomic term for the land to be occupied.

m *zĕbul*, "exalted dwelling," qualifies *bayit*, "house" cf. 1 Kgs 8:13 = 2 Chr 6:2; from the root meaning, one could translate "princely dwelling."

n MT pl. could be retained as an abstract term; 1QIsa[a] lacks *plene*, probably sing. with ancient versions.

o The meter (3:3) suggests the following verse division:

ʾayyeh qinʾātĕkâ ûgĕbûrōtekâ
hămôn mēʿêkâ vĕraḥămêkâ
ʾal titʾappāq kî ʾattâ ʾābînû

1QIsaiah[a] supports MT; LXX and Tg. have pl. for MT sing. (*ʾēlay*) and Vulg. sing. (*super me continuerunt se*). However, the emendation proposed is justified because (1) *ʾēl* cannot mean "from"; (2) the verb *hitʾappeq* never takes an object direct or indirect; (3) 1st-person sing. occurs elsewhere in the poem only in the conventional psalmic opening (63:7).

p MT *yākkîrānû* is anomalous in tense (Imperfect) and suffix, though on the latter, see GKC §60d; 1QIsa[a] has the normal Perfect form, *hikkîrēnû*.

q MT of this verse bristles with problems; *miṣʿār* (NRSV "for a little while") is never used temporally (Gen 19:20; Ps 42:7; Job 8:7; 2 Chr 24:24), and even if the sense were temporal here, the complaint that the people had possessed the temple, or the land, "for a little while" would make no sense (pace Hanson: 1975, 84–86); further, the verb *yārĕšû* ("they took possession") would have no object. The verse is obscure enough to make the ingenious emendation proposed independently by Torrey (1928, 464), and accepted by Westermann (1969, 390) and Whybray (1975, 261–62), attractive: *lammâ ṣiʿărû rĕšāʿîm qodšekâ*, "Why have the reprobates made light of your holy place?" The consonantal text remains the same, with the omission of two vowel letters and substitution of yod for vav, letters easily confused, and allowing for different word division. This reading also balances the second half of the verse.

r MT *nazollû* → *zll* Niphal, as in 64:2 and Judg 5:5; Vet. Lat. and Vulg. *defluerent* → *nzl*, "flow," "melt"; LXX has both "quake" and "melt"; 1QIsa[a] *nzlv* remains uncertain because there is no vowel letter after the second radical.

s The widely different renderings in the ancient versions were probably due to the hapax *hămāsîm* ("kindling," "brushwood") close to *mss* = "melt,"

e.g., LXX "As wax melts before the fire, and fire will burn up your enemies";
perhaps also a reminiscence of Ps 97:5: *hārîm kadôneg nāmassû millipnê
YHVH*, "The mountains melt like wax in the presence of YHVH." The
verse interrupts the flow, introduces different metaphors, and is probably
an addendum.

[t] 1QIsaiah[a] omits negative particle *lo'*.

[u] A misplaced repetition of the last four words of 63:19b in disregard of the
sense.

[v] MT has 3d-masc. pl.; literally, "they had not heard, they had not given ear."

[w] LXX omits "who rejoice"; "the one who rejoices" and "the one who does
what is right" (literally) are taken together as hendiadys.

[x] LXX omits the 2d-person masc. sing. suffix to the verb *yizkĕrûkâ*; hence,
"They will remember your ways"—an unnecessary simplification, since
the preposition in *bidrākêkâ* can be taken as *beth instrumentalis*.

[y] The second half-verse of v 4b (literally, "in them a long time and we will
be saved") makes no satisfactory sense, and most agree that it is corrupt.
For Tg. and Jewish interpreters, including Ibn Ezra, *bāhem 'ôlām vĕniv-
vāšea'* refers to the doctrine of salvation through the merit (*zĕkût*) of the
ancestors; LXX *dia touto eplanēthemen*, "on that account we strayed," is not
close; Syr. takes *bāhem* in an adversative sense: "against them [i.e., your
ways], yet we will be saved"; Vulg. stays even closer: *in ipsis fuimus semper
et salvabimur*, "We were always in them [i.e., our sins] and [yet] we will be
saved"; among the many modern conjectures, I mention Torrey 1928, 466:
bāgod mē'ôlām ûpāšoa', "betraying of old and transgressing"; Westermann
1969, 391, after Köhler: *vĕnipša' bĕma'alênû*, "because of our unfaithful-
ness we transgressed"; and Volz 1932, 267: *bĕhē'alemkâ vanniršā'*, "when
you hid yourself we transgressed," accepted by Whybray 1975, 264; a modified form of this proposal, *bĕhit'alemkâ* Hithpael, is adopted here as best
fitting the context.

[z] Reading 1QIsa[a] *vannibbol* → *nbl*, "fade," "wither," for MT *vannābel* → *bll*,
"confuse," "be thrown about."

[aa] Reading *yiśśā'ēnû* for MT *yiśśā'ûnû*.

[bb] MT *vattĕmûgēnû*, "you make us melt [away]," does not make good sense;
Tg. (verb *msr*) and LXX (*kai paredokas hēmas*, "you handed us over") correspond to the sense required by the context; perhaps, therefore, *vattĕmaggĕnēnû* → *mgn*, "hand over" cf. Gen 14:20; Hos 11:8; Prov 4:9; cf. 1QIsa[a]
vtmgdnv, perhaps from a verbal form *mgd*, "bestow" cf. *meged*, "precious
gift," and Arab. *mjd*, "bestow gifts."

[cc] 1QIsaiah[a] has *vĕ'attâ*, "you" (masc. sing.), for MT *vĕ'attâ*, "and now," probably due to 'aleph-'ayin confusion.

[dd] A Christian interpretation seems to underlie both LXX *polis tou hagiou sou*
and Vulg. *civitas sancti tui* = "the city of your Holy One." The pl. of MT is
supported by 1QIsa[a], Syr., Tg.

[ee] Though *maḥămad* occurs in a similar context in the pl. in Lam 1:7, 10, and
pl. would be more likely following *kol-* ("all"), Syr., Tg., and some Hebrew

MSS read sing. *maḥămadēnû*, "our precious thing," for MT pl. because the accompanying verb is sing.; additionally, *maḥămad* appears to be a synonym for the temple in Ezek 24:21.

COMMENTS

This long, psalm-like composition has no obvious connection with the preceding poem about the divine anger and vengeance visited on Edom (63:1–6) which, as we saw above, is structurally and thematically the counterpart to 59:15b–20. On the other hand, the questions with which the present composition concludes (64:11[12]) and which remained without an answer up to that point, are answered in the verses that follow 65:1 (65:1–12), at least in the sense that an explanation is given for the question of why no answer was forthcoming. The juxtaposition of 63:7–64:11[12] with 65:1–12 was no doubt part of the editorial arrangement of the material in 56–66, but this need not imply either that the entire section 65–66 is an answer to the psalm and essentially ordered to it, or that chs. 65–66 are compositionally parallel to the five sections into which 63:7–64:11 can be divided (Steck 1991a, 34–44).

It also seems unnecessary, and therefore undesirable, to read the psalm as a composite of different strata: as an original poem in 63:7–16 and an expansion in 63:17–64:11[12] (Duhm 1922, 469); or as a poem composed according to the more complex explanation of Pauritsch (1971, 144–71), who distinguished four levels or strata: 63:11b–14a, 15–19a; 64:4b–8; 63:19b–64:4a, 9–11; 63:7–11a, 14b; or as a poem explained by Sekine (1989, 148–64) with a somewhat different stratigraphy: 63:11b–64:3, 9–11; 64:4b–8; 63:7–11a and 64:4a. With the exception of what appear to be glosses in 63:11 and 64:1–2, the composition reads quite smoothly, without any obvious break in meaning. The five sections or strophes into which I have divided it in the translation simply follow the sense and logic of the composition without either implying serial composition or excluding alternative divisions—for example, the six sections of *Textgraphik* of Imtraud Fischer (1989, 32–72, 205–23).

The speaker or writer—identified explicitly in the Targum as a prophet—first proposes to recite what YHVH did for his people in the past: those foundational benevolent deeds celebrated in the liturgy, the recital of which was designed to inspire undivided allegiance and fidelity (63:7–9). The people's failure to respond in a positive manner induces rueful consideration of the great days of the Exodus, guidance through the wilderness under Moses, and the occupation of the land of Canaan (63:10–14). The experience of moral failure leads to lament and prayer of petition addressed to God as Father from the other side of disaster (63:15–19a). The prayer eventuates in a passionate appeal to God to show his hand, to set aside the angry silence that, the writer hints, is itself an incentive to further sinning (63:19b–64:6). The psalm concludes with a final attempt to motivate God to act in view of the destruction of Jerusalem, its temple, and the cities of Judah (64:7–11).

All commentators note the close affinity of this composition with the canonical psalms of community lament. Following the standard analysis of Gunkel (1933, 125) and Mowinckel (1962, 1:195–219), the principal components of this type of liturgical composition are identified as: historical reminiscence, usually in the form of a recital of past benefits conferred by God; praise of God; description of the present miserable condition of the nation or community, leading to complaints and attempts to motivate God to act; petition; assurance of a hearing; and commitment to offer a vow, a thanksgiving sacrifice, or something of the kind. It is not always easy to distinguish between the numerous psalms in which an individual complains of sickness, hostility, the infliction of psychic or physical harm by witchcraft, or other ills (perhaps about 1 in 5 of the 150) and the relatively few in which the psalmist is clearly speaking in the name of the nation.

Confession of sin, when present in either the individual or communal type of lament (e.g., Pss 25:7, 11; 35:11–14; 41:5; 79:9), is much less in evidence than the protestation of the sufferer's innocence (e.g., Pss 7:4–6; 17:3–5; 44:18–23; 59:4–5; and the entire Psalm 26), often combined with reproach directed at YHVH for failure to honor what the psalmist regards as his (YHVH's) commitments. The lament should therefore be distinguished from the penitential psalms, in which confession of sin, personal or communal, is more clearly in evidence. Beginning with Cassiodorus's *Expositio Psalmorum* in the mid–sixth century, Western Christianity has identified, commented on, and made liturgical use of the Seven Penitential Psalms (Pss 6, 32, 38, 51, 102, 130, 143) as a distinct collection.

Comparison with the communal laments (Pss 44, 60, 74, 79, 80, 83, 85, 89, 90, 94) shows that Isa 63:7–64:11 has much in common with them but also some significant differences. It contains historical reminiscence in the form of a recital of YHVH's great deeds on behalf of Israel together with Israel's inadequate response, it describes the deplorable condition in which the community now finds itself as a result of its infidelity, and it gives expression to lament and complaint. There is also petition, though YHVH is not addressed directly until 63:14. It succeeds in conveying a strong and vivid sense of collective spiritual disorientation but also goes some way toward attributing its sinful condition to the anger and indifference of the deity. But the most significant peculiarity of the passage read as a psalm of communal lament is the absence of an assurance of a hearing with which these psalms invariably conclude; for example, Pss 69:31–37[30–36]; 79:13. There is no response to the impassioned final appeal. The skies do not open, God does not come down or even look down, and there is no answer to the complaint.

Isaiah 63:7–64:11 has one other feature in common with these lament psalms, namely, the difficulty of assigning to it even a proximate date. The only clue it offers is the reference to foreign occupation, widespread destruction in Jerusalem and other Judean settlements, and the destruction and profanation of the temple (63:18; 64:9–10). The only situation known to us prior to 70 C.E. that corresponds to this description is the one that resulted from the Babylonian punitive campaign of 589–586 B.C.E.

The occupation of Jerusalem by Ptolemy I in 302 or 301 B.C.E. does not qualify, since the temple was not burnt down and whatever devastation took place was not nearly as widespread as is assumed in 64:9–10[10–11]. Josephus (*Ant.* 12.4–10; *Ag. Ap.* 1.210) relates that Ptolemy took the city by guile, but also speaks of his liberality toward the Jewish people (pace Steck 1989a, 398–400; 1991a, 38–39). The reading of the passage as a Samaritan or Proto-Samaritan (Samarian?) complaint against the *gôlâ* Jews has long been abandoned, and Neh 1:3, referring to disturbances in the province shortly before 445 B.C.E., speaks only of damage to the city wall and gates (*pace* Duhm 1922, 470; Watts 1987, 331). Hanson begins by dating it to the mid–sixth century B.C.E. but then goes on to interpret it as a protest against "the normative Zadokite community" in control of the temple, which would be impossible in the mid-sixth century before the temple was rebuilt (Hanson 1975, 86–87, 93).

The only remaining issue in the commentaries is whether to opt for the early post-destruction period (say 586–539), as Muilenburg (1956, 729–30), Fohrer, for whom it is the earliest passage in Isa 40–66 (1964, 246–47), Westermann (1969, 386), and others have done; or somewhat later (post 539), as in Elliger (1928, 94–99), Bonnard (1972, 445), and Williamson (1990a, 48–58: some time after 586 and later than Lamentations).

Given its psalm-like character, it is natural to think that Isa 63:7–64:11[12] was composed for liturgical recital, either on the site of the ruined temple or at some other religious center in southern Palestine. Several interpreters have made this suggestion, most recently Williamson, who compares it in this respect with Ps 106 and Neh 9:6–37 (1990a, 1990b). The proposal is plausible if unprovable, but the structural and metrical irregularity of the composition and its close connection with the passage that follows could with equal plausibility favor the hypothesis of a purely literary work that imitates the language and themes of the psalms of lamentation.

The affinity with these psalms is apparent from the recital of the benevolent acts and praiseworthy deeds of YHVH on behalf of his people (63:7–9). The language used in these opening verses is significant. The Hebrew term *ḥesed* means not just benevolence in a general sense but benevolence exercised in the fulfillment of commitments solemnly undertaken; hence, its frequent use in connection with covenant (*běrît*). The relatively infrequent plural (*ḥăsādîm*, also Isa 55:3; Pss 17:7; 25:6; 89:2, 50; 107:43; 119:41) therefore presupposes the existence of a covenant relationship.

The connection with covenant is reinforced by the possibility that Israel will "play false" (*šqr* Piel), since one meaning of this verb is to renege on agreements solemnly entered into; see, for example, Gen 21:22–24, Abimelech's proposal of a sworn agreement with Abraham, in which the same language (*ḥesed*, "loyalty," and *šqr*, "deal falsely" occurs. The same verb appears in connection with covenant in Ps 44:18 (*věloʾ-šiqqārnû bibrîtekâ*, "and we have not been false to your covenant") and in one of the Aramaic treaties from Sefire (Fitzmyer 1967, 107). Israel's rebellion, which elicits an angry response from YHVH (63:10), is also in conformity with the treaty-covenant pattern.

Covenant-making and covenant-breaking come into clearer focus in the affirmation "Surely they are my people," alluding to the formulaic "You will be my people, and I will be your God" (Deut 29:13; Lev 26:12; Jer 7:23; negated in Hos 1:9). In a traditional, patrilineal society such as Israel, moreover, it was natural that reflection on covenant would move on the father-son axis (cf. Isa 1:2), even though the practice of addressing God as Father, which appears later in the lament, developed significantly only in the post-destruction period.

It is important that these elements of a narrative tradition be not only remembered mentally but enacted and re-presented—that is, made present, actualized. The verb hazkîr (Hiphil of zkr, "remember") has this fuller sense of a significant retrieval of the past, a bringing of the past into the present by means of liturgical action, whether recited (verb spr Piel, Pss 9:15; 78:4) or sung (šîr, Ps 89:2). It is apparent from the reference to redemptive action, to YHVH as Savior, frequent in the second part of Isaiah (43:3, 11; 45:15, 21; 47:15; 49:26; 60:16), and to his carrying the people in his arms (Exod 19:4; Deut 1:31; 32:11 cf. Isa 40:11; 46:3–4) that the tradition in question is the Exodus from Egypt and the journey through the wilderness to the land of Canaan, especially in its Deuteronomic formulation.

I note in passing an interesting issue involved in the much-disputed verse, 63:9a (see Note d). According to the LXX, Israel was saved not by a messenger or an angel but by the Lord himself. Duhm (1922, 466) reproduced this reading: Nicht ein Bote und ein Engel, sein Angesicht rettete sie ("It was neither a messenger nor an angel; his Face rescued them"), preferring the LXX to the Masoretic reading represented by the Qere, which corrects the consonantal text. The reason given, that the expression mal'ak pānîm, "the messenger of the Face/Presence," is unattested, was enough to convince many commentators to follow Duhm's example, among them J. Fischer (1939, 191), Kissane (1960, 291, 296), McKenzie (1968, 188), Westermann (1969, 385), and Whybray (1975, 257).

The alternative reading, reproduced in this translation, was adopted by Ibn Ezra and was well represented in the modern period prior to Duhm. Among its proponents were Lowth (1833, 392), Bredenkamp (1887, 350), Dillmann (1890, 521) and Whitehouse (1908, 309). What is at stake is the interpretation of certain statements in the Pentateuch about the divine guidance of Israel from Egypt to Canaan. According to the best represented view, the Israelites were guided and protected by YHVH's angel (mal'āk, Exod 23:20–23; 32:34; 33:2; Num 20:16; Judg 2:1–5). However, a problem arises in Exod 33, in which YHVH promises Moses that he will send the mal'āk (v 2), then Moses speaks as if no such promise had been made (v 12), and then YHVH assures him that "my Face [pānîm, that is, "Presence"] will go with you" (v 14). These statements may be taken to reflect learned theological discussions about the historical traditions going on among scribes, including Deuteronomic scribes (cf. Deut 4:37,

"He led you out of Egypt by means of his *pānîm*"). The phrase *mal'āk pānîm* ("the angel of the Face") in Isa 63:9a may therefore represent a compromise solution to the exegetical problem posed by Exod 33, one which consisted in reconciling these alternative expressions of divine agency.

In keeping with the pattern of the psalms that rehearse the vicissitudes of Israel's history, especially Pss 78, 105, and 106, the benevolent divine acts elicit only rejection and rebellion (vv 10–14). According to the Deuteronomic didacticism reproduced in these psalms, the wilderness was the paradigm epoch during which this drama of gratuitous benevolence, rejection, punishment, and new beginnings was played out. Rebellion, a term closely associated with covenant-making and covenant-breaking, is a key concept in Deuteronomy (the corresponding verb *mrh* Hiphil appears in Deut 1:26, 43; 9:7, 23–24; 31:27; see also Ps 78:8, 17, 40, 56; 106:33, 43). It is also an important aspect of the Deuteronomic reading of Israel's religious history from the other side of the disaster of 586 B.C.E.

In the Hebrew Bible the expression "the Holy Spirit" appears only here (vv 10–11) and in Ps 51:13[11]: "Do not cast me off from your presence, do not take away from me your holy spirit (*rûaḥ qodšĕkâ*)." The association of the Spirit with the Presence or the Face of God (also in Ps 139:7) indicates that the Spirit (*rûaḥ*) has now become the object of theological reflection, a kind of hypostasis similar in that respect to the Face (*pānîm*), the Angel (*mal'āk*) and, later in the Targum, the Word (*memra'*). We are at the beginning of a development that will eventuate, on the one hand, in the Christian doctrine of the Holy Spirit and, on the other, the rabbinic concept of the *rûaḥ haqqodeš* as the spirit of prophecy (*rûaḥ hannĕbû'â*).

The first step toward restoring the broken relationship between people and their God is to remember (v 11), an injunction in keeping with one of the most prominent motifs in Deuteronomy—recollection of, in the sense of active engagement with, the historical traditions of Exodus and wilderness journey (Deut 5:15; 7:18; 8:2; 9:7; 15:15; 16:3,12; 24:9, 18, 22; 25:17). The catalog of events to be recalled comes in the form of questions lamenting the absence of evidence of such divine involvement at the present time. The emphasis is on the role of Moses, perhaps because of a crisis of leadership at the time of writing (cf. 56:9–12). With the help of two minor emendations, and taking *yām* to refer to the Nile (cf. Isa 18:2; 19:5 and Arab. *al bahr*), some commentators take v 11b to refer to the infant Moses, providentially saved from death (Exod 2:5–10).

Though possible, this may not be the best option, but Moses' endowment with the spirit of God, mentioned in the verse following, is a basic traditional postulate. The focus is on the miracle at the Papyrus Sea, and the language suggests familiarity with the traditional accounts, more or less as we have them: YHVH cleaves the water (*bq'*, Exod 14:16, 21; Ps 78:13), and they go down into the watery depths (*tĕhōmôt*, Exod 15:5, 8; Ps 106:9). Just as the Song at the Papyrus Sea ends with entrance into the land of Canaan (Exod 15:17), so in this Isaian psalm, passage through the watery depths and the desert ends with "respite," that is, settlement in the land (*nûaḥ* Hiphil cf. the corresponding substantive *měnûḥâ*, "rest," the Deuteronomic expression for occupation of the land, Deut 12:9; Ps 95:11).

The lament proper that follows (63:15–64:11) begins and ends with a prayer that YHVH not stand aloof from his people (63:15; 64:11[12]). It would be form-critically too positivistic to make this second section into a distinct composition, especially since we have no assurance that it was written for liturgical use. Petition and complaint (63:15–19a) are standard features of the canonical lament psalms (e.g., Pss 79 and 83), which complain, as people have been doing since time immemorial, of the silence, inattention, and indifference of their gods. In this instance, the lament is for the absence of the qualities—zeal, power, compassion—manifested so abundantly in the events just narrated. The initial petition directed to YHVH's heavenly abode, identical with Ps 80:15[14], reflects a shift in thinking to which the destruction of the temple must have contributed (cf. Isa 57:15; 66:1–2). It also gives expression to the feeling, much in evidence in chs. 56–66, that God had moved away from his people.

It was no doubt this sense of alienation from the traditional religious assurances that inspired the author to address YHVH as Father. That this attribute, which seems so natural, is of relatively rare occurrence in Israel of the biblical period, in contrast to ancient Mesopotamia, may be due to the need to avoid the idea of physical paternity, the god as begetter of his devotees. Jeremiah 2:27 denounces those who address a tree or a stone—symbols of deities—as father. The paternity of the god was common elsewhere (for example, El, supreme deity of the Ugaritic pantheon, was addressed as father) but is present only residually in Israel, in theophoric personal names (e.g., Abijah, Joab) and, rarely, in poetic compositions (e.g., Deut 32:6).

Where the relationship between YHVH and his devotees is expressed in the language of paternity, the expression will therefore be either metaphorical or in terms of adoption. During the time of the kingdoms, the Judean dynast was considered the adoptive son of YHVH, following Egyptian court protocol (2 Sam 7:14; Isa 9:5[6]; Ps 2:7; Ps 89:27–28). The tradition could speak of Israel as YHVH's son because YHVH had created Israel (Exod 4:22; Hos 11:1; Jer 31:9). This conventional language transported aspects of the exercise of paternity in that society into the sphere of religious thinking—primarily the power and authority of the paterfamilias in a patrilineal social organization. The result, much in evidence in biblical texts (e.g., Isa 45:9–11; Mal 1:6; Prov 3:12), has proved to be problematic for Christian and Jewish people who favor the promotion of equality in general and gender equality in particular in the religious sphere.

Isaiah 63:15–16, however, looks at other aspects of the metaphor of fatherhood including tenderness, affection, and availability. In this sense, appeal to God as Father became an important part of personal piety in the late biblical and postbiblical period (Sir 23:1, 4; Tob 13:4; 3 Macc 5:7; Wis 2:16; 14:3). According to the witness of the Gospels, Jesus prayed to God as Father ("Father in heaven," Matt 5:48; 6:9), and fatherhood seems to have characterized the way he and his first followers thought and spoke about God.

The following verse, v 16, has occasioned a great deal of discussion. Duhm (1922, 469) took it to mean that the speaker's contemporaries had appealed in vain for assistance to these distinguished ancestors by means of necromancy, and now had only YHVH to turn to. Hanson (1975, 92–100) took "Abraham" and "Israel" to stand for Judeo-Babylonian Zadokites, the "reprobates" and "adversaries" of 63:18, who had taken over the temple and disenfranchised the Levitical-prophetic minority among whom the psalm originated. He therefore read Isa 63:16 as providing one more indication of a schism within the Palestinian-Jewish community. It is tolerably clear, however, that the writer is speaking throughout in the name of the community as a whole (as is especially evident in 64:8), and there would be no precedent for such a pejorative use of the names "Abraham" and "Israel"—this quite apart from the problem of a Zadokite hierocracy controlling the temple in the mid–sixth century B.C.E., the date Hanson assigns to this passage (1975, 87).

If the verse is read straightforwardly in the indicative mood (hence, "For Abraham does not know us, Israel does not acknowledge us"), we could take it as expressing a sense of disorientation and alienation from the traditions of origins. I have preferred to read the first phrase as a counterfactual ($k\hat{\imath}$ meaning "if," GKC §159aa, bb), which has the advantage of rendering explanations like those of Duhm and Hanson superfluous.

The complaint gathers strength with the charge that in some way YHVH himself is responsible for the people's conduct and obduracy. The standard explanation for this kind of language is that the God was seen to be responsible for everything—good and bad, indifferently—so that no distinction is made between the absolute and the permissive will of God (e.g., Amos 3:6). This is no doubt the case, but we should not underestimate the willingness of biblical authors to charge God with indifference to or even complicity in human evildoing, a point made forcibly in Isa 6:9–10 and even more so in the book of Job.

The point has been made and is reinforced by the parallel reference to the tribes inherited by YHVH that the term "servants" ($\text{‘}\bar{a}b\bar{a}d\hat{\imath}m$) alludes to the community as a whole and therefore indicates a different historical context from that of the "Servants" in the last two chapters of the book. The lament for the ruined temple dates the composition sometime after 586 and before 520 but probably closer to the latter than the former ($m\bar{e}\text{‘}\hat{o}l\bar{a}m$, "from a long time ago," v 19a).

The impassioned plea for God, not just to look down (63:15) or to reach down (Pss 18:7–15[6–14]; 144:5–8), but to come down (Isa 63:19b[64:1]) marks the beginning of the second half of the poem, which falls into two stanzas: 63:19b–64:6[64:1–7] and 64:7–11[8–12]. It was inevitable that Christian readers and hearers would give this plea a messianic interpretation; and, so interpreted, it came to be used together with Isa 45:8, read according to the Vulgate, in the Advent liturgy. In the first of the two parts—63:19b–64:6—there is a notable change of mood between 63:19b–64:a and 64:4b–6, and the distinctive character of 64:4b–6 is marked by the inclusive reference to the self-concealment of God as the occasion for sin at the beginning and the end (vv 4b and 6b).

The plea is for God, whose abode is in the sky (63:15), to break through the domed firmament and the clouds and intervene. The particle *lû'* ("would that") followed by the Perfect usually, but not invariably (see Deut 32:29), refers to the past, but the writer knows from the tradition that God did rend the heavens long ago and come down at Sinai. The pleading therefore is for action in the present—a request that the Sinai theophany, with its all-consuming fire and earthquake shaking the mountains, be repeated (Exod 19:16–20).

But the wording of 63:19b also sends back an echo of the Song of Deborah, in which the coming of YHVH, "He of Sinai" (Judg 5:5), from Seir/Edom is accompanied by earth tremors, violent precipitation, and the mountains' shaking (*hārîm nāzĕlû [nāzollû] mippĕnê YHVH*, Judg 5:5—emended text in square brackets); compare Isa 63:19b, *mippānêkā hārîm nāzollû*, "that the mountains might quake in your presence." This instance of intertextual linkage is particularly apposite in view of the description at the beginning of the chapter (Isa 63:1) of YHVH striding out of Edom (verb *ṣ'd* emended text, as in Judg 5:4a) after fulfilling his pledge to carry out judgment on his enemies.

Continuing in the same train of thought, the poet looks for a repetition of the awesome deeds (*nôrā'ôt*) of which the historical traditions speak. Here, too, he takes up a theme of frequent occurrence in psalms and prayers (Pss 66:3; 139:14; 145:6; 2 Sam 7:23), with special reference to the Exodus and wilderness experience (Deut 10:21) and the miracle at the Papyrus Sea (Exod 15:11; Ps 106:22). The thought of these great deeds induces praise for the incomparability of the God of Israel, a theme of frequent occurrence in Isa 40–55. Forgetting his complaint for the moment, the author adds that this God is always ready to meet halfway those who are prepared to wait for God—this, too, a prominent Isaian theme (Blenkinsopp 2000a, 420).

The transition to the confession of sin in 64:4b[5b] marks an abrupt change of mood. The textual corruption of the second half of v 4b obscures the point that the writer wishes to make. Translated literally, the verse begins: "Behold, you became angry, and we sinned." The many functions performed by the conjunction in Hebrew leaves open the possibility of translating: "You became angry, and so we sinned." If the emendation proposed for the last verse of the strophe is correct ("for you have hidden your face from us, you have handed us over to our iniquities," 6b), this translation would gain in plausibility. Blank (1952, 149–54) makes an even stronger case against YHVH by translating *ḥṭ'* (usually "sin") and *rš* (usually "act wickedly") as "bear the blame" and "stand convicted," respectively, but this does not make as good a fit with the passage as a whole as the more common rendering.

The complaint that God has hidden himself or his eyes or his face from the suppliant is often heard in the Psalms (Pss 10:11; 13:2; 27:9; 30:8; 44:25; 69:18; 88:15; 102:3; 143:7), as it is throughout the book of Isaiah (Isa 1:15; 8:17; 54:8; 57:17; 59:2). The breakdown in contact, communication, and interactivity induces a feeling of uncleanness (*ṭāmē'*), using the metaphor of a cloth stained with menstrual blood (*'iddâ* hapax), juxtaposed somewhat incongruously with the insubstantiality of a shriveled leaf driven by the wind. In writings from the post-destruction period, there is no more poignant expression of abandonment and godforsakenness induced by the disaster of 586 B.C.E.

The lament proper continues in 64:7–11[8–12], ending as it began with a plea to YHVH not to stand aloof (64:11; 63:15). Speaking in the name of the people as a whole ("We are all your people," 64:8), and therefore not as the representative of an oppressed minority, the writer addresses God as Father once again. But, as Muilenburg points out (1956, 743), whereas in 63:16 fatherhood is associated with the redemptive acts celebrated in worship, at this point fatherhood is attributed to YHVH as Creator. While this association is by no means confined to Israel, it could be seen as a more acceptable alternative to the idea of a begetter deity. The point is made unambiguously by the metaphor of the potter, as in 45:9–10:

> Should one take issue with one's Maker,
> one sherd among others made of earth?
> Should the clay say to the one who shapes it,
> "What are you doing?". . .
> Should one say to a father,
> "What is this you are begetting?"

As signifying a relationship of dependence between Creator and creature and between parent and child, the metaphor was in wide use (Isa 29:16; Jer 18:1–11; Gen 2:7; Job 10:9 etc.). Here, the prayer is, in effect: Do not destroy what you have made!

The plea becomes more specific to the situation with the reminder that the holy cities of Judah (holy because the land is held in fief from YHVH) including Jerusalem and its temple have been turned into a wilderness. The archaeological record attests to extensive but far from wholesale destruction inflicted by the Babylonian army during its punitive campaign of 588–586 B.C.E. Some of the fortified cities, Jerusalem and Lachish in particular, were severely damaged or destroyed, but the claims for total or near-total destruction made by William Foxwell Albright and still heard in some quarters are now recognized to be greatly exaggerated. Moreover, some of the damage attested in the Negev and Shephelah and laid to the charge of the Babylonians could have resulted from Edomite encroachment. Furthermore, we should not underestimate the resilience of a population in such a crisis in picking up the pieces and restoring a semblance of order. At the approach of the Babylonian army, many would have taken refuge in one or other of the inaccessible retreats and refuges with which Judah is liberally provided, to reemerge once the immediate crisis had passed. In any case, most of the population did not live in cities, so the country was by no means depopulated.

This last strophe is close enough to Lamentations to practically eliminate the later dates proposed by Morgenstern and Steck, among others. Both texts end with desperate questioning and the plea that YHVH not punish or remain silent or be angry "beyond measure" (*'ad mě'od*). They have in common the theme of divine anger (Lam 1:12; 2:2, 4, 22; 3:1, 43), unanswered prayer (3:8, 44), confession of sin (3:42), waiting for God (3:25–26), and a prayer for God to look down, or come down, from his place in heaven (3:50). Both lament the entry of foreigners into the temple (1:10) and the reduction of Jerusalem to a desolation (šĕmāmâ, Isa 64:9b; Lam 5:18, verb šmm). There are also close linguistic parallels with Lamentations. The term tip'eret, "splendor, pride and joy," is used of the temple in Isa 64:9 and Lam 2:1; the loss of Jerusalem's maḥămad-dîm (maḥămudîm, "precious possessions") is lamented in Lam 1:7, 10 (cf. Isa 64:10b), perhaps with reference to the temple vessels; and both texts convey the sense of pollution by means of menstrual blood (Isa 64:5, beged 'iddîm; Lam 1:17, niddâ).

The lament of Isa 63–64 and the book of Lamentations set the tone for a kind of penitential piety, both public and private, both mainstream and sectarian, that came to be a characteristic feature of Jewish religious life throughout the Second Temple period. Other instances, principally the prayers attributed to Ezra in Ezra 9:6–15 and Neh 9:6–37, replicate much the same pattern as the Isaian lament and would eventually have a significant impact on the liturgy of the synagogue. Later examples are the penitential prayer of Dan 9:4–19 and, in less fully developed form, 1 Macc 2:49–70, the Prayer of Manasseh, and 4Q504, published under the title "Paroles des Lumières" by M. Baillet (1982, 137–68).

JUDGMENT ON THE SYNCRETISTS (65:1–7)

(Barthélemy 1986, 452; Beuken 1991, 204–21; Brownlee 1964, 234–35; D. Conrad 1968, 332–34; Dahood 1960, 400–409; G. R. Driver 1967, 43–57; Emerton 1980b, 437–51; Hanson 1975, 134–50; Jefferson 1949, 225–30; Lewis 1989, 158–60; Lipiński 1973, 358–59; K. Nielsen 1989, 201–22; Pauritsch 1971, 171–94; Rubinstein 1953, 94–95; Steck 1987c, 103–16 = 1991a, 217–28; Webster 1990, 89–102)

TRANSLATION

65   ¹I was ready to be sought out,[a] but they did not ask for me;[b]
I was ready to be found,[a] but they did not seek me.
I said, "Here I am, here I am"
to a nation that did not invoke[c] my name.
²All day long I spread out my hands
to a stubborn, rebellious[d] people,
who go their evil way,
following their own devices;
³a people that provokes me
continually to my face.
They offer sacrifices in gardens,
they burn incense upon bricks;[e]
⁴they squat among the tombs,

pass the night among the rocks.[f]
They eat the flesh of pigs,
with broth of unclean things in their pots.[g]
⁵They say, "Keep your distance;
do not approach me, for I have been set apart from you."[h]
These are smoke in my nostrils,
a fire that burns all the time.
⁶Observe: it is recorded in my presence!
I shall not be silent; rather, I shall requite,
I shall requite in full measure[i] ⁷their iniquities[j]
and those of their forebears[j] together.
[A saying of YHVH]
Since they burn incense on the mountains,
and on the hills they insult me,
I shall first[k] take stock of their deeds
and then requite them in full measure.

NOTES

[a] Tolerative Niphal (GKC §51c) and so understood by Tg. but not LXX *emphanēs*, *heurethēn*, "I was made manifest," "I was found."

[b] Suffix omitted by haplography in MT; added with 1QIsaᵃ, LXX, Syr., Tg.

[c] Reading Perfect Active *qārā'* with LXX, as more in conformity with the context cf. 64:6; MT *qōrā'* Pual Perfect is supported by 4QIsaᵇ (*qvr'*), unless it is an Active participle; 1QIsaᵃ *qr'* could be either identical with MT or Perfect Active, orthographically more likely the latter.

[d] 1QIsaiahᵃ is unclear but more likely *mōrē* than *sōrē*, "contumacious"; LXX adds another adjective, *antilegonta*, "gainsaying" (cf. Rom 10:21), perhaps therefore add *ûmōre* → *mrh*, *metri causa* cf. Deut 21:18, 20; Jer 5:23; Ps 78:8.

[e] LXX adds *tois daimoniois ha ouk estin/estai* ("to the demons that do not / will not exist,") probably not → Luc. *oikousin* → *yōšĕbîm* (Goshen-Gottstein 1995, 286 contra Seeligmann 1948, 30); 1QIsaᵃ reads *vynqv ydym 'l h'bnym* in place of MT *umqṭrym 'l hlbnym* (consonants only), close enough to suggest a variant of the same original text; for the meaning, see Comments.

[f] *nēṣûrîm* is by some scholars derived from the verb *nṣr*, "watch," "guard," in the sense of "vigils" or places where the night was passed in vigils; others read "in secret places"; I read MT *ûbannĕṣûrîm* as *ûbên ṣûrîm*.

[g] MT *pārāq* is hapax; the related verb *prq*, "break off," "tear off," could suggest a reference to broken-up bits of the unclean food in question; but Q *mārāq*, "soup," "broth," "stew," is supported by LXX *zōmon thusiōn*, "broth of sacrifices," and 1QIsaᵃ *vmrq* cf. Vulg. *ius profanum*. "In their pots," reading *bikĕlêhem*, that is, adding the preposition, as in 1QIsaᵃ, Tg., Vulg.

[h] Some commentators read *qiddaštîkâ* Piel, meaning "consecrate," "dedicate," with direct object (transitive) for MT *qĕdaštîkâ* Qal; however, there

are cases in which an indirect object is expressed with a direct object suffix; hence Qal may be retained (GKC §117x; and see Emerton 1980b, 437–51); the use of this cultic term in expressing distance is no doubt ironic.

i   "Full measure" renders *ʿal-ḥêqām* ("into/on their laps") in 6b and 7c; the metaphor is based on the practice of receiving and carrying goods in the fold of the outer garment.

j   With LXX and Syr. 3d-person pl. suffix for MT 2d-person pl.

k   Torrey (1928, 468) makes the interesting suggestion that *ri'šonâ ʿel* is a textual note that found its way into the text, making the point that the first occurrence of the phrase is correct; Westermann (1969, 399) reads *běrō'šām*, "on their heads." On the whole, it seems better to take *ri'šonâ* as adverbial.

COMMENTS

The diatribe addressed to an unresponsive, contumacious, and idolatrous people in *oratio recta* of the Deity has been read by many commentators as a response to the agonizing questions with which the previous lament ends. The response would be by way of explaining why the lament did not conclude, as liturgical lamentations generally conclude, with an assurance of divine assistance. Actually, an explanation was given in the course of the lament, in the complaint that "there is none who invokes your name" (64:6a[7a]). But Duhm (1922, 474–75) was certainly correct to point out that those addressed in 65:1–7, who are practicing "pagan" cults, eating pork, and so on, have little in common with the plaintive penitents on whose behalf the psalm immediately preceding was composed. This would suggest that, though a connection does exist, with chs. 65–66 we are in a quite different situation.

The pattern of alternating words of reproof with reassurance, in evidence in successive units beginning with 56:1–8, continues nevertheless throughout ch. 65 (vv 1–7, 8–10, 11–12, 13–16, 17–24). The alternation is highlighted by the call-response, seeking-finding motif, first heard in 50:2 ("Why was no one there when I came? Why did no one answer when I called?"), a complaint that anticipates 65:1 and is repeated at intervals throughout the last 11 chapters of the book (58:9; 64:6[7]; 65:1, 10, 12, 24; 66:4). Since 65:25 is an addendum to the chapter, as I shall argue, the same theme also serves as an inclusio binding the chapter together (65:1, 24). The distinction between the elect and the reprobate in the Jewish community also comes increasingly into focus in these last two chapters. It corresponds to the contrast between the nation that does not invoke YHVH's name mentioned in the present passage and "my people who seek me" in the passage following (65:10). Likewise, the honorific title "servants of YHVH," used of the people as a whole in the preceding lament (63:17), is restricted in the last two chapters to the elect, that is, those who, in the writer's view, constitute the faithful minority.

Recent commentary has given much attention to the question whether ch. 65 can be read as a literary rather than an editorial unity. Marti (1900, 400) argued for a collection of small units in chs. 65–66 held together by a common theme (65:1–7, 8–12, 13–20, 21–25; 66:1–4, 5–11, 12–18a, 18b-22, 23–24). Budde (1922, 713–14) and Volz (1932, 281) read ch. 65 as one literary unit, as also do Muilenburg (1956, 757) and Hanson (1975, 161–63), though for different reasons. Pauritsch (1971, 173) used the expression "kerygmatic unit" for the chapter. It seems advisable in general to approach this and other texts with the expectation of compositional unity rather than to anticipate a work of editorial bricolage.

The conventional prophetic formulas, helped out by repetition of significant phrases, function to articulate the chapter. The first of these—'āmar YHVH, "a saying of YHVH," 7a—may at some point have concluded the first unit, since the indictment unexpectedly starts up again, and does so in repetitive fashion, in v 7b–c. The following section (8–12), is clearly delineated by the introductory "these are YHVH's words" in vv 8 and 13, reinforced by the repetition of the call-answer motif at its conclusion (v 12). The same motif wraps up vv 13–24, even though some commentators assign the brief apocalypse, vv 17–25, a distinct and later origin. The only indication of disturbance in vv 1–7 is the final, repetitive accusation and anticipation of judgment (v 7bc) that follows the closing prophetic formula (*'āmar YHVH*) in v 7a.

That these markers, though useful, cannot by themselves answer the question posed at the beginning of the previous paragraph is confirmed by the great variety of solutions proposed in recent years. Some of these are unduly elaborate and speculative. I am thinking of Sekine (1989, 165–78), who extracts from the chapter a Trito-Isaian core (vv 16b–23, 25) and assigns the rest to redactors. Vermeylen (1978, 492–503) identifies seven editorial layers in chs. 65–66 and two in 65:1–7, the first deriving from a pietist group in the fourth century B.C.E. (vv 1–2, 6–7a), the second from the Hellenistic period (vv 3–5, 7b). Attention to incipits and excipits of the conventional prophetic type, in addition to subject matter, suggests the following articulation of chs. 65–66: 65:1–7, 8–12, 13–16, 17–24, 25; 66:1–4, 5, 6–11, 12–16, 17, 18–24. The interesting suggestion of P. A. Smith (1995, 129–31) that 66:17 forms an inclusion with 65:1–7 will call for discussion, as also will 66:18–24, the conclusion to the entire book as well as to chs. 56–66.

The meter of the poem is for the most part (11 out of 16 verses in MT) a regular 3:3, with the exception of 2:2 in the middle (vv 3b, 4a), which was perhaps intended to draw attention to the unacceptable cults being practiced.

Seeking God and calling on his name (65:1) is, for these Isaian texts, the essence of religion. Compare 55:6–7a, which uses the same language as 65:1–2 (seeking, invoking, going one's own way, following one's own devices):

> Seek YHVH while he may be found,
> invoke him while he is near;
> let the wicked forsake their ways,
> the sinful their devices.

Depending on the context, seeking (*drš*, *bqš*) and asking (*š'l*) can also imply consultation of the deity through a designated intermediary (e.g., Isa 8:19; 11:10;

19:3) and participation in worship, as in the phrase "to seek the face of YHVH" (Pss 24:6; 27:8; 105:4, with *bqš*). Invocation of YHVH's Name, the cults mentioned in vv 3, 4 and 7, and the language of ritual sequestration in v 5 suggest rather strongly that the complaint is about neglect of the orthodox cult of YHVH, and this conclusion is reinforced by the attack in the following passage on the equally unresponsive people who forsake YHVH and ignore his holy mountain, that is, the Jerusalem temple (65:11–12).

As the diatribe proceeds and gathers strength (2–3a), the natural Godward direction of prayer is reversed. Stretching out the hands or, more commonly, the palms of the hands, is the typical attitude of the one praying (Exod 9:29, 33; 1 Kgs 8:22, 38, 54; Isa 1:15; Ezra 9:5; Pss 44:21; 143:6 etc.). At this point the language is conspicuously Deuteronomic in character. For the Deuteronomists, sin is preeminently rebellion (Deut 21:20; 30:1; Jer 5:13; 6:27–28) and a provocation of God (*kʿs* Hiphil: Deut 4:25; 9:18; 31:29; 32:16; and often in the History). The wording of the denunciation is also similar to Jer 18:12—"We will follow our own devices, and each of us will act in the stubbornness of our evil heart"—which appears in the context of the incomprehension about and therefore rejection of YHVH's purposes in the affairs of Israel.

With the help of LXX, perhaps quoted from memory, Paul in Rom 10:20–21 presents an interesting interpretation of Isa 65:1–2. Those who, without seeking, have found God and to whom, without asking, God has become manifest are the Gentiles, and their attitude is in contrast to the disobedient and contrary Jewish people to whom in vain God holds out his hands. This Pauline reading of Isa 65:1–2 has had unfortunate consequences. One particularly scandalous example is Pius IX's command that the text be inscribed in Hebrew and Latin over the entrance to the church of San Gregorio a Ponte Quattro Capi, facing directly into the Roman ghetto, where it can still be seen.

Beginning with v 2b, the attitude and practice of the rebellious people are spelled out by means of seven active participles. The first of five cultic practices listed is participation in sacrificial rites in gardens. The garden (*gannâ*, feminine form) as a sacred *temenos* is also mentioned in 1:29 in a passage (1:27–31) from the same milieu as 65:1–7 (Blenkinsopp 2000a, 187–88). It is noteworthy that 1:29 associates sacred trees with gardens, and the frequent condemnation of worship "under every green tree" (Deut 12:2; 2 Kgs 16:4; Hos 4:13) would lead us to suspect that such a "tree of life," situated in the center of a garden, as in the Garden of Eden, was the focus of cultic action. Comparison with the deviant cults practiced "under every green tree" in 57:5 would be appropriate. Association with the cult of Asherah is also suggested. From the numerous biblical references to the *ʾăšērâ* we deduce that this symbol of the goddess could be planted (Deut 16:21) and uprooted (Mic 5:13), cut down and burned (Judg 6:15–26; 2 Kgs 18:4 etc.). It was therefore a sacred tree, a "tree of life," that served as the focus for rituals in honor of the goddess. And, in general, the idea of the garden as the sacred *temenos* and place for cultic activity was widespread in the Near East (for an example from Assyria, see Lipiński).

In a later, apparently fragmentary allusion to such practices (66:17), we witness the adepts' sanctifying and ritually cleansing themselves before entering the gardens following a female hierophant. There is no need to limit such practices either to the Hellenistic period or the time of the kingdoms.

The accusation of burning incense upon bricks has exercised the ingenuity of exegetes for some time. Unsupported emendation of *lĕbēnîm* ("bricks") to *hārîm* ("mountains") or *'ăbānîm* ("stones") is no solution, and reading *malbēnîm* ("brick molds," "brickworks," "brick pavement" [?]; see 2 Sam 7:21; Jer 43:9; Nah 3:14) is a case of *obscurum per obscurius* (Hanson 1975, 140). Some have suggested that the fault lay in the use of bricks instead of earth or unworked stone in the construction of an altar (Exod 20:24–25), which would be a fault, but not the kind being castigated here. Based on Hos 4:13, Marti (1900, 401) proposed (but without much conviction) the plural of *libneh*, "white poplar," while D. Conrad (1968, 232–34) found a parallel in Babylonian rooftop offerings in earthenware vessels or on bricks.

Perhaps the most plausible of the many proposals on offer, and one calling for the least alteration in MT, is to read *ûmĕqaṭṭĕrîm ʿal hallĕbōnâ*, "and burning incense on the incense altar." While *lĕbōnâ*, "frankincense," nowhere means "incense altar" in the Hebrew Bible, this meaning is attested in an inscription on an incense altar from Lachish: *lbnt 'yš bn mḥly*, "incense altar of Iyas son of Mahlay" (Dahood 1960, 406–9). The equivalent term in Biblical Hebrew is *hammān*, and it is perhaps worth noting that these incense altars are elsewhere associated with Asherah symbols (Isa 17:8; 27:9; 2 Chr 34:4–7). But it remains true that there is nothing intrinsically improbable about burning incense on bricks, under circumstances unknown to us that could have rendered it reprehensible in the eyes of the writer.

Even more puzzling is the alternative rendering of 1QIsa^a which, literally translated, reads: "They suck hands on the stones." In the Note on this Qumran reading, it was suggested that this text has enough letters in common with MT (11 out of 17), and in the same order, to suggest textual corruption in either the Qumran scroll or MT. Attempts to circumvent a reference in this alternative version to an obscene rite are understandable but unconvincing. (For *yād* = "penis" and possibly *'abnayim*, reading dual = "testicles," see Isa 57:8; Exod 1:16; Qoh 3:5). Hanson (1975, 141) reports Cross's rendering, "They empty their incense spoons on stones" which takes the verb to be *nqh* rather than *'nq*. But there seems to be no basis in Classical Hebrew for the verb *nqh* = "to empty" or for *yād* = "incense spoon," and this would in any case be a rather odd way of referring to a reprehensible cult act (see further Rubinstein 1953, 92–95; Brownlee 1964, 234–35).

Squatting among rocks and spending the night in tombs, perhaps in tomb chambers like the one mentioned in a tomb inscription from the Kidron Valley (*hdr bktp hṣr*, "chamber on the slope of the rock," Dahood 1960, 408–9), belong to the same category of necromantic practice as those referred to in 57:5b–6. Ritual incubation, spending the night in a holy place in the expectation of obtaining a communication from the numen of the place (e.g., Gen 28:10–22; 1 Sam 3:2–18), was a normal religious practice throughout the Levant and Near East. In this instance the purpose was to communicate with the ancestors, "the spirits of the dead and the ghosts that chirp and mutter" (Isa 8:19), a practice that, though contrary to Yahvistic orthodoxy (Lev 19:31; 20:6, 27; Deut 18:11), was a well-attested feature of the religion of the household and clan.

The prohibition against eating pork (Lev 11:7; Deut 14:8) was due less to the perceived insanitary habits of this animal or to the danger of contracting trichinosis, the pathogen for which was discovered only in the nineteenth century, than to its role in the sacrificial rituals of neighboring peoples. The reference here is most likely to a sacrificial meal in which pork was consumed, especially since in other cultures the pig was associated with chthonic deities. (de Vaux 1971[1958]: 252–69). "Unclean food" (*piggûl*, Lev 7:18; 19:7; Ezek 4:14) is also mentioned together with pork in 66:17, which lists a witch's brew of insects and vermin, consumed during the ritual in the garden.

These reports from the Judean underworld do not require us to identify the participants in these rituals as members of Hellenistic mystery cults (*Kultgenossenschaften*, as Volz 1932, 279–80 describes them and several scholars since have proposed). As I noted in the discussion on the similar practices condemned in 57:3–13, it is rather a case of continuity with religious practice, at both the popular and state level, during the last century of the Judean kingdom. In his supernaturally guided tour of the Jerusalem temple in 592 B.C.E., Ezekiel witnessed a ritual in progress analogous to the one to which the Isaian texts refer (Ezek 8:10–12). The location was a dark corner of the Jerusalem temple, the room was decorated with images of all sorts of creeping and crawling things (*remeś, šeqeṣ*), incense was burned, and a certain Jaazaniah, the leader of the liturgy, stood in the midst of the participants.

The injunction spoken by the members of the conventicle or cult group (v 5a) appears, in the context, to be directed at YHVH rather than at YHVH worshipers in the community. "Keep your distance"—literally, "approach to yourself" (*qĕrab 'ēleka*)—could be understood as an insolent rejoinder to YHVH's invitation in 57:3 to draw near (*qirĕbû hēnnâ*), addressed to the children of the sorceress. However, no translation of the second part of the verse featuring the verb *qdš* is entirely above suspicion. In the Masoretic pointing, the verb is intransitive and would therefore not have a suffix indicating direct object, though there are a few cases in which an indirect object is expressed by a direct object suffix (GKC §117x). But it is doubtful that this construction would permit a comparative, such as "I am too holy for you" (NRSV and frequently in the commentaries, e.g., Beuken 1989a, 67; Lau 1994, 189–90) or "I am purer than you" (as in the Targum). Even more dubious is "do not touch me, or I will communicate holiness to you" (Hanson 1975, 147–49), because *kî* cannot mean "or," and the tense of the verb must be either past or present but not future. If the Masoretic punctuation is maintained (Qal rather than Piel conjugation) the idea may be that, as a result of participating in the rituals mentioned, the speaker has been made holy, that is, set apart, *with respect to* YHVH.

Smoking nostrils and fire are usually manifestations of divine anger and danger:

> Smoke went up from his nostrils,
> a consuming fire from his mouth. (2 Sam 22:9 = Ps 18:9)

In Isa 65:5, however, the imagery applies to the transgressors whose offenses are as distressing as smoke blowing into one's face from a fire. The idea of heavenly record-keeping was familiar throughout the ancient Near East, as also was the idea of tablets of destiny in which the future was recorded (cf. Ps 139:16). The ledger would contain either the names of all the living (e.g., Exod 32:32–33) or the names of the righteous together with their tribulations and good deeds (Ps 56:9; 69:29; Neh 13:14; Isa 4:3; Mal 3:16; Dan 12:1). Here, in Isa 65:6, we are closer to the court records detailing deeds good and bad, on the basis of which judgment will be passed in the final reckoning (Dan 7:10; *1 En.* 90:20).

The theme of YHVH's silence or inactivity appears frequently in the latter part of Isa (42:14; 57:11; 62:1), and this latest announcement that the silence will be broken could be taken as an answer to the lament about YHVH's silence in 64:11[12], but not the kind of answer that was anticipated. The verb *šillēm*, here translated "requite," is used for the fulfillment of vows (Isa 19:21), making restitution (Exod 21:34, 36–37), or making payment. Paying or requiting in full measure (literally, "into their laps") makes use of the image of filling the fold of the outer garment (used in lieu of pockets) with goods. Due to the prophetic *excipit* at the end of v 7a and the repetitions in 7bc, several commentators regard the final two verses as textually suspect. This may be so, but the text makes sense as it stands, and the repetitions do not materially affect the meaning.

WHO ARE AND ARE NOT GOD'S PEOPLE (65:8–12)

(Baldacci 1978, 189–91; Baltzer 1992, 114–19; Beuken 1990, 67–87; 1991, 204–21; Lau 1994, 193–98; W. A. Maier 1992: *ABD* 2, 863–64; Pauritsch 1971, 171–75; Ribichini 1999: *DDD* 339–41; Sperling 1999: *DDD* 566–68; Steck 1987c, 103–16 = 1991a, 217–28; Stegemann 1969, 161–86)

i

65   [8]These are YHVH's words:
When there is still some juice in a bunch of grapes,
people say, "Don't destroy it; there's a blessing in it."
So shall I do for the sake of my servants,
so as not to destroy all the people.[a]
[9]I shall bring forth descendants from Jacob,
from Judah heirs[b] to inherit my mountains.[c]
My chosen ones will inherit the land,[d]
my servants will have their abode there.

[10]Sharon will be grazing for flocks,
the Vale of Achor pasture for cattle;
they will be for my people who seek me.

ii

[11]But you who forsake YHVH
and neglect my holy mountain,
who spread a table for the god of good luck
and fill bowls of mixed wine for the god of destiny,[e]
[12]I shall destine you for the sword;
you will all crouch down to be slaughtered—
because, when I called, you would not answer;
when I spoke, you would not listen;
but you did what was evil in my sight,
you chose what did not please me.

NOTES

[a]   In clarification of MT *hakkol*, "the whole."
[b]   Reading MT *yôrēš* as a collective sing.
[c]   LXX has sing. *to oros to hagion mou*, "my holy mountain" cf. 57:13c, but
       the fem. suffix in *vîrēšûhâ* immediately following, referring to *'ereṣ*, "land,"
       counsels retaining MT as in parallelism with "land." See Comments.
[d]   Taking fem. suffix in MT *vîrēšûhâ* to refer to *hā'āreṣ* (fem.) = "land."
[e]   "The god of good luck" and "the god of destiny" translate "Gad" and
       "Meni," respectively in MT; see Comments. LXX translates *tō daimoniō*,
       "for the demon," and *tē tuchē*, "for [the god of] Good Luck," respectively;
       Vulg. *Fortuna* for both and Syr. *gaddē* for both.

COMMENTS

In 65:1–7 the preacher addressed all the community without distinction in traditional terms. The logical connection between 65:1–7 and the present passage,
however created, is that the impression of a totally corrupt people destined for
an annihilating judgment in vv 1–7 now calls for qualification. The preacher's
intent was grasped by the Targumist, who refers at this juncture to the salvation
of the righteous Noah out of a sinful world at the time of the great deluge. To
make the point, the preacher invokes the traditional prophetic theme of the
holy remnant expressed under different metaphors throughout Isaiah (1:8–9;
6:13; 17:4–6; 30:17–18). The remnant theme is one of the most radical contributions of eighth-century prophecy, because it rejects the idea that the traditional, ideal Israel and its current political embodiment are identical. From the
prophetic point of view, institutions are always under judgment.
    While acknowledging the unity of ch. 65 as a whole, Pauritsch (1971, 171–
75) divided it into three segments (vv 2–10, 11–16, 17–23) which ignore the
prophetic markers at vv 8 and 13 and the important, repeated contrasting of

those who are and those who are not considered to be God's true people. Vermeylen (1978, 492–95) also severed 8–10 from 11–12 in arguing that 8–10 with 16–24 (minus 17–18a, 20b, 22b, and 24) formed the original response to 1–7. Vermeylen's elaborations at this point seem to me to be typical of much redactional work on Isaiah, in that his work consists in stating a possibility rather than a serious probability—and one that is both unnecessary and unfalsifiable.

We can get an idea of the momentous nature of the change of perspective at this point by noting the different functions assigned to traditional Isaianic designations for the people of Israel in this passage. In the word of assurance addressed to the resident foreigners and eunuchs (56:6), and in the community lament (63:17), the term "Servants" (*'ăbādîm*) designates the community as a whole, following Deuteronomic and earlier Isaianic usage (41:8–9; 42:19; 43:10; 44:1–2, 21; 45:4; 48:20; 54:17). In both 65:8–12 and 65:13–16a, however, this term is restricted to the genuine core of Israel, for whom alone the relief and salvation promised from the early post-destruction period is reserved. The same is true for "the elect of God," "the chosen" (*běḥîrîm*, v 9b), a term formerly applied to the community as a whole (Isa 43:20; 45:4) but here limited to a part of it, implying a drastic change in what we might call the doctrine of election (verbal stem *bḥr*: Isa 41:8–9; 43:10; 44:1–2; 49:7).

It is, finally, no longer obvious that when God, speaking through his prophet, refers to "my people" (*'ammî*, Isa 40:1; 43:20 etc.), the reference is to Israel as a whole. The author of the lament psalm protested that "we are all your people" (64:8), but this must be qualified, because now the promises are restricted to "my people who seek me" (65:10b). "Seeking God" (verbal stem *drš*) indicates, within this prophetic tradition, here too in debt to the Deuteronomists, fundamental religious attitude (Isa 55:6; 58:2; Deut 4:29).

We see, then, that vv 8–12 and 13–16a register important modifications with respect to the undifferentiated condemnation in vv 1–7. Both passages draw invisible lines through the community, each in its own way, and present different interpretations of an eventual salvation and judgment, the first within history, the second beyond it.

The remnant idea is here expressed in the figure of a bunch of grapes, deliberately evocative of the traditional metaphor of Israel as vineyard (8a). The term *tîrôš* is usually rendered "must" or "new wine," as differentiated from the more common *yayin*. But in only one instance is the distinction apparent: where *yayin* and *tîrôš* occur together in Hos 4:11. It is the latter also that gladdens both gods and human beings (Judg 9:13). Commentators are divided concerning the point of the metaphor. The idea could be that there are some good grapes in this particular bunch, so save them and discard the rotten ones. This would make a good fit with the preternaturally large grape cluster (*'eškôl*) which, according to one of many etiologies in the narrative tradition, was picked by the spies in the Vale of Eshkol (Num 13:23–24) and served to symbolize the land, as it does still, for the State of Israel (cf. the conventional description of the land as *'ereṣ dāgān větîrôš*, "a land of grain and wine": Deut 33:28; Jer 31:12; Hos 2:10; 7:14).

However, it seems to fit the context better to read the grape cluster metaphor as implying that there is at least one good bunch among the rotten grapes, so the one good bunch must not be destroyed with the rest. The figure therefore modifies the previous passage, in which no such exception was apparent. It serves, moreover, as commentary on the definitive judgment passed on Israel as YHVH's vineyard in the "Song of the Vineyard" (Isa 5:1–7) with which the author was surely familiar. There may also be an echo of Ezekiel's haggadic teaching on moral accountability. When a land, Judah for example, sins and is punished by famine and other disasters, the righteous in it will themselves be saved but will be unable to save the others, among whom only a small group will survive (Ezek 14:12–23). It will be clear that this solution is quite different from that of Gen 18:22–33, in which Abraham pleads with YHVH for the inhabitants of Sodom.

The quotation, "Don't destroy it; there is blessing in it," may conceivably reflect a proverb about the blessing of the vine (Westermann 1969, 404), though in truth it doesn't look much like a proverb. It looks even less like a vintage song, in spite of the curious title 'al-tašḥēt ("Do not destroy") appended to Pss 57, 58, 59, and 75. This title more likely refers either to Moses' intercession ("YHVH God, do not destroy the people who are your own possession," Deut 9:26) or, in the context of the entire title to the vicissitudes of David (David to Abishai: "Do not destroy him, that is, Saul," 1 Sam 26:9).

The servants, the elect, the people who seek YHVH (v 8b, 10b) are promised not only exemption from the general judgment reserved for their fellow-Jews but more immediate and concrete benefits (9–10). Like the prophetic Servant of Isa 53, they will have descendants (zera', "seed"); in other words, from them YHVH will bring into existence a new people. From the wording of this promise, repeated often in chs. 40–66 (44:3–5; 48:19; 49:19–21; 54:1–3; 60:4–9, 21–22), we gather that proselytes are included among the descendants:

I will pour out water on the thirsty ground,
streams of water on the parched land;
I will pour out my spirit on your descendants,
my blessing on your offspring.
They will flourish like well-watered grass,
like willows by the runnels of water.
This one will say, "I belong to YHVH,"
another will take the name Jacob,
yet another will write YHVH's name on the hand,
and add the name Israel to his own. (44:3–5)

Inseparably connected with the promise of descendants is a land to settle and live in. This territorial promise, too, is repeated often throughout these chapters (49:8; 54:3; 57:13; 58:12; 60:21; 61:4). "My mountain" stands, by metonymy, for "my land" (cf. Isa 14:25; Ezek 38:21).

I do not see any reason for relegating v 10b (*lĕʿammî ʾăšer dĕrāšûnî*) to the status of a gloss on metrical grounds (as Duhm 1922, 477; Fohrer 1964, 263; Pauritsch 1971, 180 et al.). The incidence of the half-verse, either as closing a passage or simply as variety, is quite common in these chapters (e.g., 56:8b; 57:6c; 59:18b; 63:6b; 65:6b). The Plain of Sharon to the west and the Vale of Achor to the east (probably the Buqeiah northwest of the Dead Sea) represent the totality of the land of Judah, the more easily in that both names are elsewhere given a symbolic valency (for Sharon, Isa 33:9 and 35:2; for Achor, Josh 7:24–26; 15:7; Hos 2:15). This is therefore a statement about the land as a whole, comparable to "from Dan to Beersheba"—that is, from north to south rather than, as here, from west to east.

This dual assurance of survival as a people and land tenure echoes, deliberately and repeatedly throughout chs. 40–66, the promises made to the first ancestors, beginning with Abraham (Gen 12:1–3 etc.). The relationship between the narrative traditions in Gen 12–50 in which the promises are embedded and these prophetic texts from the early Persian period is not as straightforward as may appear. In texts datable prior to the destruction of Jerusalem, we hear nothing of Abraham apart from the name in the formulaic "Abraham, Isaac, and Jacob." The earliest allusions to him in prophetic texts (Isa 29:22; 51:2; 63:16; Jer 33:26; Ezek 33:24; Mic 7:20), none of which is thought to be preexilic, suggest that the Abraham narrative in Genesis was constructed to reflect the vicissitudes and crises facing Jewish communities documented directly or indirectly in biblical texts from the Neo-Babylonian and early Persian periods.

Among the major issues are immigration from Mesopotamia to Judah, contact between Judeo-Babylonian immigrants and native Judeans and their neighbors, relations with Arabs (Edomites, Kedarites) in the Negev, contractually valid title to land (cf. Abraham's purchase of a plot from the "Hittites" of Hebron, Gen 23:1–20), intermarriage with local populations, and the very possibility of surviving as a people (cf. the "Binding of Isaac," Gen 22:1–19).

Once the possibility of immigration to Judah from Babylon and other diaspora centers was opened up in the early Persian period, the issues just listed would have become acute. Among these the two most important would have been land tenure and the restoration of Jerusalem as a political and religious center. The expropriations, redistributions, and breakup of large estates following the deportations would have been a major source of conflict once descendants of the previous title-holders began to arrive. The locals claimed to follow Abraham's example in taking over territory (Ezek 33:23–29) and argued on religious grounds that, in moving outside of YHVH's jurisdiction, the deportees had forfeited title to their lands (Ezek 11:14–17). The other issue, the rebuilding of the temple (and the related question of who would control its assets and operations), comes more clearly into view in ch. 66. But we saw in the opening defense of resident aliens and eunuchs that access to and support of the temple went hand in hand with civic status and title to real estate (see Comments on 56:5).

Over against the Servants and the elect are those who forsake YHVH and neglect (literally, "forget") his holy mountain (v 11). Forsaking YHVH (verbal stem *ʿzb*) means abandoning normative Yahvism, specifically Yahvism as defined by the Deuteronomists, for a syncretistic form of religion. It is condemned at the beginning of the book (1:4, 28), and in 58:2 the hearers are condemned for having forsaken the *mišpaṭ ʾĕlohîm*, that is, the customary and normative way of worship (cf. *mišpaṭ hammelek*, "the custom of the king," 1 Sam 8:11).

What is meant by neglecting YHVH's "holy mountain" is not so clear. The "holy mountain" (*har qodšî*) can refer to Jerusalem (Isa 11:9 = 65:25; 66:20) but refers more often to the temple (Isa 27:13; 56:7; 57:13). The meaning would then be that those addressed are being denounced either for opposing the project of restoring the Jerusalem temple cult or for not frequenting the temple, depending on the date assigned to this passage. But if we take this entire section into account, especially 66:1–4, it appears more likely that the accused were participating in temple worship, and perhaps even officiating in the Jerusalem cult, but were doing so abusively and neglectfully while engaging in cults to other deities. The gravamen is therefore directed against syncretistic religious practice.

At this point the prophet-preacher adduces only one example of these non-Yahvistic cults: sacrificial meals in honor of the gods of good fortune and destiny—Gad and Meni, respectively (v 11b). Recourse to these deities may have been occasioned by a sense of disorientation and insecurity, so often reflected in these chapters; somewhat comparable, therefore, to the covenant with death (the deity Mōtu) denounced in Isa 28:14–22. Failure to solve the problem of theodicy, reflected in one way or another in all the biblical texts from the immediate post-disaster period, could easily have led people to turn to such cults.

In the Hebrew Bible, the deity Gad is mentioned only here and, possibly, Gen 30:11 (the birth of the tribal eponym, Gad), if Leah's exclamation (*bĕgad*) implies that the birth came about with the assistance of that deity. Perhaps people had recourse to Gad especially at the dangerous moment of childbirth. Gad corresponds in function but not gender with the Hellenistic deity Tyche, Good Fortune, as we see from a bilingual (Aramaic-Greek) inscription from Palmyra from the mid–second century B.C.E. However, LXX identified Meni with *tuchē*, "good fortune," and used the more generic term *daimōn* for Gad. Gad was also known and worshiped in the Phoenician homeland and colonies, and his name occurs in Punic inscriptions in Tunisia, Spain, and Sardinia. His veneration continued well into the common era. As late as the fifth century C.E., the Syriac ecclesiastical writer Jacob of Sarug reports that people were preparing meals (corresponding to the Latin *lectisternia*) for Gad, "the Lord of Fortune." That he was venerated in Syria, Palestine, and the Levant in general long before the Hellenistic period is not in doubt, since it is attested in Ugaritic and Amorite as well as Phoenician and Punic onomastics. In the Hebrew Bible we have the place-names Baal-gad (Josh 11:17; 12:7; 13:5) and Migdal-gad (Josh 15:37) and the personal names Gaddi (Num 13:11), Gadi (2 Kgs 15:14, 17), Gaddiel (Num 13:10), and Azgad (Ezra 2:12 = Neh 7:17;

Ezra 8:12; Neh 10:17[16]). The last of these at least is of a familiar theophoric type (cf. ʿzbʿl, ʿzmlk).

The name Meni is related to the Hebrew verb mnh (count," "assign," "appoint") and the corresponding substantive mānâ, "portion," "lot," and its cognates—for example, Arabic manīha, with a meaning similar to the Greek moira, "fate." As is often the case, there may be an astral aspect to both deities in presiding over human destinies. Meni appears to be related to Manāt, one of the three pre-Islamic Arabic goddesses mentioned in the Qurʾan (Sura 53:20), who is identified with Venus, known as the Lesser Fortune, just as Jupiter is the Greater Fortune among the Arabs. The same deity appears under the name Manūtu in Nabataean theophoric names and tomb inscriptions.

In pronouncing the verdict on the syncretists (the sword, slaughter, v 12a), the author does not have any particular event or eventuality in mind. The wording is chosen to permit a bitter pun on their addiction to the cult of Meni. YHVH destines them not for good times but for the sword, employing the verb mnh (ûmānîtî), and they will bow down (krʿ, e.g., in the worship of Baal, 1 Kgs 19:18) not to offer cult to Gad and Meni but for the coup de grâce (e.g., Judg 5:27).

The last two verses (12bc) are often demoted to secondary status because they appear in practically identical form in 66:4. But it seems to me more likely that they have been placed at these two points deliberately—by whom and at what stage of composition we do not know. We have heard the call-response theme more than once (50:2; 58:9), and it functions in this last section of the book to articulate the literary unit 65:1–66:4 (65:1, 12, 24; 66:4). Moreover, 65:8–12 and 66:1–4 are structurally similar. Both play out the contrast between the true YHVH-worshipers and the syncretists, the verdict on the latter is suffused with irony, and both conclude in practically identical form.

ESCHATOLOGICAL REVERSAL (65:13–16)

(Beuken 1990, 67–87; 1991, 204–21; Blenkinsopp 1983, 1–23; 1997, 155–75; Kessler 1956–1957, 335–58; Lau 1994, 198–202; Steck 1987c, 103–16 = 1991a, 217–28; Stegemann 1969, 161–86)

TRANSLATION

65 [13]These, therefore, are the words of the Sovereign Lord[a] YHVH:
My servants will eat, while you go hungry;
my servants will drink, while you go thirsty;
my servants will rejoice, while you are put to shame;
[14]my servants will exult with heartfelt joy,
while you cry out with heartache
and wail[b] with anguish[c] of spirit.
[15]You will leave your name behind as a curse for my chosen ones,
[May the Sovereign Lord YHVH put you to death!][d]

but his servants will be called[e] by a different name,
[16]so that the one who blesses himself[f] in the land
will do so by the God whose name is Amen,[g]
and the one who swears an oath in the land
will do so by the God whose name is Amen,[g]
for the former troubles are forgotten
and are hidden from my sight.

NOTES

[a] "Sovereign Lord" (*'ădonay* = *kurios*) omitted in LXX; in 1QIsa[a] written superscript.

[b] MT *tĕyēlîlû* → *yll*: the Preformative has been added to the contracted form of the Hiphil (GKC §70c), hence no need to emend with BHS.

[c] 1QIsaiah[a] has a late form, *šbrvn*, for MT *šēber*.

[d] A gloss that interrupts the train of thought rather violently; there is also a change from pl. to sing. form of address. Perhaps the scribe wished to supply the wording of the curse, though this does not correspond to the curse formula; more likely he simply got carried away with just indignation; cf. 2:9, *'al-tiśśā' lāhem*, "Do not forgive them!" Torrey (1928, 468) proposed, rather too adventurously, to emend *'ădonay* to *'āmar* and *'emîtkâ* to *'etmōk*, giving "but my chosen ones I will uphold, says YHVH." 1QIsaiah[a] adds *tmyd*, "continually," and omits 15b, 16a, leaving most of the line blank, then adds *vhyh hnšb' b'lvhy 'mn*, "and the one who swears an oath by the God Amen"; this probably due to a defect in the copy with which the scribe was working.

[e] Reading Passive with LXX *klēthēsetai* for MT Active *yiqrā'*.

[f] *brk* Hithpael with Reflexive sense (Gen 22:18; 26:4; Deut 29:18[19]; Jer 4:2).

[g] None of the proposed emendations (*'ēmet*, *'omen*, *'ēmûn*) is necessary, and the ancient versions support MT. Torrey (1928, 470) kept *'āmēn* but as an adjective "true, faithful, dependable," comparing it with the epithet *al-amin*, "the trustworthy one" assigned to Mohammed. See Comments.

COMMENTS

The prophetic incipit introducing the passage marks a new stage in the unfolding panorama of salvation and reprobation, while the initial "therefore" (*lākēn*) preserves continuity with what precedes, reinforced by the reference to the final destiny of the "Servants" (cf. v 9b) and perhaps also the hungering and thirsting contrasted with meals in honor of the gods (v 11). The conclusion is not so clear. Many commentators (e.g., Westermann 1969, 407–8; Whybray 1975, 275) read v 16c as the beginning of the next section, which therefore links the passing of the bad times with the promise of an age of renewal. But the repetition of 16c in 17b in slightly different form suggests, rather, a deliberate linking of successive strophes, a transition from one stage to the next of an unfolding panorama of the future.

The continuities in the chapter are reinforced by the repetition of the call-response motif at key points (vv 1, 12, 24). The comprehensive judgment of 1–7 is differentiated in 8–12 and 13–16 by different frames of reference, the former within and the latter beyond history. The destiny of the "Servants" likewise moves from the historical to the metahistorical plane. The eschatological scenario viewed from this plane—new heavens, new earth, new Jerusalem, new name—is described in terms familiar from the earlier stages of this Isaianic tradition (e.g., 43:18; 62:2).

This prophetic utterance is addressed to the people denounced in vv 1–7 and 11–12, those who forsake (the cult of) YHVH—in other words, the syncretists. The antithesis between their destiny and that of the "Servants" is expressed economically and elegantly in three balanced bicola, ending in a kind of rallentando in v 14. The theme, a familiar feature of revolutionary movements and sects, is eschatological reversal, a vision of the future in which roles are reversed, power and authority (the power to coerce) radically redistributed, and the redemptive media redefined.

An attempt to probe beneath the surface of these antitheses might begin with an allusion to the theme of the eschatological banquet. Rooted in the mythic image of the banquet of the gods (e.g., *Enuma Elish* III 129–38; VI 69–94; the Ugaritic Baal text 51 IV 35–59), it developed in the postbiblical period into an elaborate scenario involving immortality-conferring food and drink (ambrosia, the water of life) and feasting on the flesh of Leviathan (e.g., *1 En.* 34:4–35:7; 60:24; *4 Ezra* 6:52; *b. B. Bat.* 74b). It seems likely that at Qumran and in early Christian churches the sacramental meals of the respective communities were considered proleptic celebrations of the eschatological banquet (1Q28a 2:17– 21; Matt 26:29: Jesus anticipates drinking the fruit of the vine anew in his Father's kingdom). The theme is anticipated in Isa 25:6–8, which speaks of rich food, wine well aged, and the final defeat of misery and death. The provision of grain and wine promised in 62:8 has, however, a different background (pace Lau 1994, 199).

The antitheses also send back an echo of the blessings and curses attached to treaties and covenants. Since curses are functionally more important in this context, it is not surprising that the closest parallel is to be found among the curses listed toward the end of Deuteronomy:

> Since you did not serve (*'ābadtâ*) YHVH your God with heartfelt joy (*běsimḥâ ûběṭûb lēbāb*) for the abundance of all things, you shall serve your enemies . . . in hunger, thirst, nakedness and lack of everything. (Deut 28:47)

Here we have the essential features of the opponents' destiny—hunger, thirst, shame (nakedness), and general misery—expressed in much the same language. Isaiah 65:13–14 represents, therefore, an eschatologized version of this anticipated outcome of the refusal to serve.

We can dispel some of the obscurity surrounding the identity of the Servants and their opponents referred to here by noting the connection of this denunciation with the anonymous prophet's address to those who tremble at YHVH's word (*haḥărēdîm 'el-dĕbārô*) in 66:5:

Hear the word of YHVH, you who tremble at his word!
Your brethren who hate you,
who cast you out for my name's sake have said,
"May YHVH reveal his glory, that we may witness your joy!"
But it is they who will be put to shame.

In this instance the opponents are referred to obliquely rather than directly. The antithesis between the ultimate destiny of the Servants and the destiny of their opponents in 65:13–14 can be read either as the occasion for or the reply to the taunt of the opponents in 66:5: "May YHVH reveal his glory, so that we may witness your joy!"

If this is so, the *'ăbādîm* ("Servants") of 65:13–14 would be identical though perhaps not contemporaneous with the *ḥărēdîm* ("Tremblers") of 66:5, and they would be a group excommunicated by their opponents, at least partly on account of their eschatological beliefs. For this to happen, the opponents must have included the religious authorities—in other words the men who controlled the Jerusalem temple. This in its turn confirms our suspicion that those who have forsaken YHVH and neglected his holy mountain (65:11) include the temple authorities. This issue of the identity of the Servants and their opponents will be discussed further in the Commentary on 66:5.

The opponents are then told that after their disappearance from the scene their name will continue in circulation as a curse. What this means can be seen from the terrible fate of the Judeo-Babylonian prophets Ahab ben-Kolaiah and Zedekiah ben-Maaseiah, during the reign of Nebuchadrezzar, whom the Babylonians roasted to death and whose names passed into common usage in a curse formula: "May YHVH make you like Ahab and Zedekiah, whom the king of Babylon roasted in the fire" (Jer 29:21–23). A psalmist who has suffered some serious misfortune also claims that his name is being used as a curse (Ps 102:9[8]), and the same prospect is used as a threat against the woman accused of marital infidelity (Num 5:21). It remains unclear whether the threat in Isa 65:15 involves personal names or whether the author is thinking of a collective designation, either real or symbolic. If a collective designation, we are given no clue what it was.

The different name to be assigned to the Servants is equally obscure. It may simply mean that their name, and therefore their destiny, will be different from their opponents', a name with which to bless rather than with which to curse. If the anomalous relative pronoun *'ăšer* at the beginning of v 16 may be translated "so that . . . ," we might be led to conclude that they are to bear the name of the God Amen—that therefore they are to be known as the Amen people, the people that say Yes to God. This appellation—the God Amen—is often emended out of existence, but early Jewish and early Christian readers did not regard it as implausible (see 2 Cor 1:17–20; Rev 3:14; and Jepsen 1974), and no one has taken exception to the equally strange appellative *'ehyeh* in Exod 3:14 and Hos 1:9.

This interpretation of the Servants' new name is tempting but, pace Blenkinsopp (1990, 10), the temptation should be resisted. The idea of a new name is consistent with a major theme that informs this post-destruction Isaianic tradition from its earliest stages—new events (42:9; 48:6), a new intervention of God (43:19), a new song to be sung (42:10)—and is taken up in later stages of development. Zion's old name, Azuvah (= Abandoned), will give way to the new name Hephzivah (= My Delight is in Her); the old name of the land, Shemamah (= Desolation) will give way to the new name Beulah (= Married; 62:2–4). In a continuation of the reversal theme, the Servants' new name, which is to be conferred in the future, will be symbolic of a new epoch, different from the time of the former troubles. This play upon curse and blessing has undertones of Abraham's story. YHVH's name is invoked in both curse and blessing, and the Name Amen signifies that he gives reliable warranty for both, as he did with Abraham (Gen 12:1–3).

New Heaven, New Earth, New City (65:17–25)

(Beuken 1991: 204–21; Koenen 1990, 168–83; Lau 1994, 134–42; Martin-Achard 1979, 439–51; Mauser 1982, 181–86; Monaci 1982, 337–48; Pauritsch 1971, 171–94; van Ruiten 1992, 31–42; Sehmsdorf 1972, 517–62; P. A. Smith 1995, 144–52; Steck 1987c, 217–33 = 1991a, 217–28; 1992b, 104–13; 1997[b], 349–65; Sweeney 1997, 455–74)

TRANSLATION

65   [17]See, I am about to create new heavens and a new earth;[a]
the former things will no more be remembered,
nor will they come to mind.
[18]Rejoice, rather, and take delight[b] unending
in what[c] I am about to create!
I shall create Jerusalem as a delight,
her people as a source of joy;
[19]I shall take delight in Jerusalem
and rejoice in my people.
No more will the sound of weeping be heard in her,
no more the cry of distress.
[20]No child[d] there[e] will ever again live but a few days,[f]
no old man fail to live out his full span of life.
Whoever dies at a hundred will be just like a youth,
whoever falls short of a hundred will be reckoned accursed.[g]

²¹When they build houses, they will dwell in them;
when they plant vineyards, they will eat their produce;
²²they will not build for others to live in,
they will not plant for others to eat.
Like the life-span of a tree[h] will the life-span of my people be,
my chosen ones will long enjoy the work of their hands.
²³They will not toil in vain
or bear children destined for disaster;
they will be a race blessed by YHVH,[i]
they and their offspring with them.
²⁴Before they call out, I shall answer;
while they are yet speaking, I shall hear their prayer.
²⁵The wolf and the lamb will graze together,
the lion will eat hay like the ox.
[As for the snake, dust will be its food.][j]
No longer will they hurt or destroy
on all my holy mountain.
This is what YHVH says.

NOTES

a   LXX, *estai gar ho ouranos kainos kai hē gē kainē* ("For the heaven will be new and the earth new,") perhaps a deliberate avoidance of the idea of a new creation.

b   1QIsaiah[a] has sing. *śyś, gyl* for MT and 1QIsa[b] pl.; LXX "Rather, they will find joy and exultation in her"; Vulg. also has future: *sed gaudebitis et exultabitis* ("But you will rejoice and exult"), but MT need not be emended.

c   We would expect *ʿal-ʾăšer* for MT *ʾăšer*, but the elliptical use of the relative pronoun is attested (e.g., Isa 31:6).

d   1QIsaiah[a] has *ʿvyl* (*ʿăvîl*), "young boy," for MT and 1QIsa[b] *ʿûl*, "infant," only here and Isa 49:15 (fem.); the fuller spelling is common in 1QIsa[a].

e   MT *miššām*, literally, "from there" (also 1QIsa[a] and 1QIsa[b]), is unusual, but the prefixed preposition need not be elided; the sense is "No infant from that place. . . ."

f   *yāmîm* pl. for "a few" (GKC §139h).

g   MT may be exploiting the double meaning of the verb *ḥṭʾ*, "miss the mark," "fall short" (Job 5:24; Prov 8:36; 19:2), more often "sin" cf. LXX (*hamartōlos*) and Vulg. (*peccator*); this would help to explain *yĕqullāl* (Pual), "will be reckoned accursed," not to be emended with BHS to *yēqāl* (Qal), "will be reckoned of little account."

h   1QIsaiah[a] lacks the article; both LXX and Targ. gloss "the tree" as "the tree of life."

i   1QIsaiah[a] *brk* (Piel 3d-masc. Perfect) and LXX *sperma eulogēmenon* have sing. in contrast to pl. in MT and 1QIsa[b].

j   A scribal insertion; see Comments.

COMMENTS

Commentators in the modern period have raised questions about the literary integrity of this passage, its relation with the preceding pericope, and its place in ch. 65 in general. It is common to begin with v 16b—thereby understanding the new creation to be the reason for forgetting former troubles (kî understood causally). Another reason for doing so is the repetition of 16c in somewhat different words in 17b. But it would be entirely characteristic of Isa 40–66 to connect two sayings by a catchword (in this instance *hāri'šōnôt*) or the repetition of a phrase, and *kî* appears with great frequency at the beginning of a verse throughout chs. 40–66 (nine times in 65:16–25), as a connective particle with no particular charge. We would, finally, expect a solemn pronouncement such as 17a to open a new section.

In any case, the division at this point is not of great importance, since ch. 65 is made up of thematically linked passages. Thus, the prospect of the future vindication of YHVH's Servants and chosen ones is enlarged to take in the renewal of the cosmos, and the new name of these chosen ones is taken up into a new heavens, new earth, and new city. Since v 24, together with vv 1 and 12, structures the chapter around the theme of call and response, the final verse, based on Isa 11:6–9, would appear to be a scribal afterthought. If so, it is by no means inappropriate, which has led several commentators to read it as integral to the passage (Beuken 1989a, 91–92; van Ruiten 1992, 31–42; P. A. Smith 1995, 148–49). The suggestion that vv 17 and 25 were added to provide an apocalyptic framework for the promise of a renewed city and people (Westermann 1969, 326) is an unnecessary elaboration and removes any logical or thematic hiatus between vv 16 and 18.

On the subject of unnecessary elaborations, we might mention the redactional analysis of Vermeylen (1978, 492), who identifies the original core of the passage as vv 18b–20a, 21–22a, 23 and assigns the rest to the work of editors. Another redactional maximalist, Sehmsdorf (1972, 517–61), limits the core promise to 16b–19a, which was then filled out with three successive expansions from adherents of the Deuteronomistic school (i.e., 20, 21–22a, 24–25) and one *Zusammenfassung* (i.e., 22b–23). This reading follows from his conviction, based on linguistic and thematic overlap, that chs. 56–66 have been subjected to a thorough Deuteronomistic reworking (especially in evidence in 56:1–8; 58:13–14; 60:18a; 62:8–9; 66:1–4). In most instances, however, the vocabulary and themes on which Sehmsdorf based his argument are attested outside of the Deuteronomistic corpus, a good example being the blessing formulas in vv 21–22 and the corresponding curses, as we shall see. It seems that the similarities he adduces can be adequately explained by the pervasive influence of the Deuteronomists on chs. 40–66 in general, often noted and commented on in this section of the book.

The most striking difference between 17–25 and 1–16 is that there is no distinction between the elect and their opponents in the audience of 17–25. If the passage is read without reference to its context, its affinity with chs. 60–62 (the core of this third section of the book) and therefore indirectly with chs. 40–55, becomes apparent. In this situation, however, it is important to note that much of the language in which the renewed cosmos is described does not appear in chs. 60–62 — conspicuously the verb br' ("create"), hāri'šōnôt ("the former things"), and bĕḥîrîm ("chosen ones"). But if the context of the passage is taken seriously, whatever one thinks about its original form or location, we see that the regenerated world with Jerusalem at its center is promised not for the Jewish people as a whole but for "my people who seek me" (65:10b), the Servants (65:8–9, 13–15), the elect of God (65:9, 15).

The passage consists essentially in two solemn pronouncements beginning kî hinnĕnî bôrē' ("See, I am about to create"). That the second of these (18b–24) is much longer than the first (17–18a) suggests that the new heavens and earth are thought of more as the context for social and political transformation and therefore are not the focus of attention in themselves, as is the case in apocalyptic writings from the Greco-Roman period. The line of continuity with the preceding verses is not difficult to trace. In vv 13–16 YHVH's Servants are promised a different, therefore a new, name and a transformed existence in which past misfortunes will be forgotten. The prospect held out in vv 17–25 simply enlarges on this panorama, and we shall find the same association between cosmic renewal and a renewed Jerusalem toward the end of the book (66:22–23).

The author of the poem is drawing on and sometimes reinterpreting sayings that now form part of chs. 40–55. The idea of new heavens and earth may have been suggested by the prediction of the end of the present cosmic order in 51:6:

> Raise your eyes to the sky,
> look at the earth beneath—
> for the sky will be dispersed like smoke,
> the earth will wear out like a garment,
> its inhabitants will die like gnats;
> but my salvation will endure for ever,
> my triumph will not be eclipsed.

Whether this language of endings and new beginnings can be described as *apocalyptic* depends, of course, on how one defines this elusive term. There is here no dogma of the two ages, no dominion of Satan, and the sense of crisis communicated in such texts as 2 Pet 3:5–13 and Rev 21:1 is lacking.

The threefold use in vv 17–18 of the verb bārā', a technical term for divine creative activity, indicates dependence on chs. 40–48, which speak of the creation of darkness and light (45:7), the heavenly bodies (40:26), the earth and its inhabitants (40:28; 42:5; 45:12, 18), and Israel (43:1, 7, 15). The author of the poem is also giving fresh content to the theme of renewal that is pervasive throughout chs. 40–48, especially in the contrast between "former things" and "new things" now coming into existence (42:9; 48:6). Here, in 65:17b, "the former things" are reinterpreted in the light of "the former troubles" at the end of the preceding saying. The injunction to put the past aside, to forget it, is also taken over from the same source (43:18).

While the creation recital of Gen 1:1–2:4a and Isa 65:17–25 may well have been roughly contemporaneous and may well have shared elements of the same *Weltanschauung*, it has proved impossible to establish with a reasonable degree of assurance a relation of dependence in either direction (pace Steck 1997b, 349–65, who argued for the dependence of 65:17–25 on Gen 1–3). Isaiah 40–66 has indeed much to say about creation but more often than not in terms quite different from Gen 1. Rather than forming a dome or bell-shaped solid cover (*rāqîʿâ*, Gen 1:6), for example, the Deutero-Isaian heaven is stretched out (*nṭh*) like a curtain or tent (40:22; 42:5; 44:24; 45:12; 51:13, 16). In contrast to Gen 1, in these Isaian texts God creates both light and darkness (45:7), and the celestial elements are not simply made, as in Genesis, but called forth (40:26; 48:13).

The idea of a return to the first creation, to the paradisal existence of Eden, is present marginally in the allusion to the snake in the scribal addition in 65:25, as it is in the LXX and Targum glossing of the tree as the Tree of Life in v 22, and obliquely in the longevity theme in v 20. These and other allusions to motifs from the primeval history—Eden the garden of God (51:3), Noah and the flood (54:9)—demonstrate the currency at the time of writing of these narrative themes and traditions without amounting to proof of an intertextual relationship between Gen 1–11 and Isa 40–66.

In chs. 56–66 Deuteronomic echoes are frequently heard, and of these several examples have been noted. In this first pronouncement, the phrase *ʿālâ ʿal-lēb*, "come to mind," appears, which also is used several times in prose passages in Jeremiah, assigned by many scholars to a Deuteronomistic editor and usually occurring in the context of syncretistic cults (Jer 3:16; 7:31; 19:5; 32:35).

This first pronouncement, then, urges those addressed to put the troubles of the past behind them and to rejoice in the prospect of a new situation. The address is presented in an elegant ring composition (*kî hinnĕnî bôrēʾ . . . ʾăšer ʾănî bôrēʾ*, 17, 18a). Here, too, there is linkage with the previous saying in which the future rejoicing of YHVH's Servants is foreseen (vv 13d–14a), leading to the main theme of the renewal of Jerusalem and its people. Rejoicing (verbs *śîś, gîl*) is a major theme in the Trito-Isaian core (60:15; 61:10; 62:5) and in passages dependent on it (66:10, 14; 35:1–2). It appears, then, that 65:17–25 has drawn independently on both chs. 40–48 and chs. 60–62.

The second pronouncement prolongs the note of joy and does so to make it clear that YHVH joins in the rejoicing and that the cause of joy is not so much the physical city as its inhabitants (vv 18b–19a). This I take to be a more sober or neutral expression of 62:5: as the bridegroom rejoices over the bride, "so will your God rejoice over you." It can be illuminating to compare the description of the future condition of the city and its inhabitants (19b-20) with other Isaian projections into the future. These include ecological transformation, the end of violence and oppression, and the removal of physical disabilities (29:17–21);

justice, peace, and security in a utopian rural environment (35:1–10); and harmony in the animal world, implying a return to the first creation (11:6–9), a motif picked up and developed by the scribe who added v 25.

Particularly moving is the prospect that weeping and cries of distress, or cries for redress (Gen 18:20), will come to an end (Isa 65:19b)—the reversal of a theme repeated at intervals throughout the first part of Jeremiah (7:34; 16:9; 25:10). A later Isaian text predicts the wiping away of tears from every face and the abolition of death itself (25:8). The author of our poem is not prepared to go so far but contents himself with announcing the end of infant mortality and a return to the longevity of the ancestors, taking examples from the two extremes of the age spectrum (v 20).

We are unfortunately not well informed on the physical conditions of life in the biblical period, for example, on such matters as diet, health and sickness. Estimates of life expectancy that do not take into account the dangerous first 5 years of life are practically useless. In preindustrial societies, modern as well as ancient, probably at least one-third of babies born live died before reaching the age of 6, and it has been calculated that in peasant societies in medieval Europe life expectancy *at birth* was about 33 years. This may give us a very rough idea of the situation in Palestinian peasant society during the Iron Age and down into late antiquity. Now we are told that this major source of grief, the premature death of children, is to be removed in the Jerusalem of the future. There will be no *'ûl yāmîm*, literally, "infant of (a few) days." This is a somewhat unusual term for a child prior to weaning (more commonly *'ôlāl*, *'ôlēl*, or *yônēq*), meaning therefore ages birth to about 3 or 4 years old (1 Sam 1:22–24; 2 Macc 7:27).

At the other end of the age spectrum, none will die without "fulfilling their days." The formulation is reminiscent of the blessing attached to the "covenant code": "No one shall have a miscarriage or be infertile in your land; I shall fulfill the number of your days" (Exod 23:26). It is not stated that 100 is the ideal age at which to die but that a person will reach the century mark without suffering the ills usually attendant on aging. The idea seems to be that of a return to the ideal represented by the ancestors, whose ages were in the 100–200 range, from Isaac at 180 to Joseph and Joshua at a mere 110. According to *1 En.* 25:6 the elect will live a long life such as their ancestors lived. Perhaps with Isa 65:20 in mind, the author of the book of *Jubilees* (23:27–28) sets the ideal at 1000 and predicts that "there shall be no old man, nor one who is not satisfied with his days, for all shall be as children and youths."

In the damaged postdiluvian world, the maximum is 120 years (Gen 6:3), in keeping with a common Near Eastern topos based on the Sumerian sexagesimal system (60 × 2). Very clearly, life expectancy has a moral dimension: a long life is correlative with a morally upright life; sickness or premature death is diagnostic of moral disorder. In the dawn of history, the life-span is reduced to 120 years as a result of promiscuous relations between divine males and human females (Gen 6:3). The moral correlation inevitably led to problems when an ostensibly righteous individual died at a young age (Josiah at 39) or an ostensibly wicked person died in the fullness of years (Manasseh at 67). Surprisingly, perhaps, the moral dimension is not in evidence in 65:20, though both LXX and Vulg., understandably but incorrectly, found a reference to sin in the Hebrew text.

The promise that God's elect will remain in possession of their houses and vineyards (vv 21–22a) represents the reversal of a common curse attached to covenant formulations and, indirectly, to international treaties:

You will build a house but not live in it;
you will plant a vineyard but not enjoy its fruit. (Deut 28:30)

This kind of formulation, which became part of the common stock of prophetic diatribe (Amos 5:11; Mic 6:14; Zeph 1:13), reflects the bitter experience of people subject to military occupation, deportation, sequestration of property, and the impositions of an oppressive state system, either their own or that of a colonial power (for this last see, for example, Neh 5:3: the complaint of the common people that they are obliged to mortgage their vineyards and houses). Reassurance about having a place to live and the means of livelihood, especially in the troubled and uncertain time following the Babylonian conquest and the deportations, would be an important element in any vision of a different future (cf. Amos 9:14).

At this juncture (vv 22b-23) it is important to reiterate a point made earlier, that these predictions of a blessed future are addressed to God's elect (*běḥîray*, 22b) and that therefore the people in the community who are addressed as "my people," who are assured of long life, are "my people who seek me" (65:10), the elect, the Servants of YHVH (65:9,15), and they alone. As it occurs in 40–55, this expression "my people" (*'ammî*) refers unproblematically to the Judean community as a whole (40:1; 47:6; 51:4; 52:4–6; 53:8). God's people is also addressed as Israel, Jacob, Zion (51:16), or "my chosen ones" (43:20). This undifferentiated usage appears in the early chapters of section 56–66 (57:14; 58:1) and in the community lament (63:8), but in section 65–66 these designations are restricted to those in the community who, from the prophetic-eschatological perspective of the writer or speaker, are responsive to the message. This is to all intents and purposes a sectarian perspective.

In vv 22b–23 the longevity theme is repeated, as it were, in a different key. The hearers are also assured that they will not toil in vain (*lārîq*, Deut 28:33; Jer 3:24) and will not bear children who will have to live through disastrous events (*běhālâ*, Lev 26:16; Ps 78:33; Jer 15:8). This, too, is the reversal of a covenant curse:

I will bring sudden disaster (*běhālâ*) on you . . .
You will sow your seed in vain (*lārîq*), for your
enemies will eat it. (Lev 26:16)

The call-response theme (v 24) recapitulates vv 17–24 and serves to enclose and unify the entire chapter. The chapter begins by reiterating YHVH's openness to dialogue and interactivity (65:1 cf. 58:9) and, after excluding those who failed to respond to the invitation (v 12), ends by an even stronger affirmation of an openness to listen and respond (24), with the qualification that the dialogue partner is now "my people who seek me" (*'ammî 'ăšer dĕrāšûnî*, 65:10b).

The scribal addition to the poem (v 25) is an interesting example of prophetic intertextuality, the reuse or "recycling" of existing prophetic sayings by adapting them to new situations. In this instance the scribe has inserted a somewhat abbreviated version of Isa 11:6–9, perhaps reproduced from memory. Only two out of the six pairings of unlike animals (predator and prey) were considered necessary to make the point, omitting therefore leopard and goat; lion cub and calf, together with stall-fed beast; bear, and cow.

The scribe also omitted the infant playing in close proximity to cobra and viper, and mention of these dangerous reptiles suggests an addition, drawing on Gen 3:14b. But whoever added this further note was not just presenting an alternative to cobra and viper, as if to say that snakes are to become just ordinary, harmless animals (as Volz 1932, 287). He was apparently convinced that, having been cursed from the very beginning, snakes are the one exception to this ideal scene of harmony in the animal world. The snake is therefore excluded from this transformation of the natural world, this return to the first creation, in which humans and animals are to live in harmony and none will kill for food (Gen 1:29–30). From this perspective, the new creation is an *apokatastasis*, a restoration, a return to origins, to the lost world of innocence that came to an end with the great deluge.

VINDICATION OF THE TRUE WORSHIPERS OF GOD (66:1–6)

(B. W. Anderson 1988, 17–38; Beuken 1989c, 53–66; Blenkinsopp 1981, 1–26; 1983, 1–23; 1990, 5–20; 1997, 155–75; Carr 1996, 188–218; Ebach 1992, 85–113; Fohrer 1970, 101–16 = 1981, 81–95; Koenen 1990, 183–96; Lack 1973; Lau 1994, 168–81; Liebreich 1955–1956, 259–77; 1956–1957, 114–38; Pauritsch 1974, 195–218; Rofé 1985, 205–17; Sasson 1976, 199–207; Schramm 1995, 161–70; Smart 1935, 420–32; P. A. Smith 1995, 128–32, 153–65; Steck 1987c, 103–16 = 1991, 217–33; Webster 1986, 93–108)

i

66 [1]This is what YHVH says:
Heaven is my throne, the earth is my footstool.
What kind of house[a] could you build for me?
What kind of place[a] for my abode?
[2]Did not my hand make all of these,
and all these things came to be?[b]

[A pronouncement of YHVH]
But on these I look with favor;
the poor, the afflicted in spirit,[c] and those who tremble at my word.

ii

[3]He who slaughters an ox kills a man;[d]
he who sacrifices a sheep wrings a dog's neck;[e]
he who makes a cereal offering (offers) the blood of a pig;[f]
he who makes a memorial offering with frankincense
pronounces a blessing over an idol.
They too have chosen to go their own way,
they take delight in their idols;
[4]so I will choose to punish them[g]
and bring on them the things that they dread;
for when I called, there was no one to answer;
when I spoke, they would not listen,
but they did what was evil in my sight,
choosing what was displeasing to me.

iii

[5]Hear the word of YHVH, you who tremble at his word![h]
Your brethren who hate you
and cast you out for my name's sake, have said,[i]
"May YHVH reveal his glory,[j] that we may witness your joy!"
But it is they who will be put to shame.

iv

[6]That sound of tumult from the city,
that thundering from the temple,
it is the sound of YHVH dealing out
retribution to his enemies!

NOTES

[a]   The interrogative particle *'ê-zeh* more commonly equals "where?" (e.g.,
Isa 50:1; Job 28:12, 20) and is so translated here by many commentators,
for example, Duhm 1922, 481; but the meaning "which?" or "what kind
of?" is also attested (1 Kgs 22:24; 2 Chr 18:32), and in this instance is supported by LXX *poion oikon . . . poios topos* cf. Acts 7:49, and Vulg. *quae est
iste domus . . . quis est iste locus*; also, for "Where would you build me a
house?" we would expect *'ê-zeh tibnû-lî bayit*.

[b]   NRSV "All these things are mine" goes back to Bishop Lowth ("For all
these things my hand hath made / and all these things are mine, saith Jeho-
vah"), who used the LXX version *kai estin ema panta tauta* cf. Syr., probably
influenced by Ps 50:10–11; but MT is supported by 1QIsa[a], 1QIsa[b], Vulg.,
Theod., Aqu., Symm.

c   MT *ûnĕkēh-rûaḥ*, perhaps with several MSS, 1QIsaᵃ and 1QIsaᵇ, read *ûnĕkê-rûaḥ* cf. Prov 15:13; 17:22; 18:14.
d   The four appositions ("The one who does X is the one who does Y") are often turned into comparisons, as NRSV, following 1QIsaᵃ (*kĕmakkēh 'îš*, "like one who strikes [kills] a man"), Targ. (*kqtyl gbr, knqyp klb*), LXX, and Vulg.(*qui immolat bovem quasi qui interficiat virum*); but MT, which is deliberately abrupt and elliptical, should be retained (see Comments).
e   LXX conflates its first two comparisons, perhaps to avoid the implication of human sacrifice: "But the lawless one who sacrifices to me a bullock is like one who kills a dog."
f   The word "offers" is added for the sense; the Hebrew of 66:3 is extremely elliptical.
g   Literally, "So I will choose their punishments."
h   1QIsaiahᵃ has pl. *dbryv*.
i   LXX: "Speak, our brethren, to those who hate us and ban us, that the Lord's name may be glorified and may be seen in their rejoicing; but they will be ashamed"; cf. Tertullian: *Adv. Marc.* IV: *dicite: fratres nostri estis, eis qui vos oderunt* ("Say 'You are our brethren' to those who hate you").
j   Reading *yikkābēd* Niphal for MT *yikbad* Qal with LXX (*doxasthē*), Syr. (*nštbh*), Vulg. (*glorificetur*), and most modern versions.

COMMENTS

The last chapter of the book gives the impression of being a loose collection of short sayings or a series of appendices introduced or rounded off with a variety of prophetic rubrics ("This is what YHVH says," "A pronouncement of YHVH," "Says your God") or calls for attention ("Hear the word of YHVH"). In this respect Isa 66 is comparable to Zech 14, with about the same number of sayings, many introduced with the familiar eschatological rubric "On that day" and presenting an equally impressive apocalyptic scenario. On the breakdown of the chapter into distinct sayings, only a sample of opinion can be given. On the basis of rubrics and meter, Duhm (1922, 481–90) divided it into six sayings (1–4, 5–11, 12–17, 18–22, 23, 24), Westermann (1969, 411–29) into five (1–4, 5, 6–16, 17, 18–24), and Whybray (1975, 279–94) into seven (1–4, 5, 6, 7–14, 15–16, 17, 18–24). Taking a more integrative approach, Webster (1986, 93–108) reduced the units to three (1–6, 7–14, 15–24), identified with the help of key words and concentric arrangement, and the same division is accepted by Oswald (1998, 665). Muilenburg (1956, 757–73) divided the chapter into a poem composed of seven strophes (1–16) and an eschatological summary (17–24), and other variations of this basic division into 1–16 and 17–24 can be found in Kissane (1960[1943]:314– 20) and Hanson (1975, 161–63). Torrey (1928, 471–72) is one of the few who read the chapter as a single composition. Further indications will be given in the comments on individual passages.

A closer inspection will reveal interconnections among the individual segments of the chapter and between the chapter and other parts of the book.

The volume of editorial comment in evidence in all parts of the book would lead us to expect even more intense activity of this kind toward its conclusion. Beginning with Liebreich in the 1950s, several scholars have drawn attention to linguistic parallels between the first and the last chapter of Isaiah of a frequency to suggest a deliberate framing device. The implication is that the book is to be considered in some sense a unity (Liebreich 1955–1956, 259–77; Lack 1973, 139–41; Carr 1996, 188–218; and Beuken 1991, 218–19 for a computer-generated concordance of chs. 1 and 65–66). Not all the parallels noted by these and other commentators are equally significant, but those appearing in 1:27–31 are consistent with other indications that this distinctive passage was added at a late stage in the formation of the book (Blenkinsopp 2000a, 187–88). They include the reference to "rebels" (*pōšĕ'îm*, 1:28; 66:24), the inextinguishable fire (1:31b; 66:24), and garden cults (1:29; 66:17) and insinuate a reading of the entire book as, in some sense, one unified composition dominated by certain important themes.

Structural and thematic parallels between 66:7–14 and 54:1–17 suggest that the former is the conclusion or epilogue to 56–66, as the latter is to 40–54, with ch. 55 serving as a link between these two major sections. Both passages begin with Jerusalem and end with the Servants of YHVH. In both, the destiny of the Servants is described in positive terms, what YHVH will do for them, and with reference to their vindication vis-à-vis their opponents (66:14b; 54:17c). The theme developed in both passages, with much of the same vocabulary, is Zion's miraculous childbearing and the granting of *Lebensraum* for her new family, of which it is understood that the Servants form the nucleus. The intent is not just to round off these two major sections of the book but to link them together by means of the twinned themes of Mother Zion and the Servants of YHVH that they have in common.

Up to this point I am in agreement with Beuken, who reads 66:7–24 as a series of epilogues: vv 7–14, an epilogue to Third Isaiah, 15–21 to Second and Third Isaiah together, and 22–24 to the entire book (Beuken 1991, 204–21). But in keeping with a characteristic feature of the book as a whole, vv 15–16 read rather like a further stage in a process of cumulative and incremental editing. In other words, these verses develop the thought of YHVH's indignation in the previous verse (*za'am*,14), and do so in language that draws on the entire Isaian repertoire: the coming of God in salvation and judgment (30:27; 40:10), divine anger under the image of fire (9:18; 10:16–17; 33:12–14) and of flames of fire and whirlwind (29:6; 30:30), and judgment executed by YHVH's sword (27:1; 31:8; 34:5–6) on all flesh (40:5–6; 49:26; 66:23–24). These verses also, no doubt, had a recapitulatory intent similar to that of vv 7–14. In much the same way, v 17 could be read as an isolated comment on "those slain by YHVH" in the preceding verse, reminding the reader that the slain are to be identified with the practitioners of transgressive cults mentioned in 65:3–4.

In some respects vv 18–21 could be regarded as forming an inclusion with 56:1–8. Leaving aside the inserted v 20 (see Comments on this verse), both passages share a broad and inclusive approach to membership in the Jewish community. The penultimate paragraph vv 22–23 (24) reads like a recapitulation of 65:13–25, repeating the prediction of new heaven and new earth as a guarantee of the permanence of the progeny, and therefore the name, of the Servants (53:10; 54:3; 56:5; 65:9, 23). It is even possible that vv 12–16 and 22–24 served *at some stage* as alternative endings to the book, comparable therefore to the two conclusions to the book of Job (38:1–40:5; 40:6–42:6).

We come now to the first of the segments of this concluding chapter: it is at least beyond dispute that 66:1–6 is polemical writing reflecting a deep and apparently irreconcilable division in the community addressed. Still very much subject to dispute, however, is the precise identification of the issues and the parties involved.

The first of the four paragraphs into which I have divided this first section of the chapter (vv 1–2) has been interpreted as a radical rejection of temples as the loci of sacrificial cult (or at least of animal sacrifice), considered as the antithesis of "the true religion of heart and life" (Smart 1935, 420; also 1965, 281–88; Volz 1932, 288–89; Lau 1994, 168–77 et al.). Quite apart from the confessional prejudices about what constitutes genuine religion that commentators bring with them to their task, this conclusion seems implausible in view of what is said elsewhere in chs. 56–66 about YHVH's holy mountain (56:7; 57:13; 65:11), his holy and beautiful house (64:11; also 60:7, 13), the place where his feet rest (60:13), and so on. One would also have to account for 43:23–24, a complaint about the failure to sacrifice, and 60:6–7, the offering of sacrificial animals for YHVH's "glorious house" in Jerusalem. The image of divine judgment emanating from the temple in 66:6 constitutes an additional problem for this interpretation.

A similar point is made in Solomon's sermon delivered at the dedication of the First Temple: "Will God indeed dwell on earth? Even heaven and the height of heaven cannot contain you, how much less this house that I have built!" (1 Kgs 8:27). The sermon in which this statement occurs is acknowledged to be postexilic. It embodies the Deuteronomistic disavowal of a false overvaluation of temples but, given the context assigned to it, could hardly be read as a radical rejection of the temple and its cult.

For much the same reasons, the rhetorical questions in 66:1 do not necessarily connote outright opposition to the project, supported by Haggai, Zechariah and other prophets, of rebuilding the temple (as in Hanson 1975, 173–74), though they might well be questioning the link between temple-building and political emancipation (Hag 2:6–9, 20–23), and the idea that, once the temple is built, peace and prosperity will automatically and, as it were, magically be brought about (Hag 2:9, 19).

In view of the situating of 66:1–4 within the Deutero- and Trito-Isaian *traditio*, it is extremely unlikely that the passage refers to any cult center other than Jerusalem. An alternative cult center may have been set up after the Babylonian conquest, in association with the provincial administration in Mizpah, perhaps at nearby Bethel, but we would expect the passage to provide some clue that the writer had such a place in mind. The problem lies really with vv 3–4: once it is admitted that syncretistic practices of the kind referred to there could have been going on in Jerusalem, the need for an alternative location disappears. For the same reason, Duhm's option for a reference in vv 1–2 to a Samaritan (Samarian?) proposal to build their own temple during the period of Ezra and Nehemiah, while not in itself impossible, is unsupported by evidence (Duhm 1922, 481–82), and nothing in chs. 56–66 lends plausibility to an allusion to a temple in Babylon, Egypt, the Transjordanian region, or anywhere else outside of the province of Judah.

The statement that no temple can provide an adequate residence for the God who created the world reflects the influence of the Deuteronomistic rejection of the materialistic and superstitious idea that a temple is quite literally the house of a deity. In place of this ancient, persistent, and widely held belief, the Deuteronomists substituted the idea of the temple as the location of the divine Name invoked in worship (Deut 12:5, 11; 14:23 etc.)—the Name (*šēm*) being a kind of hypostasis of the deity, comparable to the Glory (*kābôd*) of the Priestly scholiasts. The Name-theology and Glory-theology may then be regarded as different attempts to express divine transcendence without surrendering immanence. A more traditional approach, which satisfies the apparently endemic need to give spatial expression to divine presence, can be found in the liturgical hymns that speak of YHVH enthroned in the heavens (Pss 2:4; 11:4; 33:13–14; 102:20; 150:1), a representation also found throughout Isaiah (e.g., 6:1; 33:5, 16; 58:4; 63:15).

The very similar affirmation about the presence of God in 57:15 provides another indication that 66:1–2 is not a foreign body within chs. 56–66:

> For thus says the Exalted One,
> who dwells in an eternal place,
> whose name is holy:
> "I dwell in a high and holy place
> and with the contrite and humble in spirit,
> reviving the spirits of the humble,
> reviving the hearts of the contrite."

The footstool (*hădôm raglayim*) is variously represented as the earth (Isa 66:1), the land of Israel (Lam 2:1), and the ark (Ps 132:7; 1 Chr 28:2). As in the great vision scene of Isa 6:1–13, the basic image is that of the royal audience chamber (cf. Pss 99:5; 110:1). The Persepolis relief representing Darius I's throne room (*ANEP* #463) and the same monarch using Gaumata as a footstool on the Behistun carving (*ANEP* #249) will give a good idea of the visual impression conveyed by this imagery, associated with absolute royal power.

But the question now arises why another warning against overvaluation of the temple, or wrong understandings about its function, was called for at this point. A connection with the preceding chapter can be found in the indictment of opponents, including cult personnel, who were engaging in syncretistic practices and in consequence were neglecting the temple (see Comments on 65:11). This would be consistent with 66:1–2 as a lead-in to the extremely elliptical indictment of the same temple personnel in the following paragraph (vv 3–4).

The principal accusation leveled against the opposition in chs. 56–66 from a Yahvist-alone perspective is cultic irregularity, syncretistic practice. Nothing that we know about the situation in Judah at any time during the first century of Persian rule excludes this reading of 66:1–4. The first high priest, Jeshua (Joshua) ben Yehozadak, is described as a brand plucked from the burning, who has to be symbolically purified from the contamination of idolatry (Zech 3:1–5). The leading priests, including members of Jeshua's family, married foreign women and were in consequence involved in the "abominations of the peoples of the land" (Ezra 9:1–2; 10:18). At the time of Nehemiah, the high priest's family intermarried with the Sanballats of Samaria (Neh 13:28–29). Malachi talks about abominations going on in Jerusalem, denounces the sad state of worship, and even wants the temple closed down (Mal 1:10; 2:11).

The gravamen was therefore not against the temple itself, or the project of rebuilding it, depending on the date assigned to the paragraph; it was instigated by opposition to those who controlled, or were about to control, the operations of the temple. Polemic against "temples made with hands" was a phenomenon of late antiquity, no doubt inspired by philosophical ideas (e.g., Pythagorean ideas in Apollonius of Tyana), as we see in the discourse of the deacon Stephen in Acts 7:48–49. Stephen's affirmation that the Most High God does not dwell "in things made with hands" (*en cheiropoiētois*), a term used for temples and idolatrous objects, is dependent on Isa 66:2 LXX, "My hands made all these things," but it would be anachronistic to draw the same conclusion from this text that Stephen did (cf. Acts 17:24; Heb 9:11, 24; *Sib. Or.* 14:62).

That the speaker's animus is directed more against temple personnel than against the temple itself sets up the contrast between these opponents and the poor, the afflicted, and those who tremble at God's word. As a survey of biblical usage shows, and as one would expect, the poor (*ʿăniyyîm*) are the economically disadvantaged, but their condition is almost always the result of injustice and oppression (e.g., Isa 3:14–15; 10:2; 32:7; and 58:7, where they are bracketed with the homeless). Of particular relevance for the interpretation of 66:1–2 are the numerous references to the "poor," the *ʿānî*, in Psalms. The context is always religious: the poor are the righteous (*ṣaddîqîm*, Ps 109:16, 22), God's own people (Ps 72:2, 4, 12), and their enemies are reprobates, oppressors, the proud, the impious (Pss 9:19[18]; 10:2, 9; 18:28 [27]; 35:10; 37:14 etc.).

In some instances the term appears to be used as a self-designation for a particular marginalized group in the community. The accompanying epithet "afflicted in spirit," like "oppressed and dispirited" in 57:15, expresses the effect of destitution very aptly. The poor and afflicted are also those who tremble at God's word. This designation appears again in the following verse, where we learn that these people have been expelled or excommunicated. The implications may be inferred from the attempt to address the problem of marriage out-side the *gôlâ*-community in Ezra 9–10. The people who failed to take part in the plenary assembly called to resolve the matter were threatened with expulsion from the community and forfeiture of (presumably immovable) property (Ezra 10:8). In the great majority of cases, therefore, ostracism, loss of civil and religious rights, would have resulted in economic destitution, consistent with the profile of the one on whom, in 66:1–2, YHVH looks with favor.

The four extremely elliptical and gnomic pairs of participial clauses that follow (vv 3–4) have elicited a wide range of response from the commentators. The addition of a *kaph comparationis* allows the reading "the one who slaughters an ox is like (the one who) kills a man," as if to say that the temple personnel are no better than murderers or, if all four statements are taken into account, practitioners of degenerate cults. While the emendation is supported by the principal ancient versions and the Qumran *Isaiah Scroll*, and renders acceptable sense, MT also makes sense and should be retained as the more difficult version.

Accepting the Masoretic Text as it is, then, what sense can it be made to render consistent with correct grammar and the context in which these two verses occur? The first and most obvious point is that the eight active participles put the emphasis directly on the agents rather than on what is done or where it is done. The question then is how to relate the first with the second participial phrase in each of the four verses. The proposal of Sasson (1976, 199–207) to read "He who slaughtered an ox would now kill a man," implying an abandonment of traditional Israelite cultic use for pagan practices, is contextually acceptable but grammatically dubious. The participles require contemporaneity and therefore favor the meaning that the one who slaughters an ox *also* kills a man, the one who sacrifices a sheep *also* wrings a dog's neck, and so on (Rofé 1985, 205–17; Blenkinsopp 1990, 9–10). This would be consistent with indications elsewhere in chs. 56–66 of the involvement of temple personnel in syncretistic cult practices, in continuity with officially sponsored practice prior to the fall of Jerusalem (2 Kgs 23:4–7, 10–12; Jer 7:9; Ezek 8:1–18).

In the first statement the phrase "kills a man" (*makkēh 'îš*, "the killer of a man") is never used of a cultic act but does occur in a forensic context (Exod 21:12: *makkēh 'îš vāmēt môt yûmāt*, "The one who strikes a man so that he dies must be put to death"). This might suggest that the sacrificing priest or official is being called a murderer (Koenen 1990, 190–91; Lau 1994, 175–76), but the context requires that all four predications be cultic. In a passage that is in some way related to 66:1–4, namely, 57:3–13, one of the accusations directed against the opponents is child sacrifice in honor of the god Molech, which would imply that *'îš* is here used, exceptionally, in a generic sense for a human being (see Comments on 57:5, 9).

Dogs feature together with pigs in Hittite rituals (Sasson 1976, 199–207), they are associated with the goddess Hecate in ancient Greece, and have a role in Lamaštu exorcisms in Mesopotamia (Firmage 1992). But the only thing at all close to the time and place of Isa 66:1–4 is the cemetery with 700 dog burials discovered at Ashkelon from the Persian period, then under Phoenician control. Since it is unlikely that this was a pet cemetery of the California type, it may indicate a cultic function, though unfortunately the neck bones of the animals are intact. Here, too, however, in spite of the huge gaps in our knowledge, it is better to assume that the action referred to in 66:3 has some ritual significance (cf. breaking the neck of a donkey in the context of a cult act, Exod 13:13; 34:20; and of a heifer, Deut 21:4, 6) than that it is simply another gross insult.

The procedure governing the offering of a *minḥâ* is set out in Lev 2:1–16 and 6:7–11[14–18]. The *minḥâ*, originally simply "gift," consisted in an offering of flour and oil together with frankincense that the priest burned on the altar. The association with pig's blood was probably due to the wine libation (*nesek*) at some point that became a mandatory adjunct to the *minḥâ* (Num 15:5–10). On pork as part of a ritual meal in which the opponents are accused of participating, see the Comments on 65:4.

The fourth and final apposition features the obscure, no doubt technical, term *mazkîr lĕbōnâ*. In a cultic context the verb (*zkr* Hiphil participle) means to recite the praises or invoke the name of a deity (Exod 23:13; Josh 23:7; Isa 26:13; 48:1). In the ritual to which a wife suspected of adultery was subjected there is mention of a memorial offering that brings iniquity into the open (*minhat zikkārôn mazkeret ʿāvôn*, Num 5:15), which may point to one aspect of the memorial offering in question. Frankincense (*lĕbōnâ*) accompanied the cereal offering (Lev 2:1, 15 cf. Jer 41:5), and one type of *minhâ* was known as the *ʾazkārâ* or memorial offering that was burnt with incense to make a sweet savor for the deity (Lev 2:2, 9, 16; 5:12; 6:8[15]. We are now told that those who routinely carry out this pleasing ceremony in honor of YHVH are also involved in rituals of a quite different nature involving the recital of blessings over another deity, using the dysphemism *ʾāven*, "harm," "mischief," but also "idol" (1 Sam 15:23; Hos 10:8; Zech 10:2).

We should add that 66:1–4, together with the related accusations in 57:3–13; 65:1–7; and 66:17, belongs to the category of polemical writing comparable, therefore, to the kind of diatribe used against the early Christians and, later, early Christian dissidents, by their opponents. While we have no reason to doubt that syncretistic religious practice was a basic factor in the conflict going on at that time, an objective view of the situation, and especially a grasp of the mind-set of the opponents, would call for evidence of a different kind.

The pronouncement of YHVH is rounded off with a statement of disapprobation (3c–4) framed by the theme of making the wrong choice, a choice displeasing to YHVH, a pursuit of their own inclinations (*gam-hēmmâ bāḥarû bĕdarkêhem* at the beginning, *ûbaʾăšer loʾ ḥāpaṣtî bāḥārû* at the end). The language is for the most part typically Trito-Isaianic: choosing (*bḥr*) what is or is not pleasing (*ḥpṣ*) to YHVH (56:4; 58:2; 65:12 cf. 1:29b from the paragraph 1:27–31 closely related to chs. 65–66), call and response (58:9; 65:1, 24) or lack of response (65:12 cf. 50:2). What is, for this tradition, characteristic of the God of Israel, and not of alien deities (see 46:7), is responsiveness and openness to dialogue. From the perspective of the group represented by the speaker, YHVH no longer had a dialogue partner among those denounced in this passage.

The call for attention in v 5a sets vv 5–6 apart as the address of an anonymous prophet to a specific group (5) with a brief sequel indicating the fate of the opponents (6). While no introductory rubric follows, the subject matter of 7–14 is quite different. Continuity of theme and no doubt also authorship with vv 1–4 is seen in the identity of the people addressed in 66:5 with those on whom YHVH looks with favor ("those who tremble at his word"). It would be of interest to know who these people are.

In the sense of religiously-inspired terror or awe, the verb *ḥrd* ("tremble") is not of frequent occurrence. The Israelites at Sinai trembled during the manifestation of the divine presence (Exod 19:16), and the Philistines were overtaken by panic inspired by the holy ark (1 Sam 14:15). Used as a designation in the participial-substantival form (*ḥārēd, ḥărēdîm*), it appears only in 66:2, 5 and in Ezra 9:4 and 10:3, the juxtaposed accounts of the attempt to resolve the issue of intermarriage between the *gôlâ*-group and the "peoples of the land." These variants may be set out as follows:

- *ḥārēd ʿal-děbārî* ("The one who trembles at my word," 66:2)
- *haḥărēdîm ʾel-děbārô* ("Those who tremble at his word," 66:5)
- *kol-ḥārēd bědibrê ʾělohê-yiśrāʾēl* ("All those who tremble at the words of the God of Israel," Ezra 9:4)
- *haḥărēdîm běmiṣvat ʾělohênû* ("Those who tremble at the commandment of our God," Ezra 10:3)
- With LXX, Vulg., 1 Esd 8:72 and cf. Ezra 10:3.

As an expression of intense religious emotion, trembling is a familiar phenomenon in the history of religious movements (Quakers, Shakers, Pentecostals, and Ultra-Orthodox *ʿēdâ ḥārēdît*). Taken together, the different forms of the modifier point to the law as the occasion for the trembling, certainly in Ezra, though we cannot exclude intense commitment to the prophetic word in both, especially in Isaiah. It is fundamentally erroneous to assume an opposition between the prophetic and the legal; witness the insistence on observance of the covenant and Sabbath in 56:1–6 and 58:13–14 by a writer who indubitably thought of himself as a prophet.

From 66:5 we learn that those addressed, the *ḥārēdîm*, have been expelled from the community by their "brethren" (*ʾaḥîm*), that is, their fellow-Jews, and more specifically by the religious and civil authorities. This action is expressed in the strongest and most explicit terms. "Hating" (verbal stem *śnʾ*) implies active dissociation rather than a merely emotional state; for example, the verb occurs in the legal phrase for marital separation in use in the Jewish military colony on the island of Elephantine at the first cataract of the Nile in the Persian period ("I hate my wife / my husband"). The other verb *niddâ* (Piel) occurs only here and Amos 6:3, in the latter instance apparently with the sense of exorcizing, driving away by magic. In Mishnaic Hebrew it was one of the terms in official use for excommunication from the synagogue (e.g., *Mo'ed Qaṭan* 81d). We saw that this condition of excommunication helps to explain that the *ḥărēdîm* are also the poor and the afflicted in spirit.

The speaker attributes the ostracism of the "Tremblers" to their devotion to the divine Name, a frequent characterization of the devout in post-destruction prophetic writings (Isa 56:6; 59:19; 60:9; Mal 1:6–7, 11, 14; 2:5; 3:16, 20), and one taken up and adapted in the Gospels (e.g., Matt 10:18, 22). But more revealing in this regard is the taunt that the speaker puts into the mouth of the opponents—"May YHVH reveal his glory, that we may witness your joy!" It is directed at their eschatological faith and, more specifically, at the belief that they would rejoice on the day of judgment, while their opponents would be put to shame.

The final situation contemplated here, in which the rejoicing of the elect is set over against the shaming of their opponents, reflects the prophetic assurances addressed to the "Servants" in the previous chapter:

> My servants will eat, while you go hungry;
> my servants will drink, while you go thirsty;
> my servants will rejoice, while you are put to shame;
> my servants will exult with heartfelt joy,
> while you cry out with heartache
> and wail with anguish of spirit. (65:13–14)

The situation presupposed in 66:5 is identical with that of 65:13–14, whether the bold claim in 65:13–14 is the occasion for the taunt of the adversaries in 66:5 or the response to it. In either case, the conclusion is unavoidable that *ḥărēdîm* ("Tremblers") and *'ăbādîm* ("Servants") are alternative designations for the same group, and that, at a minimum, the polemical passages in chs. 56–66 derive from this source.

A word must be said about the appearance of the same category (Tremblers), or at least the same or similar designation, in the account of the marriage crisis in Ezra 9–10. The situation described there is consistent with the situation implied by the polemic in Isa 65–66. Many people with Babylonian connections, including priests, had married local women and were involved in local "abominations" (Ezra 9:11, 14), a Deuteronomistic code name for non-Yahvistic cult practices (e.g., Deut 18:9; 2 Kgs 16:3; 21:2 cf. Isa 44:19). This would suggest that the polemic in Isa 65–66 is not between Judeo-Babylonians and the native Judean population, as some have proposed. We may note in passing a similar scene described in Mal 2:10–12: "abominations" being practiced in Jerusalem, the sanctuary profaned, Judah married to "the daughter of a foreign god." Conspicuous among Ezra's support group are the *ḥărēdîm*, and conspicuous by their absence are priests. The reform is to be carried through following the instructions of Ezra and "all those who tremble at the commandment of our God" (Ezra 10:3).

Ezra's supporters insist that everything is to be done "according to the law (*kāttôrâ*, 10:3)" which, since there is no law requiring divorce, means according to a strict interpretation of the law. Legal rigorism is therefore combined with prophetic intensity. Though there can be no certain answer, we may ask whether the narrative would not have us believe that Ezra was himself one of "those who tremble at the word of the God of Israel." His emotional reaction to the bad news (9:3–5), his asceticism (10:6), penitential prayer (9:6–15), and fasting and mourning (9:4; 10:6) would lead us to suspect that he was. We have seen that at several points throughout Isa 56–66 the devout minority is referred to as "mourners" (*'ābēlîm, mit'abbĕlîm*, 57:18; 61:2–3; 66:10). At any rate, since the marriage "reform" evidently failed, when Ezra disappeared from the scene his supporters would have found themselves in a vulnerable position. Those who were threatened with the social death of ostracism and loss of property for failure to support Ezra's measures (Ezra 10:8) would then have been in a position to confront their critics with the same threat.

Relevant to this situation is the complaint of certain God-fearers in Mal 3:13–21, and therefore from about the same time as Ezra, that God makes no distinction between the devout and the reprobate. The God-fearers then confer together, and a document is written containing the names of those who fear God and esteem his Name. They will be his special possession (*sĕgullâ*) on judgment day, when the distinction between the righteous and the reprobate will be made clearly manifest. Then those who revere the name of YHVH, and now lead a penitential life (*hālaknû qĕdorannît*, "we go about mourning," 3:14), will triumph and rejoice. The situation described here allows us to associate these God-fearers and God-servers, who revere the Name of YHVH and mourn in the present age, who look forward to a dramatic reversal of fortune in the future judgment, with the *'ăbādîm* and *hărēdîm* of Isa 65–66. Their conferring together and the writing of their names in a *sēper zikkārôn* (a book of records) reads like an anticipation of the Qumran sect constituting itself in a covenant as the true Israel.

The eschatological shaming of the opponents leads to a final word about judgment (v 6). A loud and threatening voice or sound like thunder emanating from the temple is a familiar prophetic topos (Amos 1:2; Joel 3:6; Jer 25:30–31; the Hebrew *qôl* = "voice," "sound," "thunder," depending on the context). Read without regard to context, the epilogue (v 6) would be a typically Isaianic figure for YHVH's punitive action against Israel's external enemies (cf. Isa 13:4; 17:12–13; 25:5), and so it is understood by several exegetes (Muilenburg 1956, 764–65; Westermann 1969, 419). But read in context, the enemies in question are the opponents whose taunt we have just heard. The saying would therefore be comparable to 59:18–20, in which the same correlation between the external and internal enemies of YHVH appears.

MOTHER ZION AND HER CHILDREN (66:7–16)

(Beuken 1991, 204–21; Darr 1994, 221–24; Koenen 1990, 196–205; Lau 1994, 126–34; Pauritsch 1971, 195–218; Sekine 1989, 54–65; P. A. Smith 1995, 159–67; Sweeney 1997, 455–74)

TRANSLATION

i

66   [7]Before she went into labor, she gave birth,
      before the birth pangs came on her, she bore a son.[a]
      [8]Who ever heard the like?
      Who ever witnessed such events?
      Can a land come to birth[b] in a single day?
      Can a nation be born all at once?
      Yet, as soon as Zion was in labor,
      she gave birth to her children!
      [9]Shall I open the womb and not bring to birth?
      [YHVH says]
      Shall I, who bring to birth, close up the womb?[c]
      [says your God]

ii

      [10]Rejoice with Jerusalem, take delight in her,
      all you who love her![d]
      Be exceedingly joyful with her,[e]
      all you who now mourn over her;
      [11]that you may nurse and be satisfied
      at her consoling breast;
      that you may drink deeply[f] with delight
      at her splendid bosom.[g]

iii

      [12]For this is what YHVH says:
      I will extend prosperity to her like a river,
      the wealth of nations like a torrent in full spate.[h]
      Your infants[i] will be carried on the hip,
      dandled on the knees.
      [13]As a mother comforts her son,
      so will I comfort you;
      you will find comfort in Jerusalem.
      [14]You will witness it, your hearts will rejoice,
      your bones will flourish like grass.
      YHVH's power will be known among his servants[j]
      and his indignation[k] among his enemies.

iv

¹⁵See, YHVH comes in fire,
his chariots like the whirlwind,
to requite with his furious anger,
to rebuke with a flame of fire.
¹⁶For with fire YHVH enters into judgment,[l]
and with his sword[m] on all humanity;
those slain by YHVH will be many.[n]

NOTES

a   LXX "She escaped (*exephugen*) and bore a son," misunderstood Hebrew *mlṭ* Hiphil, "cause to escape," with reference to birthing; compare with Isa 34:15, of owls laying eggs; LXX was taken up into the apocalyptic scenario of Rev 12:5–6, *kai eteken huion arsen . . . kai ephugen* ("She gave birth to a male child and fled"); Tg. gives the end of the verse a messianic sense: "Her king shall be revealed."

b   LXX has *gē*, "the earth," for "a land"; MT *hăyûḥal*, 3d-person sing. Imperfect masc. Hophal → *ḥîl* does not agree with *'ereṣ* fem., which suggests that 1QIsa^a *hthyl* fem. may be the original reading.

c   The versions are very paraphrastic at this point: LXX "For I gave this expectation, but you did not remember me, says the Lord. Is it not I that made the fertile and the barren? says your God"; perhaps reading *śbr*, "wait for," for *šbr*, "break through," and *'azkîr*, "call to mind," for MT *'ôlîd*, "bring to birth"; Tg. reinterprets the verse to refer to creation, the dispersal of the nations, and future return from the diaspora; Vulg. applies it to the Lord himself: "Shall I who cause others to give birth not myself give birth? says the Lord. Shall I who enable others to give birth be barren? says the Lord your God."

d   LXX: "Rejoice, O Jerusalem, and keep solemn assembly (*panēgurisate*), all you who dwell in her."

e   Translating *śîśû . . . māśôś*, internal Accusative.

f   The verb *mss* is hapax, but cf. Ug. *mss*, "slurp," "take the breast."

g   The translation is speculative; the substantive *zîz* appears only in Pss 50:11 and 80:14[13], where the contexts suggest an animal species of some kind; on the basis of an Arab. cognate the meaning here is probably "teat, nipple"; the versions are paraphrastic: LXX *apo eisodou doxēs autēs*, "From the entering in of her glory" (?); Syr. "abundance"; Tg. "the wine of her glory"; Vulg. "From her glory of every kind." 1QIsa^a has a slightly different form, *mmzvz*.

h   LXX parses differently but not implausibly: "Behold, I incline toward them like a river of peace and like a torrent that overflows the glory of the nations"; similarly Vulg.

i   MT *vînaqtem*, "and you will nurse," does not make good sense in the context; LXX *ta paidia autōn*, "their children," understood MT *vînaqtem* as a substantive *yônaqtām*, "their infants" (literally, "suckers"), and is supported by 1QIsaᵃ; read *věyôněqôtêhem*, "and your infants."

j   LXX *tois sebomenois auton*, "To those who worship him."

k   MT *vězāʿam* is a verbal form, but in the context a substantive, *vězaʿămô*, would be expected, as in NRSV and NEB but not NJPSV.

l   An attempt to render the technical forensic sense of *špṭ* Niphal (also Ezek 38:22; Joel 4:2[3:2] cf. 1QIsaᵃ *ybvʾ lšpvṭ*, "will come to judge"; LXX adds *pasa hē gē* ("all the earth").

m   Syriac *vbḥr bh → bḥr* = "test," "probe," requires only a slight difference in word division from MT, but *ûběḥarbô*, "and with his sword," should be maintained; see Comments.

n   1QIsaiahᵃ substitutes *ḥllyv*, "his slain"; in Tg. they are slain *qdm YHVH*, "before the Lord."

COMMENTS

In spite of the abrupt change of subject matter, the logical thread joining vv 1–6 and vv 7–14 is maintained by means of the close association between the new Zion and the new people, a connection made explicitly at the end of the present passage (v 14b). The passage consists in a distinct saying about Jerusalem with its own prophetic rubric (7–9), a summons to those who now mourn (cf. 61:2–3; 57:18; 60:20) to rejoice (10–11), a further saying (vv 12–14) that continues the description of the transformed Jerusalem as mother, and a final threatening vision of the final judgment that enlarges on the image of YHVH venting his anger against his enemies in the preceding verse (14b). These two final verses, or alternatively vv 15–17, are sometimes taken together with v 5 or vv 5–6 as the framework for vv 7–14 (Fohrer 1964, 274–82; Pauritsch 1971, 202–3; Koenen 1990, 196–205; P. A. Smith 1995, 159–67), but in fact v 6 and vv 15–16 have little in common. It seems more productive to read vv 15–16 as parallel with the finale of the book as a whole (66:22–24). In both passages fire is the agent of divine punishment, the victims of final judgment are much in evidence, and the perspective is that of "all flesh" (*kol-bāśār*). Perhaps the parallelism points to a conflation of alternative universalizing conclusions to the book, not unlike the two endings to the book of Job (38:1–40:5; 40:6–42:6).

As was noted earlier, 66:7–14 is the conclusion to the third major segment of the book, which consists in chs. 56–66. It runs parallel with 54:1–17b, the conclusion to the second segment, a passage that contains an apostrophe to Jerusalem/Zion (2d-person sing. fem. suffixes) and that ends in the same way as 66:7–14, by identifying the "Servants" as the beneficiaries of the promises about Jerusalem. The parallelism also binds these two major segments of the book together, consistent with the numerous indications that chs. 56–66 represent a deposit of expansive commentary on the core of chs. 40–54, adapted to new situations. Literary dependence is, moreover, best explained by postulating a relation between prophetic master and disciples.

It will therefore not be surprising to find in these last two chapters of the book numerous instances of thematic and linguistic dependence on the core Trito-Isaianic passage chs. 60–62 and, beyond it, on chs. 40–54. This process of creating new prophecy out of old, of the inspired interpretation of older prophecy in place of direct prophetic inspiration of the classical kind, is a characteristic feature of writings from the post-destruction period. (cf. Lau's *Schrift-gelehrte Prophetie*). The main instances will be noted as we proceed with the commentary.

The first statement about the miraculous childbearing of Mother Zion (vv 7–9) concludes with two brief oracles of YHVH in *oratio recta* about the opening and closing of the womb. It is constructed elegantly in ring composition, with the relevant verbs (*hyl*, "to be in labor," *yld*, "to give birth") at the beginning, in the middle, and at the end. The metaphor encloses the realia to which it refers, namely, land and population. These were clearly major concerns during the first century of Persian rule.

The image of Zion giving birth to children without labor pains clearly draws on the core passage, chs. 60–62, which represents Zion as a mother whose children return from far away (60:4, 9) and who rejoices in having a new family (62:4–5). The writer is also aware of the reassurances in 49:14–26 addressed to Zion, who will have (1) so many children she will wonder, incongruously, where they all came from and (2) enough space for them to settle. Even closer to 60–62 is the summons to Zion, who has not yet experienced childbearing and the accompanying labor pains, to rejoice at the prospect of a new and numerous family and a land for them to live in (54:1–8). Isaiah 66:7–14 reproduces many of the key themes and vocabulary of this passage: rejoicing, labor pains, numerous children, abundant land, comfort, and well-being. There may also be a reminiscence of Queen Babylon, the polar opposite of Zion, who is destined to lose her husband and children "in a single day" (*běyôm 'eḥad*, 47:9; 66:8). Finally, the rhetorical questions in 66:8 are reminiscent of the same literary feature that is so prominent in chs. 40–48 (40:21; 42:19, 23–24 etc.).

The present passage does not, however, simply reproduce these motifs and features. One indication is that the birth of the children is now instantaneous and miraculous, perhaps to make the point that the restoration of Jerusalem will come about by direct divine action and therefore without the intervention of a world ruler such as Cyrus or Darius. In this respect, the writer must have had the story of Abraham and Sarah in mind, especially since the Abrahamic promise of descendants, land, and blessing underlies so much of chs. 40–66. In Isa 51:2 the community's attention is directed to Sarah "who gave you birth" (another conjugation of the verb *hyl*, "to be in labor," as in 66:7–8). Sarah's story is of a woman who, after complaining that "YHVH has closed my womb" (*'āsā-ranî*, as in 66:9), preventing me "from giving birth" (*milledet*, Gen 16:2, identical with Isa 66:7), miraculously conceived and gave birth to a son. God promised it and brought it about without human agency. Life is elicited from the dead womb of Sarah and from the dead loins of Abraham, thus demonstrating that nothing is too wonderful for YHVH (Gen 18:14).

The change to direct address, the summons to rejoice (vv 10–11), does not require postulating a different source, much less a different author. The concentration in this short poem of the language of rejoicing (śmḥ, gyl, śyś, māśôś), of comforting (nḥm, an Isaian leitmotif), of satiety (śbʿ), of nursing at the breast (ynq cf. 60:16; mss), and of pleasure (ʿng, elsewhere associated with eating, 55:2; 58:14; here with drinking) is unparalleled and may well appear to the modern reader excessively Freudian. The change from mourning to rejoicing looks back to the claim of the Servants and those who tremble at God's word that those who now mourn will rejoice on judgment day (65:13–14, 18–19; 66:5); beyond that to the core text of 56–66 (60:5, 20; 61:10–11); and beyond that again to the summons to rejoice at the prospect of the end of suffering in 49–54 (49:13; 51:11; 54:1). Here, too, we see a continuum created by a cumulative and incremental process of textual reinterpretation.

This prospect of exuberant joy is addressed to the people who are still in mourning for the destruction of the city and, with it, of their hopes (cf. ʾăbēlê ṣiyyôn, "the mourners for Zion," 61:3). These are no doubt in some way associated with the people whose faith is wavering and who go about in mourning (qĕdorannît) in Mal 3:13–18, a passage discussed in the previous section. Mourning is expressed in the practice of community fasts (58:3–9; Zech 7:1–7; 8:18–19), and therefore in abstention from the pleasures of eating and drinking, and mourning and fasting add another dimension to the prospect of joyful excess in 66:10–11.

Direct citation alternates with the speaker's own words in this section, as indicated by the rubrics introducing vv 9a, 9b and now 12–14. The river image (kĕnāhār šālôm) draws on 48:18 ("Your prosperity would have flowed like a river, / your vindication like the waves of the sea") and is consistent with the use of this image in the frequently occurring theme of ecological transformation in Isa 40–55 (e.g., 41:18; 43:19–20). Another messianic passage, certainly postexilic, even refers to Jerusalem itself as "a place of broad rivers and streams," 33:21. The wealth (literally "glory" cf. 60:5; 61:6) of nations is compared to "a torrent in full spate" (naḥal šôṭēp). The expression occurs in 30:28, but in the quite different context of divine judgment. Elsewhere in Isaiah, water flowing in full spate (šôṭēp) is a threatening image rather than a metaphor for abundant well-being. In general, the mere recurrence of a word or phrase does not by itself constitute a case of conscious and deliberate modeling or, much less, of intertextuality, especially when the contexts in which the words or expressions occur are quite different.

The prospect of return from the diaspora, principally but not exclusively the Babylonian diaspora, was a central theme of the core material in chs. 60–62 — here too in continuity with earlier Deutero-Isaian prophecy. This is one aspect of a larger scenario, within which foreigners will serve Israel in menial capacities, including child-minding (61:5 cf. 49:23), their kings will be obliged to do homage in Jerusalem (60:11, 14), their wealth will be at the disposal of the

Judean Jewish community (60:5–7, 11, 16; 61:6), and they will be charged with repatriating the dispersed of Israel (60:4, 9). The younger children are to be carried on the shoulders (49:22) or on the hip (60:4; 66:12), a common practice in rural societies that has the advantage of leaving one hand free. The dandling on the knees probably refers back to the fantasy of foreign kings and queens serving as child-minders or (in the case of the queens) wet nurses for Jewish children, functions assigned to slaves (49:23). The resentment that fuels these "fantasies of the oppressed" is understandable, and parallels could easily be cited. But history also shows that they can have injurious consequences for both people who continue to cherish them and those with whom people who cherish them come in contact.

The promise of mother comfort which, a scribe adds, will be experienced in Jerusalem, ushers in the new period of rejoicing and flourishing. It may seem strange that the text speaks of the bones flourishing—so much so that the modern versions paraphrase with "you" (NEB), "your limbs" (NJPSV), "your bodies" (NRSV), "votre corps" (Bible de Jérusalem). Yet we speak of feeling something in our bones, and in liturgical hymns, especially individual lamentations, a sense of psychological disintegration or depression, and emotions deeply internalized (e.g., of joy or terror) are felt in the bones (*ʿăṣāmôt*, Pss 6:3[2]; 22:15; 31:11[10]; 32:3; 35:10; 38:4[3]; 51:10[8], etc.).

The stanza ends by affirming that all of this will manifest beyond doubt the truth of the earlier oracular statement about the respective destinies of the Servants and their opponents (65:13–16). This final verse also serves as the original conclusion to chs. 56–66, corresponding to the conclusion of chs. 40–54 in 54:17c.

Though the final stanza in this section (vv 15–16) ends with no concluding rubric and v 17 begins with none, 15–16 have nothing in common with 17. The latter, moreover, is clearly prose, while 15–16 (with the possible omission of the initial *kî-hinnēh*, literally, "for behold . . .") are in metrically regular tricola and are therefore correctly written stichometrically in BHS, as also in NRSV and other modern versions. On the other hand, 15–16 can be read as prompted by the mention of YHVH's venting his anger on his enemies in the previous verse (14b), and we have seen that it has a theme in common with the last verse of the book (66:24).

In this final statement, the language of theophany—the coming of the deity accompanied by fire and extreme meteorological and sometimes tectonic phenomena (e.g., the Sinai theophany, Exod 19:16–25)—is transposed into the idiom of apocalyptic. YHVH's coming signifies both salvation and judgment, but where the imagery of fire appears the accent is generally on judgment:

> Observe: the name of YHVH comes from afar
> blazing with anger,
> heavy with a sense of doom;
> his lips are charged with wrath,
> his tongue is a consuming fire. (Isa 30:27)

In keeping with the thrust of ch. 40–55 in general, in these chapters YHVH's *parousia* is also associated with salvation, the exercise of the royal prerogative of mercy:

See, YHVH is coming with power,
his strong arm affirms his rule;
see, his reward is with him,
his recompense precedes him. (40:10)

With the increasing fracturing of the community, and the emergence of internecine polemic, however, the emphasis on condemnation tends to predominate,

Behold your God!
Vengeance is at hand,
fearsome retribution;
it is he who comes to save you (35:4),

leading to the apocalyptic scenarios of 66:15–16 and 66:24.

The expression "like the whirlwind (are) his chariots" (*kassûpâ markĕbōtâv*) is borrowed from Jer 4:13, but the figure of YHVH riding a chariot through the sky, drawing on descriptions of Near Eastern storm- cloud deities, is a familiar component of theophanies (e.g., Ps 18:10; 68:5, *rōkēb ʿărāpôt*, emended text "chariot rider in the clouds"; Isa 19:1, *rōkēb ʿal-ʿāb qal*, "riding on a fast cloud"). That the final theophany involves a judicial process (*nišpāṭ*), that it will be with "all flesh" (*kol-bāśār*), and that judgment will be executed with the sword (thereby confirming the MT reading in v 16)—these ideas also derive from Jeremiah (Jer 25:31). And, finally, the introduction of this phrase "all flesh" in vv 15–16 and v 24 suggests the important conclusion that these verses have been added to locate the destinies of the elect and the reprobate within the Jewish community, the principal theme of chs. 65–66, in the context of the destiny of all humanity, whether for salvation or for reprobation.

A SENSE OF AN ENDING (66:17–24)

(Beuken 1991, 204–21; Cheyne 1882, 125–32; Duhm 1922, :485–90; Emerton 1980a, 21–25; Fohrer 1964, 282–85; Kellermann 1991, 46–82; Koenen 1990, 208–14; Lack 1973, 139–41; Lau 1994, 143–51, 183–85; Lowth 1833, 404–6; Muilenburg 1956, 769–73; Odeberg 1931, 281–85; Pauritsch 1971, 206–18; Rinaldi 1961, 109–18; Seitz 2001, 547–52; Sekine 1989, 43–45, 55–58; P. A. Smith 1995, 166–86; Steck 1987c, 103–16; Tomasino 1993, 81–98; Torrey 1928, 473–75; Volz 1932, 298–300; Webster 1990, 89–102; Williamson 1994, 1–29)

TRANSLATION

i

66 [17]As for those who consecrate and purify themselves to enter[a] the gardens following the one in the center,[b] who partake of swine's flesh, unclean things[c]

and rodents, their deeds and their devices will together come to an end:[d] a declaration of YHVH.

ii

[18]I am coming[e] to gather together nations of every tongue,[f] so that they can come and witness my glory. [19]I shall place a sign[g] among them,[h] and I shall send some of them, the survivors,[i] to the nations, to Tarshish, Put[j] and Lud, Meshech[k] and Tubal, Yavan and the distant coastlands and islands, those who have neither heard about me nor witnessed my glory. They will proclaim my glory among the nations. [20]They will bring all your brethren from all the nations as an offering for YHVH. They will bring them on horseback, in chariots and covered wagons, on mules and dromedaries, to Jerusalem[l] my holy mountain, says YHVH, just as the Israelites themselves bring the cereal offering in ritually clean vessels to the house of YHVH. [21]Some of them I shall take as priests, as Levites,[m] says YHVH.

iii

[22]For, as the new heavens and the new earth that I am about to make will endure in my presence—YHVH declares—so will your posterity and your name endure. [23]And each month at the new moon, and each week on the Sabbath,[n] all flesh will come to worship in my presence:[o] YHVH declares.

iv

[24]They will go out and gaze on the corpses[p] of the men who rebelled against me; for neither will the worm that consumes them die nor the fire that burns them be quenched;[q] they will be an object of horror[r] to all flesh.

[[23]And each month at the new moon, and each week on the Sabbath, all flesh will come to worship in my presence: YHVH declares.][s]

NOTES

[a] The verb is supplied.

[b] MT K has masc. *ʿaḥad*, Q fem. *ʿaḥat*, as also 1QIsa[a] and 1QIsa[b]; Barthélemy 1986, 461–62 reports that his committee was equally divided between K and Q. The ancient versions provide no certain answer: the origin of LXX *en tois prothurois* ("in the forecourts") is unknown; Vulg. *post ianuam intrinsecus* ("behind a door inside") is equally mysterious, though *post ianuam* is probably an error for *post unam*, "after one (female)," which would support Q; Syr. *ḥd btr ḥd*, "one after the other"; Tg. *ṣîʿāʾ bātar ṣîʿāʾ*, "one company after another"; and, according to Jerome, Theod. and Symm. (*alter post alterum*) suggest *ʾaḥad ʾaḥar ʾaḥad*, taken up by NEB, "one after another in a magic ring"; for the view that *ʾaḥar ʾaḥad* (*ʾaḥat*) entered on account of vertical dittography, see Emerton 1980a, 21–25; I adopt MT (Q) with some hesitation.

[c] The temptation to emend MT *šeqeṣ*, "abominable object or food," to *šereṣ*, "ritually unclean crawling creatures" (insects, reptiles, Lev 11:29), with

Duhm 1922, 486 and many others, is strong since the other two foods are specific, but MT is supported by all ancient versions, and outside of Leviticus, *šeqeṣ* appears only here and in Ezek 8:10, on which see Comments; 1QIsaᵃ has *šqvṣ* (*šiqqûṣ*), with the probable meaning of "abominable food."

d   I follow the suggestion of Duhm 1922, 486 that *maʿăśêhem ûmaḥšĕbôtêhem*, "their deeds and their devices," immediately following and unintelligible in its present location, has been misplaced.

e   This opening sentence is unintelligible as it stands and cannot be construed as aposiopesis ("And I—as for their deeds and devices . . ."); RSV adds "I know," following Syr.; for the phrase *maʿăśêhem ûmaḥšĕbôtêhem* ("their deeds and devices"), see Note c, above; the displacement must have taken place at an early date, because it is in 1QIsaᵃ; for MT *bāʾâ* 3d-person fem. sing., read *bāʾ* masc. with LXX, Syr., Vulg., Tg.; it is unclear why 1QIsaᵃ has *bʾv* 3d-person pl.

f   Literally, "all nations and tongues": hendiadys.

g   Both 1QIsaᵃ (*ʾvtvt*) and LXX (*sēmeia*) have pl.

h   Or "on them"; see Comments.

i   LXX "I shall send from them those that are saved" (*sesōsmenous*)" cf. Vulg. "Who shall have been saved" (*qui salvi fuerint*).

j   MT "Pul" may be a place unknown, but dependence on Jer 46:9 and the occurrence of Put and Lud together (Ezek 27:10; 30:5) counsels emending to Put (*pût*).

k   MT *mōšĕkê qešet*, "they who draw the bow," emended to "Meshech" cf. LXX *Mosoch*; *qešet* could have been added following Jer 46:9, referring to the Ludim *dōrĕkê qešet* ("those who draw the bow"); also, Meshech and Tubal are invariably linked (Ezek 27:13; 32:26; 38:2–3; 39:1).

l   Reading *ʾel* ("to") with 1QIsaᵃ for MT *ʿal* ("on"); LXX reads *eis tē hagian polin Ierousalēm*, "to Jerusalem the holy city."

m   The conjunction, absent in MT and 1QIsaᵃ, is supplied in LXX, Vulg., and Tg; 1QIsaᵃ adds *lî*, "for myself," before *lakkōhănîm halĕviyyîm*, cf. LXX *emautō*.

n   Rendering *middê* cf. *middê šānâ bĕšānâ* (1 Sam 7:16; 2 Chr 24:5; Zech 14:16), where it is the question of an action repeated at the same time year after year; for MT *bĕšabbatô*, 1QIsaᵃ has fem. *bšbth*.

o   LXX adds "in Jerusalem."

p   LXX has *kōla*, "limbs," perhaps visualizing disarticulated limbs, as in Ezek 37.

q   Literally, "their worm," "their fire"; Syr. "coals" and Tg. "spirits" are clearly interpretive.

r   LXX *eis horasin* ("as a spectacle") may be due to deriving the rare word *dērāʾôn* from *rʾh*, "see," cf. Tg. "the wicked shall be judged in Gehinnam, until the righteous say about them, 'We have seen enough'" and Vulg. *usque ad satietatem visionis* ("until sated with looking").

s   In the *haftara* for the Sabbath that coincides with the New Moon, v 23 is to be repeated after v 24.

COMMENTS

The rubrics attached to this last section of text divide it into four brief sayings: v 17 (*nĕ'um YHVH*), 18–21 (*'āmar YHVH*), 22–23 (*'āmar YHVH*) and 24. The accumulation of successive appendices or addenda at the end of a large and complex text such as the book of Isaiah is neither surprising nor unprecedented. Allow me to summarize one explanation of the way this could have come about: the original conclusion to chs. 56–66, that is, vv 12–14, was given an apocalyptic dimension by the addition of 15–16; v 17 was appended to make it clear that those referred to in 15–16 who are to be subject to judgment by fire and sword are the devotees of deviant cults referred to in 57:3–13 and 65:1–7; vv 18–19, 21 were intended to round off the section by reiterating the open admissions approach of 56:18, an attempt countered by the "correction" added in v 20 from a more integrationist perspective; vv 22–23 take up the theme of new heavens and new earth from 65:17 in order to reaffirm the promises to the Servants (65:9, 15–16) and affirm the centrality of Jerusalem, the two dominant themes of chs. 56–66; and, finally, v 24 adds the image of judgment by fire, parallel with 15–16, by identifying the worshipers of 23 as witnesses to that judgment.

Some commentators have, predictably, argued that v 17 has been accidentally moved from its original position, following either 65:5a (on account of the verb *qdš*, "consecrate") or 66:5. Such hypotheses can be neither proved nor falsified, it seems more important to explain v 17's actual location in the text. Following immediately on the scene of judgment by fire and sword, it reminds the reader that this destiny awaits the devotees of non-Yahvistic cults denounced in 57:3–13 and 65:1–7. Very likely, 66:17 belongs to the same source as these passages; at least all three describe the same phenomena from the same religious point of view.

We are shown participants in a cult preparing themselves for ceremonies in a garden by a ritual of consecration and purification. We are given no details, but such mandatory preparation could include sprinkling with water (Num 8:7), bathing (Lev 14:8), washing or changing clothes (Gen 35:2; Exod 19:14–15; Lev 14:8; Num 8:7), and sexual abstention (Exod 19:15). In the Comments on 65:3, we saw that the garden as a cultic enclosure (*gannâ*) is a place of trees and therefore more a grove than a garden in the usual understanding of the term (see also Num 24:6; Qoh 2:5; Cant 6:11). In 1:29 the garden cults are associated with sacred oak trees or terebinths (*'ēlîm*). The goddess Asherah was also represented by a tree (e.g., Isa 17:8; 27:9; Jer 7:9; Hos 11:10). Her association with oak or terebinth is explained by the fact that *'ēlâ*, sing. of *'ēlîm*, can mean "goddess" as well as oak or terebinth.

Commentators have cast their nets far and wide in an attempt to find parallels to the ceremony in which the initiates are about to participate. Marti (1900, 411) appealed to the sacred dances of early Christian Gnostic sects, Whitehouse (1908, 335) to the Sufi dervishes, and Volz (1932, 292) to the Eleusinian and Mithraic mystery cults, in keeping with his Hellenistic dating for the passage.

Cheyne (1882, 125) is one of several scholars to suggest a parallel with the cult of Tammuz-Adonis which, in its Mesopotamian form, featured a procession with the statue of Ishtar, the god's sister and lover, who brings him back to life. The suggestion at least has the advantage over others that this cult was known and practiced in Judah (Ezek 8:14–15; Isa 17:10; Zech 12:11; perhaps Jer 22:18 and Dan 11:37).

Comparison with the series of tableaux in the Jerusalem temple revealed to Ezekiel in vision has often been proposed (Ezek 8:1–18). The first, at the north gate of the inner court, is a ceremony in the presence of "the lustful image that impels to lust" (8:3)—namely, the representation of the goddess Asherah. In the following cameo, Ezekiel witnesses 70 elders, with a certain Jaazaniah in their midst (bĕtôkām), engaged in cult with incense in a room, the walls of which are decorated with representations of insects or reptiles (remeś), animals (bĕhēmâ), and unclean things (šeqeṣ; 8:7–13). Further along, he comes upon women engaged in ritual mourning for Tammuz-Adonis (8:14) and, finally, 25 worshipers of the sun-god at the eastern entrance of the temple (8:16). Isaiah 66:17 is reminiscent of this account at several points: the goddess theme the (sacrificial) food; outside of Leviticus, šeqeṣ appears only in Isa 66:17 and Ezek 8:10; and the function of Jaazaniah as hierophant. More importantly, it demonstrates continuity between the cult practices described in Isa 56–66 and the situation obtaining in the last decades of Judean independence and therefore provides a further disincentive to dating these practices in the Hellenistic period.

At all events, the probability that the cult referred to here was addressed to a goddess is increased if, following the Qere, the one in the center is a woman ('aḥar 'aḥat bĕtôk; see Notes). The phrase "after one (female) in the center" excludes the possibility of a procession led by the female hierophant, since even a goddess cannot be at the center and at the head of a procession at the same time. The preposition 'aḥar ("after") must therefore be taken in the well-attested sense of attachment (e.g., "following after a deity"). The meaning may then be that "the one in the middle" is the goddess symbolized by her 'ăšērâ, her tree in the middle of the garden (cf. "the tree of life in the middle of the garden," Gen 2:9), and represented by the priestess who directs the liturgy. Interestingly, Ibn Ezra came close to this conclusion in explaining that the text refers to gardens of trees, not kitchen gardens; that 'aḥat agrees with 'ăšērâ in gender; and that the initiates surround the tree in the midst of the garden.

The initiates are also condemned for using the meat of the domestic pig or the wild boar as sacrificial material (cf. 65:4 and 66:3). Another ritually unclean animal mentioned is the 'akbār, probably the jerboa or leaping mouse, which occurs as a personal name in Phoenicia, Edom, and Israel (Gen 36:38–39; 2 Kgs 22:12, 14; Jer 26:22; 36:12). The miscellaneous unclean material referred to as šeqeṣ (Lev 7:21; 11:10; Ezek 8:10) corresponds to the piggulîm ("unclean foods") in 65:4b.

The next section (vv 18–21) has nothing in common with what immediately precedes it. Continuity is, rather, with vv 15–16, in presenting another aspect of the apocalyptic scenario, the final coming of YHVH, the *parousia* (cf. v 16). It remains unclear how this ingathering of the nations was seen to fit with the annihilating judgment described in vv 15–16. If the survivors (*pĕlêṭîm*) of v 19 who are sent out on a mission are those who have survived judgment by fire and sword, the assembling of all humanity in Jerusalem would follow the judgment as a prelude to the final revelation of the glory of YHVH in Jerusalem. There is also a scenario in which judgment is carried out in one of the valleys near Jerusalem (Isa 66:24; Joel 4:2[3:2]) and is therefore subsequent to the mission. But since vv 18–21 speak of the goal of the ingathering only as witnessing YHVH's glory and taking part in worship, the negative aspect of judgment seems simply to have been left out of account.

The theme of the ingathering is, in the first place, developed on the basis of the Trito-Isaianic core in chs. 60–62. Jerusalem, therefore, is the center of the world, the place of the ultimate revelation of the glory of God (60:1; 62:2) and the establishment of his eschatological kingdom. A signal (*nēs*) will be raised over the peoples (62:10) for them to come to Jerusalem, led by their kings, bringing tribute; and with the prospect of being, whether willingly or otherwise, at the disposal of the people of Israel as slaves. They will come from far distant places such as Midian, Ephah, Sheba, Kedar, and Nebaioth (60:6–7), and they will be charged with the task of repatriating diaspora Jews (60:4, 8–9). As we would expect, this vision or futuristic fantasy, far removed from religious universalism as it obviously is, draws in its turn on one aspect of the complex message of chs. 40–55 (43:5–7; 45:14; 49:22–23).

In spite of the obscurities and uncertainties of 66:18–21, it is at least clear that in taking over this perspective it goes some way beyond it. To begin with, the mission to those who have not yet heard of YHVH or witnessed his glory implies a receptivity to proselytes. In this respect, 66:18–21 recalls the opening passage of chs. 56–66, especially the commitment of YHVH to gather yet more to him than the people already gathered (56:8). We saw that this statement is, in its turn, a comment on Isa 11:11–12, which expands the scope of the ingathering of dispersed Israelites mentioned in that text to include non-Israelites. Isaiah 56:1–8 and 66:18–19 are therefore aligned with the more open and universalistic perspective that comes to expression elsewhere in the book of Isaiah: all nations will stream to the mountain of YHVH to receive religious instruction and unlearn warfare and violence (2:2–4); Egypt and Assyria, traditional enemies of Israel, will also be people of God and will share a blessing with Israel (19:24–25); on the mountain of YHVH a banquet will be spread for all peoples, and YHVH will wipe the tears from all faces (25:6–8).

What does it mean that all nations will see the glory of God? In the Philistine war narrative (1 Sam 4:21–22), the glory (*kābôd*) is associated with the ark (*'ărôn*), symbol and palladium of YHVH as king and warrior. In Israel's journey through the wilderness, the *kābôd* is likewise associated with the ark-sanctuary (e.g., Exod 16:10; 40:34–35; Num 14:10) and with YHVH enthroned on Sinai (Exod 24:9–11, 17), homologous with the temple throne in Jerusalem (1 Kgs 8:11; Isa 24:23; Ezek 44:4). The theme keeps on reappearing throughout Isaiah

(4:5; 6:1–5; 24:23; 33:20–22; 52:7) and suggests that in 66:18 the nations are coming to witness the proclamation of YHVH's kingship and his ascent to the throne as king of the universe (Volz 1932, 298).

The sign ("signs" in the Great Isaiah Scroll and LXX, perhaps with the meaning "miracles") is the signal for convergence on Jerusalem. Here, too, the writer is dependent on an Isaian topos, though using a different term ('*ôt* rather than *nēs*):

> Observe: I raise my hand to the nations,
> I lift up a signal for the peoples;
> they will carry your sons in their laps,
> your daughters will be borne on their shoulders. (49:22)

> He will raise a signal for the nations,
> and gather the dispersed men of Israel;
> he will assemble the scattered women of Judah
> from the four corners of the earth. (11:12)

This is the signal for the mission to the Gentile world to begin. The question who are charged with this mission has caused considerable discussion. In the context, the only possible antecedent of *mēhem* ("some of them") is the phrase the "nations of every tongue," and this is confirmed by the appositional phrase "the survivors" (*pĕlêṭîm*), practically identical with "survivors of the nations" (*pĕlîṭê haggôyîm*) in Isa 45:20. But according to what follows, these emissaries or missionaries are to make YHVH known among the nations, which requires that they are in some way adherents to the Jewish faith from the Gentile world, in other words, proselytes.

Since the mission is to those who have not heard about the God of Israel, the emissaries are sent to the west, north, and south, but not to the east, that is, the Mesopotamian location of the principal Jewish diaspora center. There is no reason to relegate the list to the status of a scribal insertion, nor is there reason to believe that the writer had anything more than a vague and general idea of the location of these places. All six are mentioned in Ezekiel's poem about Tyre or in the prose addendum to it (Ezek 27:10, 12–13), as also in the so-called "Table of the Nations" in Gen 10:2–5, 6, 12), either of which could have been known to the writer in one form or another. For discussion of the names and possible locations, the reader is referred to the biblical encyclopedias and dictionaries. The order is of some interest. Put (Somalia?) and Lud (Libia?), descended from Ham and therefore North African, are almost always named together (Jer 46:9; Ezek 27:10; 30:5; 38:5). The same is the case with Meshech and Tubal in Anatolia (Ezek 27:13; 32:26; 38:2–3; 39:1). These twinned pairs are bracketed by Tarshish (Tartessos in SW Spain? Sardinia? Carthage?) in the first place and Yavan (the Greek-speaking Ionian littoral) in the last.

A major problem with this passage is that of determining who are the ones charged with repatriating diaspora Jews. The natural antecedent of the verb "and they will bring" (*vĕhēbî'û*, v 20) would be the aforementioned envoys, but this task does not fit well with that of making YHVH known and proclaiming his glory among the nations, in other words, preaching the Jewish religion. Furthermore, as we have seen, in order to discharge their mission, the envoys, taken from among Gentiles, must be proselytes. It seems, then, that Westermann (1969, 423) was correct in insisting that v 20 has been inserted into the passage, and this conclusion is reinforced by the following statement (21) that "some of them" (*mēhem*) will be priests and Levites, which links with "some of them" (*mēhem*) who were sent on the mission (19).

If this is so, the situation seems to be that v 20 is intended as a correction to the extraordinary claim that a mission to the Gentiles must precede the final consummation, and the even more disturbing claim (in v 21) that priests and Levites will be recruited from converts to the Jewish faith. These claims go beyond anything in the Trito-Isaian core (chs. 60–62), but they could be seen as the working out of the Servant's mission to be a light to the nations (49:6 cf. 42:6) and to bring righteousness to many (53:11).

The interpolated v 20 offers a solution more acceptable to the traditionally-minded by limiting the liturgical function of Gentiles to providing sacrificial material: their *minḥâ* consists in repatriated Israelites, for whom they provide every conceivable form of transportation, while Israelites alone offer the real cereal offering (and the other offerings), and do so in keeping with the laws of ritual purity. The alternative view, expressed in vv 18–19 and 21, makes a fitting parallel with 56:1–8. There, too, the situation unfolds against the expectation of an imminent *parousia*. The conditions under which the proselyte (*hannilveh 'el-YHVH*, 3a, 6a) may enjoy secure status as a member of the Jerusalem cult and civic community are laid down, and the temple is open to all peoples (7c).

What for many must have been the most controversial claim of 56:1–8, more than the assurances addressed to foreigners and the sexually mutilated, is that proselytes are now authorized to serve in the temple (6b). It is not stated in what capacity they will serve but, apart from secular usage (e.g., Elisha serving as Elijah's disciple, 1 Kgs 19:21; Abishag serving David, 1 Kgs 1:4, 15), the verb *šrt* is limited to cultic service offered by priests (Ex 28:35; 29:30; Num 3:31; 2 Chr 29:11; 31:2; Ezek 40:46 etc.) and Levites (Num 1:50; 3:6; Jer 33:22; Ezek 44:11–12; 2 Chr 8:14). Both 66:18–19, 21; and 56:1–8, therefore, testify to the existence within the Persian province of Judah of beliefs on the nature of the Jewish community, its relationship to outsiders, and the function of leadership within it, fundamentally at odds with the beliefs of those in authority, the temple priesthood in particular.

The last two paragraphs (22–23, 24) are prosodically irregular enough to justify setting them as prose. The prophetic rubric *'āmar YHVH* ("YHVH declares") distinguishes 22–23 from 24, though the phrase *kol-bāśār* ("all humanity," literally, "all flesh") appears in both, and the permanence of posterity and name in 22–23 is matched by permanent punishment in 24.

The first of these two final paragraphs (vv 22–23) takes off from the prospect of new heavens and new earth in 65:17 in recapitulating the promise of posterity and a new name for the Servants of YHVH (65:9, 15). This promise is itself

based on the *conditional* promise addressed to the community as a whole toward the end of chs. 40–48. If they had been faithful to the commandments,
then:

> Your descendants (*zera*ʿ, "seed") would be as countless as the sand,
> your offspring like its grains in number;
> their name would never be extinguished
> or effaced from my sight. (48:19)

We may also be hearing an echo of the "name better than sons and daughters"
promised to the sexually mutilated in 56:5. But behind all this anxiety about
stability and permanence in evidence throughout chs. 40–66 (41:8; 44:3; 48:19;
53:10; 59:21; 61:9; 62:2; 65:23) and in other post-destruction texts (e.g., Jer
31:35–36; 33:25–26) lies the Abrahamic promise (Gen 12:1–3 etc.). The assurance offered to the elect in Israel in v 22 is not rationally demonstrable; as
Duhm pointed out in typical fashion (1922, 489), one cannot base one unknown (i.e., the permanence of Israel) on another unknown (i.e., the permanence of a world not yet in existence). It is a question here of eschatological
faith, according to which, to envision a future is to set in motion the process by
which it comes about.

One aspect of this eschatological scenario is that all humanity will worship
the one true God, the God of Israel, in Jerusalem (v 23). It is too literalistic to
restrict the scope of the phrase *kol-bāśār* ("all flesh") to the Jewish people on
the grounds that only people living close to Jerusalem could go there on a
weekly basis (Duhm 1922, 489). As described, the scene closely parallels the
conclusion of Zechariah (Zech 14:16–19) and may have been influenced by it.
The participants in the year by year (*middê šānâ bĕšānâ*) celebration of Sukkoth are the survivors of the nations (cf. Isa 66:19), the families of the earth (cf.
"all flesh"), and they come to worship YHVH as king and lord of the heavenly
hosts, which we may take to be the equivalent of seeing YHVH's glory (Isa
66:18). In the Zechariah text, the punishment of the reprobate by plague is
described in lurid tones not unlike Isa 66:24: their flesh shall decay, their eyes
rot in their heads, and their tongues in their mouths (Zech 14:12). One cannot
but ask, finally, whether the last paragraph (14:20–21), which insists on ritually
pure vessels and the exclusion of "Canaanites" from the temple, is not a scribal
"correction" similar to Isa 66:20.

The last verse (v 24) has not just been thrown in, as it were, to make sure that
the book does not end on a universalistic note (Whybray 1975, 293). The
much-discussed linguistic parallels with the first chapter, or at least 1:27–31
(*pōšĕʿîm*, "rebels" 1:28; *bāʿărû . . . vĕʾên mĕkabbeh*, "they will burn . . . and there
will be none to extinguish," 1:31), reveal the intention of presenting the book
as a unified composition. Isaiah 66:24, or perhaps 66:22–24, is therefore the
excipit to the book as a whole, just as 66:15–16 was the original conclusion to
ch. 56–66. If the intention was to emphasize divine judgment in the last as in
the first chapter of the book, the same intent is in evidence at the conclusion of

other major sections: "There is no well-being (peace) for the wicked" (48:22 and 57:21).

This final verse presents the spectacle of worshipers going out, perhaps processionally from the temple, to view the corpses of the rebels. The idiom used (verb r'h with preposition bĕ) elsewhere expresses a strong sense of Schadenfreude, gloating over defeated, humiliated, or dead enemies (Judg 16:27; Ps 22:18[17]; 54:9[7]; Ezek 28:17). The scene is no doubt the Valley of Hinnom (or the Valley of the Sons of Hinnom, now Wadi er-Rababeh) south of the city (Josh 15:8; 18:16; Jer 19:2; Neh 11:30); appropriately, since this had been a cult site for Molech and human sacrifice (2 Kgs 23:10; 2 Chr 28:3; 33:6; Jer 7:32–33; 32:35). The location could also have been suggested by Jeremiah's prophecy that its future name would be "the Valley of Slaughter" (gê' hahărēgâ, Jer 7:32 = 19:6). We know from rabbinic sources that it also served as the city rubbish dump, but from what point in time we do not know.

A reading of Isa 66:24, together with texts from Jeremiah that identify the Valley of Hinnom as a place of punishment for the wicked (7:30–34; 19:6–7), contributed to the idea of eternal punishment involving fire and worms (Sir 7:17, Greek text; Jdt 16:17) and to the transformation of the Valley of Hinnom (gê' hinnôm) into Gehenna, familiar from the Gospel sayings of Jesus (Matt 5:22, 29–30; Mark 9:43–48, where the influence of Isa 66:24 is apparent).

Several scholars have lamented that the book had to end on such a note. Whitehouse (1908, 339) observed sadly that we have here descended far below the level of Deutero-Isaiah and the towering peaks of the Servant poems. Westermann (1969, 429) was convinced that this theology of eternal damnation is alien to the core of the Old Testament. In the final paragraph of his commentary, Duhm (1922, 490), with his customary mordancy, expressed sadness that a book containing the most splendid and elevated writing in the Old Testament should end on a note of such dämonischen Missklang ("fiendish discordancy"). While the "fiendish discordancy" may not be the exclusive property of the commentator, as Torrey (1928, 475) alleged with equal mordancy in the last paragraph of his commentary, something of this disquietude is reflected in the liturgical practice (in the haftara of the Sabbath that coincides with the new moon) of repeating v 23 after v 24 to provide the book with a more suitable conclusion.

INDEX OF SUBJECTS

◆

INDEX OF BIBILICAL AND OTHER ANCIENT REFERENCES

◆

THE ANCHOR BIBLE

Commentaries (C) and Reference Library (RL) volumes on the Old and New
Testaments and Apocrypha

THE CONTRIBUTORS

Susan Ackerman, Dartmouth College. RL17

William F. Albright, Johns Hopkins
University. C26

Francis I. Andersen, Professorial Fellow,
Classics and Archaeology, University of
Melbourne. C24, C24A, C24E

Markus Barth, University of Basel. C34,
C34A, C34B

Adele Berlin, University of Maryland. C25A

Helmut Blanke, Doctor of Theology from
the University of Basel. C34B

Joseph Blenkinsopp, University of Notre
Dame. C19, C19A, RL5

Robert G. Boling, McCormick Theological
Seminary. C6, C6A

Raymond E. Brown, S.S., Union Theological
Seminary, New York (Emeritus). C29,
C29A, C30, RL1, RL7, RL15

George W. Buchanan, Wesley Theological
Seminary. C36

Edward F. Campbell, Jr., McCormick
Theological Seminary. C7

James H. Charlesworth, Princeton
Theological Seminary. RL4, RL13, RL14

Mordechai Cogan, Hebrew University,
Jerusalem. C11

John J. Collins, University of Chicago. RL10

James L. Crenshaw, Duke Divinity School.
C24C, RL16

Mitchell Dahood, S.J., The Pontifical
Biblical Institute. C16, C17, C17A

Alexander A. Di Lella, O.F.M., Catholic
University of America. C23, C39

David L. Dungan, University of Tennessee,
Knoxville. RL18

Joseph A. Fitzmyer, S.J., Catholic University
of America. C28, C28A, C31, C33, C34C

J. Massyngberde Ford, University of Notre
Dame. C38

Michael V. Fox, University of Wisconsin,
Madison. C18A

David Noel Freedman, University of
Michigan (Emeritus) and University of
California, San Diego. General Editor.
C24, C24A, C24E

Victor P. Furnish, Perkins School of
Theology, Southern Methodist University.
C32A

Jonathan A. Goldstein, University of Iowa.
C41, C41A

Moshe Greenberg, Hebrew University,
Jerusalem. C22, C22A

Louis F. Hartman, C.SS.R., Catholic
University of America. C23

Andrew E. Hill, Wheaton College. C25D

Delbert R. Hillers, Johns Hopkins
University. C7A

Luke Timothy Johnson, Candler School of
Theology, Emory University. C35A, C37A

Craig R. Koester, Luther Seminary. C36

Bentley Layton, Yale University. RL11

Baruch A. Levine, New York University. C4,
C4A

Jack R. Lundbom, Clare Hall, Cambridge
University. C21A

P. Kyle McCarter, Jr., Johns Hopkins
University. C8, C9

John L. McKenzie, De Paul University. C20

Abraham J. Malherbe, Yale University
(Emeritus). C32B

C. S. Mann, formerly Coppin State
College. C26

Joel Marcus, Boston University. C27

J. Louis Martyn, Union Theological
Seminary, New York. C33A

Amihai Mazar, Institute of Archaeology of
Hebrew University, Jerusalem. RL2

John P. Meier, Catholic University of
America. RL3, RL9

Carol L. Meyers, Duke University. C25B,
C25C

Eric M. Meyers, Duke University. C25B,
C25C

Jacob Milgrom, University of California,
Berkeley (Emeritus). C3, C3A, C3B

Carey A. Moore, Gettysburg College. C7B,
C40, C40A, C44

Jacob M. Myers, Lutheran Theological
Seminary, Gettysburg. C12, C13, C14, C42